PUBLIC
RELATIONS

'As the title suggests, this text is a comprehensive introduction to public relations theory and practice. It offers the reader a selection of contemporary case studies in all areas of public relations practice, along with discussion starters and exercises that allow you to explore the theoretical concepts in more depth. It is an excellent resource for people interested in learning about the public relations profession.'
—*Liz McLaughlin, President, Public Relations Institute of Australia*

'An excellent overview of the practice of public relations as well as insight into the theory building in the field . . . This text places research and ethical issues where they should be—central to practice.'
—*Mai Hansford, University of Technology Sydney*

'A very readable introductory text . . . The book is popular with students and prepares them for more advanced treatments of the key PR debates.'
—*Dr Malcolm Kennedy, Monash University*

'Public relations practitioners, along with undergraduate and postgraduate communication students, will find it a welcome addition to their reading. The authors draw on the collective experience of practitioners and academics, and the focus on Australian cases and issues makes it an invaluable text.'
—*Maggie Walsh, RMIT University*

'I have to say your book makes teaching PR a dream! So many good things in the text . . . so many references for students to look-up for assignments!'
—*John Cokley, James Cook University*

PUBLIC
RELATIONS
THEORY AND PRACTICE

EDITED BY JANE JOHNSTON AND CLARA ZAWAWI

2ND EDITION

First published in 2000

This edition first published in 2004

Allen & Unwin
83 Alexander Street
Crows Nest NSW 2065
Australia
Phone: (61 2) 8425 0100
Fax: (61 2) 9906 2218
Email: info@allenandunwin.com
Web: www.allenandunwin.com

National Library of Australia
Cataloguing-in-Publication entry:

Public relations: theory and practice.

  2nd ed.
  Bibliography.
  Includes index.
  ISBN 1 86508 922 2.

  1. Public relations. 2. Communication. I. Johnston, Jane,
  1961– . II. Zawawi, Clara.

659.2

Set in 11pt Caslon 540 by Midland Typesetters
Printed by Ligare Book Printer, Sydney

10 9 8 7 6 5 4 3 2 1

CONTENTS

CONTRIBUTORS

John Allert is Public Relations Coordinator and Senior Lecturer in Public Relations in the School of Marketing at the Curtin University of Technology, Perth. John is also Director of his own public relations consultancy, Westline Communications. John's background has been in writing, journalism and public relations. Before joining Curtin, he was a Director of International Public Relations, Australia, and he ran the Western Australian operations for Shandwick International PLC. His main research areas involve Australian Indigenous economic development and he sits on the Western Australian Government's Aboriginal Economic Development Council as one of only two non-indigenous people on the council.

Susan Boyd is the managing director of Infront Communications Pty Ltd, a boutique consultancy specialising in tourism and leisure public relations. She has more than 15 years' industry experience and organised logistics and public relations for some of Australia's largest mass participation sporting events including traithlons, fun runs, yachting, paddling and cycling. Susan holds a BA in Journalism from the University of Southern Queensland and an MA in Public Relations from Bond University.

Dr Jeff Brand is Associate Professor of Communication and Media, and Co-director of the Centre for New Media Research at Bond University. His research has explored electronic media news and entertainment content and the social–psychological effects of electronic media on young audiences. This program of research has focused specifically on stereotyping in the media and stereotypic attitudes of youth, on effects of advertising on the materialistic values of youth, and on the effects of news on youth knowledge about social and political reality. More recently, he has undertaken a program of research centred on computer and video games as a dominant form of communication. Jeff Brand regularly serves as a consultant to industry and government. Most recently he co-authored two published studies: for the Australian Broadcasting Authority, *Sources of News and Current Affairs*; for the Special Broadcasting Corporation, *Living Diversity: Australia's Multicultural Future*.

Rhonda Breit lectures in journalism at the University of Queensland. A graduate of Melbourne University Law School, Rhonda has extensive experience teaching media law to journalism and public relations students. She has completed post-graduate studies in media law at Melbourne University and is currently completing her PhD in media ethics. Before joining the University of Queensland, Rhonda co-ordinated the journalism program at Deakin University. During her six and a half years lecturing at Deakin University, Rhonda developed many courses in media law and ethics, including a course entitled Legal Principles for Public Relations Practitioners. She was also instrumental in designing a course-work masters program in professional communication. Rhonda's research interests include media law and ethics and she has published extensively in these areas.

Kristin Demetrious is a lecturer in the School of Communication and Creative Arts at Deakin University. An experienced public relations practitioner, Kristin has worked in both the education and cultural tourism sectors and operated her own communication consultancy. Kristin has a Bachelor of Arts from Deakin University, a Graduate Diploma in Applied Film and TV from Swinburne University and a Diploma of Education from La Trobe University. She is currently undertaking a PhD on citizenship and public communication. In 2003 Kristin was awarded the Centenary of Federation Medal for community service and also received an Online Teaching and Learning Fellowship to develop an innovative pedagogical approach to a new course that looks at contemporary developments in public relations. In 2002 she received the Faculty of Arts Award for Excellence in Teaching.

Leanne Glenny is a Lecturer in Public Relations at the University of Canberra. Prior to joining the university, Leanne worked in Defence Public Affairs and completed postgraduate studies in Marketing Communication and Management. Her current research interests include Public Relations internship programs and government communication strategies following the ACT bushfires. She is a council member of the PRIA (ACT).

Marian Hudson is Group Manager, Public Affairs for one of Australia's largest national energy companies, Energex, based in Brisbane. She has more than 25 years' experience in public affairs, communication and media in both government and the private sector. At Energex she is responsible for all aspects of public affairs, including corporate positioning, the website, media relations, issues and crisis management, sponsorship and public education programs. Marian has also worked as a journalist in Australia and overseas as well as a Press Secretary to two Queensland Government cabinet Ministers. Marian is a Fellow of the PRIA, a Past President of the PRIA (Qld) and author of *The Media Game: An insider's guide to powerful publicity.*

Jane Johnston is convenor of the public relations major at Griffith University's School of Arts, where she also lectures in journalism studies. Following an industry career in print journalism and public relations, she has developed a particular research interest in the relationships between the news media, the courts and public relations. She is also interested in media relations and co-authored *Breaking into Journalism* with Mark Pearson (Allen & Unwin, 1998).

Lelde McCoy is Managing Director of Lelde McCoy and Associates, specialists in reputation management and public relations strategic planning. Previously she was Deputy Chairman of Porter Novelli, one of Australia's major national public relations consulting firms. She also set up Western Pacific Communications and worked in corporate communications roles in the food and beverage and utility industries. With more then 25 years' experience in public relations, Lelde has received numerous awards for her work from Australian and international public relations professional associations and has published in journals in the corporate communications field. Her research interests are in corporate reputation management, ethics in public relations and corporate branding. She was educated at Melbourne University and RMIT University and has undertaken postgraduate studies at the Newhouse School of Communications at Syracuse University in New York State. Lelde is a Fellow and former National President of the PRIA.

Dr Steve Mackey followed ten years as a London journalist and seven as a press officer in London's County Hall, with thirteen years as a lecturer in public relations at Deakin University in Victoria. His PhD is in public relations theory. He gives papers regularly at national and international conferences and is a Research Associate at Bournemouth University, which in 1989 was the first to run undergraduate degrees in public relations in the UK. Steve researches and writes in the areas of the critical theory of public relations and in the areas of crisis and issues management.

Severin Roald is Account Manager at Cox Kommunikasjon, an affiliate of Edelmann PR Worldwide and one of the largest public relations agencies in Norway. His work involves consulting in public relations, media relations, analysis and evaluation. He has studied Political Science at the University of Bergen (Norway), Communication at Volda University College (Norway) and he holds a Master of Arts degree in Communication Management from Bond University.

Raveena Singh is Course Convenor and Senior Lecturer in Public Relations and Marketing Communication at the University of Canberra. Her main interest of research is in international marketing communication and public relations. She was founding editor of the Asia Pacific Public Relations Journal.

Marianne Sison is Program Manager of the Master of Arts (Communication) by coursework at RMIT University's School of Applied Communication. As a senior lecturer, she has taught public relations courses in the undergraduate and post-graduate programs since 1992. She holds a BA (Broadcast Communication) from the University of the Philippines and an MA in Mass Communication (Public Relations) from the University of Florida. She has worked in consultancy and in-house public relations in Melbourne, Los Angeles and Manila. Her research interests include public relations roles and organisational communication.

Dr Stephen Stockwell is Senior Lecturer in Journalism and Communication at Griffith University's Gold Coast campus. He is author of *Political Campaign Strategy* (forthcoming) and co-author of *All Media Guide to Fair and Cross-Cultural Reporting* (2000). He was previously a journalist with 4ZZZ, JJJ and the ABC's *Four Corners* and worked as a press secretary for state and federal politicians and media manager for the Queensland ALP. His research interests include political campaigns, media management, investigative journalism, new communication technology and trash culture.

Clara Zawawi is Director, Client Relationships for Professional Public Relations, Australasia's largest public relations consultancy group. She is also responsible for the PPR Academy, PPR's internal staff training and knowledge management organisation. She joined PPR in early 2001, after spending ten years as Assistant Professor of Public Relations Studies at Bond University, where she was responsible for the accreditation of the first Masters degree in public relations in Australia. Beginning her career at Mojo Corporate, the public relations arm of advertising agency Mojo, in the mid 1980s, Clara has extensive experience in consumer public relations as well as particular strengths in complex issues management. Her doctorate is on the relationship between public relations practitioners and journalists, a topic on which she is often called to comment in the media and at industry forums.

PREFACE

Public relations is not a static profession. It is fast moving, developing and far reaching. For these reasons and more, *Public Relations: Theory and practice* has now moved into its second edition, growing in size and scope to better reflect the profession. Our aim has been to provide a solid foundation and reference for students and practitioners in Australia and the Pacific, and to present insights into organisations at a range of levels—corporate, political and NGOs—as they interface with a variety of publics, from the media to internal and community. The ideas, concepts and examples in this book have come from a broad base of experienced public relations practitioners and communication academics. These experts have presented a multiplicity of insights, all drawn together in a uniform style, to provide a broad perspective on current best practice in this dynamic profession.

The book has been divided into five parts and 16 chapters, and represents a larger, more comprehensive coverage of the profession than the first edition. The 14 original chapters have all been completely revised and updated, and two new chapters, 'Ethical practice' and 'Public relations and the Third Sector', have been introduced. These two new chapters are exciting and fulfilling additions to the book, and were carefully chosen to reflect development and growth in the profession in these key areas. Ethics in public relations is central to its effective practice, and the Third Sector covers that part of society that is neither corporate or political, but inclusive of community-based, not-for-profit organisations and activist groups which increasingly utilise public relations strategies and tactics to achieve their goals. In keeping with this, we have chosen to broaden the term 'organisation' to better reflect groups at all levels, from the highest-profile corporate multinational to the local suburban activist group.

The five parts of the book take the reader from a theoretical base through to the wide range of processes and applications and the main areas of practice. Part One introduces the reader to the nature of public relations, its history and the theories underpinning it. Part Two covers the law and ethics. Part Three looks at management of public relations campaigns and programs, covering research and evaluation, strategy, tactics, planning and scheduling. It examines these concepts in practice, and explains how to apply content from previous chapters through the use of information and communications technologies. Part Four looks at public relations in action, and Part Five examines public relations practice in a variety of key professional areas. Throughout each chapter, there are pointers to other relevant chapters that develop a similar theme or topic, recognising that no one area of public relations works in isolation. We have taken up suggestions from the first edition to increase the coverage of theory, choosing to incorporate it at relevant stages throughout the text, as well as in the dedicated theory chapter. It has remained, however, an introductory book and the aim has been to provide a balance between theory and practice.

We most gratefully acknowledge the work of the many contributors in this edition. Many of the first contributors have painstakingly revisited their chapters to update material, some to the extent of a virtual re-write. We are eternally grateful to these people for working so hard on their chapters and for proudly sharing the successes and challenges of the book with us. We would also like to welcome and thank those new contributors who have joined the team. The new authors have worked tirelessly to research and write new material, all producing first-rate work to complete the book. They are an impressive line-up of contributors representing senior practitioners and academics, many of whom have written about their own area of specialisation, bringing to their chapter years of research and insight. We are proud to be among this wonderful list of contributors who, among other things, wrote and re-wrote these chapters while juggling full-time practice or academic jobs, caring for small children and elderly parents, having babies (we welcome three new babies), living overseas or travelling extensively throughout the production of their chapter. Indeed, the contributors are testament to the saying that if you want something done, ask a busy person to do it! In addition, we would all like to thank the various research assistants and office support staff for their tireless help.

Our thanks to our families for their patience and support, especially over those weekends and public holidays which should have been theirs. And, as always, thanks to our publisher Elizabeth Weiss, who tried to warn us how much work a new edition would be but supported us nevertheless and has always been there for advice, and to Catherine Taylor, who has done a magnificent job in editing the manuscript. Our employers, the School of Arts at Griffith University and Professional Public Relations, have been extremely supportive of this book and we thank them too.

Since publishing the first edition, the literature of public relations in this region has grown. We are proud to be part of this growth, which continues to expand the breadth of literature in public relations, both in the Australian/Pacific region and beyond.

Jane Johnston and Clara Zawawi
July 2003

PART 1
THEORY

1 WHAT IS PUBLIC RELATIONS?

Jane Johnston and Clara Zawawi

In this chapter

Introduction
Defining public relations
The role of public relations practitioners
Public relations activities
Relationship to marketing and advertising
From publics to markets
Skills needed in public relations
Trends in public relations
Public relations in university curricula
Conclusion
Career paths

Introduction

One of the most common questions asked by first-time public relations students is: 'What is public relations?' Students are not the only ones unsure of the boundaries of the profession. The term 'public relations' is often misunderstood, leaving many people, including senior management, unsure of the profession's parameters. One reason for the confusion is that it is often used inappropriately. For example, Queensland's Gold Coast meter maids—attractive women in very short skirts or bikinis who walk around the main streets of Surfers Paradise and put coins into parking meters that are about to expire, thus helping motorists (often visitors from interstate) to avoid a fine and giving them a good impression of the holiday city—have described their job as being in 'public relations'. Further confusion comes from the enormous array of titles used to describe jobs in the field: in 1994, 74 different titles were used in job advertisements for people performing public relations roles (Foster 1995: 6). Some of the more common terms are Corporate Affairs Manager, Public Affairs Executive, Communications Manager and Media Liaison Director. Many professionals use these titles to try to distance or differentiate themselves from, for instance, the meter maids—who may more accurately be described as 'goodwill ambassadors'. Sometimes the phrase 'public relations' is avoided in job titles because, to many people, the term is synonymous with 'spin' or 'spin doctoring', which has negative connotations of putting a slant on a subject or disguising or hiding information in order to have something appear in a favourable light.

Another reason for the range of titles and names has been the need to identify the various types of public relations—the 'specialisation' required for a particular role. An analysis of the range of public relations activities that exists follows later in the chapter, and we can see the use of key words from these activities in some of the job descriptions. Such a range of activities is consistent with other professions that foster both specialisation and generalist practitioners. Take medicine, for instance. Doctors may be general practitioners, orthopaedic surgeons, ear, nose and throat specialists, cardiologists, obstetricians, and so on. Similarly, public relations provides for the specialist and the generalist, and usually the title of the position reflects this. Such a range of activities and specialisations within the industry is now being paralleled by a range of different theories to describe public relations. The next chapter includes such a range of diverse theories which have application to different activities in public relations. We can therefore see that theories are not 'right' or 'wrong', but perhaps more appropriate to one field of public relations than another.

Whatever the nomenclature, these roles fall under the banner of public relations as examined in this text. The peak professional body for the industry, the Public Relations Institute of Australia (PRIA), similarly brings all the different activities and titles under one banner.

Defining public relations

So what is public relations? Public relations practitioners and academics have been explaining the term for a long time. In 1967 Don Barnes, then president of the New

South Wales chapter of the Public Relations Institute of Australia, published a paper entitled *What is Public Relations?* He described the purpose of public relations officers and consultants as maintaining an organisation's relations with its various publics—the groups of people who are important to it. He further described the functions of public relations practitioners as being:

- to advise management on policy and its effect on public relations;
- to channel and coordinate within an organisation the activities that affect public relations;
- to provide the mechanics for explaining an organisation and its policies to its various publics through communications media;
- to ascertain and explain to management what various publics think about the organisation (Barnes 1967: 2).

Twenty years later, in 1987, the chairman of one of the world's largest public relations firms, Harold Burson of Burson-Marsteller, listed what he believed to be the four most important functions of public relations in society. His list shows that basically little had changed (see 'Definitions of public relations tasks' box). Aspects of Burson's view of the function of the public relations practitioner hold true today (Burson 1987).

Definitions of public relations tasks

- *Sensor of social change.* The public relations professional perceives the rumblings at the heart of society that augur good or ill for the organisation, and helps management prepare for the onslaught and impact of those issues.
- *Corporate conscience.* Henry David Thoreau wrote: 'It is truly enough said that a corporation has no conscience; but a corporation of conscientious men is a corporation with a conscience'. These are powerful words—ones that the public relations professional should always bear in mind. Such qualities are basic to the job description of public relations officers.
- *Communicator.* Many people think communications is the main public relations role. Most likely, they think that way because they spent a lot of time mastering communication skills and little time

honing their social judgement. Communications is not the main role: it is one of four important roles.

- *Corporate monitor.* This function seeks to make corporate policies and programs match public expectations. The spirit of the ombudsman should pervade the public relations person's job. And this is perhaps the best reason for the senior public relations officer to report to the highest level of management.

Source: PR Reporter, 'Tips and tactics', 23 March 1987.

More recently, academic definitions have developed. In 1984 Grunig and Hunt, while acknowledging that a single definition was difficult, defined it as the 'management of communication between an organisation and its publics' (1984: 6). More than a decade on, McElreath described it as 'a management function that uses communications to facilitate relationships and understanding between an organisation and its publics' (1996: 3).

While these are excellent ways of understanding the public relations function from the point of view of the organisation, they do not take into account the growing trend in democratisation of communication. Additionally, the very use of the word 'organisation' in these definitions has tended to place the existence of public relations practice too firmly within the corporate context.

This traditional connection is no longer adequate. The advent of cheap mass communications in the form of the internet, and the growing sophistication of the smallest community groups or individuals to leverage this and traditional media has limited our understanding of the range and depth of public relations activity. Developments such as the growth of anti-globalisation coalitions, which by their very nature are anti-organisational but which use these same tools against the corporations, make a new approach and a new definition necessary. This is discussed further in Chapter 16.

We therefore define public relations as *the ethical and strategic management of communication and relationships in order to build and develop coalitions and policy, identify and manage issues and create and direct messages to achieve sound outcomes within a socially responsible framework.*

This activity can be carried out by organisations, groups or individuals as they interact with their various publics or stakeholders to pursue objectives and goals. This view recognises that communication should not be simply strategic, because this implies the potential exploitation of the imbalance of power between the communicator and the recipient. Ethical parameters allow the practitioner to ensure that public relations programs and activities remain fair to those involved in the communication relationship.

Coalitions and relationships are central. Without these foundation stones, it would be impossible for the practitioner's efforts to have any effect. Thus the focus of much public relations activity is to create and recognise strong bonds at all levels.

Finally, these theoretical considerations should inform practical activity, resulting in outcomes which are equitable, balanced, just and considerate as far as possible to all parties.

This definition allows us to see public relations as a process that can occur at many levels, and can explain the way in which practitioners, whether they be in government, corporations or working for a community group, can use the same basic sets of skills and techniques, even though this may occur for widely different purposes.

The role of public relations practitioners

Both the type of business and the position of the public relations practitioner will influence what type of public relations is practised within an organisation. The two primary roles public relations practitioners hold are those of technician and problem-solver/manager. *Technicians* provide services such as producing publications (e.g. news releases and newsletters). *Problem-solvers* ask clients or senior management to rethink or clarify problems and to look for solutions. Technicians hold lower positions within organisations than problem-solvers. Problem-solvers belong to management, with accompanying responsibility for decision-making and policy formation. They are part of what is known as the *dominant coalition of management.* In some cases, one person may perform both functions, but in organisations employing a team of practitioners, the more junior staff member will perform the technician's role and the more senior the problem-solver or manager's role.

This difference in roles is quite clearly demonstrated by the public affairs department of ENERGEX, one of the largest electricity corporations in Australia and based in Queensland. Owning assets worth $3.7 billion and employing 3100 people in Queensland, Victoria and New Zealand, it is a large and complex organisation which manages the public relations function through its Public Affairs Group. The group has a staff of seven—the Group Manager, Public Affairs, two Senior Public Affairs Consultants, two Public Affairs Consultants, a web developer and an office manager who acts as personal assistant to the Group Manager.

The Public Affairs Group has responsibility for all external relations, including the development and maintainance of the corporation's website, and as part of this responsibility manages all of ENERGEX's sponsorship initiatives. It is heavily involved in community liaison on major capital works programs, such as the building of new substations, and is responsible for producing the company's annual report and other publications. These duties require communication with a large and varied set of publics, from state and federal government to businesses, individual householders and employees. Members of the public affairs team need to be aware of all their varied publics, and able to communicate easily with them all.

The Group Manager is a very senior executive who reports directly to the General Manager Legal & Corporate Affairs and is in direct liaison with the Chief Executive Officer. She oversees all activities carried out by the group, including sponsorship, advertising and community education campaigns, and also advises the board and the CEO on communication matters. As a manager, her role is a strategic one which involves defining key messages and providing themes. For example, she is ultimately responsible for accepting sponsorship proposals that fit with the corporation's goals. Her role as a strategist also requires her to provide advice to the board on any communication issues raised through a major acquisition. It is a varied job—in any one day she may spend the morning preparing briefing papers for the Chief Executive on environmental initiatives and trends, and the late afternoon in crisis management mode making regular media appearances advising customers on safety as a major thunderstorm rolls across Southeast Queensland, blacking out thousands of homes.

Her staff work at the technical level of researching, writing and supervising production of publications, updating and maintaining the website and ensuring that exposure and leverage are gained for the corporation's sponsorship activities. While the Group Manager is the company spokesperson and therefore in constant contact with the media as a problem-solver, it is the responsibility of the Public Affairs Consultants to identify, prepare and update all media material, as well as organise any media conferences at which she may appear.

Large as it is by corporate standards, ENERGEX's Public Affairs Group also occasionally uses the services of external consultants to provide extra 'arms and legs' or specialist expertise when necessary. During the recent takeover of Allgas, an external public relations consultancy was used to provide specialist financial relations advice, and another specialist consultant was retained to help develop and test the corporation's crisis management plan (Hudson, 24 October 2002).

Hard Rock Cafes, on the other hand, are much simpler organisations with fewer publics—customers, employees, entertainers and their management. The four cafes in Australia and New Zealand and the Hard Rock Hotel in Bali share a single Public Relations Director, whose primary responsibility is to gain media exposure for the cafes. As each cafe opens, she is also responsible for the organisation of each launch event. While she writes and disseminates all media releases, appears on behalf of the cafes as spokesperson when necessary, and creates and manages the invitation lists and running sheets for each event, the format and content of these are determined by senior management, either in the cafes or at Hard Rock HQ in the United States. Though she carries the title of Director, her role is primarily that of a technician (Davidson, August 2002).

An organisation's employment pattern of problem-solvers and technicians therefore depends on its size and complexity and the number and range of publics that it needs to communicate with. The fact that people who hold very different jobs with widely varying levels of responsibility are all called public relations practitioners makes it difficult to define who a public relations practitioner is and what a public relations practitioner does. The activities listed in the next section indicate the wide range of functions within the profession.

Public relations activities

Public relations work may be undertaken as a consultant or as an in-house practitioner. As consultants, practitioners have several or many clients or accounts, balancing their time among these. One obvious benefit is the variety of work this allows in terms of job locations, people to work with and the development of different accounts. In-house practitioners work solely for one organisation. The major benefits of this type of employment are the chance to get to know an organisation 'from the inside out' and the ease of access to management, facilities, and so on.

In either capacity, the public relations practitioner's job is a multifaceted one in which many roles overlap. The roles and key activities may be broadly summed up in the following areas:

- *communication*—imparting or exchanging thoughts, opinions or messages through visual, oral or written means;
- *publicity*—disseminating purposefully planned and executed messages through selected media, without payment, to further the particular interests of an organisation;
- *promotions*—activities designed to create and stimulate interest in a person, product, organisation or cause;

- *press agentry*—generation of 'soft news' stories—sometimes through stunts—usually associated with the entertainment industry;
- *integrated marketing*—public relations functions that support the marketing or advertising aims of an organisation;
- *issues management*—identification, monitoring of and action on public policy matters of concern to an organisation;
- *crisis management*—dealing with a crisis, disaster or negative unplanned events and maximising any positive outcomes these might have;
- *press secretary/public information officer*—acting as liaison between political representatives or government departments and the media;
- *public affairs/lobbyist*—working on behalf of private organisations in dealing with politicians and public servants who determine policy and legislation to either maintain the status quo or effect change;
- *financial relations*—dealing with and communicating information to shareholders of an organisation and the investment community;
- *community relations*—establishing and maintaining relationships between organisations and community groups affected by each other;
- *internal relations*—establishing and maintaining relationships with the people involved in the same organisation;
- *industry relations*—establishing and maintaining relationships with, or on behalf of, companies within an industry group;
- *minority relations*—establishing and maintaining relationships with, or on behalf of, minority groups and individuals;
- *media relations*—establishing and maintaining relationships between the media and an organisation;
- *public diplomacy*—establishing and maintaining relationships to enhance trade, tourism and general goodwill between nations;
- *event management*—preparing, planning and carrying out significant events spanning a limited time frame;
- *sponsorship*—offering or receiving financial or in-kind support in return for public exposure;
- *cause/relationship marketing*—establishing and maintaining relationships to engender customer loyalty and support;
- *fundraising*—establishing and maintaining relationships on behalf of the not-for-profit sector to stimulate public donations and support.

Relationship to marketing and advertising

Students new to public relations often ask the question: 'How exactly is public relations different from marketing and advertising?' Marketing is usually understood to relate to the buying and selling of products and services, and is thus the function of the organisation devoted to gaining profit through those products and services. A useful definition is 'a social and managerial process by which individuals and groups obtain what they need and want through creating and exchanging products and value with others' (Kotler et al. 1998: 6). Some of the tools and functions of public relations can be used to assist the promotion and sales of products and services, and are thus included in the 'marketing mix'. This is often known as 'integrated communications' or 'marketing public relations'. However, as can be seen from the list above, this is by no means the sum of the many roles and activities of public relations. And, as Hunt and McKie (1998) point out, one of the big differences between marketing and public relations is that marketing has a profit focus, which does not necessarily apply to public relations.

Confusion also often arises among students over the difference between advertising and public relations in the mass media. Advertising is the buying of space—in newspapers or magazines, or on radio and television—for the purpose of transmitting a message to an audience. The distinguishing feature of advertising messages in the mass media is that they are *controlled*. This means that both the content of the advertisement (wording, artwork, etc.) and its placement and frequency (lower quarter of page three in Saturday's *Sydney Morning Herald*, or during Channel 9's *Sixty Minutes*) are determined by the organisation buying the space. Few restrictions apply so long as the organisation can afford the price, the product is legal, and the wording and graphics are not offensive. By contrast, the mass media space achieved by a public relations practitioner's publicity is 'free'. The media outlets do not charge the practitioner for printing all or part of a press release or a newsworthy photograph. However, the practitioner has no control over whether such material will be used, how favourable the usage will be, or whether a competitor's or opponent's views will be aired or even given more prominence or sympathetic treatment. In this sense, publicity is considered to be *uncontrolled*. (The differences between controlled and uncontrolled media are further discussed in Chapter 8.)

Naturally, modern media-savvy readers or viewers perceive the information that they receive through advertisements or in editorial completely differently. Understanding that advertisers, having paid considerable amounts for the privilege of doing so, will naturally extol the virtues of their product, consumers discount or distrust much of the positive information provided in advertisements. Similar information coming from a journalist in the pages of a newspaper or magazine carries far more conviction. It is in this independent third-party endorsement that much of the power of public relations lies. As Van Meter puts it: 'Advertising is visibility, public relations is credibility.' (1999: 6)

One of the best ways to explain how an integrated marketing communications program can work is to build on some student work that didn't quite hit the target. A group of first-year public relations students presented their plan for the launch of a new European car in Australia. The plan was strong on marketing: it included details of the television and magazine advertising planned for the launch; it targeted a specific buyer and made sure the chosen media was directed at the buyer; it even included a competition to give away one of the new cars and provided a cost estimate of $5 million for the three-month advertising campaign, a realistic figure when considering the cost of national advertising.

The plan did not, however, consider how to use public relations to maximise exposure beyond the $5 million or truly develop an image for the car. A public relations campaign could have been integrated into the marketing campaign. Uncontrolled publicity could have included articles in the motoring sections of newspapers; staging road tests on national television lifestyle programs could have achieved prime-time exposure; write-ups in specialist magazines could have gained further exposure; a sponsorship package could have been developed linking the car to an upmarket sport such as polo; a well-known person who related to the target market could have been signed to endorse and drive the car; and a spectacular party could have been planned for its launch. All of this would have further developed the image of the sought-after European car in a new market niche. Public relations and marketing working together on such a campaign would complement each other, both to improve sales of the vehicle and to create a longer-term position for it in the marketplace. (Some further examples of integrated marketing are discussed in Chapter 14.)

The roles of public relations and marketing are summed up in Figure 1.1, which shows the areas of discrete responsibility and intersections.

Very often, a variety of skills, tactics and techniques are necessary in a campaign. This requires the roles of the public relations, marketing and advertising practitioners to come together. So, while these three areas may be independent, they are also often interdependent. It is therefore beneficial for practitioners to not only acknowledge the importance of the roles played by the other parties, but to be informed of and knowledgable about these roles in order to produce the best outcomes for clients.

Figure 1.1 Public relations and marketing often overlap—this figure shows separate and overlapping areas

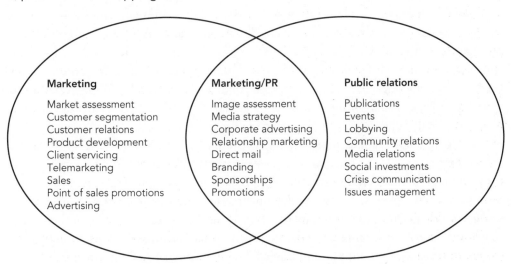

Marketing

Market assessment
Customer segmentation
Customer relations
Product development
Client servicing
Telemarketing
Sales
Point of sales promotions
Advertising

Marketing/PR

Image assessment
Media strategy
Corporate advertising
Relationship marketing
Direct mail
Branding
Sponsorships
Promotions

Public relations

Publications
Events
Lobbying
Community relations
Media relations
Social investments
Crisis communication
Issues management

One way in which the relationship-building aspects of public relations are used to enhance an organisation's marketing objectives is known as 'data mining'. Sophisticated computer software allows the information stored on databases (made up of banking transaction records, warranty cards, competition entries or even phone orders for pizza) to be sorted in order to allow a company to tailor its marketing messages, customising its relationship with the consumer. According to the Commercial Economic Advisory Service of Australia, the use of data-mining techniques has meant that, for the first time, the amount of money spent on direct marketing in 1999 overtook that of mainstream advertising (Sexton and Hornery 1999: 63). The aim is to use information to strengthen the bond between the organisation and the customer—not necessarily to increase sales in the short term, but to engender loyalty, selling more by building commitment over the long term.

An example is that of a London photographer who, on several visits to Hong Kong, had always stayed at the Mandarin Oriental Hotel. On his first trip to Bangkok, he decided to stay at the Oriental Hotel in that city. After he checked in, he went to have a drink at the bar. He handed over his room key to the bartender, who swiped it on the register. The bartender turned to him—he had not introduced himself or uttered a word—and asked: 'Your usual, Mr Randall?' The accumulated information about him on the hotel's database was being used to make him feel welcome, comfortable, recognised, appreciated and at home—precisely the effect that a five-star hotel strives for. The photographer is now a convert to Oriental

Hotels: if there is one in a city he's visiting, he will now stay there in preference to anywhere else (Evans, in Sexton and Hornery 1999: 63).

Another example is that of Hoyts Cinemas, which gather customer information on their website and use that information to extend tailored offers to moviegoers. For example, if you go online to the Hoyts website, you are invited to join a special club that allows you to receive cut-price tickets, an email newsletter and other special discount offers. Hoyts use the information provided by club members to SMS special deals, including a recent co-promotion with Pizza Hut that offered recipients of the message a special 'dinner and movie' deal.

The activities of some data miners, particularly in selling private information about their customers to other corporations, has meant that in recent years the privacy regulations in Australia have been strengthened significantly. It is now a legal requirement for those seeking private information from their customers to inform those customers whether or not that information will be passed on to any other party, or whether it will be maintained confidentially by the organisation. They must give customers the ability to 'opt out' of having their private information used for further marketing purposes, including receiving further marketing information from that same organisation. Failure to comply attracts strong penalties from the ACCC.

The amendment to the privacy legislation also identifies the issue of data matching, which is the sharing of databases between organisations. You can find further information on the Australian Direct Marketing Association's website: or <www.adma.com.au/site/privacyPolicy.htm> and <www.privacy.gov.au/act/datamatching/ index.html>.

This issue of privacy demonstrates that, although the use of data mining can offer similar results to those of public relations activities, it is not public relations. The Australian Consumers' Association has warned that data mining can be a double-edged sword, and is concerned that it can also be used by companies to get rid of undesirable customers, such as the aged or the poor (Bun, in Sexton and Hornery 1999: 63). This can lead to consumer backlash against the organisation. It is the role of the public relations practitioner to ensure that such damaging uses do not occur and that information is used to protect and enhance relationships between the organisation and its publics.

From publics to markets

Just as there is a need to examine the differences and intersections between public relations, marketing and advertising, there is also a need to consider the groups of people who are at the centre of this activity. These groups are usually referred to as publics, stakeholders, audiences and markets.

Publics and stakeholders

A public is any group of people who share interests or concerns. Publics may be active or latent/passive. An *active public* consists of individuals who know that they share interests or concerns with others. For example, property owners affected by the erection of a mobile telephone tower at the end of their street and who combine as a citizens' action group are an active public of the telephone company. The same group of people, before notification of the telephone company's plans for the mobile telephone tower, are a latent or passive public. This particular citizens' action group may combine with other similarly affected groups and proceed to lobby local, state or federal government, thus becoming an active public for these government organisations as well as the telephone company.

Sometimes groups are called *stakeholders* instead of publics. This term tends to be used to describe people who have a stake or an interest in an organisation or its actions. In this respect, the terms stakeholder and public are reasonably interchangeable, so long as they are used in a consistent manner. However, one of the important attributes of publics—the ability to change from active to passive and back again—is not assigned to stakeholders. A stakeholder's interest is always active.

Publics can be internal or external. An *internal public* is the group of people who exist within an organisation. These can be the employees of an organisation, members of a group or club, or volunteers of a not-for-profit group. *External publics* are all others—including customers, community groups, lobby groups, the mass media, voters, competitors, legislators and other special-interest groups.

Markets and audiences

Additionally, the terms 'audiences' and 'markets' are used to describe groups affected by, and affecting, organisations. These two groups are more narrowly defined than publics. *Audiences* are the groups of people who receive messages, either from the mass media or through other communications channels. Simply put, to have an audience you must also have a message. A public can be made up of several audiences, who may receive messages through different media.

Markets are identified and targeted by organisations as part of the process of making a profit. To have a market, you must have a product or service that requires an economic exchange. Dealings with a market require the focus to be on this exchange.

Skills needed in public relations

So what skills do public relations practitioners require? Whether they are employed in-house or within a consultancy, in a large organisation as part of a team or in a small organisation as sole practitioner, there are certain skills needed by all graduates entering and remaining successful in the profession. At a meeting of public relations educators in 1998, the following list of desirable skills gained during public relations education was devised, and has been summarised and developed for this book. The public relations graduate should strive for:

- an understanding of how public relations and communications theory informs public relations practice;
- the capacity to plan and analyse while developing a problem-solving approach;
- strong technical and communication skills;
- strong relationship/interpersonal skills;
- a strong social, political and ethical appreciation with an understanding of the big picture and the interconnectedness of events;
- industry knowledge and perspective with knowledge of applications and processes.

Further to this list, certain key words and phrases were listed as desirable or critical in graduates. These were:

- possessing *vocational skills*—research, writing, listening, presentation and media;
- possessing *relationship skills*—interpersonal skills, political nous, networking ability, listening;
- possessing *professional skills*—the ability to meet deadlines and plan ahead;
- having a strong *ethical perspective*;
- *understanding technology* and how it can be used as a tool;
- possessing *industry knowledge*—undergoing professional experience, understanding how theory informs practice, keeping abreast of current affairs, developing the ability for lifelong learning;
- being *thinkers*—analytical, critical, strategic, evaluative, creative and lateral.

These give public relations students an insight into what they will need to achieve during their education, ensuring they are well equipped to cope in the job market and to maintain quality within the profession.

Trends in public relations

In 2002, one Australian public relations scholar noted that 'the face of public relations is female' (Rea 2002: 1). While empirical research in this area has been undertaken primarily in the United States, course coordinators in Australia anecdotally report that over 80 per cent of public relations students are women (Rea 2002). The reasons for this trend were identified by Donato as 'women being a "better-buy" than male employees, women being the new "consumer" public to whom practitioners could communicate . . . and a gender ideology of society that defined public relations as "women's work"' (in Toth 2001: 240). Feminist studies of public relations have considered public relations in the context of the 'glass ceiling'—that is, the invisible ceiling that restricts women from reaching the upper levels of organisations. Studies have shown that, while it was once considered that men moved from the technician's role to the manager's role more easily, women tended to do both roles rather than moving from one to the other (Toth 2001).

Another trend in the industry is the emergent practice of working from home. Due to the mobility required in the industry, it is often not necessary for the practitioner to be based in a commercial office, and this trend to small and boutique consultancies has opened up opportunities for the practitioner who wants to work part time or wishes to combine parenting with work.

It would appear that this trend towards flexible work practices is resulting in a further development: the emergence of women at the senior levels of the public relations industry as women return to full-time work after 'juggling' small children and part-time work. Added to this has been the first and second generation of graduates from specialised university courses, which has resulted in the creation of highly skilled, in-demand professionals, most of whom are women. Additionally, the other traditional 'breeding ground' for public relations practitioners—journalism—is now itself far from being male dominated. This layering of change needs to be taken into consideration in any theorisation of the feminisation of public relations.

As public relations establishes a firm foothold at the management level of organisations, a further trend is the need to work alongside other professionals and advise them accordingly. In the days where public relations centred on press agentry, there was little need for practitioners to work in tandem with other professionals. Today's practitioners communicate with and advise IT professionals, lawyers, accountants and financial advisers, marketing managers, environmental experts, graphic designers, advertising executives, human resource managers and psychologists, who in turn feed back into the public relations knowledge bank. The trend toward specialised knowledge increasingly demands that these channels remain open to reduce risk for the organisation.

Public relations in university curricula

Public relations is a relatively new discipline to Australian universities. The first degree courses were introduced in the late 1960s by four institutions: Mitchell College of Advanced Education, Bathurst; Queensland Institute of Technology; NSW Institute of Technology; and Royal Melbourne Institute of Technology. It is now taught at most universities and many colleges (Anderson 1999).

The degrees on offer at these various institutions are not identical. This is because public relations is not housed in the same faculty, department or school in every university. For example, Curtin University's course is taught in the School of Marketing and Deakin University's in the School of Literature and Communication, while at Bond University it is taught in the School of Humanities and Social Sciences. At Griffith University in Queensland, public relations is taught in the School of Arts and at Edith Cowan University it is offered by the School of Communication and Multimedia.

Predictably—and sensibly—many students are combining their public relations degrees with other study, undertaking double degrees or double majors. The combinations chosen by students will vary according to their interests and will be important in determining their career options (see box below). It is important for first-year students to think carefully about the double major or double degree options available to them. Many students get well into their degrees before they consider this, wasting precious time, money and energy studying subjects that end up being of little or no use to them. The best advice is to keep your options open. Of course, choices will depend on the university: popular double majors include public relations/marketing; public relations/advertising; public relations/journalism; public relations/media studies; public relations/management; and public relations/ international relations. It is possible to do a double degree—for example, in public relations and law—depending upon specific university offerings. New students should discuss options with career advisers or course convenors.

Many degrees which offer public relations as a major are accredited by the PRIA. In 1991 the PRIA introduced a formal accreditation for undergraduate and postgraduate degrees. The guidelines for accreditation are updated every five years, establishing an ongoing benchmarking system for each accredited tertiary institution. Accreditation of degree courses requires a thorough analysis of courses, teaching resources and educators. Some basic principles of accreditation are summed up in the guidelines:

> The fundamental purpose of an undergraduate public relations education is to provide the student with a well-rounded program of study . . . it should be aimed at developing the intellectual and problem-solving capacities of students as well as giving them a sound understanding of the theory and practice of communication and public relations. (PRIA 2002: 3)

As this passage clearly indicates, the focus of quality education in public relations needs a combination of theoretical and practical input. The following chapters aim to present a careful mix of these two ingredients.

Conclusion

Predicting the future of any industry is always tricky—in the communications industries, such as public relations, this is even more so. Increasing fragmentation of messages and media make consumers and audiences harder to reach. Growing cynicism about messages also makes publics harder to motivate or influence. What we do know, however, is that in this environment the public relations industry appears to be strengthening its foothold as it competes with other communication industries, particularly mainstream advertising. According to John MacGregor, Managing Director of Edelman Public Relations Australia, 'the hottest marketing trend in the US is to devote more of your budget to PR than to booked advertising space' (in Callaghan 1999). As the public relations industry continues to expand, job opportunities in this exciting and dynamic profession will expand with it.

Career paths

Tamara Morris

Tamara majored in public relations and marketing. Months before graduating, Tamara was running a busy media relations and event management consultancy while the senior executive spent four weeks in Manchester heading the media unit at the 2002 Commonwealth Games. When she finished her studies, Tamara worked on a range of accounts including the Asia Pacific Masters Games, the Surfers Paradise International Criterium, a large specialist medical practice and a state Member of Parliament.

Julie O'Dell

Julie majored in marketing and public relations and, upon graduation, immediately took up a position as a communications officer with the not-for-profit group Lifeline. She began as a publicity officer but rapidly moved into the role of Promotions Coordinator, heading the busy Fundraising and Promotions Department. She organises high-profile events such as the Lifeline Sporting Heroes Dinner, writes grant applications to Australian and international philanthropic and government organisations (and has been successful with the likes of Paul Newman's Own and the federal government), and writes all advertising and brochure copy for the regional office where she is based.

Todd Balym

Todd Balym graduated with a Bachelor of Communications majoring in Public Relations and Journalism. While completing the three-year degree, he was heavily involved in the public relations of elite-level swimming events. A consultancy PR position for Australian Swimming involved work in Melbourne promoting the international World Cup. He also provided research services to various media for the Commonwealth Games. He now writes full time as a specialist sports writer for the *Gold Coast Bulletin*.

Sebastian Kowalski

Sebastian graduated with a Bachelor of Communications and followed a path in political public relations as Assistant Electorate Officer to the state Member for Surfers Paradise. In this role he writes all the press releases for the MP, attends meetings that relate to the electorate of Surfers Paradise and assists the MP at Parliament House when Parliament is sitting. His role includes liaising with local police and community groups and gaining feedback on topical issues such as shark meshing. In addition, he deals with any concerns from constituents within the electorate.

Discussion and exercises

1   Some products, such as condoms, are difficult to advertise. Discuss how public relations can be used to convey the benefits of such products and devise a campaign that uses only public relations tools and techniques and not advertising.

2   Identify and discuss key phrases of the following definition: the ethical and strategic management of communication and relationships in order to build and develop coalitions and policy, identify and manage issues and create and direct messages to achieve sound outcomes within a socially responsible framework. How might these different elements work together in a public relations program for Coca-Cola or McDonald's?

3   Identify and discuss which of the twenty public relations activities listed in this chapter would be utilised by the graduates in the 'Career paths' box in their different jobs.

4   Using Figure 1.1, identify and analyse a promotional program that combines marketing and public relations activities.

Recommended reading

Baskin, O., Aronoff, C. & Lattimore, D. (1997) *Public Relations: The Profession and the Practice*, 4th edn, Brown & Benchmark, Madison.

Cutlip, S., Center, A. & Broom, G. (1985) *Effective Public Relations*, 6th edn, Prentice Hall, Englewood Cliffs, New Jersey.

Grunig, J. & Hunt, T. (1984) *Managing Public Relations*, Holt, Rinehart & Winston, New York.

Heath, R. (ed.) (2002), *Handbook of Public Relations*, Sage, Thousand Oaks, California.
Newsom, D., VanSlyke Turk, J. & Kruckeberg, D. (1996) *This is PR*, 6th edn, Wadsworth, Belmont.
Wilcox, D., Ault, P.H. & Agee, W.K. (1997) *Public Relations Strategies and Tactics*, HarperCollins, New York.

References

Anderson, M. (1999) *Public Relations Education*, PRIA, Sydney.
Barnes, D. (1967) *What is Public Relations?*, PRIA, Sydney.
Burson, H. (1987) 'Tips and Tactics', in Jackson, P. (ed.), *PR Reporter*, 23 March.
Callaghan, G. (1999) 'Sultans of spin', *Weekend Australian*, 24–25 July, p. 26.
Davidson, C. (2002) Personal interview, Sydney.
Dozier, D., Grunig, L. & Grunig, J. (1995) *The Manager's Guide to Excellence in Public Relations and Communication Management*, Lawrence Erlbaum, New Jersey.
Foster, C. (1995) *The Crowe Communication Report*, Crowe Communications, Sydney.
Grunig, J. & Hunt, T. (1984) *Managing Public Relations*, Holt Rinehart & Winston, New York.
Hudson, M. (2002) Personal interview, Brisbane.
Hunt, M.L. & McKie, D. (1998) *Staking Claims: Marketing, Public Relations and Territories*, paper presented to public relations educators session at the 1998 PRIA Convention, 7–10 October.
Kotler, P., Armstrong, G., Brown, L., & Adam, S. (1998) *Marketing*, 4th edn, Prentice Hall, Sydney.
Lee, R. (1999) 'Belittling of culture disguised as debate', *Sydney Morning Herald*, 10 July, p. 47.
McElreath, M. (1996) *Systematic and Ethical Public Relations*, 2nd edn, Brown & Benchmark, Madison.
Public Relations Institute of Australia (PRIA) (2002) *Guidelines for the Accreditation of Courses in Public Relations at Australian Tertiary Institutions*.
Rea, J. (2002) 'The feminisation of public relations: What's in it for the girls?', conference proceedings of Australia and New Zealand Communications Association, Gold Coast, June.
Sexton, E. & Hornery, A. (1999) 'The baiting game', *Sydney Morning Herald*, 17 July, pp. 59, 63.
Toth, E.L. (2001) 'How feminist theory advanced the practice of public relations', in Robert Heath (ed.), *Handbook of Public Relations*, Sage, Thousand Oaks.
Van Meter, J. (1999) 'Why advertising increasingly doesn't work and public relations does', <www.fleishman.com/cybercafe/zinestory_0.3.html>.

2 A HISTORY OF PUBLIC RELATIONS IN AUSTRALIA

Clara Zawawi

In this chapter

Introduction
Promotion through press agentry—the emergence of public relations
Publicity to public relations
Changes in Australian public relations
Public relations and the media
External environment and social responsibility of the press
Conclusion
Chronology of the development of public relations in Australia

Introduction

The whole notion of public relations as described in this book is relatively new in Australia. The first listing for public relations practitioners appeared in the Sydney phone book in 1952, the Public Relations Institute of Australia (PRIA) was founded in 1959, and the first degree course in public relations was offered at Mitchell College in Bathurst (now Charles Sturt University) in 1969. Like all professions, public relations has experienced a period of development into its final form and many of the activities and functions of public relations (as described in Chapter 1) have quite a long history, even prior to the 1950s. People and events, together with social and technological factors, have all had an impact. A strong influence is apparent from the United States, though public relations in Australia is unique, not only in the way in which it developed but in the way it is practised today. This chapter provides an overview and a chronology for the development of public relations in Australia.

Promotion through press agentry—the emergence of public relations

Between the 1840s and 1890s, three significant developments occurred which had implications for the development of the public relations industry in Australia. The first was the implementation of the *Education Act 1872*. With the development of schools and schooling programs over the next twenty years, nearly all young Australian men could read and write by the 1890s (Ward 1958: 196). This enlarged the audience for newspapers, which had until this time been largely reserved for a small, educated, politically aware elite with a primary interest in politics and business, to one with a much broader spread of interests. This led newspapers to cover a wider range of issues with a greater variety of content.

The second development was the creation of a technology that would allow the production of daily newspapers (the *Sydney Morning Herald* became Australia's first daily in 1841). Daily publishing created an interesting problem for the press. In the sixteenth century, the publishers of America's first newspaper could simply say that they would publish once a month or more regularly if there was more news. But in the mid-nineteenth century, newspapers had to satisfy advertisers' demands for regular publication. As is still the case today, the size of the publication was determined by the amount of advertising sold. This economic fact, and the demand by readers to have something new for their money each day, put publishers under pressure to find more editorial material to fill the spaces between the advertisements.

The earliest advertising agencies were well placed to help the newspapers out. Two of Australia's first advertising agencies, Gordon & Gotch in Melbourne and Greville's in Sydney, were press agencies as well. They bought advertising space in country newspapers in exchange for news. As a great deal of advertising in country papers was for products available only from the city by mail order, this was an arrangement that suited everyone very well. Edward Greville in particular would have found providing editorial copy easy, as he had press interests himself, owning the *Sydney Evening Mail* for a short time.

The third development lay in the depoliticisation of newspapers. The earliest newspapers had been highly political, often owned or heavily subsidised by political parties. However, newspapers that targeted political factions could not attract a wide enough audience to satisfy the requirements of advertisers. In fact, they ran the risk of encouraging other factions to boycott the products advertised in their pages. By increasing their financial reliance on advertising, newspaper proprietors were able to end their dependence on political factions, and stopped slanting their stories ideologically. Taking their cue from the international news agencies, which had been forced to report objectively in order to sell their stories widely, newspapers began to print objective stories that would not alienate readers and would offer advertisers the largest possible audience (Granato 1991: 18).

It did not take long for the new-found principle of objectivity from political involvement to come into conflict with the interests of advertisers. Entertainment had become important to newspapers. The theatre, vaudeville and, later in the century, movies used newspapers extensively, not just for advertising but to gain editorial coverage. Promoters sent in so-called puff pieces—promotional material barely disguised as editorial copy—and journalists were accused of cooperating too closely with advertisers in seeing to it that such material got into print. In 1864, *Sydney Punch* lambasted the providers of such puff pieces as people whom it 'hates, abjures, abhors, detests and spurns' (17 September 1864: 131).

There is no hard evidence for it, but we can speculate that the advertising agencies that were also press agencies were the source of some of these puff pieces. If so, these were the first companies in Australia to employ the one-way communication model of press agentry (discussed further in Chapter 3). By all accounts, their efforts were successful—by the 1890s, the *Bulletin* magazine was complaining that such advertisements, disguised as news, were common (Mayer 1964: 157).

As people became aware of the demand to fill editorial space, puffery gave way to publicity, the earliest form of public relations. As with puffery, entertainment was the inspiration, and the first great publicists whose antics were covered in Australian newspapers appeared in America. Leading the field in the United States was Phineas T. Barnum, who staged stunts to achieve press coverage for his circus. In 1835, for example, Barnum exhibited a black slave named Joice Heth, whom he claimed had nursed George Washington 100 years earlier. Newspapers ran the story and Barnum achieved extensive publicity for his circus (Bernays 1952: 38–39).

Barnum's methods of attracting attention and press coverage were widely copied. In 1868, W.W. Duran, who worked for a rival circus, was the first person to formally use the title 'press agent'—meaning one who 'provided representation to the press'—trying to get news coverage for his circus (Irwin 1911: 24–25). Press agents and publicists found ready employment in all areas of entertainment. The growth of the new film industry and its requirements for promotion and publicity provided an enormous impetus to growth in press agentry.

Promotion was possibly more important to the film industry than to any other, because of the high costs of production and distribution. Each film, being unique, needed extensive individual promotion in order to attract an audience and recover costs. In Australia before World War I, however, selling and promoting films was an uncoordinated activity undertaken by individual, independent exhibitors. This changed when the US production/distribution companies entered the Australian market. By the 1920s, almost all the major Hollywood studios had offices in Australia and the contract system, which linked control of production to distribution, meant that they had automatic control of exhibition and, of course, publicity (Collins 1987: 13).

The predominance of American film companies in Australia had an immense effect on the way Australian publicists viewed and carried out promotion and publicity. During the 1920s, it was usual for the Australian operation of such companies as Paramount, Fox and Selznick to be headed by Americans, who introduced American-style publicity, sales and motivational concepts and techniques. Each company had its own advertising department, designing posters and newspaper and magazine advertisements, as well as a department of 'ballyhoo' or 'exploitation', which specialised in thinking up headline-grabbing stunts, and a department of 'publicity', in which employees spent time thinking up exciting stories to plant in the press (Collins 1987: 142). From 1921 onwards, Australian publicity staff travelled regularly to the United States for training, and at this time talented publicity men (and they *were* all men!) were among the highest-paid and most sought-after employees in the Australian film industry (Collins 1987: 146–49).

The Australian press apparently took a dim view of film publicists, accusing them of regurgitating 'American dope-sheets' provided by head offices in the United States. Australian publicists such as Ken Hall (later a prominent film director) defended their actions, pointing out that they provided a kind of cultural translation service. Translation was as far as they went in adapting their work to Australia, however. They were, after all, using American publicity as their model, with the same techniques, the same visual and literary styles and the same marketing devices. The image or the name of the star dominated promotional design and superlative-laden film advertising was overwhelmingly targeted at women (Collins 1987: 152–57). It was stunts, however, that achieved free editorial copy. To publicise *Ben Hur*, a man in Roman costume drove in a chariot from Sydney to Melbourne, and as part of the promotions for a Western, *The Iron Horse*, half a dozen 'Indians' on piebald ponies pursued a model of a train through Australia's cities (Collins 1987: 163).

Publicity to public relations

In the 1930s, movie promoters changed direction. The impact of the Depression required a more restrained treatment of promotion, and by the mid-1930s extravagant stunts were rare. Not only did such stunts sit badly with an impoverished audience, but their box office return was often hard to measure, and newspaper advertising was far more easily monitored (Collins 1987: 167). The female angle was pursued even harder, and with good reason. By 1935 women were an important part of newspaper audiences, leading the English press baron Lord Northcliffe to advise his editors: 'Always have one woman's story at the top of all the main news pages of your paper.' (Moseley 1935: 304) A growing range of publications aimed at women were utilised to place Hollywood publicity stories. Through the 1930s and 1940s, Australian newspapers and magazines contained beauty hints, short stories, fashion photos and studio news about Hollywood stars (Collins 1987: 171). These publicity stories were not necessarily linked to a particular film, but described the lives of the stars, their marriages, homes and leisure activities (1987: 173).

The publicists enjoyed success for their efforts, proven by an article in the publication *A.M.* in 1930 which said: 'The Press has a first duty to the public, but it does also owe something in the way of honest and justifiable support to advertisers. That obviously is recognised by the amount of free editorial publicity which is now to be found in the pages of almost every newspaper.' (September 1930: 31–32) This was the case even though many Australian businesses still avoided promotion (Collins 1987: 146). Society in the 1930s was very different from society today. Reputable middle- and upper-class people did not appear in the newspapers unless it was in the social pages. The antics dreamed up by the publicists to gain coverage for entertainers did not help that prejudice. Serious businesspeople did not consider using publicists at all—the publicists were linked too closely to entertainment (Joel 1995).

In the United States, however, things had changed. The founding of the first National Consumers' Group in America in 1899 and the emergence of 'muckraking' journalism, dedicated to exposing corruption in business and politics, meant that businesses had to change their style to begin to communicate with the public. Ivy Lee pioneered this type of public relations in his work for the Pennsylvania Railroad, among other clients, in the 1920s and 1930s (Newsom et al. 1993: 42–44). An alternative to the 'ballyhoo' style of publicity for more conservative Australian business did exist, but it was not yet being utilised in Australia.

The combination of mass circulation and the growing importance of entertainment, advertising and news brought newspapers large profits, attracting the interest of the Packer family—still a dominant force in the Australian media industry. They bought and closed down the last Australian Labor Party-owned newspaper, the *World*, on 14 November 1932, and used its presses to begin production of the *Australian Women's Weekly* (Cook 1969: 55–57; Whitington 1971: 122). Enormously popular and profitable with the female audience, the *Weekly* used Hollywood publicity extensively. In 1936, some 25 per cent of its page space—twelve pages— was given over to a 'Movie World' feature containing material exclusively provided by Hollywood publicists (Collins 1987: 172). This enormous quantity of free, ready-made editorial material meant that the *Weekly* needed to employ fewer journalists—contributing significantly to its profitability.

In 1936, the prominent British writer R.C.K. Ensor published a complaint that news was being 'doctored' by owners, editors and journalists. In his opinion, the daily press had changed the way in which it handled news and editorial opinion. According to Ensor, in the past these two had been kept very separate, with 'news' being a list of facts from which readers could form their own judgment and editorial opinion provided by separate articles written by the most senior people in the organisation, or sometimes by good outside writers. Ensor argued that opinion had now crept into news, which meant that instead of having points of view openly argued, the news was slanted to present opinions, preventing readers from drawing their own conclusions and leading to a proliferation of propaganda (Ensor, in Burns 1979: 52). The aim of much modern public relations effort is to influence the news in exactly this way, and it is in the 1930s that we first find proof of such activity.

Changes in Australian public relations

The arrival of General Douglas MacArthur in Brisbane in 1943 with a public relations staff of 35 was the catalyst for change in Australian public relations. Asher Joel, at that time a journalist who had joined the Navy (he was later knighted), became a member of MacArthur's public relations staff, working under Brigadier General LeGrande Diller. Apart from his journalism experience, Joel had another insight into the way in which publicists operated—his brother had been the publicity officer for a major studio before the war. According to Joel, MacArthur and Diller both realised the power and influence that the media could exert and both worked hard to ensure that they maintained strategic control of every piece of information that went out to the huge media contingent that accompanied MacArthur as Allied Commander-in-Chief.

Joel saw the influence that could be exerted through the media and how that influence was used by MacArthur and his team. He saw how news was suppressed and manufactured for journalists, news photographers and broadcasters. Most importantly, he learned that public relations was not just about getting publicity. Rather, public relations was often based on *not* getting publicity. He began to understand that public relations was about messages and how these were conveyed.

MacArthur and Diller, like the movie publicists before them, introduced American methods of public relations practice to Australia. Accustomed to the realisation that organisations—especially the Army—could not afford to ignore public opinion, they worked assiduously to ensure that public opinion remained on their side. Steinberg considers World War II to be the catalyst that allowed public relations to develop into a 'full-fledged profession' (Steinberg, in Newsom et al. 1993: 27).

The US Office of War Information was responsible exclusively for disseminating information and disinformation worldwide. Allied to the War Advertising Council, it won support for the war effort in America and overseas, sold war bonds and got the cooperation of the public, industry and labour (Newsom et al. 1993: 50). The distinguishing characteristic of the public relations practitioners working for the Office of War Information, as opposed to the earlier publicists, was their focus on 'news management'. This was different from publicity. Instead of regarding any publicity as good publicity, the new approach stressed that press coverage must be managed, controlled and influenced to achieve an end that might have nothing to do with product sales but everything to do with public opinion. This was the concept that MacArthur and Diller brought to Australia in 1943. To Joel, this idea was a revelation (Joel 1995). Newsreels, radio and newspapers—the media through which all Australians received their war information—became important tools in building morale and garnering support for the war effort.

When Joel returned to Sydney after the war, he set up a business that made use of the techniques he had learnt during his service with Diller. George Freeman, who described himself as a persuader of public opinion rather than a publicist, and whose main business interest was as fundraiser for the Dalwood Home for Children, agreed to join Joel in a *Yellow Pages* listing as Australia's first public relations practitioners (Joel 1995).

Over the next ten years, Joel worked hard to promote an understanding of how his business differed from that of publicist, both to clients and to publicists. He founded the Public Relations Institute of Australia (PRIA), hosting lunches designed as forums for describing public relations practice as a part of business management strategy. While only a handful of practitioners were members in the early 1950s, the PRIA now boasts around 2000 members, affiliates and student members.

In the early 1950s, however, most of the so-called public relations businesses still offered only publicity or press agentry, under a fancier name: 'It was merely a change of name and not a change [of activity] . . . It was still just publicity.' (Joel 1995)

Much of the early development of public relations took place within government departments. In 1949, the New South Wales Public Service Board appointed public relations officers to a number of departments and also began to train practitioners to provide a pool for future appointments (Barnes 1957: 5). Many organisations and businesses—notably the airlines and the banks—established internal public relations departments (Barnes 1957: 5). Public relations consultancies were slower to develop—in 1950, there were only three PR consultancies in Sydney. They belonged to Asher Joel, Eric White & Associates and an American, Dr Winchester (Hike) Hiker. By 1957, the number of consultancies in Sydney had risen to around 30, with about the same number in Melbourne. By the late 1950s, Eric White & Associates had set up six offices in Asia and one in London, becoming Australia's first international public relations consultancy. Its clients, among which were the Commonwealth Banking Corporation and the Australian Finance Industry Association, were a far cry from the vaudeville clients of the early publicists. By 1959, the concept of a wide range of businesses wanting press coverage was familiar enough for the magazine *Advertising* to publish an article arguing for the provision of more non-financial business news by the press.

In 1961, an estimated £3 million was spent by Australian business on public relations consultants, and 'a much greater amount spent on internal consultants employed inside industry' (*Australian Financial Review*, 27 July 1961). Women were beginning to move into the industry. Esther Morrish, an ex-journalist, was a prominent consultant at Eric White during the 1960s and later. Peter Lazar, who was appointed as manager of Eric White's Sydney office in 1969, employed that company's first female consultant without a background in journalism in 1970 (Lazar 1999).

The introduction of television in 1956 added new elements to public relations practice. Though relatively few business and corporate stories appeared on TV news programs, placing or managing those that did required new skills on the part of the public relations practitioner. For example, events and launches had, until now, been geared towards print deadlines. Practitioners wanting to gain TV coverage had to reschedule events to allow the cameras to get to them, and allow time for editing in order to make the evening news. In many cases, the timing problems meant that practitioners had to think seriously about which audiences were more important for their message—those delivered by print (either morning or evening newspapers) or by television. The fact that the first owners of commercial television stations to be licensed were often the press proprietors in the regions and that in the earliest days local content was 'radio with pictures' (Cunningham 1997: 96) made delivering public relations content on television not much different to doing so in the other, more familiar, media.

Television's challenge to practitioners—to produce visuals more attractive than a talking head—proceeded to foster a climate of creativity not previously demanded by print and radio. Additionally, the importance of television spawned a need for media training of spokespeople, and this business became quite important in Sydney and Melbourne. Grooming services for corporate spokespeople and politicians became popular: the technology of the day demanded, for example, that people appearing on television wear blue rather than white shirts, and no stripes in case they 'strobed' or flickered disturbingly on the screen (Lazar 1999).

By the 1970s, the growing importance of TV news services gave rise to the making of video clips for the use of the networks. These videotapes were distributed by the public relations practitioners. Some networks even provided their studio and camera facilities to make these 'news release clips'. There was also an emphasis on providing community service announcements for television; although practitioners were accustomed to providing these for radio, they had now to become conversant with video technology (Lazar 1999).

The large multinational public relations firms moved into Australia in the early 1970s, with Eric White selling his firm to Hill & Knowlton, at that time the biggest of the internationals (Myers 1999). Advertising agencies began to look to buying public relations consultancies, seeking to consolidate client services. International advertising group Saatchi & Saatchi bought Neilsen McCarthy in the early 1970s. Other advertising agencies, such as J. Walter Thompson, maintained publicity departments to ensure that clients received in-house product promotion and marketing public relations support. This trend has continued, with nine of the ten top public relations consultancies in the world being bought by advertising agencies during the 1990s (Callaghan 1999).

The establishment of the first public relations degree courses (Mitchell College, Bathurst and Queensland Institute of Technology, Brisbane) not only allowed businesses to employ trained junior staff but helped open the profession to women. In the early 1970s, only around 10 per cent of public relations practitioners were women. It is estimated that the ratio of men to women hit the 50/50 mark some time in the early 1980s. In 1997, a survey of Queensland members of the PRIA (Zawawi 1997) showed that two-thirds were women. A quick examination of gender distribution finds this proportion echoed in the offices of Professional Public Relations, a national consultancy, where, out of 61 staff, only seventeen are men (Lazar 1999).

The 1980s and 1990s have seen continuing development and emphasis on public relations education at tertiary level, with a corresponding growth in the body of knowledge of the profession. The public relations industry showed an annual growth of 25 per cent between 1994 and 1999 (Callaghan 1999), and competent and well-trained graduates are much in demand. Many universities in all states offer PRIA-accredited courses, and many more are in the process of gaining accreditation. Both a cause and a result of education has been the desire of today's public relations practitioners to demonstrate that, though the roots of the industry may lie in publicity and sometimes questionable behaviour, modern practice has evolved into something far different.

Public relations and the media

In the mid-1950s, most of the people calling themselves public relations practitioners were ex-journalists. Journalists dealt daily with public relations practitioners and publicists and could see the difference between the two. Many journalists were well suited to becoming public relations advisers to business, being knowledgable about political, social, economic and industrial issues. In this phase of public relations, Australian practitioners became business advisers and news management became only part of the service being offered. Former political reporters, for example, were much in demand to give organisations advice related to government or politicians (Myers 1995).

The public relations practitioner's news management expertise lay in understanding how to achieve news coverage in the quality press—the publications important to business interests. A public relations news manager, being within the business information loop, could identify story ideas that would appeal to journalists. He (and they were all men until the 1960s) could then plant the idea for the story by issuing a company statement that would appeal to a journalist's news sense. The statement would either provide the angle for a story that the public relations news manager wanted to have published, or contain quotes that a journalist could legitimately use that would influence the slant of the story. The crucial difference from the efforts of earlier publicists was that, instead of providing finished editorial copy to the newspaper for unedited insertion, the public relations news manager understood that a journalist would write the story. The reward was access to the quality press for Australian business (Myers 1995). Because of this ability in news management, public relations news managers were accepted by business as publicists and press agents had not been.

This is not to say that public relations news managers had open access to news columns. Journalists who became public relations practitioners were looked down on by those who remained in journalism. The stereotype of the journalist who abandoned a low-paid but honourable job to become a well-paid mercenary of business was formulated at this time and remains strong today. Editors and press owners looked askance at public relations news managers' attempts to place material in their editorial columns. Their attitude was that, by printing stories prompted by public relations, their newspapers were giving free exposure, and if people wanted exposure they should pay for it through advertising.

Frank Packer in particular gave public relations practitioners a poor reception at the *Daily Telegraph* during the 1950s and 1960s. Practitioners of the time recall Sir Frank putting an active ban on public relations people entering the doors of the office, as well as on any material that came from public relations sources. He was known to go into the newspaper's offices and pull a front-page story because he believed it had been fed to the *Telegraph* by a source of this kind. This antagonism made the *Telegraph* difficult to deal with at the time.

But Packer's opposition to printing public relations material did not put the *Telegraph* completely out of bounds. The competitiveness between newspapers was then, as it is now, a major driving force for selection of news. No newspaper could afford to be consistently 'scooped' by its opposition. This competition underlies much of the success of news management. There were two morning newspapers in Sydney at the time, the *Sydney Morning Herald* and the *Telegraph*, and if the *Telegraph*'s owner would not print a newsworthy story because it happened to come from a public relations source, the *Herald* would. As the public relations profession grew, so too did the range and number of companies and organisations using the opportunities it had to offer. Important and newsworthy stories were being offered to the press by public relations practitioners and the *Telegraph* could not afford to cut itself off completely from the flow of information. Editors at the *Telegraph* learnt to keep public relations-sourced material away from Packer (Myers 1995).

In any case, newspapers were willing to provide editorial support to advertisers, as indicated by an interview given by the managing director of the Armidale Newspaper Company:

> I say without hesitation that where manufacturers or givers of service advertise with papers they get generous treatment in our news columns. The moral

is clear. We must never forget, however, that if a handout for a new detergent has to struggle with an item relating to the establishment of a nudist colony at Bourke or Booligal, the nudist colony will win. (*Advertising*, October 1959: 19)

It is telling that the support for advertisers was not uncritical. Material received from interested sources would be published only if it met the criterion of newsworthiness. The implication that many advertisers thought their editorial contributions should be published irrespective of newsworthiness is confirmed by the public relations manager of Felt & Textiles Australia, who in 1961 said that 60–70 per cent of advertisers believed that high-volume advertising entitled them to editorial space (Blanch 1961: 20). The already existing tensions between journalists and public relations practitioners, discussed above, were exacerbated by this attitude. The world was changing, and the public relations industry had to recognise this and keep up.

External environment and social responsibility of the press

The development of the role of public relations and the expectations placed on practitioners' activities took place over a long period of time. The world was changing dramatically, and many of the changes either assisted or actively promoted the development of public relations. A primary factor was the change in society's attitudes towards newspapers and other media. The expectations placed on journalists and editors as to how they should deliver news and comment had changed since the first newspapers were published. The concept of an impartial press dates from the early nineteenth century, but a truly impartial press had never really existed. The power and arrogance of such press barons as Britain's Lord Rothermere, who had boasted that he could ensure election of a political party by supporting it through his newspapers, and the increase in the range and reach of the new media of film and radio, contributed to widespread concern in the United States, England and Australia about the nature and direction of the press.

The role of newspapers is different (and the difference was even more marked in the early 1950s) from that of other media such as radio, television or film. Journalists have a unique socio-political role as the fourth estate, acting as watchdogs over those in power and reporting on their activities to inform those who vote for them, in order to allow the public to make informed decisions in the political process—the underpinning of democracy. Historically, journalists had done so through newspapers, and therefore the watchdog political role was adopted by the newspapers as well. The entertainment function was secondary in newspapers to the news function. The primacy of the news function and the watchdog role of newspapers have also meant that, to a great extent, newspapers were held to be independent of government control, for how could an institution established to ensure democratic freedom of speech be contained by any democratic government without risking that government's becoming authoritarian? Freedom of the press was argued to be synonymous with freedom of speech, a fundamental right enshrined in many democratic constitutions. The broadcast media—radio, television and film—by contrast, were held to be primarily entertainment media, with the news function being secondary. This distinction allowed governments in democratic nations such as Australia and the United States to charge licence fees and apply censorship to these media in a way that was not possible for newspapers.

The basis for a libertarian press system had been developed by Milton and Locke in the seventeenth century. As democratic political systems were established in the eighteenth and nineteenth centuries, libertarian theories were embedded in their constitutions or fundamental laws. Libertarian theorists assumed that, out of a multiplicity of voices in the press, some information reaching the public would be false and some opinions unsound. They argued, however, that the people could be trusted to accept that which served the needs of the individual and society. Libertarians also argued that the state did not have the right to suppress the publication of information, as this would inevitably lead to interference with arguments or opinions contrary to those held by the state (Seibert 1965: 50–51).

Such total freedom of the press never existed in reality. A range of prior restraints, from charges of seditious libel to obscenity, were imposed on newspaper publishers in Great Britain, the United States and Australia. During World War I, censorship of the press in areas that could be construed as obstructive to the war effort was imposed in all three countries. In 1919, US Supreme Court Justice Oliver Wendell Holmes advocated that the 'clear and present danger test' could be applied to allow government interference with freedom of expression when such freedom presented an urgent and real danger of bringing about evils that Congress had the right to prevent (Granato 1973: 210).

When film and television were developed, however, their primary function was entertainment and not news. Although radio was seen as an educational medium, it too was used extensively for entertainment from the earliest broadcasts, particularly in the United States and Australia. This crucial difference meant that governments licensed, censored and controlled radio, television and film from the very beginning. Another good reason for licensing was that the infrastructure costs of setting up a television or radio station meant that no one would do so unless they were assured that no other station could come along and broadcast on their frequency or interfere with their broadcasts in any way.

Extensive discussion about the nature of freedom of the press and the responsibilities held by the press in exercising these freedoms took place in the United States and in England during and after World War II. In America the privately funded 1945 Commission on Freedom of the Press, instigated and largely financed by Henry Luce of *Time* magazine, examined the issue in its report, *A Free and Responsible Press* (Hutchins, in Leigh 1947: v). In England, the 1949 Royal Commission on the Press, suggested by the National Union of Journalists to study concentration of ownership of the press and to consider means of improving press performance, supported and supplemented the US Commission's findings (Seibert et al. 1956: 75). Australia, still very much in the colonial thrall of Britain, looked to the British Commission's findings. In summary, the findings of these various commissions were that:

- Freedom of expression is vital in a free society. Both the press (as an issuer of news, opinions and so on) and the audience as consumers of news have interests that need to be honoured in the process of communication. But as to protect the freedom of the issuer is to protect the interests of the consumer and in general the community, it is sufficient to protect only the 'freedom of the press' as the freedom of issuers.
- Freedom of expression cannot be made costless by limiting hostile response, as free expression is destined to liberate social conflict, not repress it. But the intention should be for social conflict to be lifted from the plane of violence to the plane of discussion.
- The government, through its monopoly on physical force, must protect press freedom by maintaining order and personal security as well as protecting by law against sabotage, blackmail and corruption. By the same token, the government must set limits on its own capacity to interfere with, regulate, control or suppress the press, or manipulate the data on which public opinion is formed.
- The press has a duty beyond the state, to truth, right or justice—and this duty means that freedom of speech and the press are moral rights with which the state must not interfere. All ideas deserving of a public hearing should receive that hearing, and the decision about what ideas deserve such a hearing should rest not only with the particular biases of editors and owners but with consumers or the audience. If information is worthy of being put in front of the community, press owners should not stop the information from becoming public. But the duty of the press to morality means that freedom of expression is not unconditional.

- Because the consumer or audience of news is dependent on the quality, proportion and extent of news supply to judge public affairs, news outlets have a public responsibility to perform the function of information properly. It is important that press performance be guided by a sense of duty to this public responsibility. Somehow, the press must reconcile the facts that, though it is a private business, its efforts to define and realise its standards are a community concern.
- Governments have responsibilities to ensure that the press can be free. For example, governments need to act to ensure that distribution is more universal and equitable; that legal measures are available to stop abuses of the press; and that supplementary sources of press comment and news supply are provided, particularly in educational and non-commercial areas of the media.
- The problem that concentration of power in the hands of the few presents in respect of the news media is that it limits the ability of other, opposing voices to gain a hearing. (Leigh 1947: 107–33)

These findings gave rise to what is known as *social responsibility theory*, which accepts the role of the press in servicing the political system, in enlightening the public and in safeguarding the liberties of the individual. It accepts the role of the press in servicing the economic system, but would not have this task take precedence over such other functions as promoting the democratic process or enlightening the public. It accepts the role of the press in furnishing entertainment, but stipulates that the entertainment should be 'good'. It accepts the need for the press to be financially self-supporting but it would exempt certain media from having to earn their way (Seibert et al. 1956: 74). It reinforces the notion that the press has a responsibility to produce accurate, fair, good-quality information on which an increasingly complex society could base decisions.

When social responsibility theory was formulated, it focused on the press as the dominant media form of the day. Today, however, there is an expectation that all media will conduct themselves in a socially responsible fashion. Thus, for example, the television presenter Mike Willesee found himself the focus of negative comment when he disregarded police requests and made a phone call to the child victim of a kidnapping, preventing police from continuing negotiations with the kidnappers and possibly endangering the child. Famously, he even asked the child if he had witnessed any murders—and broadcast the conversation (Putnis 1996: 208). And the radio talkshow host John Laws sparked what is now known as the 'Cash for Comment' affair when it was revealed by ABC TV's *Media Watch* (12 July 1999) that he had made an agreement to promote banks on his show in return for payment of over a million dollars, even though his previous stance on the banking industry had been uniformly negative. *Media Watch* revealed that Laws had been retained by the Australian Bankers' Association to speak positively on air about the banks, and after an inquiry by the Australian Broadcasting Authority, regulations were promulgated requiring disclosure of any financial relationships between a business and a media personality who promoted that business. This case is discussed in greater detail in Chapter 5.

For public relations practitioners, a public expectation of social responsibility in the media has meant that they too need to behave in a socially responsible fashion—particularly, though not only, when dealing with the media. Research indicates that approximately 65 per cent of stories in the front news section and up to 90 per cent of stories in the business news section of prominent daily newspapers in Australia come from public relations sources (Zawawi 1994), and a straw poll conducted by *Sydney Morning Herald* journalist Bernard Lagan in 1999 demonstrated that publication depended on trips, free tickets or other gifts provided by public relations practitioners in order to gain the information necessary to write stories for the paper (Cameron et al. 1999: 41). Social responsibility, however, demands that the line between assistance and bribery must not be crossed.

Since the early 1980s, much of the focus of the PRIA has been on developing the social responsibility aspects of the public relations profession. One of the big questions facing the industry at that time concerned government licensing of public relations practitioners. Some debatable public relations tactics used in a Victorian state election in the early 1980s prompted then premier Joan Kirner's government to discuss mandatory government licensing for public relations practitioners in that state. Recognising that it is essential for a profession to be self-regulated, the PRIA embarked on a strategy aimed at raising standards and creating accountability. The strategy—which encompasses accreditation of professionals by the PRIA; encouragement of tertiary education in public relations; encouragement of continuing professional development through self-education; adherence to the PRIA code of ethics and enforcement of sanctions for matters in breach of the code; and an emphasis on professional accountability through the publishing of papers such as the 1999 *Position Paper on Research and Evaluation*—has moved public relations from an industry towards professional status. The extent to which this shift has been effective can be seen in a media statement issued by the PRIA's then National President, Lelde McCoy, in which she emphasised that demanding adherence to the code of ethics by PRIA members provided 'a valuable safeguard to the community and to clients using the services of PRIA members' (1999).

Conclusion

Modern practitioners of public relations work in areas as diverse as media relations, sponsorship, crisis and issues management, shareholder or financial relations, marketing communications and community relations. They may send messages out over the internet, through film and television, or on good old paper news releases. The different areas of practice and the skills that each area employs have developed as Australian businesses, society and media have grown and changed over the past century. But the principles of public relations, introduced to Australia by Sir Asher Joel, Eric White and others in the 1950s just after World War II, practised ethically and professionally, remain the same. The tools and their expression may change, but the essence of public relations—managing communication between an organisation and its publics—has not changed.

This chapter has tracked some of those changes and shown that the seeds of modern practice lie in the past. The range and diversity of jobs that public relations practitioners can hold—as publicists, shareholder relations specialists, media relations specialists, event managers or sponsorship coordinators, detailed in Chapter 1—have arisen from this rich and diverse background.

Chronology of the development of public relations in Australia

1840s–90s	Newspapers begin to develop objectivity, so as to avoid alienating readers and to offer advertisers the largest possible audience. Press agencies provide editorial copy to country newspapers. Some press agencies owned by advertising agencies may have provided editorial copy to country newspapers as payment for advertising space. Entertainment promoters send puff pieces to newspapers to obtain free advertising for their shows.
1920s	Film promotion well established in Australia, with almost all Hollywood studios having offices in Australia, working hard to produce 'ballyhoo', headline-grabbing stunts and exciting stories to place in the press. Australian publicity staff travel regularly to America for training. Publicity is completely product-related to specific films.

1930s	The Depression leads to more restrained use of promotion. Women emerge as an important audience and a growing range of publications appear to cater to the female market. Publicity about celebrities is not necessarily linked to particular films but describes the lives of the stars, their marriages, home and leisure activities.
1940s	World War II becomes the catalyst to allow public relations to develop into a fully fledged profession. The American Office of War Information focuses on news and perception management to garner full support for the war. General Douglas MacArthur brings a large public relations staff to Brisbane, and Australian naval officer Asher Joel is seconded to this group. On his return to Sydney in 1949, Asher Joel and George Freeman list themselves in the *Yellow Pages* as public relations consultants.
1950s	Public Relations Institute of Australia (PRIA) is founded. Public relations consultancies proliferate in Sydney and Melbourne. Eric White & Associates sets up offices in Asia and London.
1960s	Women begin to move into the public relations industry. First public relations degree is launched at Mitchell College, Bathurst.
1970s	International consultancies begin to move into Australia. Advertising agencies begin to buy up public relations consultancies in order to consolidate client services. Television has an impact on the advisory nature of public relations, bringing new audiences and new approaches.

Discussion and exercises

1   Search out some of the companies described in this chapter on the internet and see what you can discover about their history and the way in which they have developed specialist expertise in particular areas.

2   Interview a senior practitioner in your city and, from the information gained from that person, write a short report on how public relations practice has changed over the course of their professional life.

3   Search the weekend edition of your local newspaper and see if you can find a story or a photograph that may have been provided by a publicist or a press agent.

4   Analyse an edition of a national women's magazine and estimate what proportion of space is devoted to stories about celebrities.

Further reading

Bonwick, J. (1890) *Early Struggles of the Australian Press*, London.
Boorstin, D.J. (1961) *The Image or What Happened to the American Dream*, Penguin, Chicago.
Leigh, R.D. (ed.) (1947) *A Free and Responsible Press*, University of Chicago Press, Chicago.
Quarles, J. & Rowlings, B. (1993) *Practising Public Relations: A Case Study Approach*, Longman, Melbourne.
Seibert, F.S. (1965) *Freedom of the Press in England, 1476–1776*, University of Illinois Press, Urbana, Illinois.

References

Barnes, D. (1957) 'Just what is public relations?', *Rydges*, April–May–June.
Bernays, E. (1952) *Public Relations*, University of Oklahoma Press, Norman.
Blanch, J. (1961) *Newspaper News*, 27 October, p. 27.
Burns, T. (1979) 'The organisation of public opinion', in Curran, J., Gurevitch, M. & Woolacott, J. (eds), *Mass Communication and Society*, pp. 44–69.
Callaghan, G. (1999) 'Sultan of spin', *Weekend Australian*, 24–25 July, p. 26.
Cameron, D., Lagan, B. & Davies, A. (1999) 'His master's voice', *Sydney Morning Herald*, 24 July, pp. 33, 41.
Collins, D. (1987) *Hollywood Down Under*, Angus & Robertson, Sydney.
Cook, P. (1969) 'The end of the world', *Labour History*, no. 16, pp. 55–57.
Cunningham, S. (1997) 'Television', in S. Cunningham & G. Turner (eds), *The Media in Australia—Industries, Texts, Audiences*, Allen & Unwin, Sydney, pp. 90–111.
Granato, L.A. (1973) Prior Restraint: Resurgent Enemy of Freedom of Expression, unpublished PhD Thesis, Southern Illinois University.
—— (1991) *Reporting and Writing News*, Prentice Hall, Sydney.
Irwin, W. (1911) 'The press agent, his rise and decline', *Colliers*, 2 December, pp. 24–25.
Joel, Sir Asher (1995) Personal interview, 16 May.
Lazar, Peter (1999) Personal interviews, 1, 3, 9 March.
Leigh, R.D. (ed.) (1947) *A Free and Responsible Press*, University of Chicago Press, Chicago.
Mayer, H. (1964) *The Press in Australia*, Lansdowne, Melbourne.
Moseley, S.A. (1935) *The Truth About a Journalist*, Routledge, London.
Myers, A.H.H. (1995) Personal interview, 16 May.
—— (1999) Personal interview, 3 March.
Newsom, D., Scott, A. & VanSlyke Turk, J. (1993) *This is PR: The Realities of Public Relations*, Wadsworth, Belmont.

PRIA National Secretariat (1999) *Position Paper on Research and Evaluation*, PRIA, Sydney.

Putnis, P. (1996) 'Police media relations: issues and trends', in D. Chappell & P. Wilson, (eds), *Australian Policing: Contemporary Issues*, 2nd edn, Butterworths, Sydney.

Seibert, F.S. (1965) *Freedom of the Press in England, 1476–1776*, University of Illinois Press, Urbana, Illinois.

Seibert, F.S., Peterson, T. & Schramm, W. (1956) *Four Theories of the Press*, University of Illinois Press, Urbana, Illinois.

Ward, R. (1958) *The Australian Legend*, Collins, Melbourne.

Whitington, R.S. (1971) *Sir Frank: The Frank Packer Story*, Melbourne.

Wilcox, D., Ault, P.H. & Agee, W.K. (1994) *Public Relations Strategies and Tactics*, HarperCollins, New York.

Zawawi, C. (1994) 'Who feeds the watchdogs?' *Australian Journalism Review*, vol. 16, no. 1, pp. 67–73.

—— (1997) Survey of members: Queensland Chapter of the PRIA, unpublished study.

3 THEORETICAL PERSPECTIVES

Steve Mackey

In this chapter

Introduction

Theories can be thought of as imaginary road maps that are used to help gain understanding. To think theoretically is to use a set of assumptions about how the world works in order to be able to predict and make conclusions about what happens. Theoretical approaches provide a framework through which questions are raised and the nature of events and processes is probed and analysed. But theories are varied and different theories about the same things can be based on quite different assumptions.

When public relations is theorised, an approach based on certain assumptions is offered from a particular perspective. Of course, another theory based on another set of assumptions may make this view seem impossible or perhaps laughable. For instance, theories premised on the idea that public relations always has a positive effect on society deflect us from seeing any problems with the industry, while those originating from criticism of public relations may show public relations activity in a negative light. Theories based on the idea that public relations lies within the field of communication direct us to look only at the communicative aspects of public relations. In the same way, viewing public relations through the prism of organis-ational theory reveals only those aspects of activity. Theories about public relations originate from all of these standpoints and many others.

It is no wonder that a profusion of definitions and considerable disagreement exist about exactly what public relations is. In this chapter, a range of the most important theoretical approaches to public relations will be considered. As we look at these different approaches, we will review how they enable us to imagine public relations in certain ways and not in other ways and thus why it is important to understand different and contrasting theories of public relations.

Until fairly recently, most public relations theories were borrowed from adjacent disciplines. One theory borrowed from communication studies is agenda setting. Systems theory came from organisational studies after originating in phil-osophy and sociology. Semiotic approaches and Habermas's critical theories emerged from cross-disciplinary studies of communication, culture and sociology. After looking at these four examples of 'borrowed' theories we will contrast them with more recent theoretical suggestions developed specifically from within public relations studies, followed by a collection of theories in brief. Elsewhere in the book, other theories will also be considered—for example, the legal and ethical environments (Chapters 4 and 5), information and communication technologies (Chapter 9), and public relations in government (Chapter 15) and the Third Sector (Chapter 16) provide further sets of theories.

Agenda setting

What is it?

Agenda setting theory originated as a critique about the way news is selected. It suggests that selection results in prominence or omission of news. Agenda setting indicates that, although the news media do not tell you *what* to think, they do strongly influence what you think *about*. According to this theory, prominent news stories which are splashed across the front pages of newspapers and which dominate TV news bulletins with graphic images make us think they are more important than other things that are not gaining such attention. Matters which are not reported, or which are reported briefly, tend to drop off the public 'agenda' and are forgotten by most people.

How can it be used?

Public relations people are usually trying to set the agenda by getting prominent, positive attention in the news for their clients. Occasionally the opposite is true when they are trying to play down stories—for instance, in a crisis situation. Agenda setting theory maintains that articles generated by public relations work are competing against many other articles which may have a higher priority. The theory reminds us that there are editorial policy hurdles which a story has to jump to receive 'top of the page' treatment or lots of seconds of TV time. This theory reminds us to think carefully about the sorts of stories the publication or program prioritise and the pecking order of the different journalists who might be approached—which journalists usually get 'headline' coverage?

Agenda setting theory also gives us a reality check. It says that, however massive the coverage of our organisation or point of view, target publics are unlikely to be talked around by the 'loudness' of our message. The message has to be in line with the existing beliefs and attitudes of those people. Our target publics also need to receive the same message from other people in their community whose views they respect. Research indicates that people usually make up their minds on important matters based on the views of the communities of which they are a part, following face-to-face discussion with people they trust.

Importance and limitations

Agenda setting theory draws attention to the relationship between the news media and public relations practice. It is a theory about the social construction of news which provides important understandings about the role and power of the media in society. But this theory does not deal with the full mental processes which people go through in making their minds up during a public relations program.

General systems theory

What is it?

General systems theory originated in the 1930s. The theory considers that organisations can be viewed as operating within either 'closed' or 'open' systems. A *closed system* indicates that the organisation is sealed off from all external influencing factors, as if in a vacuum. An *open system*, on the other hand, takes into account the fact that organisations must interact with the world around them in order to be successful. This notion of vulnerability to outside events helps us to see the 'inside–outside' role of public relations. This is because public relations deals with interactions and messages which flow both *inside* an organisation as well as to people and groups *outside* that organisation (see Figure 3.1).

Figure 3.1 Open and closed systems of communication

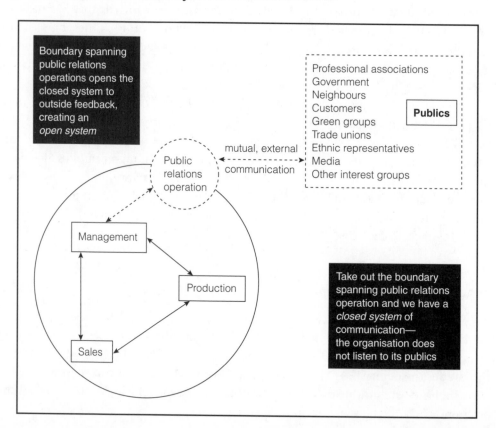

How can it be used?

Open systems theory suggests that we can draw a picture of communication which can help us map the public relations and other information processes of an organisation. The map will show the routes of inputs, throughputs and feedback of messages and opinions which affect understandings and relationships. Used intelligently by public relations strategists, this analysis can help discover where and how an organisation talks to itself and others, and what needs to be done to keep all this conversation 'on message'.

A 'closed system' model for an Australian car company would show communication only circulating around inside the different departments of the company. An open system model would show the same thing, but in addition it would reveal relevant communication flowing outside the company and where aspects of communication flow 'inside–outside' across the organisation's boundary. Outside communication might include such things as criticism from vehicle consumer groups, discussion by government departments on safety and financial policy or reviews about car design among motoring writers and car buffs. The open system model shows the point at which these external voices can be channelled into the company for consideration and where the company's communication can be channelled outwards to influence these external discussions. Much of this communication in and out past the boundaries of the company is via the public relations or public affairs office of the company. This is why 'open systems' theory depicts the public relations role in an organisation as a 'boundary-spanning' role.

You can conclude from this systems modelling exercise that:

- the role of public relations, when it is used properly, is as a strategic function in close cooperation and in constant two-way communication with senior managers; and
- this strategic public relations or communication function often straddles the organisational boundary.

With a leg in both the internal and the external communication environments, the public relations function interprets the organisation and its intentions to both internal and external groups. It also interprets internal and external groups and their intentions to the organisation's leaders.

Importance and limitations

There are problems with both closed systems theory and open systems theory. Both help us model the flow of information. But closed systems theory does not take into account external factors around the organisation which may threaten or provide the organisation with opportunities. Open systems theory shows public relations is very much concerned with monitoring and linking the organisation to external factors. Systems theory implies that public relations is an organisational process, but it does not necessarily go into the psychology and power relations of discussants. It does not require analysis of the content, validity or ethics of the messages which circulate.

Semiotics

What is it?

The study of semiotics or semiology is the study of signs. Signs, in this sense, may be made up of words, pictures, symbols or sounds, which represent something. For instance, the words you are reading in this book stand for concepts which you are thinking about. The fashions which you wear and see others wear carry a meaning about how people want themselves to be thought of. Pictures and paintings—that is coloured and lighter and darker areas arranged in a particular way on paper or canvas—convey soothing rural scenes, jagged modern art effects, strident commercial or political messages, or perhaps biting political satire. These representations—these images, designs, words or sounds—all draw on the existing language understandings which we hold in our heads in order to deliberately cause us to trigger certain thoughts.

Proponents of semiotics and semiology draw from the work of early twentieth century philosopher C.S. Peirce and linguist Ferdinand de Saussure to argue that, in this way, our verbal, written and visual languages and codes are constantly manipulated by advertisers, film-makers, authors, designers and other media producers to conjure up particular understandings of who we are and how the world works. Public relations practitioners are clearly among this group.

How can it be used?

This theory can be used to explain how our thoughts can be manipulated through the use of particular symbols. For instance, if a product is dressed up in a gold-coloured packet, or the word 'gold' is used when naming or describing it, in most

Saussure's model is one which is commonly associated with the study of semiotics. He suggested a 'dyadic' or two-part model of the sign which was composed of a 'signifier', which is the **form** the sign takes; and the 'signified', which is the **concept** it represents. According to Saussure's theory of semiotics, a sign must have both a signifier and a signified.

If we take a linguistic example, the word 'Open' (when it is invested with meaning by someone who encounters it on a shop doorway) is a *sign* consisting of:

1. a *signifier*: the word **open**;
2. a *signified concept*: that the shop is open for business (Chandler 1994).

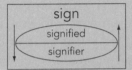 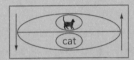 

For Saussure, the signified was not the 'thing' but the **idea** of the thing. The signifier is the word 'cat', the signified is the mental concept of a cat—a furry animal with whiskers. Similarly, the word 'hat' makes a mental picture of something we wear on our head.

But Saussure is not without his critics, who argue that the signified/ signifier model is detached from social context, that the bar that separates the signified and the signifier in the model should be blurred or erased, or that the signifier has primacy in the model despite the pre-existence of the signified (Chandler 1994).

cultures this conveys the notion that it is luxurious, top of the range, highest quality and so on. Consider the semiotics of the Public Relations Institute of Australia Golden Target Awards, or the use of gold cigarette packets. Consider the repeated advertising images of fun, sun and youth which are deliberately associated with a dark, sweet, caffeinated liquid called cola. The advertisements attempt to naturalise a way of thinking by supporting codes or sign-relations in our mind which try to make us understand cola in a certain way.

The same process is at work in vivid speeches which are rich in metaphor— such as Queen Elizabeth I's speech when rallying her troops: 'I may have the body of a weak and feeble woman, but I have the heart and stomach of a king.' Elizabeth's intention was to reposition her image in the minds of her subjects. She wanted them to see her as strong rather than weak, and she had to play with the semiotics of gender stereotyping in order to do this. George W. Bush also enlisted semiotics when he used the phrase 'the Axis of Evil'. This was rather like former president Ronald Reagan's phrase 'the Evil Empire'. These US presidents' speeches tried to enlist a notion of 'evil' which is held deep within our cultures in order to label countries in a negative way.

The semiotic approach reminds public relations people and designers to be aware of the negative as well as the useful constructions people can put on messages and symbols. A salutary example concerns a well-known Australian university. For a new logo, the university adopted a large triangular symbol which incorporated the university's name. In the designer's mind, this stood for the university 'pointing the way ahead to the future'. When the logo first appeared on signage outside the university, some people took it to be an arrow pointing the way ahead literally. They thought it meant the university was further down the road so they drove past it! Semiotics must also be considered in intercultural contexts because the meanings of signs may vary from culture to culture. For example, in some Asian cultures, white is the colour of mourning. In most European societies, it is black. In some cultures, head shaking and nodding have different meanings.

Importance and limitations

Semiotics reminds us of the ways meanings can be shifted and manipulated by words, metaphors and images. It helps us to understand the role of perception in communication, and how perceptions are culturally determined. It also helps us to understand how powerful associations can be created and maintained between images and words. In literary and film studies, it has become fashionable to 'deconstruct' the semiology of books, films and passages of writing. This is done to try to reveal hidden meanings and to identify cultural codes which work on the unconscious, sometimes with deliberate propaganda effects. In public relations processes, it is important to be aware of these processes both as a check on ethics and in the course of striving to achieve best communication practice.

Habermas, critical theory and the notion of the 'public sphere'

What is it?

Critical theory is a movement within sociology and cultural studies which criticises the way citizens are influenced to think by their surrounding capitalist culture.

Some signs (or in this case, symbols) are culturally specific, but some signs are cross-cultural. Road signs generally do not need words to convey their meaning. A combination of colours, letters, pictures and shapes can indicate conditions or driving behaviour for the motorist. These signs tell the driver: stop; winding road; road workers ahead; and children crossing. Even the stop sign, which uses language as well as colour and shape, could still be identified as 'stop' in another language.

Critical theorists are concerned about the capture and displacement of the 'public sphere'—the way citizens would normally debate and discuss freely in public—by the rhetoric of big business, big government and other powerful organisations. These powerful players overwhelm the news media and dominate other means of communication and cultural expression. They swamp what is referred to as the 'lifeworld'—the meanings and cultures of ordinary people who try to understand the world and express themselves and their relation to the world in terms of their own community interests.

Habermas is an important theorist in this school of thought. He suggests that the best qualities of civilised society are maintained if people are allowed to make up their minds about things in a rational way when the following ideal speech conditions apply (Habermas 1991: 25):

- The discussants genuinely want to reach understanding.
- They discuss rationally—they use reason rather than emotion in their discussion.
- The discussion produces cogent arguments—careful reasoning allows opinion to be validated as either correct or not.

Habermas maintains that these conditions can only be met when discussants meet on an equal footing in terms of power relations. If this 'ideal speech situation' is disregarded or undermined, communication becomes, in his term, 'strategic'—that is, used as an instrument for enforcing unequal power relations. Habermas says society has a more healthy 'lifeworld' if its organisations strive to keep as close to the 'ideal speech situation' as possible. Communication that aims to observe the ideal speech situation promotes fairness and enriches democratic community life.

How can it be used?

Habermas's critical theory suggests guidelines for an ethical check on a public relations program. Is the public sphere of free communication being overwhelmed and distorted by the communication approach which is being proposed by a powerful organisation? What are the consequences for that community whose existing ways of reasoning are damaged or destroyed in this process? One only has to think of the fate of indigenous cultures, or the lamented replacement of social, community and collegial values by commercial, winner-takes-all and *laissez faire* attitudes in many spheres of contemporary life. Habermas is sometimes mentioned in relation to the symmetrical model of public relations (see Grunig's theories below). Habermas does call for level playing fields in communication, but his theories are far more complex than this.

Importance and limitations

Habermas only refers to public relations directly a few times in his extensive writings. These references are generally negative and brief. He is more concerned, and far more expansive, about the modern use of the terms 'publicity' and 'public opinion'. Habermas says 'public opinion' once meant 'the will of human communities', but this term has now become the tool of the marketer, the politician and big business. It is a concept for theorising how to manipulate democracies in ways that serve the people who hold financial power. He thinks that, freed from the public opinion 'work' of manipulative corporations and other unscrupulous powermongers, citizens will become much more enlightened about the world and how they should relate to each other. This does not assist an immediate theoretical understanding of public relations activity such as promoting health, education, environmentalism and prudent economic activity within our current style of society. It is an argument for a different sort of society. The implication is that public relations is an integral expression of the contemporary capitalist style of society, a style of society which is unfair and unbalanced.

Grunig's models and the 'symmetrical debate'

The best known theory of public relations is the 'four models' approach taken by Grunig and Hunt (1984). They explain the development of public relations from its origins at the end of the nineteenth and beginning of the twentieth century to current practice.

* *Model 1: press agentry* describes the activities of people who would do anything to get attention for their organisation, event or product.
* *Model 2: public information* describes public relations becoming more sophisticated and evolving into accurate one-way information on behalf of organisations.
* *Model 3: two-way asymmetric* describes two-way public relations work which is biased to propagating the organisation's view, rather than responding to messages from publics.
* *Model 4: two-way symmetric* is Grunig and Hunt's ideal model for public relations. In this model, the publics' views are respected and are given the same importance as the views of the organisation sponsoring the public relations work.

Model 1

Grunig and Hunt say work corresponding to the press agentry/publicity model involves 'a propaganda function . . . Practitioners spread the faith of the organisation involved, often through incomplete, distorted, half true information' (Grunig and Hunt 1984: 21). They say work along these lines is associated with gaining editorial space for sports promotion, the entertainment industry and product promotion. This model is associated with stunts and explicit publicity-seeking. The following example shows that the press agent/publicity model is alive and well in the twenty-first century. *Promotions for sales increase*

Richard Branson rolled into Sydney's Pitt Street mall yesterday [3/9/01] in a tank, breaking through a giant red Virgin Mobile 'Break out' banner, spraying the crowd with water from a plastic machine gun pistol, and ceremoniously cutting the handcuffs of four actors 'tied' to the four major mobile phone carriers—Telstra, Optus, Vodafone and Orange—by their mobile phone number prefixes. Branson used the publicity stunt to inform the public about the upcoming advent of mobile phone number portability later this month, and also to announce a cross-promotional marketing deal between airline Virgin Blue and Virgin Mobile to the value of $3m. (<www.bandt.com.au/articles/35/0c006f35.asp> 7/6/02)

Model 2

Grunig and Hunt (1984) say: 'For the public-information model, the purpose is the dissemination of information, not necessarily with a persuasive intent. The public relations person functions essentially as a journalist in residence . . .' They objectively report information about the organisation to the public (Grunig and Hunt 1984: 22). This model is particularly useful for describing public sector and other non-commercial public relations activity, or any information propagated along strictly professional and ethical guidelines. Examples might be where an organisation is issuing news releases to openly and honestly convey what is going on in a crisis, when financial commentators are given accurate market-related information or when sports results at Olympic, Commonwealth or Pan Pacific Games are released.

Models 3 and 4

Grunig and White (1992) agree that most people believe mainstream public relations is best described as operating asymmetrically (Model 3) rather than symmetrically (Model 4). What this means is that public relations programs are thought to be mostly aimed at advancing the standing and the projects of the organisation which pays for public relations work. The programs are not aimed at advancing the interests of targeted publics to the same extent:

Some critics of the symmetrical worldview—both practitioners and theorists—claim that the approach is unrealistic or idealistic. They argue that organisations hire public relations people as advocates to advance their interests and not as 'do-gooders' who 'give in' to outsiders with an agenda different from that of the organisation. In short, these critics believe that organisations would not hire a public relations person who does not practise asymmetrically. (Grunig and White 1992: 46)

Grunig and Grunig (1992) nonetheless find that symmetrical public relations— that is, public relations programs that make sure the targeted publics benefit as much as the programs' sponsors or originators—*are* the most effective. They say research confirms both that programs which conform to the two-way symmetrical model are more ethical and that ethics helps the bottom line. Grunig and Grunig go on to say: 'Several studies have shown the ineffectiveness of the press agentry, public information, and two-way asymmetrical models.' (Grunig and Grunig 1992: 308)

What is the debate?

There has been much academic debate about the notion that it is possible for everyone to benefit from a symmetrical approach to public relations. Opponents say the political theory which the symmetrical model is based on—'interest group liberalism' (Grunig 1989)—only applies if a society is fair and everyone has equal power. Even affluent societies with strong democratic traditions do not enable all groups to have an equal say. For instance, how powerful are the voices of poor students when governments make them pay more for university education? If we consider Third World countries, the impracticality of the symmetrical model becomes more striking. Leitch and Neilson (1997) point out:

> It is simply absurd to suggest that an interaction between, for example, the Shell Oil company and a public consisting of unskilled workers in a developing country can be symmetrical just because the interaction is symmetrical in form. It is even more absurd to suggest the reverse, that the interaction between this worker public and Shell Oil can be symmetrical if the workers adopt the correct attitude and are willing to compromise. (Leitch and Neilson 1997: 19)

L'Etang (1996) also argues that symmetry in public relations is flawed:

> There is . . . a problem in the attempt which some make to maintain the idea of 'symmetry' alongside the role of public relations as advocate. Surely symmetry and advocacy are in opposition. The only way round this tension is to argue that public relations ensures that all world views are held, i.e. that the playing field is level. Whether this sort of pandering to the liberal

conscience is justifiable is a matter for debate: a debate which has yet to take place within public relations. (L'Etang 1996: 96–97)

Grunig has responded to such criticisms, arguing that symmetrical public relations brings groups together to protect and enhance self-interests:

> Argumentation, debate and persuasion take place. But dialogue, listening, understanding and relationship building also occur because they are more effective in resolving conflict than are one-way attempts at compliance gaining. (Grunig 2001: 18)

How can the models be used?

As Grunig and Hunt's models of public relations have constituted the only theory arising from within public relations for many years, it is natural that they have attracted criticism. This controversy should not prevent students of public relations from analysing public relations case studies by comparing them to any, or a combination, of models 1 to 4. Nor should students be discouraged from modelling their own public relations programs on what they consider to be the appropriate model. These models can differentiate different approaches or aspects of a public relations campaign with clarity.

Importance and limitations

The four models approach has been the benchmark public relations theory for two decades. It has provided guidance for those who want to think about how public relations can be practised and changed in ways which might justify the designation 'profession'. However, simplistic application of the concept of 'symmetry'—borrowed from communication theory—does not acknowledge the power relations which are implicit in any public relations activity. This is where an understanding of Habermas's theories is complementary to a use of Grunig's preferred approach.

Heath and 'rhetorical theory'

What is it?

Heath (2001) has taken a major initiative to try to make rhetorical theory the primary perspective through which public relations should be understood. He champions commitment to rhetorical dialogue as the process for forging conclusions and influencing actions. The process is a two-way one. Through statement and counterstatement, people test each other's views of reality, value and choices relevant to products, services and public policies (Heath 2001: 31).

'Rhetoric', like 'public relations', has negative connotations for many people. However, the term originated as the very welcome mode of persuasive communication which accompanied the advent of relatively civilised democracy. It essentially means reaching agreement on what is true through the use of the most convincing, reasoned argument. This was an important aspect of the way complex, ancient Greek society governed itself through public debate and persuasion, rather like our present court and parliamentary processes, reducing the need for oppression and violence. It was the revolutionary new way of managing society. For Heath, public relations practitioners are engaged—rather like ancient rhetoriticians such as Aristotle—in a 'wrangle in the marketplace': 'Professional communicators have a major voice in the marketplace of ideas—the dialogue on behalf of various self interests.' (Heath 1992: 20)

Like Grunig, and to some extent Habermas, Heath says this 'wrangle'—that is, this rhetorical battle by public relations people to have their point of view accepted—must be conducted on the basis of a level playing field in order for it to constitute ethical public relations practice: 'A rhetorical view presumes that, in terms of their right to speak, all parties are symmetrical.' (Heath 2001: 35). Heath suggests that: 'Rhetoric is symmetrical because each idea placed in the marketplace or public policy arena stands on its own merits.' (Heath 2001: 49)

How can it be used?

The advantage of the rhetorical theory approach to public relations, as explained by Skerlep (2001), is that it allows public relations people to take radically new perspectives on situations. Commonsense notions of what is 'true' can be overturned. Skerlep suggests:

> The naïve belief in truth, objectivity and impartiality as the normative criteria of validity of public relations discourse that is professed by public relations textbooks does not elucidate on the discursive dimension of polemical confrontations . . . the positivistic concept of truth [has] become controversial with the ascent of postmodern relativism . . . (2001: 183)

What Skerlep's 'postmodern-speak' means is that a rhetorical theory approach gives permission for the public relations person to think outside the square of what is normally thought of as 'true'. In a pro-corporate sense, this approach would imply that it was valid for an organisation to mount a public relations program which seemed to fly in the face of established 'truths'. For instance, it would validate a public relations program aimed at showing that genetically engineered (GE) crops are good. It would hold that there is no absolute rightness or wrongness in assumptions about GE crops other than what could finally be shown by the most exhaustive, rational debate on the topic. By the same token, it recognises the right of George Washington University Law Professor John Banzhaf to argue that it is possible to sue fast food companies for making us fat (salon.com 2002). In other words, under this theory 'normality', or the accepted view, is only contingent on the current best arguments for how we should think.

Importance and limitations

In considering rhetorical theory, one should bear in mind that Heath's other major works include writings on issues management. Heath is concerned about public relations at the major, strategic, corporate management levels. Rhetorical theory is not readily adaptable to theorising public relations as marketing support for the fashion industry or as part of not-for-profit fundraising programs. Rhetorical theory—or 'rhetorical enactment rationale', as Heath calls it—presumes that thinking in contemporary society can be fluid and capable of being won over by the best rational argument. However, it is not clear how 'rhetorical enactment rationale' makes public relations more ethical or acceptable. Heath says that those engaged in contesting their views rhetorically should be equally resourced. But we have seen that the critics of Grunig argue that this is often impossible to achieve. We are led to the conclusion that, like 'symmetrical public relations', 'rhetorical enactment rationale' is another 'ideal type' for describing how public relations should work in an ideal society. As with Grunig, an understanding of Habermas's ideal speech situation, where people must be empowered to reason on an equal footing, complements Heath's rhetorical theory.

The 'relationship management' approach

What is it?

Another important public relations theory initiative has been Ledingham and Bruning's (2000) edited book on relationship management. In their introduction, the editors claim that:

> The emergence of relationship management as a paradigm for public relations scholarship and practice calls into question the essence of public relations—what it is and what it does or should do, its function and value within the organisational structure and the greater society, and the benefits generated not only for the sponsoring organisations but also for the publics those organisations serve and the communities and societies in which they exist.
> (Ledingham and Bruning 2000: xiii)

The 'relational management' approach to public relations is centred on the 'dimensions' or 'parameters' of a relationship. These dimensions or parameters are aspects in the relationship between the organisation sponsoring the public relations work and the target of that project. They are factors in the relationship such as:

- the ability of parties to adapt in the relationship;
- the balance of power;
- whether people are trying to be constructive;
- whether people are being open about things;
- each party's level of commitment to the relationship;
- how cooperative each party is;
- the credibility of the different parties;
- whether synergy is produced in the relationship;
- how intimate or frosty the relationship is;
- how much time and effort each party invests in the relationship;
- whether the relationship is legitimate to everyone;
- whether the parties have mutual goals;
- whether there is some legal requirement for cooperation;
- whether the parties have mutual friends;
- the sorts of satisfaction attained;
- whether the use of shared resources is facilitated;
- whether the parties can unite to tackle a common task;
- whether there are existing social or organisational bonds or structures in place;
- whether change is advantageous or best avoided by either or some parties;
- whether the parties trust each other; and
- whether the parties understand each other and each other's needs.

Advocates of the relationship management approach say that when the term 'relationship' is used in public relations textbooks, often authors do not say which of the above aspects of 'relationship' they are referring to, or which they do not mean. The implication is that better analysis of public 'relationships' through the framework of the above listed components would enable people to understand public relations better.

How can it be used?

The intention of the relationship management approach is to encourage both scholars and practitioners to break down a 'relationship' they are concerned with in public relations into its component parts and to devise some way of measuring each aspect. A proper understanding of each aspect of the relationship would enable the analyst to make more satisfactory inferences about just what sort of a relationship is being dealt with and a better analysis of how that relationship changes (or does not change) as the result of a public relations program.

Importance and limitations

The 'relational management' approach to public relations makes a valuable contribution. However, as with the Grunig and Heath approaches, a Habermasian perspective might help to deal with some objections. If we look again at the list of relational aspects, many of them do not have to develop rhetorically as the product of rational, dialogic debate. Nor is there a need for symmetry between the parties involved. The critique of 'relationship management' which Ledingham and Bruning claim penetrates to the 'essence' of public relations casts public relations in a rather different light from that indicated by Grunig and Heath. Relationship management would seem to indicate that public relations may be steered by relational circumstances which exist prior to dialogue, or which may be constructed external to dialogue. The theory underlines that relational circumstances are often not symmetrical. Relationships may be built on pre-existing structural bonds, shared interests and the need for synergy. But just because organisations and publics are in relationships does not mean that they are equal partners in those relationships or that they unreservedly embrace those relationships. If we bear this inequality in mind, then the relationship management approach is useful in helping to create a better picture of what actually goes on in public relations processes.

Theoretical implications of postmodernism and the internet: the future of public relations theory

Some recent theories offer alternative viewpoints on public relations. Holtzhausen, for example, advocates a postmodern perspective (2000). She implies that management thinking within major organisations needs to be critiqued by public relations people to challenge dominant ideas which overlook the diversity of views and perspectives current in the postmodern condition of society. By 'postmodern society' we mean a society where political, cultural, social and economic views and mores are very diverse.

In postmodernism, there is no one guiding principle as there is in a theocracy, or a society guided by 'scientific progress', or as is implied by the expression 'the American Dream'. Holtzhausen revisits the concept of the public relations practitioner as keeper of the corporate conscience. She argues that, in this role, the responsibility for keeping the organisation abreast of postmodern thinking importantly resides in the public relations department. She says:

> Postmodern theories urge public relations practitioners to acknowledge the political nature of their activities and to be aware of the power relations inherent in everyday practice. Public relations is about change or resistance to change, these political acts are manifest in the everyday use of organisational language and symbolism and are influenced by the organisation's cultural and social environment. This redefines the boundary spanning role. Instead of claiming objectivity, practitioners are forced to choose which side they are on. (Holtzhausen 2000: 110)

Holtzhausen gives examples from South Africa of an internal corporate communications department persuading a tourism board to align with animal rights activists to campaign against a government policy to cull elephants. The same department assisted in a trade union-linked campaign to oppose discrimination against black people and women within the tourist board. Interestingly, James Grunig sees Holtzhausen's 'internal revolutionary' ideas as being in line with his own strictures for organisations to be symmetrical with their publics, even if asymmetry looks more obviously to be the way to go: 'I concur with Derina Holtzhausen that public relations is a postmodern force in organisations that gives voice to public in management decision making—an in-house activist.' (personal email 2001)

Another element challenging established public relations thinking is the omnipresent internet. Authors such as Blood (2000) suggest that the internet has not just made global protest against corporations and other dominant organisations easier, it has also created a new class of protesters. Blood refers to the 'micro-activists'. These are individualists opposed to capitalism, but also opposed to big organisations such as political parties of the left and organisations such as Greenpeace. Micro-activists believe such campaigning organisations compromise and 'sell out'. They are all part of the 'oppressionism' of a violent and environmentally malfunctioning world. While rejecting macro organisations, the internet enables micro-activists to cooperate very effectively as they have done in a number of radical political protests against the World Trade Organisation and the World Economic Forum. Examples include the Seattle protest in 1999, the Melbourne demonstration of 2000, protests in Sydney in 2002, and the regular protests against the Davos (Switzerland) gathering of leading global business leaders and politicians:

> corporate opponents have taken the lead in using the Internet to communicate their message. It is activist and pressure groups that have proven themselves to be quickest on their feet and most sensitive to online opportunities . . . Companies must start thinking and planning now if they are serious about maintaining and building their reputations in an online environment. (Blood 2000: 177–78)

Similar 'lateral connection' changes can be observed among corporations' stakeholders, facilitated by the increasing adoption and development in sophistication of the internet (de Bussy et al. 2000).

Other theories in brief

Situational theory

Situational theory is another important aspect of theory that has been developed within public relations scholarship by James Grunig and Todd Hunt. The theory suggests that the situation in which people find themselves influences whether or not they will protest or try to get their opinions heard. The theory can be used to help an organisation classify its publics into:

- publics that are active on all issues of public concern;
- publics that are apathetic on all issues;

- publics that are active only on issues that involve nearly everyone in the population—such as drink driving or environmental pollution; and
- single issue publics such as neighbourhood activists or 'save the whale' protesters (1984: 160).

The theory suggests that it can be predicted how people fall into the above categories from an examination of three independent variables. These are:

1 *Problem recognition*: do people recognise a problem which should be fixed (for instance, global warming) and do they think about it?

2 *Constraint recognition*: do people think there is very little they can do about an issue (for instance, global warming) because of the political complexities and their inability to understand those complexities or to assert any political power?

3 *Level of involvement*: the extent to which they are affected by the problem (for instance, people on low-lying Pacific atolls may *recognise* and feel very *involved* in the issue of global warming even though they see big *constraints* on what they can do about it in terms of protesting to overseas governments and polluting industries)

According to this theory, the levels of recognition, involvement and ability to affect the situation determine people's active and passive communication behaviour—that is, whether and how they protest and/or gather information on the problem. More recent development of this theory adds that recognition, constraint and involvement affect the cognition (types of understanding), attitudes and behaviour which they adopt towards the problem. (Grunig 1997: 9)

One implication of situational theory is that it can be used by substantial organisations to identify which groups of people are unlikely to protest even if their interests are harmed, because they do not feel they have the literacy, unity or because they fear retaliation in a political or economic sense. High constraint may exist among populations in developing countries and among some First World, socially disadvantaged groups. This situation clearly has ethical implications when a powerful organisation is dealing with powerless or disadvantaged groups. Derville and McComas (2003) make suggestions for how such situations may be made more equitable in order to facilitate ethical public relations. They advocate community based interventions to reduce the barriers of severely constrained publics. They say disadvantaged groups should be protected, compensated and given training and communication resources in order to change such situations.

Opinion, attitude and belief

These are useful concepts for charting how firmly people hold particular views relevant to a particular subject. Knowing that a person holds one opinion often enables us to predict correctly that he or she also holds another opinion. For example, a Green party voter might predictably be in favour of the Kyoto Agreement, and be against migrant detention centres or mandatory sentencing. Daryl Bem (2003) says this is possible, in part, because opinions appear to follow a common set of beliefs, attitudes and values based on an underlying ideology.

Studies of public opinion are well known for their input into political and marketing research. Zaller (1992) developed a theory to explain how people convert information from the mass media and political élites into voting behaviour. His theory suggested that people make opinion preferences as they confront specific issues. In addition, people make the greatest use of ideas that are most relevant or salient to them. Opinions, then, might be reversed by a convincing argument.

Alternatively, individuals might have a more substantial attitude built up by information and experience over a longer period or in greater depth. Bem (2003) says attitudes are made up of likes and dislikes—favourable or unfavourable reactions to objects, people, situations or any other aspects of the world. But even though attitudes are feelings, they often depend in part on underlying 'evaluative' beliefs.

Beliefs may be broken down into three levels: zero-order, first-order and higher-order. Zero-order beliefs are those which we learn as children—things that our senses tell us are true. These are the strongest beliefs. First-order beliefs are based on zero-order beliefs but we can imagine alternatives to them, so they are chosen beliefs: 'Most religious . . . beliefs are first-order beliefs based upon an unquestioned zero-order faith (Bem 1970: 7)'. Higher-order beliefs are based on an authority or reasoning. Over time, our higher-order beliefs can change.

We tend to think of our belief system as being the hardest of all to change, but some beliefs are clearly stronger than others. Some people hold their beliefs so dearly that they go to war to express them. They will be shattered if these beliefs are exposed as false in some way and may not even accept such exposure as true.

By distinguishing and categorising the different strengths of people's opinions, attitudes and beliefs, a practitioner will more easily be able to determine how much effort is needed to influence them. This will also help to assess the solidarity or weakness of views that support public relations objectives. The practitioner will be able to assess whether it is at all practicable to try to influence the views of a particular public on certain matters.

Audiences and media effects

A number of theories have been used to determine how the mass media process and distribute messages to their audiences. These include the *magic bullet theory* (one-way messages sent from a single point of origin that find their target), the *two-step flow theory* (use of opinion leaders in communicating media messages) and the *uses and gratifications theory* (people using different media for different purposes). Essentially, while all have their limitations, all these theories looked at getting the message to the right audience through selected media.

Constant changes and fragmenting of the mass media environment, including the popular media becoming 'pictorialised' (Hartley 1992: 6), have made it more important than ever to know your audience. Balnaves and O'Regan argue that 'knowledge about media audiences is integrally tied up with the strategies and plans of action of industry players, campaigners, professional bodies and interest groups who take up and apply this knowledge to prosecute their own agendas' (2002: 10). Among the audiences studied in the Australian market has been the often-cited 'Generation X'. This generation has been seen as difficult to pinpoint because of its diversity: 'Generation X is *homogenised* in the very face of diversity to produce a classless youth culture, where socio-economic, racial, geographical, gender and sexual differences seem to go "on holiday".' (Mungham and Pearson in Balnaves et al. 2002: 95). Nevertheless, Generation X has become a 'hot target audience' with estimates of 32 million US teenagers spending about $100 billion on themselves annually, and their parents spending half that much on them again (Merchants of Cool in Balnaves et al. 2002). While Sternberg does not identify specific media used to target this diverse audience, the internet has become synonymous as 'the media' of Generation X.

By identifying audiences that share similar patterns of media usage, media and cultural planners can develop behavioural profiles of media consumers for their clients (Balnaves et al. 2002). Knowing behavioural patterns of audiences, as well as having an understanding of media segmentation and effects, are essential in this complex process.

Edward Bernays, in the 1920s, cited three elements of media effects as they apply to public relations. These elements, which are still relevant today, are:

1   The practitioner must be a careful student of media to know how people develop their 'pictures of the world'.
2   The practitioner should be knowledgable about sociology and anthropology to know how attitudes are formed through culture and social structures.

3   The practitioner should be knowledgable about the individual's psycho-
    logical processes; practitioners can then tailor their efforts to maximum
    effect. (in Olsen 2001: 278)

Social learning theory

Social learning theory (also known as social cognitive theory) suggests that people
modify their attitudes and behaviour to emulate or fit in with the attitudes and
actions exhibited by others. This theory deals with how people observe and model
the behaviours, attitudes and reactions of others.

In 1977 cognitive psychologist Albert Bandura explained human learning
according to this theory:

> Learning would be exceedingly laborious, not to mention hazardous, if people
> had to rely solely on the effects of their own actions to inform them what to
> do. Fortunately, most human behavior is learned observationally through
> modeling: from observing others one forms an idea of how new behaviors are
> performed, and on later occasions this coded information serves as a guide for
> action. (Kearsley 2003: 22)

Television advertisements are among the most common, and pervasive, examples
of modern social learning. These advertisements suggest that drinking a certain
soft drink, using a particular shampoo or driving a specific car will make people
popular with others. The aim is to model the behaviour and buy the product in the
advertisement (Kearsely 2003).

Kearsley (2003) notes that in social learning theory:

- individuals are more likely to adopt a modelled behaviour if it results in
  outcomes they value; and
- individuals are more likely to adopt a modelled behaviour if the model is similar
  to the observer and has admired status and the behaviour has functional value.

Social exchange theory

Social exchange theory holds that social life is a series of exchanges. We give and
receive affection, respect, labour, goods and services for reward, and we pay money
for goods and services. The outcome of any interaction is the combination of
rewards and costs involved in the interaction:

People strive to minimize costs and maximize rewards, as with economics, and then base the likeliness of developing a relationship with someone on the perceived possible outcomes. When these outcomes are perceived to be greater, we disclose more and develop a closer relationship with that person. (Thibaut and Kelly 1999)

Designing a public relations campaign along these lines might mean listening to the views of protesters, for example, in exchange for fully briefing them on the proposed development project. Employees might respect employees in return for their attention and genuine interest. Support for the arts or community projects might bring government policy support or customer loyalty.

Critics of exchange theory suggest that there are some social phenomena which cannot be explained by the theory, such as tradition, political dominance and gender discrimination. However, exchange theory would seem to be useful for public relations purposes: it rings true that most people feel obliged to act reciprocally in all sorts of relationships (Abercrombie et al. 1994; Jary and Jary 1991; Ritzer 1988).

Conclusion

This chapter has briefly explained a number of different theoretical approaches to public relations. Some of the approaches are borrowed from other disciplines, other more recent ones have arisen from within public relations studies. The chapter has suggested that public relations is a difficult, contested and controversial area of study. This is because it is used by powerful organisations to influence the way we think and thus the way the world works. It has different meanings depending on the particular political and intellectual perspectives from which it is viewed. Because of this, it is important that students and practitioners are able to understand and use a number of theoretical approaches based on contrasting philosophical and political assumptions. Different approaches critique each other and help us to become clearer about the kinds of public relations practices which are legitimate in genuine democracies.

Discussion and exercises

1   Agenda setting: over a period of one week, compare the media coverage of a pressure group in your neighbourhood—perhaps campaigning for a better child care centre or something similar—with the coverage of a major corporation, the

coverage of a national politician and the coverage of a disadvantaged group of people far away in Australia or overseas. What is the prominence or invisibility of these four groupings in various types of news media and what are the consequences? How does the public opinion 'agenda' become affected with respect to each group? Do they benefit or suffer because of the ways media agendas are set? How could public relations work change the media agenda in each situation?

2   Closed and open systems: a university is likely to be an organisation familiar to most people reading this book. On a large piece of paper, draw 5 cent-sized black circles scattered around to represent all the departments and groupings which you think exist in your university. Then draw lines between each circle and the other departments or groupings where you think information currently goes. If you think there is a one-way communication along this line, use a red pen for your line. If you think there is two-way communication, use a blue pen. The crazy matrix you end up with will give you a starting point for an internal communication audit if you want to research the nature of the communication system in the university. Systems theory does not tell you anything about the content and quality of the messages, but it shows you where to go to find this out. A communication systems matrix like this will be very different from the formal organisational structure charts which the organisation might have. Now, on a separate piece of paper, draw circles representing all the groups of people *outside the organisation* who also might communicate with, or at least receive messages from, the university. These circles will represent such groupings as the news media, governments and their departments, different sorts of potential employers of graduates, suppliers, parents, professional associations and so on. Now put the two pieces of paper next to each other and draw red or blue lines to where you think these outside people communicate with the university. You should see that many of these lines through the organisational boundary of the organisation go to the senior administration of the university and its marketing, communication or public affairs office. You should also notice (if you know your university well) that there is a lot of two-way communication internally between the senior managers and their marketing or communication officers. Much of this is to cope with these outside communication demands.

3   Semiotics: the study of semiotics allows us to deconstruct images in tactics such as advertising that include pictures, words and tone. Find a colour advertisement in a magazine and list all the features included in it. Note whether the words are consistent with the picture. Are there logos or slogans that are central to the ad? Are there different levels of text? Are there subtle elements, such as a photo being out of focus, that impact on the ad?

4   Grunig and Hunt's models: this chapter provides examples of Grunig and Hunt's four models of public relations. From your own experience, find further examples. How efficient are your examples? Could they be improved? Are there examples where a range of models apply to, say, a community campaign in your area?

Further reading

Fawkes, J. & Gregory, A. (2000) 'Applying communication theories to the internet', *Journal of Communication Management*, vol. 5, no. 2.

Fiske, J. (1991) *Introduction to Communication Studies*, Routledge, London.

Grunig, J. (2001) 'Two-way symmetrical public relations: past, present and future', in Robert Heath (ed.), *Handbook of Public Relations*, Sage, Thousand Oaks.

Heath. R. (ed.) (2001) *Handbook of Public Relations*, Sage, Thousand Oaks.

Moloney, K. (2000) *Rethinking Public Relations: The Spin and the Substance*, Routledge, London.

References

Abercrombie, N. et al. (1994) *The Penguin Dictionary of Sociology*, Penguin, London.

Balnaves, M., O'Regan, T. & Sternberg, J. (2002) *Mobilising the Audience*, UQP, Brisbane.

Banzhaf, J. (2002) <www.salon.com/tech/feature/2002/05/24/fastfoodlaw/>, assessed 17/8/02.

Bem, D. (1970) *Behaviour, Attitudes and Human Affairs*, Belmont, California.

—— (2003) *Introduction to Beliefs, Attitudes, and Ideologies*, Psychology Department, Cornell University, <http://comp9.psych.cornell.edu/courses/Psych489/Introduction_to_Beliefs_&_.html>, accessed 19/5/03.

Blood, R. (2000) 'Activism and the internet: from e-mail to new political movement', *Journal of Communication Management*, vol. 5, no. 2.

Broom, G., Casey, S. & Ritchey, J. (2000) 'Concept and theory of organization–public relationships', in John Ledingham & Stephen Bruning (eds), *Public Relations as Relationship Management: A Relational Approach to the Study and Practice of Public Relations*, Lawrence Erlbaum, New Jersey.

de Bussy, N., Watson, R., Pitt, L. & Ewing, M. (2000) 'Stakeholder communication management on the internet: an integrated matrix for the identification of opportunities', *Journal of Communication Management*, vol. 5, no. 2.

Derville, T. & McComas, K. (2003) The use of community-based interventions (CBIs) to reduce the barriers of severely constrained publics, Communication to borderlands, 53rd Annual Conference of the International Communication Association, 23–27 May, San Diego.

Grace, D. & Cohen, S. (2000) *Business Ethics: Australian Problems and Cases*, Oxford University Press, Melbourne.

Grunig, J. (1997) 'A situational theory of publics: conceptual history, recent challenges and new research', in D. Moss, T. McManus & D. Vercic (eds), Public Relations Research: An international perspective, Thompson Business Press, London.

—— (1989) 'Symmetrical presuppositions as a framework for public relations theory', in Carl Botan & Vincent Hazleton (eds), *Public Relations Theory*, Lawrence Erlbaum, New Jersey.

—— (2001) 'Two way symmetrical public relations: past, present and future', in Robert Heath (ed.), *Handbook of Public Relations*, Sage, Thousand Oaks.

Grunig, J. & Grunig, L. (1992) 'Models of public relations and communication', in James Grunig (ed.), *Excellence in Public Relations and Communication Management*, Lawrence Erlbaum, New Jersey.

Grunig, J. & Hunt, T. (1984) *Managing Public Relations*, Holt, Rinehart and Winston, New York.

Grunig, J. & White J. (1992) 'The effect of worldviews on public relations theory and practice', in James Grunig (ed.), *Excellence in Public Relations and Communication Management*, Lawrence Erlbaum, New Jersey.

Habermas, J. (1991) *The Theory of Communicative Action: Reason and the rationalisation of society*, vol. 1, Polity, Cambridge.

Hartley, J. (1992) *The Politics of Pictures*, Routledge, London.

Heath, R. (1992) 'The wrangle in the marketplace: a rhetorical perspective of public relations', in Elizabeth Toth & Robert Heath (eds), *Rhetorical and Critical Approaches to Public Relations*, Lawrence Erlbaum, New Jersey.

—— (2001) 'A rhetorical enactment rationale for public relations: the good organisation communicating well', in Robert Heath (ed.), *Handbook of Public Relations*, Sage, Thousand Oaks.

Holtzhausen, D. (2000) 'Postmodern values in public relations', *Journal of Public Relations Research*, vol. 12, no. 1.

—— (2001) personal email, 24 January.

Jary, D. & Jary, J. (1991) *Collins Dictionary of Sociology*, Harper Collins, London.

Kearsley, G. (2003) 'Social learning theory', <http://tip.psychology.org/bandura.html>.

Lawson-Tancred, H. (1991) 'Translation, introduction and notes', in *Aristotle's The Art of Rhetoric*, Penguin, London.

Ledingham, J. & Bruning, S. (eds) (2000) *Public Relations as Relationship Management: A Relational Approach to the Study and Practice of Public Relations*, Lawrence Erlbaum, New Jersey.

Leitch, S. & Neilson, D. (1997) 'Reframing public relations: new directions for theory and practice', *Australian Journal of Communication*, vol. 24, no. 2.

L'Etang, J. (1996) 'Corporate responsibility and public relations ethics', in Jacquie L'Etang & Magda Pieczka (eds), *Critical Perspectives in Public Relations*, International Thomson, London.

Neuman, R. (1991) *The Future of the Mass Audience*, Cambridge University Press, Cambridge.

Olsen, B. (2001) 'Media effects researchers for public relations practitioners', in Robert

Heath (ed.), *Handbook of Public Relations*, Sage, Thousand Oaks.

Ritzer, G. (1988) *Sociological Theory*, McGraw-Hill, New York.

Skerlep, A. (2001) 'Re-evaluating the role of rhetoric in public relations theory and in strategies of corporate discourse', *Journal of Communication Management*, vol. 6, no. 2.

Thibaut, J. & Kelley, H. (1999) *Social Exchange Theory*, <http://oak.cats.ohiou.edu/~al891396/exchange.htm>.

Zaller, J.R. (1992) *The Nature and Origins of Mass Opinion*, Cambridge University Press, New York.

PART 2
THE LEGAL AND
ETHICAL FRAMEWORK

4

THE LEGAL ENVIRONMENT

Rhonda Breit

In this chapter

Introduction

When public relations students study the law, many seem to be overwhelmed. Yet law is a part of everyday life. It regulates how people treat each other, how they conduct themselves in public, how they do business—it governs just about everything people do. As ignorance of the law is no excuse for breaking it, individuals need to be aware of the laws that regulate their actions and their profession. To ensure quality public relations outcomes, practitioners need to take an active role in developing strategies to minimise the legal risks associated with the functions and roles they perform.

As outlined in Chapter 1, the profession of public relations covers many activities and roles, which can be classified into three main areas: communication, advisory/counselling and business/management. These functions must be performed in a reflective way, which requires assessing all risks, including the legal ones, and advising on how to manage them. To do this, practitioners need foundation knowledge on several bodies of law because there is no one over-arching body of law covering public relations. Practitioners must be aware of the tort of negligence, which specifies a professional's duty of care to clients and the general public. The tort of defamation is crucial to public relations as it outlaws unjustified publications, which have a tendency to harm an individual's reputation. Western society is becoming increasingly litigious, therefore public relations practitioners must be aware of the body of law protecting the administration of justice: contempt law. Contracts are an essential part of business, so practitioners must have a basic understanding of contract law. Statutory obligations regarding product liability, market controls and consumer protection will also affect how public relations decisions are made. Public relations is a creative practice and creative endeavours represent valuable business assets. Therefore public relations practitioners must understand how to protect trademarks, copyright, designs, patents and confidential information—a body of law known as intellectual property law.

These laws have different origins: some come from common law (judge-made law), while others are created by statute (parliamentary laws) at federal or at state or territory level. They have different reasons for existing, balancing competing rights, duties and obligations. These ostensibly disparate bodies of law are connected by the practice of public relations.

The legal environment

Public relations decisions must be made in context of the 'legal environment'. But when legal risks are being assessed, strategies to minimise harm must take account of the commercial and professional risks arising from the legal action. Tension exists between the legal and public relations responses to crises. Hoger and Swen (2000: 3) categorise these differences into four areas: understanding of time and timing; traditions and strategies; audience relationships; and approaches to message construction. Therefore, practitioners must take an active role in assessing and responding to legal risks. They must negotiate with lawyers on the strategies employed to minimise harm. Otherwise, public relations outcomes could be compromised.

Legal solutions alone may not be in the client's best interest. For example, the global fast-food giant, McDonald's, took offence at a campaign launched by

London Greenpeace, where pamphlets were circulated in the United Kingdom condemning McDonald's environmental policies. McDonald's brought an action in defamation, claiming the pamphlet alleged '[it had] contributed to third-world starvation, rainforest destruction, the corruption of children and . . . it exploits its workers and supplies unhealthy food' (Ackland and Florance 1996: 15). The head of McDonald's public relations department said the trial was about protecting McDonald's' reputation: 'A lot of people trust McDonald's. The allegations [in the pamphlet] challenge that trust. If we don't stand up, then it would be seen that there is some truth in the allegations.' (Ackland and Florance 1996: 15) The action went to trial and, after five years of legal wrangling, McDonald's was found to have been defamed. However, the action was perceived as 'a lose–lose case for McDonald's' (Ackland and Florance 1995: 18). Instead of being seen as the wronged corporate citizen trying to uphold its reputation, the two unrepresented defendants to this action 'turned the tables and put McDonald's on trial' (Ackland and Florance 1996: 15). So, while McDonald's won the legal battle, it lost the public relations war.

It may be better to negotiate a settlement or seek some alternative means of resolving a conflict, than to expose clients to public scrutiny as in the McDonald's defamation case. Public relations relies on good reputations, positive images and strong relationships. These matters must be factored into the cost of any legal action.

Before examining some of these legal risks in more detail, it is important to observe another important characteristic of the public relations legal environment. The emergence of an efficient global communication system and the birth of the truly transnational corporation have transformed public relations, creating a global communication and business environment. However, regulation of communication and business is far from global. The collapse of global giants—such as Enron and WorldCom—has signalled one of the greatest legal challenges facing the information age, as the laws of individual countries try to regulate global communication and business.

The global nature of business and communication means individual public relations practitioners face a minefield of legal obligations as domestic jurisdictions attempt to provide a regulatory framework for global products. Practitioners working within Australia also experience this tension, as Australian communication and business is regulated by a variety of state, territory and federal laws and regulations. For example, defences of defamation vary from state to state and territory, which means a person may be legally defamed in one state or territory but not another.

So, while the bodies of law governing public relations are diverse and complex, it is becoming increasingly necessary for practitioners to develop good working relations with their legal advisers. Practitioners need foundation knowledge of these principles to communicate and 'negotiate' appropriate responses to legal problems. Before turning to a legal solution, the public relations practitioner should consider three questions:

1   What are a public relations practitioner's legal rights and responsibilities?
2   How do these rights and responsibilities translate into everyday work practices?
3   What are the public relations implications of any legal dispute?

These questions need to be asked in an informed and reflective context. This chapter aims to provide some foundation information to help practitioners make informed choices about legal risks, focusing on these key areas:

- protecting reputations;
- protecting creative ideas;
- the practitioner's duty of care;
- legal risk management, the role of contracts in a global legal environment; and
- technology and future legal directions in a public relations context.

Protecting reputations

Reputations are seen as integral to, if not definitive of, contemporary public re-lations. Hutton, Goodman, Alexander and Genest (2001) have conducted a study into the significance of reputation management as a guiding philosophy in corpo-rate public relations. While the study noted an increasing focus on reputation man-agement within the role of corporate public relations in the sample of US firms sur-veyed, it questioned the suitability of reputation management as a guiding philos-ophy. The study could not deny the interrelationship between public relations and reputations, noting that no company with a relatively large communication budget (more than $5 million) had a poor reputation. The study also revealed that corporate reputations could be quite volatile, moving up and down in public rankings. It concluded that: 'A reputation is generally something an organisation has with strangers, but a relationship is generally something an organisation has with its friends and associates.' (2001: 9)

   Legal issues can affect both reputations and relationships. This section examines the tort of defamation and the increasing role of public relations in managing the fallout from negative litigation.

Defamation

The tort of defamation (a tort is a legal way of saying a civil wrong) aims to protect a person's reputation, a fundamental human right (Optional Protocol to the International Covenant on Civil and Political Rights 1996). However, the rights of an individual to enjoy the reputation they have earned must be balanced against the public interest in terms of freedom of speech. This tort limits what a public relations practitioner can publish, but it also provides a vehicle by which practitioners and their clients can protect their reputations.

Words, pictures, cartoons, graphics, effigies, signs, even human gestures can give rise to an action in defamation directly, or indirectly through inferences or innuendo arising from some special knowledge held by people to whom the material is aimed. To bring an action in defamation a person must show that:

* the material was published—that is, read, seen or heard by a third person;
* they were identified in the publication—that is, a person of average intelligence can identify the plaintiff as the person referred to in the publication;
* the publication was defamatory.

Under common law, there are three tests for defamation: the publication exposed the plaintiff to hatred, contempt or ridicule (*Parmiter v Coupland* 1840: 340); it lowered the plaintiff in the eyes of right-thinking members of the community (*Sim v Stretch* 1936: 669); or it caused the plaintiff to be shunned or avoided, without moral blame (*Youssoupoff v Metro Goldwyn Mayer Pictures* 1934: 581).

In deciding whether a publication is defamatory, the publisher's intention is irrelevant. A publication can be defamatory either directly or indirectly through inference or special knowledge of extrinsic (additional) facts. For example, Slater and Gordon solicitors were ordered to pay $300 000 in damages after promotional material circulated by them was found to defame two prominent surgeons. The action arose from the full-colour front cover of a booklet promoting the firm's ethical stance on medical negligence actions and its commitment to avoiding publicity to protect a doctor's reputation if proceedings for negligence were commenced against a doctor. The front cover included a photograph depicting a ground-breaking operation being performed by two surgeons. An image of a fully robed barrister was superimposed over the photograph, giving the impression of the barrister scrutinising the surgeons' work. The caption above the photograph read: 'Medical malpractice claims . . .' and below the image it read: '. . . A litigation explosion?' (*Nixon v Slater & Gordon* 2000: 3; Catlin 2000: 1, 2) The original photograph of the surgeons was acquired from *The Age* pictorial library, without the knowledge or consent of the surgeons. Directions were given to a graphic artist to digitally disguise the surgeons' appearance. One surgeon's image was altered by removing his beard and heart-shaped red marks on his head-gear. The other surgeon's image was altered by adjusting the line of his surgical cap, removing his sideburns and eyebrows, altering his eyelashes, the texture and colour of his skin and reshaping his hairline and earlobe (*Nixon v Slater & Gordon* 2000: 4). Despite these alterations, the surgeons were still recognised by colleagues in the medical profession.

Defamation law places a strict burden on publishers. A publisher is anyone involved in the publication of material from the actual author through to the printer of the material, unless they are an innocent disseminator. Authors of the material are liable even if they publish the material on the internet (*Rindos v Hardwick* 1993), and anyone who repeats the defamatory words of others (*Morosi v Broadcasting Station 2GB* 1980: 418n). The proprietors of the publication in which material appears are also liable (*Levien v Fox* 1890, 11 NSWLR 369). Even people relaying broadcasts, who have not previewed the program, can be liable for republication of a defamatory statement because they should have procedures in place to check the content of material (*Thompson v ACTV* 1996: 574). This is the case even if someone sends an internal email, or makes a statement to a third person. Public relations practitioners, who regularly communicate messages, can fairly easily fall prey to defamation action.

A public relations practitioner can defame someone unintentionally and without even knowing that person exists. For example, a defamatory inference may arise when a publication describes a joint research project, and praises one researcher and not the other. This could infer that one party has not done their share of the work. One way to minimise the threat of defamation is to make positive rather than negative statements, but even this is no guarantee against liability because a negative inference can arise from saying something positive about another person or company. For example, a broadcaster was held to have defamed a woman while he was defending her reputation, because he repeated defamatory statements from a previous broadcast and the harm of the defamatory words outweighed the effect of the defence (*Morosi v Broadcasting Station 2GB* 1980: 418n).

A person cannot be defamed unless they are identified by a publication. This does not mean they have to be named specifically. It is enough that people can identify the plaintiff from what was published. It does not matter that a public relations professional may not have intended the publication to refer to the individual identified. Fictitious names will not avoid liability if an individual is identified from the publication. The court looks at how the publication's audience/readership has interpreted the publication. In the *Slater and Gordon case*, members of the medical profession gave evidence that they identified the plaintiffs from the digitally altered photograph. This illustrates that photographs can give rise to defamatory imputations, despite attempts to disguise those depicted in the picture. The pictorial front cover was found to have defamed the doctors because it affected how others (their colleagues) perceived them. It was not simply hurtful. It does not matter what the publishers think the material means, the test for defamation is that of the ordinary, reasonable person and whether they would consider the publication to be defamatory.

In the case involving the two surgeons, Justice Merkel found that the average medical practitioner would believe Slater and Gordon were involved in a medical malpractice claim against the two surgeons depicted in the photograph (*Nixon v Slater & Gordon* 2000: 10; Catlin 2000: 3). This impression was reinforced by the image of the barrister scrutinising the operation. The court acknowledged that, when determining a publication's meaning, it must be considered as a whole. However, the meaning will be determined from the 'precise words used and the context in which they are used' (*Nixon v Slater & Gordon* 2000: 11). The judge cited several past cases and warned publishers to 'pick his or her words very carefully' if he/she 'wants to exclude the suggestion that where there is smoke there is fire' (*Nixon v Slater & Gordon* 2000: 11).

The booklet did not give rise to an imputation that the surgeons were guilty of malpractice, because the average medical practitioner would infer that the publication merely suggested there were reasonable grounds for bringing a malpractice claim against the surgeons. It also found that the booklet did not give rise to an imputation that the doctors endorsed the solicitors' campaign (*Nixon v Slater & Gordon* 2000: 11).

Defences against defamation balance the right of the individual to protect their reputation against other conflicting interests such as the need for freedom of speech and the public's right to receive information. At common law, the defences to defamation are 'truth', 'fair comment' and 'privilege', and these vary between the states and territories. National and international publications may have to conform to different defamation regimes. In 2002 the Australian High Court adjudicated on where internet publications are published. In this case, Joseph Gutnick instituted a defamation action in Victoria against United States-based publisher Dow Jones & Co. Dow Jones sought leave to have the defamation action heard in the United

States because the internet publication was predominantly uploaded there. The High Court concluded that the act of publication is not complete until the material is read. Therefore publication occurred in Victoria. The court also concluded that Victoria was the place where Gutnick's reputation was strongest, therefore he should be permitted to sue in that jurisdiction. However, four of the seven judges suggested that the reasonableness of an internet publisher's actions may be taken into account in deciding whether a defamatory imputation is defensible. This means the rules about defamation that apply in the place where the material is uploaded may be taken into account (*Dow Jones & Co v Gutnick* 2002: 10).

To rely on the *truth defence*, a publisher must prove the truth of the material at all levels. This relates back to the meaning of words. Remember, it was noted that words could assume different meanings by a person drawing inferences or having knowledge of additional information. Proving that someone is *suspected* of something falls short of proving that they have in fact *done* something. To prove the truth of a claim, the defendant must be able to establish truth by providing admissible evidence to the court. Therefore, hearsay evidence (a rule stating that only parties to a conversation can give evidence of what was said) cannot be relied upon. Several states have varied the common law defence of truth, adding some privacy protection by requiring the publication to be true and in the public interest (New South Wales) or public benefit (Queensland, Tasmania, Australian Capital Territory).

Fair comment is designed to allow people to express opinions. The law recognises that a fair comment should not be prohibited, provided the comment is a comment and not an assertion of fact. The court will look at the form of publication when deciding whether a statement is a comment or an assertion of fact. Therefore, public relations practitioners should be mindful of the way in which they express comments. To maximise protection, public relations practitioners should try to state the facts first and then draw conclusions from those facts (*Gorton v Australian Broadcasting Commission* 1974: 193). For example, instead of saying a product is defective (which would obviously be defamatory of the manufacturer), set out the facts which support the claim and state the allegation as a conclusion from those facts. Not only will this increase the likelihood that the material will be construed as a comment and not an assertion of facts, but it will also ensure the material meets another element of the defence: that the facts upon which a comment is based are stated or indicated. To rely on this defence, however, it also must be shown that:

- the facts were true or absolutely privileged. If a fact cannot be proven to be true, then it should be left out because it could undermine the fair comment defence;

- the comment was a matter of public interest;
- the comment was 'fair' in that it was an honest opinion capable of being held based on the facts set out. The comment does not have to be reasonable; the test to determine whether a comment is fair is: 'Could a person honestly hold the opinion expressed?' (Gardiner v John Fairfax 1942: 174) At common law, the defence of fair comment will fail if the publication is motivated by a malicious intention.

Privilege protects a person from liability for the publication of defamatory material. Privilege operates at a number of levels. First, some proceedings attract absolute privilege because of the fundamental importance of the free flow of information. Generally, the proceedings of parliament and the courts are protected by 'absolute privilege'. The publications arising from those proceedings are also protected by qualified privilege, where the publication is a fair and accurate record of what went on in those proceedings and where it conveys to the audience/reader the impression of being present at the proceedings (*Chakravarti v Advertiser Newspapers Ltd* 1998: 298, 309, 347). When relying on this defence, practitioners should ensure they use precise language and do not engage in commentary of their own (*Chakravarti v Advertiser Newspapers Ltd* 1998: 335, 346).

The common law also recognises that defamatory publications are protected by qualified privilege where the publisher has a legal, social or moral obligation to publish the information and the person who receives the information has a reciprocal interest to receive the information. The courts have strictly interpreted the situations where the public has a special interest to receive information, stating that publications in the mass media will rarely satisfy this requirement. There are three exceptions: where the publication is in response to some public criticism on a matter of public interest (*Adam v Ward* 1917: 309); where it is warning people of a local or national crisis (*ABC v Comalco* 1985: 83); or where it is correcting incorrect information (*Dunford Publicity Studios v News Media Ownership* 1971: 961). However, the nature of privilege means that the class of protected publications is not closed. It is dependent on the 'common convenience and welfare of society'. When determining whether there is a duty to publish to the world at large, the court will take into account:

- the extent of the publication;
- the proportion of readers who have a legitimate interest in receiving the communication; and
- whether the publication is for commercial gain (*Seary v Molomby* 1999: 4, 6).

In the landmark decision of *Lange v ABA*, the High Court also stated that the mass media have a duty to publish and the general public has a reciprocal interest to receive information of a political or governmental nature. However, because of the mass circulation of the information, the court stated that general publications of a political or governmental nature must meet the additional requirement of reasonableness of conduct. This includes that the publisher took steps to verify the information was true, did not believe the information to be untrue and, where appropriate, gave the person defamed the opportunity to respond (*Lange v Australian Broadcasting Corporation* 1997: 11–13).

This discussion highlights the complexity of defamation law, but it is also costly in terms of reputations, time and money. If a defamatory publication cannot be defended, then the publishers can be ordered to pay damages to compensate for the harm suffered to the plaintiff's reputation. The court also has power to grant injunctions against the publication of defamatory material, which will stop the material being made public. But the cost to the professional reputation of the practitioner and their client must also be factored into decisions about defamation actions. Before embarking on any litigation, the following issues should be addressed:

* Will a legal win equate to a public relations win?
* Have reputations been damaged?
* Will legal action expose you or your client to further disclosure?
* What are the likely costs of the litigation, taking into account any adverse publicity? (Todd 1997)

The responses to these questions should indicate whether litigation is a viable option.

The *Trade Practices Act 1974* (Cth) and reputation

When organising campaigns and lobbying for support for a particular campaign, care should be taken to verify claims to ensure they are not misleading and deceptive, which means looking at the way the material will be received and not what it is intended to mean.

Practitioners should pay particular attention and exercise caution in areas such as puffery, comparative advertising, character merchandising and how they promote goods and services generally.

Section 52 of the *Trade Practices Act 1974* (Cth) (TPA), and the equivalent state provisions, impose onerous obligations on corporations and the people who communicate a corporation's message. An objective test (that of the reasonable person and not the subjective test of the individual) is applied to determine whether conduct is misleading or deceptive, or likely to mislead or deceive (Stals 1997b: 3). The important features of this section are:

- Promotional activities associated with the supply of goods and services to actual or potential customers have a trading and commercial character.
- Intention is irrelevant.
- Conduct that is merely likely to mislead or deceive is banned by the Act.
- Disclaimers and exemption clauses cannot usually excuse misleading and deceptive conduct.
- Silence may constitute misleading and deceptive conduct.
- Statements of opinion may mislead or deceive.
- Conduct does not have to be continuous to be in breach of the Act and it does not have to be known to the public or a group of the public (because it only has to meet the standard of being likely to mislead or deceive).

In the *Slater and Gordon case* (2000: 17) discussed earlier, the court found that the booklet was a form of promotional activity which had a trading or commercial character. The booklet was misleading and deceptive in contravention of section 52 of the TPA because it represented that Slater and Gordon was involved in a medical malpractice action against the two doctors. Therefore, under section 82 of the TPA, the doctors were entitled to damages to compensate for injury to their reputation caused by the misleading or deceptive conduct. Damages were awarded for breaches of the TPA and an injunction was issued against further publication of the booklet in any form that used the photograph. Slater and Gordon was ordered, at its own cost, to send a letter of retraction to each of the doctors who received a copy of the original publication (*Nixon v Slater and Gordon* 2000: 17, 18).

Minimising reputational harm: legal risks of litigation public relations?

Sometimes parties to litigation or people charged with offences look to public relations to 'control the damage' of proceedings. Any practitioner engaged in litigation public relations has a duty to be aware of the legal status of any case and factor the contempt of court laws into any advice offered to clients seeking strategies to minimise potential harm. Liaising with court public information officers will help practitioners to keep track of proceedings. But practitioners also must understand the doctrine of contempt of court, particularly the *sub judice* rules.

The *contempt of court* rules exist to protect the administration of justice, and attempt to balance the need for people to scrutinise the courts with the need for the courts to be free to judge matters. They regulate many things, including:

- what can be published about matters before the court;
- what can be published about the people who sit in judgment of those matters (whether judge or jury);
- how people conduct themselves in court and how they conduct themselves in relation to people involved in the court process, including witnesses and officers of the court; and
- ensuring people do what the court orders them to do.

The *sub judice* rules restrict what can be published about proceedings that are pending. Proceedings are pending from the time of arrest in criminal charges (*AG for NSW v TCN Channel Nine P/L* 1990: 368) and at the time of the issue of the writ in civil proceedings. Criminal trials or civil trials, where there is a jury present such as in defamation actions, pose the greatest problems in terms of *sub judice* contempt. It is contempt to publish material which will have a clear tendency to substantially prejudice the outcome of those proceedings (*AG for NSW v TCN Channel Nine P/L* 1990: 379). What constitutes a 'clear tendency to substantially prejudice' is not defined, but is determined instead on a case-by-case basis. Factors taken into account include:

- the immediate circumstances of the publication, including the time of publication and the stage of the proceedings. A publication is more likely to have a tendency to prejudice if it is published close to the trial;
- the likely delay in the proceedings coming to trial;
- the status of the person making the statement which is published;
- whether the publication relates to the issues on trial;
- whether the audience is likely to contain potential jurors or witnesses; and
- the level of media coverage.

The court will permit publications which prejudice the proceedings if there is some overriding public interest justifying publication (*Hinch v AG for Vic.* 1987). However, the prejudicial information must be limited to that which is necessary to satisfy the public interest. Broadcaster Derryn Hinch was found guilty of contempt of court for publishing information about a priest being charged on several counts of sexually assaulting children in his care. The court found that, by revealing the prior convictions of the accused, Hinch was in contempt of court (*Hinch v AG for Vic.* 1987). Publications generally will be permitted if they are fair and accurate reports of proceedings.

The publisher is liable for contemptuous publications. This includes the people responsible for the publication (in media publications, this is the journalist/ broadcaster, producer/editor and proprietor) and the person who conveys the information to a journalist/broadcaster/writer, which includes public relations practitioners (*AG for NSW v TCN Channel Nine P/L* 1990: 378–79).

This discussion exemplifies the need for caution in campaigns seeking to influence 'the court of public opinion' where judicial proceedings are still pending. These dangers are highlighted in *NAALAS v Bradley*, where the court found former NT Chief Minister and Attorney General Denis Burke guilty of contempt of court for making comments which had a clear tendency to interfere with the administration of justice by putting improper pressure on the North Australian Aboriginal Legal Aid Service (NAALAS) in its action against Chief Magistrate Hugh Bradley. Comments made by the former Chief Minister at a press conference were found to have the clear tendency to deter a litigant from continuing to prosecute or defend a case and dissuading potential witnesses from giving evidence. It was noted that Mr Burke was entitled to have whatever opinion he wished about the motives and purposes of NAALAS, and he was entitled to express those opinions provided he did not transgress the rules concerning contempt of court (*NAALAS v Bradley* 2001: 16, 18).

Practitioners might need to coach clients in handling press conferences dealing with issues to be determined by the court. They should ensure that the views expressed are balanced and non-judgmental of issues before the court. The views should not threaten parties to an action (including witnesses). Answers given at a press conference should respond to questions and not set an agenda to criticise the other side's case.

A significant study into the prejudicial effect of pre-trial publicity on criminal juries by Chesterman, Chan and Hampton (2001: 1) concluded that New South Wales juries had 'a relatively successful record of resistance to publicity'. The researchers conceded that the legal restrictions imposed on pre-trial publicity helped juries resist the adverse effects of such publicity.

Property in public relations: real and creative

Clark, Cho and Hoyle (2000: 240) stress that a knowledge of intellectual property law has become 'a prerequisite for anyone doing business in what has become known as the information or digital age'. Before going into a more detailed analysis of some aspects of intellectual property law, it is important to distinguish between real, personal property and intellectual property. Big sporting events, for example, involve a variety of stakeholders who have various property interests—real, personal and intellectual. The venue owners have real property in the venue, the venue managers have personal property in the chattels they put into the grounds, such as furniture and equipment, and event organisers and sponsors have intellectual property in the logos, slogans and campaigns used to promote the event.

Real property law refers to land and things affixed to land (Clark, Cho and Hoyle 2000). Ownership of land is easily proved because it must be registered either under statutory provisions or a system recognised at common law. A titles office search will reveal who owns a particular property. Public relations practitioners may need advice on real property issues when organising events. Permission is required of the owner or occupier of land or premises. If permission is not obtained, the owner/occupier can evict those people who have entered his or her land or premises without permission. Property rights give rise to a right of quiet enjoyment of land, which is protected by a body of law known as trespass and nuisance. This chapter will not go into further detail on these bodies of law, but practitioners should be aware of the rights attaching to property ownership and occupation of land.

There is no comprehensive system for registering personal property. Yet many businesses—including public relations firms—amass personal property including cars, computers and business equipment. Proof of ownership does not become a problem until ownership is challenged. Problems could arise, for example, on dissolution of partnership or termination of business arrangements. Issues relating to ownership of personal property can be dealt with in contracts or business ledgers. But all records of purchase should be retained for taxation and proof of ownership purposes.

Each state provides a system for registering business names. The system serves a two-fold function of protecting businesses from competitors trading under their name and protecting the public by ensuring people who trade under a business name register details of the people involved. Clark et al. (2000: 243) note a number of serious problems with the scheme, including its failure to provide proprietary interests, forcing businesses to register their name as a business name and trade mark.

Intellectual property law 'protects the property rights in creative and inventive endeavours and gives creators and inventors certain exclusive economic rights, generally for a limited time, to deal with their creative works or inventions'

(Commonwealth of Australia 2001). Ideas are protected by the *Patents Act 1990* (Cth) and law of trade secrets; how those ideas are expressed are protected by the Designs Act, *Copyright Act 1968* (Cth) and *Circuits Layout Act 1989* (Cth); and trade marks and product get-up are protected by *Trade Marks Acts 1995* (Cth) and the tort of passing off (Clarke and Sweeney 2000: 9). Clarke and Sweeney (2000: 13) have summarised the type of intellectual property protection offered by statute and common law (see Table 4.1).

Copyright is regulated in Australia by the *Copyright Act 1968* (Cth), which aims to balance the rights of the creators of original material and their investors against the right of the public to access this material at a fair price (Cantwell 2000: 2). Copyright prevents people from unfairly exploiting the skill and labour of authors and creators of original work. Copyright cannot exist in ideas, only in how the ideas are expressed. For example, an idea for a public relations or advertising campaign only becomes copyright when that campaign is expressed with a specific slogan, logo and other written or oral styles.

The first question to consider when dealing with copyright is whether the material is covered by the *Copyright Act 1968* (Cth). The Act applies to works (including literary, dramatic, musical or artistic works, and computer programs) and subject-matter other than works (including sound recordings, films, television and sound broadcasts, and published editions of works) (Stals 1997b: 14). Copyright also exists in publications on the internet. Copyright protection occurs automatically when an original expression of an idea is reduced to tangible form. Although copyright protection is automatic, the Commonwealth of Australia advises copyright owners to attach a notice on their work. The copyright guide (2001: 5) provides a sample notice, which states:

> This work is copyright. Apart from any use permitted under the *Copyright Act 1968* (Cth), no part may be reproduced by any process, or any other exclusive right exercised, without the permission of (name and address of copyright owner and the year in which the work was made).

All professionals (and students) should be careful to acknowledge the source of works and obtain permission to use them. Unfortunately for people who want to use copyright material, there is no central copyright registration system; however, a number of agencies do exist which may help ascertain the copyright status of material (see <www.dcita.gov.au/Article/0,,0_1-2_1-4_14309,00.html>) which provides a list of the non-government copyright collecting societies which administer the rights of copyright owners.

Table 4.1 Intellectual property protection

	Copyright Act	Designs Act	Patents Act	Confidential information	Trade Marks Act	Passing off (protection of IP rights, not creation of right)
Source of law	Statute (Commonwealth)	Statute (Commonwealth)	Statute (Commonwealth)	Common law	Statute (Commonwealth)	Common law (Section 52 TPA offers similar protection)
What is protected?	The manner in which ideas are expressed in works and subject-matter other than works	Look and shape of product	New and inventive industrial products and processes	Commercial information that is secret and has value	Distinctive marks	Reputation in a distinctive designation or get up
Is registration required?	No	Yes	Yes	No	Yes	No
How long does protection last?	*Works:* life of creator + 50 years *Subject-matter other than works:* 50 years from publication	16 years	20 years (standard patent) 6 years (petty patent)	As long as information is secret and valuable	10 years + 10 years + 10 years indefinitely	As long as reputation in name or get-up remains distinctive

What are rights enjoyed by owner?	Exclusive right to reproduce, publish, adapt, perform in public and communicate to public the copyright work (rights vary according to the type of work)	Exclusive right to apply the design to the article in respect of which the design is registered	Right to stop others exploiting the invention (i.e. to hire, sell or otherwise dispose of the invention)	Right to stop unauthorised disclosure of trade secrets (no power to stop independent discovery)	Right to stop others using mark or any other mark that is deceptively similar in respect of goods or services in respect of which the mark is registered	Right to stop others using similar designation or get up in such a way as to indicate a connection with the complaining business
Expense	Proving copyright ownership Policing infringement	Registration Policing infringement	Registration Policing infringement Fighting revocation proceedings	Protecting secrecy Policing infringement	Registration Policing infringement	Establishing reputation and misrepresentation Policing infringement

Source: Clarke and Sweeny (2000), p.13.

If these organisations cannot help in identifying who owns copyright and there is no wording accompanying the material which reserves copyright to someone in particular, then a practitioner should apply the general principles set out in the *Copyright Act 1968* (Cth). Generally, the creator of a literary, dramatic or artistic work is the first owner of copyright in it. However, if original works are created in the course of employment, the copyright in them may be owned by the employer. Where someone commissions original works, the copyright may vest in the person commissioning the work. This is something a practitioner will need to clarify when negotiating contracts with clients—for example, in the creation of slogans, logos and other elements of campaigns.

The *Copyright Act 1968* (Cth) gives copyright owners (usually the creator) a number of exclusive economic rights, which vary according to the different types of works and other subject-matter protected by copyright. These rights include the right to copy, publish, adapt, communicate (broadcast or make available online) and publicly perform the copyright material. Copyright creators also receive non-economic rights known as moral rights, recognising the right of integrity of authorship, right of attribution of authorship and right against false attribution of authorship (Commonwealth of Australia 2001: 1, 7).

Economic rights may be exercised by the copyright owner or assigned, licensed, given away, sold, included in a will or passed on. An assignment of copyright—whether whole or in part, complete or limited in time or location—must be in writing and signed by the assignee. Economic rights can be licensed either exclusively or non-exclusively and upon specified conditions, such as the payment of a fee or the performance of particular acts (Commonwealth of Australia 2001: 12). The most common copyright licence specifies a defined and limited use of copyright material. Art banks, which provide a library of images that can be used for a fee, are a good example of this. Fees are charged for each use of an image. So, if an image is bought to use on a brochure, it cannot be used on a website unless an additional fee is paid for a licence to cover that extra use.

The personal nature of moral rights means they cannot be given to anyone else (Commonwealth of Australia 2001: 7). This means licensed copyright work must acknowledge and respect the moral rights of the copyright creator, which means acknowledging the creator and obtaining consent to deal with the copyright work in a way that may affect the creator's integrity. For example, adaptations of songs or paintings need the consent of both the copyright owner and the copyright creator. The attribution right continues for the duration of copyright protection—that is, the life of the author plus 50 years and 50 years for the first publication for a film (Department of Communications, Information Technology and the Arts 2002a: 2).

Public relations professionals should vet all public statements, press releases and promotional material for obvious breaches of copyright. Stals (1997b: 17) offers this advice on how to minimise copyright breaches:

- Mark the original work with the copyright symbol, a date of creation and the business name.
- Check the copyright status of work being used from other sources and ensure that permission to use the material (for the specific use sought) has been obtained from the copyright owner.
- Check the licence conditions of promotional material to ensure that it covers its intended use.
- Ensure that the packaging of clients' products is not copied from other packaging.
- Do not make unnecessary copies of documents.
- Do not show documents to third parties unless it is required as part of the job.
- Do not copy designs, logos or graphics belonging to other businesses.
- Verify the copyright status of material supplied by clients.

Practitioners also need to be cautious about putting information online. The *Copyright Amendment (Digital Agenda) Act 2000* (Cth) has clarified the copyright positions of online publications. The new communication right, which replaces the broadcast right, includes the right to first digitisation. Therefore permission of the copyright owner is needed to put material online. Common questions arising from online copyright include the status of emails. Emails do attract copyright but, as the Department of Communications, Information Technology and the Arts acknowledges, most authors of emails do not wish to enforce their copyright. Press releases—whether hard copy or electronic—attract copyright because they are an original expression of news. Remember, news or information itself does not attract copyright, but the original expression of it does. However, the action of sending press releases to news outlets gives rise to an implied licence to use and adapt the material. It is therefore unlikely that a public relations practitioner would take action against a media outlet which was circulating their message, since this is the intention of releasing the communication in the first place. A problem may arise, however, if another practitioner uses all or part of the press release and passes it off as their own work. It could be argued that this implied licence does not extend to other public relations professionals, and this action could be actionable under the PRIA Code of Ethics.

When advising clients on image and relationship building, public relations practitioners must be careful not to borrow too heavily from the ideas of their client's competitors. The tort of passing off and sections 52 and 53 of the TPA limit the type of representations that can be made. In addition, the *Trade Marks Act 1995* protects the 'identifying mark' of a particular good or service (not the description of the good or service). Examples of the information needed to register identifying marks as trade marks are available at <www.ipaustralia.gov.au>. Although it is not mandatory to register a trade mark, it could save time and money because registration of an identifying mark grants an exclusive legal right to use, license or sell it within Australia for the goods and services for which it is registered (IP Australia 2002b: 1). Applications for trade marks should be filed with the Trade Marks Office of IP Australia. To be registered, trade marks must be capable of distinguishing an applicant's goods or services (Clarke and Sweeney 2000: 173).

The McDonald's golden arches logo, for example, could not be registered in Australia by a business selling takeaway foods. However, a medical practice may be successful in registering a similar mark because the goods and services provided are not significantly similar to McDonald's.

Any 'trade secret' which is a patent, design or trade mark should be registered. IP Australia (2002a) explains that a trade secret is both a type of intellectual property and a strategy for protecting intellectual property. In a public relations context, trade secrets might include customer lists, new project ideas, promotion plans or financial reports, many of which may not attract protection under the areas of copyright, patents, designs or trade marks.

Trade secrets should be backed up by having all parties enter into confidentiality agreements. Confidentiality agreements provide documentary evidence of the nature of the secret, thus making it easier to prove a breach. The legal obligations to maintain the confidence derive from contract rather than common law and therefore are easily established in court. Proof of the nature and extent of the duty of confidence is far easier if it is specified in a confidentiality agreement. Problems of proof arise where the common law needs to examine the relationship to decide whether the duty of confidence is an implied condition of a contract. To establish an equitable duty of confidence it must be shown that:

- the information was confidential;
- the relationship between the parties to the action must have given rise to an obligation of trust and confidence; and
- the information was imparted without consent (Clark, Cho and Hoyle 2000: 270).

Rather than run the risk of confidential information being the subject of public litigation, it is advisable to enter into confidentiality agreements with all staff, contractors, clients and any other person who may come in contact with confidential aspects of business.

The role of contracts in public relations

Contract law plays a pivotal role in public relations. Contracts define the relationship between parties and are used in all facets of public relations from employment of staff to the supply of materials to fulfil a campaign. Most of the time, standard form contracts will be used. The standard form contract usually contains 'a uniform set of printed conditions which can be used time and time again and is oriented towards servicing a large volume of clientele as expeditiously as possible' (Harmer 1998: 17). But circumstances may arise which require additional clauses or a completely new contract. If this occurs, the practitioner should seek legal advice.

The essential ingredients of a contract are an *offer*; *acceptance of that offer* despatched to or communicated to the offeror; and *consideration*. When preparing contracts for supply of goods or services, several important risks should be identified and managed. Clark, Cho and Hoyle (2000: 113–14) identify these as:

- *securing the right provider*: conduct a due diligence test to check the financial viability, reputation and dependability of provider;
- *assessing likelihood of complete performance*: link payment to performance and the completion of meaningful milestones;
- *specifying what happens if the provider fails to provide service on time*: provide for periodic progress reports and incorporate penalty clauses;
- *specifying who bears the risk of negligence in performance of contract*: include a clause requiring the provider to accept responsibility for his/her/its negligence and requiring insurance to cover this risk;
- *specifying obligations of confidentiality*: include a standard clause preventing the provider from disclosing confidential information relating to the contract;
- *privacy*: require information to be used only for the purposes of the contract and oblige the provider to take steps to ensure the protection of privacy. Include a standard clause that specifies any privacy standards (legal or voluntary) and oblige the provider to meet those standards. Specify penalties for failure to meet standards (i.e. breach of contract);
- *providing for public feedback*: in campaigns, etc. include a clause that provides for feedback from the target public regarding the success of the campaign;

- *specifying what happens if a conflict of interest arises*: include a standard clause which sets out what will happen if a conflict of interest arises.

As this list illustrates, contracts are a useful way of clearing up uncertainty in relationships with others. For example, if contracting for materials to be supplied from overseas, a term can be included in the contract to clarify which country's laws will be applied if a dispute arises. If the contract is expected to continue over a period of time, then an arbitration clause can be included to help resolve minor disputes.

It is important to remember that a contract only becomes a problem when the parties to the contract fail to agree. Time spent on predicting possible areas of contention at the start of the agreement may result in more efficient and amicable relations in the future. When contracting with clients, it is important to maximise the amicable nature of relations to ensure continuous work.

Contract preparation should start early and ensure the following:

- *completeness*: all aspects of the service must be identified, service standards articulated, and dimensions of service identified;
- *clarity*: the purchaser and provider should have the same understanding and agreed definitions;
- *measurability*: outcomes should be identified and expressed in measurable terms. Contracts should focus on outcomes and standards rather than processes (Clark, Cho and Hoyle 2002: 113).

A common feature of standard form contracts is the exemption or exclusion clause, which is inserted to exclude a party from liability in certain circumstances. Exemption clauses are extremely common and most people would have encountered them in their everyday life. For example, a dry cleaning ticket usually states that the cleaner will not be responsible for damage to garments, or carpark tickets will state that the carpark operator is not responsible for damage to or theft of vehicles. Anyone competing in a fun-run or major event will note that the organisers exempt themselves from liability for injuries in these events. Obviously public relations practitioners who are involved in event organisation will need to ensure exemption clauses are included in their contracts. Practitioners must also guard against the risk of facing additional costs because a party to the contract has exempted themselves from liability.

Examples of overriding legal duties include a professional's duty of care to their client and the public (to be discussed in the next section) or obligations arising under the *Trade Practices Act 1974* (Cth) or tort of passing off.

This chapter has already noted that the public relations legal environment is one of global business and global communication. These factors also affect the way in which contracts are entered into. Clark et al. (2000: 295) note that the use of electronic contracts in business is growing and the *Electronic Transaction Act 1999* aims to remove obstacles to further development of e-commerce by removing legal uncertainties regarding business and commerce conducted electronically. The Act aims to ensure that the law is the same for both paper-based commerce and e-commerce and there is no discrimination between the forms of technology.

However, electronic contracts face a number of problems, including:

- proof of agreement: one of the problems facing electronic contracting is proof of its existence—that is, proof of offer, acceptance and consideration. These problems can be reduced by the use of encryption and digital signatures, but these solutions do present their own problems;
- what law applies, if this is not specified in the contract;
- whether the contract is in a proper form (where this is required to be enforceable);
- security: can you be sure with whom you are dealing and possible limitations of encryption and digital signatures, particularly in view of the recent success of hackers?
- certainty of the terms of contract;
- cultural (online and international) implications for the interpretation of the contract; and
- whether consumer law has been complied with across multiple jurisdictions. Clark, Cho and Hoyle (2000: 296–99)

The globalisation of the business environment is impacting on the legal environment. Attention to detail in the preparation of contract may minimise legal risk, but if problems do emerge it may be difficult to enforce judgments in jurisdictions outside Australia. Moves are being made at an international level to develop contracting conventions. In 2002, the United Nations Commission on International Trade Law Working Group on Electronic Commerce met to develop a draft convention on electronic contracting to help eliminate legal obstacles to the use of modern means of communication in contract formation. Working paper No 95 is available from <http://law.gov.au/wotl.html>.

Contracts—whether electronic or in traditional form—are an excellent way of defining relationships, responsibilities and reasonable hopes of people engaging in business. However, the terms and conditions agreed upon bind only the parties. What happens if a practitioner suffers damage as a result of the negligence of someone who is not party to the contract? The tort of negligence offers some help. But the tort also exposes a practitioner to liability if they fail to exercise reasonable care.

The public relations duty of care

A contract may specify a particular standard of care. If this standard is not met, then the other party has a right of action in contract. However, 'under the principles of professional negligence, a public relations firm, who owes a duty in contract to its clients . . . also [owes] a duty to third parties in relation to the giving of information or advice which is relied on by third parties' (Stals 1997a: 1).

Butler and Rodrick (1999: 3) identify three elements which must be proved to bring an action in negligence. They are as follows:

- A duty of care must be owed by the person accused of being negligent and that duty must be owed to the person claiming to have suffered damage.
- There must be a breach of that duty by failing to exercise reasonable care.
- Damage must be suffered as a consequence of that breach.

The existence of a duty of care depends on two things: foreseeability and policy consideration that the court believes should be taken into account (Butler and Rodrick 1999). In some cases, there will be no real policy considerations to take into account; therefore, reasonable foreseeability of potential harm is sufficient to establish a duty of care. In other cases involving pure economic loss, there is a level of uncertainty about the appropriate test, with some decisions suggesting the test should be foreseeability of harm, proximity and policy. Obviously, in situations where your actions could impinge on the financial viability of others, you need to exercise considerable care to ensure they do not suffer harm.

The law generally requires that a professional will act with the reasonable care and skill of an ordinarily competent member of the profession in question. Professionals are obliged to give skilled advice based on the possession of a systematic body of knowledge. In public relations, a duty of care will arise where advice is given on a serious or business matter; the adviser knows or ought to know that a person will rely on the advice given; and it is reasonable for the other party to rely on the advice given (Stals 1997a: 1, 2).

A practitioner's obligation to exercise reasonable care also extends to third parties who can reasonably be expected to rely on this information and advice, including 'shareholders and investors in client corporations' and 'other corporations or persons which have a business relationship with the client corporation' (Stals 1997a: 3).

To be liable in negligence, a public relations practitioner must breach the duty of care by not exercising the standard of care expected of a competent practitioner. Here the court will take into account the standards of professional organisations; therefore the PRIA Code of Ethics (which is considered in more detail in Chapter 5) will be a good benchmark for acceptable practice. Avoiding an action in negligence comes down to maintaining good work practices and exercising common sense. If in doubt, do not offer advice that goes beyond your expertise. Recommend or take the advice of other professionals, and make sure you limit your liability in contract.

Conclusion

This chapter identifies parts of the legal environment in which public relations practitioners must operate. This general discussion should reveal the complexity and diversity of the public relations legal environment, highlighting the necessity of good legal advice. But that legal advice must be interpreted from a public relations perspective to ensure that quality decisions are made. This means selecting a legal practitioner who respects the professionalism of their client and can ensure the best outcomes from both the legal and public relations perspectives.

Working with legal input, public relations practitioners can move towards a systematic approach to dealing with the law. Organisations should move towards developing a legal strategy for their area of specialty, setting benchmarks of best practice in potential problem areas, such as contract law, intellectual property, defamation, contempt and consumer protection law (TPA). Developing a legal strategy and compliance systems will not eliminate legal problems, but will go a long way towards minimising harm arising from these problems.

Table of cases

ABC v Comalco (1985), <www.austlii.edu.au/do/disp.pl/au/cases/cth/federal_ct/unrept2398.html> (viewed 17/8/99)
Adam v Ward [1917] AC 309
Attorney General for the State of NSW v TCN Channel Nine (1990) 20 NSWLR 368
Chakravarti v Advertiser Newspapers Ltd (1998) 154 ALR 294
Dow Jones & Co v Gutnick (2002) viewed at <www.butterworthsonline.com/cgi-bin/urjlink.pl?qstring=asf2002200207411> on 12 December 2002

Dunford Publicity Studios Ltd v News Media Ownership Ltd [1971] NZLR 961

Gardiner v John Fairfax & Sons Pty Ltd (1942) 42 SR (NSW) 171

Gorton v Australian Broadcasting Commission (1974) 22 FLR 181

Hinch v Attorney General for Victoria (1987) 164 CLR 15

Lange v Australian Broadcasting Corporation (1997) High Court of Australia, <www.austlii.edu. au.h/high_ct/unrep324.html> (viewed 19/2/98), pp. 1–18

Levien v Fox (1890) 11 NSWLR 369

McPhersons Limited v Hickie (1995) unreported, Supreme Court of NSW, Court of Appeal, NO CA 40290 of 1994, delivered 26 May

Morosi v Broadcasting Station 2GB (1980) 2 NSWLR 418n

Nixon v Slater and Gordon (2000) viewed at <http://online.butterworths.com.au/urjlink.html/ 2000200001995> on 5 August 2000

North Australian Aboriginal Legal Aid Service Inc v Bradley (2001) viewed at <http://online. butterworths.com.au/ujrlink.html/2001200104108> on 39 July 2001

Packer v Peacock (1912) 13 CLR 577

Parmiter v Coupland (1840) 6 M & W ER 340

Rindos v Hardwick (1993) Supreme Court of Western Australia (unreported) no. 1994 of 1993, judgment delivered on 31 March

Seary v Molomby (1999) NSWSC 981, viewed at <http://online.butterworths.com.au/unrep/ 99/ 9906243.htm> on 11/10/99

Sim v Stretch (1936) TLR 669

Thompson v Australian Capital Television and Others (1996) 186 CLR 574

Youssoupoff v Metro-Goldwyn Mayer Pictures Ltd [1934] TLR 581

Discussion and exercises

1   Contracts define legal relationships between various parties. The Australian Journalist's Association (AJA) has a standard contract for freelance journalists found at <http://www.alliance.org.au/freelance/stancont.htm>. Locate this contract and answer the following:

  (a) How long does the copyright licence last?

  (b) How is 'material' defined?

  (c) When should payment for 'material' be made and what additional expenses may be negotiated?

  (d) What happens if the publisher chooses not to publish or broadcast the work under contract?

2   The contempt of court laws regulate the publication of information about pending proceedings. Identify a situation where these laws could apply to public relations work.

3   Copyright restrictions exist in using some materials for public relations campaigns. Consider whether such restrictions might exist in each of the following situations:

(a) A photo taken by a photographer under contract to your organisation and a photograph located on an internet site?

(b) A music track by a well-known local group?

(c) A logo of another organisation?

(d) Factual information from the morning's newspaper?

(e) The development of an idea you once saw in a magazine?

4   Why should you consider the issue of defamation when writing and publishing an online journal? Giving consideration to the Gutnick case discussed in this chapter, discuss why communications professionals should be increasingly careful about publishing material online.

Further reading

Clark, Eugene, Cho, George & Hoyle, Arthur (2000) *Marketers and the Law*, LBC Information Services, Sydney.

Clarke, Bruce & Sweeney, Brendan (2000) *Marketing and the Law*, Butterworths, Sydney.

'The Law and New Practice Developments: Public Relations in the Litigious Nineties', seminar, Blake Dawson and Waldron Solicitors, Sydney, 27 May.

Schultz, J. (1998) *Reviving the Fourth Estate: Democracy, Accountability and the Media*, Cambridge University Press, Cambridge & Melbourne.

Walker, S. (1999) *Media Law: Commentary and Materials*, Law Book Company, Sydney.

References

Ackland, R. & Florance, K. (1995) 'More McCircus', *Gazette of Law and Journalism*, no. 33, August, p. 18.

—— (1996) 'McLibel on tap', *Gazette of Law and Journalism*, no. 38, April, p. 15.

Armstrong, M., Lindsay, D. & Watterson, R. (1995) *Media Law in Australia*, 3rd edn, Oxford University Press, Melbourne.

Breit, R. (1999) 'Defamation: does it have a future?', *Journalism Theory and Practice*, proceedings of the 1998 Journalism Education Association Conference, Journalism Education Association, Yeppoon, Queensland, pp. 31–39.

Butler, Des & Rodrick, Sharon (1999) *Australian Media Law*, LBC Information Services, Sydney.

Cantwell, H. (2000) 'Copyright', in R. Breit, H. Cantwell & J. Mullaly (eds), *The Writer and the Law*, Deakin University, Geelong, pp. 1–9.

Catlin, James (2000) 'Litigation explosion booklet blows-up in law firm's face', in *Gazette of Law and Journalism*, <www.lawpress.com.au/genews/ge114_Slater&Gordon.html>, accessed 6 September 2000.

Chesterman, M., Chan, J. & Hampton, S. (2001) 'Managing prejudicial publicity: an empirical study of criminal jury trials in New South Wales', briefing note viewed at <www.lawfoundation.net.au/jrc/reports/sum_jury.html>, accessed 15 August 2002, pp. 1–3.

Clark, Eugene, Cho, George & Hoyle, Arthur (2000) *Marketers and the Law*, LBC Information Services, Sydney.

Clarke, Bruce & Sweeney, Brendan (2000) *Marketing and the Law*, Butterworths, Sydney.

Commonwealth of Australia (2001) *Copyright in Australia: A Short Guide*, <www.law.gov.au/publications/copyrightlawaust/contents.html>, accessed 19 August 2002.

Couslon, J., Carr, C.T., Hutchinson, L. & Eagle, D. (1975) *The Oxford Illustrated Dictionary*, 2nd edn, Oxford University Press, London.

Department of Communications, Information Technology and the Arts (2002a) 'Guide to the *Moral Rights Act*', <www.dcita..gov.au>, accessed 19 August 2002, pp. 1–6.

—— (2002b) 'Moral rights—protecting the rights of creators', <www.dcita.gov.au>, accessed 19 August 2002, pp. 1–2.

—— (2002c) 'Frequently asked questions about the Digital Agenda Copyright Reforms', <www.dcita.gov.au>, accessed 19 August 2002, pp. 1–5.

—— (2002d) 'Guide to *Copyright Amendment (Digital Agenda) Act* 2000', <www.dcita.gov.au>, accessed 19 August 2002, pp. 1–4.

Doogue, J. (ed.) (1997) *The Writer and the Law*, 2nd edn, Deakin University, Geelong.

Electronic Transactions Act (1999), <www.austlii.edu.au/au/legis/cth/consol_act/eta1999256>, accessed 20 August 2002.

Harmer, S. (1998) 'The law of contract', in *Legal Principles for Public Relations Practitioners*, Deakin University, Geelong, pp. 1–21.

Hoger, E.A. & Swem, L.L. (2000) 'Public relations and the law in crisis mode: Texaco's initial reaction to incriminating tapes', *Public Relations Review*, vol. 26, no. 4, p. 425.

Hutton, J.G., Goodman, M.B., Alexander, J.B. & Genest, C.M. (2001) 'Reputation management: The new face of corporate public relations', *Public Relations Review*, vol. 27, no. 3, p. 247.

IP Australia (2002a) 'Trade Secrets', <www.ipaustralia.gov.au/ip>, accessed 19 August 2002, pp. 1–2.

—— (2002b) 'Trade Marks', <www.ipaustralia.gov.au/ip>, accessed 19 August 2002, pp. 1–3.

The Macquarie Dictionary (1985), revised edn, Macquarie Library, Sydney.

Stals, G. (1997a) 'Principles of professional negligence: to whom do public relations professionals owe a duty of care?', Public Relations Law: The Law and New Practice Developments: Public Relations in the Litigious Nineties, seminar, Blake Dawson and Waldron, Solicitors, 27 May, Sydney, pp. 1–4.

—— (1997b) 'Trade practices and copyright issues', Public Relations Law: The Law and New Practice Developments: Public Relations in the Litigious Nineties, seminar, Blake Dawson and Waldron Solicitors, 27 May, Sydney, pp. 1–17.

Todd, R. (1997) 'Media law: protection of corporate reputation', Public Relations Law: The Law and New Practice Developments: Public Relations in the Litigious Nineties, seminar, Blake Dawson and Waldron Solicitors, 27 May, Sydney, pp. 1–22.

UNCITRAL Working Group on Electronic Commerce (2002) 39th Session: Issues Paper,

Draft Convention on Electronic Contracting viewed at <www.dcita.gov.au>.

Walker, S. (1994) 'Regulating the media: reputation, truth and privacy', *Melbourne University Law Review*, no. 19, pp. 729–40.

Window on the Law (1998) 'Copyright law in Australia: a short guide', <http://law.gov.au/publications/copyrightaus98.htm>, accessed 21 May 1999, pp. 1–20.

5 ETHICAL PRACTICE

Lelde McCoy

In this chapter
Introduction
What is ethics?
Public relations ethics in practice
The role of ethics in public relations
The role of counsellor
The role of advocate
The role of corporate monitor
The role of corporate conscience
Ethical challenges for practitioners
An ethical framework
ABA inquiry
Ethics as a public relations strategy
Corporate governance
How to address ethical issues
Conclusion

Introduction

A succession of corporate and other institutional scandals involving unethical behaviour have led to new paradigms for public relations—new standards by which publics judge organisations.

In the early twenty-first century, the world suffers from a legacy of greed and excess. The depletion of natural resources, financial markets and regulations failing investors, together with controversies surrounding corporate leaders and other authority figures and increased international media scrutiny, have led citizens to question corporate ethics. The public demand for greater moral accountability from business has meant that organisations are now paying more attention to community demands and have become more responsive to a wide range of stakeholders rather than just to shareholders.

This higher level of organisational scrutiny, coupled with the move to greater professionalism in public relations, has led to concern over the public relations industry's ethical principles and practitioner standards of operation.

A growing number of people, including the news media, are questioning what constitutes appropriate public relations conduct. Books such as *Toxic Sludge is Good for You! Lies, Damn Lies and the Public Relations Industry* (1995), watchdog groups such as the Centre for Media and Democracy and public relations campaigns like the one that helped 'sell' the Gulf War have gained criticism for the industry as one that alters perceptions, reshapes reality and manufactures consent. Public relations practitioners are accused by the media and stakeholder groups of being spin doctors and describing a reality that suits their purposes.

Cutlip acknowledges that public relations has often cluttered the channels of communication with pseudo-events and phoney phrases that confuse rather then clarify (1994: xiii). This practice has led the news media and the public to regard public relations with cynicism, an attitude which Miyamoto (1996) says is encapsulated in the descriptor that an activity is merely a 'PR ploy', a 'PR manoeuvre' or a 'PR effort'.

Today's technology has further reduced the ability of practitioners to communicate truthfully with integrity, as PowerPoint slides and media news bites have reduced communications to bullet points, distilling complex issues into simple propositions.

To a large extent, the problem of inconsistent approaches to public relations work has arisen because practitioners have varying education standards and undertake different kinds of work. Some practitioners operate as technicians, implementing communications under the direction of management, who may not fully understand the role of public relations. Others operate as strategists, but find their moral agency constrained or inhibited by the actions and choices of others—for instance, when important information is not disclosed by a client.

Within the controversy and ideological opposition to public relations, there is a need for all those involved to think about how a robust and systematic ethical framework can be constructed for the profession.

Public relations theorists such as James Grunig (1992) and Seib and Fitzpatrick (1995) agree that a necessary precondition of professionalism is ethically defensible behaviour. Such a framework derives from philosophical and religious attitudes to behaviour and ethics; laws and regulations; corporate and industry codes of conduct; public relations association codes of ethics; professional values and ethics; training; and personal integrity.

Society has a keen interest in the performance of communications professionals, given the importance of accurate information as a basis for opinions and actions. As a result, practitioners have a social responsibility to maintain certain ethical standards since their work is capable of influencing others.

What is ethics?

Ethics refers to the personal values which underpin the behaviour and moral choices made by an individual in response to a specific situation. According to the Josephson Institute for the Advancement of Ethics, values considered essential to ethical life are honesty, integrity, promise-keeping, fidelity, fairness, caring for others, respect for others, responsible citizenship, the pursuit of excellence and accountability (Josephson Institute 2003). Ethics are standards of integrity—in a nutshell, ethics is about doing the right thing.

Business ethics is about prioritising moral values for an organisation and ensuring its behaviours are aligned with those values. Ethical issues touch employees in all areas of business—marketing, manufacturing, human resources, finance, corporate strategy, investor relations, corporate governance and public relations. Employees need the conceptual tools and decision-making framework for analysing and resolving the full range of ethical and corporate governance issues that arise in an organisation.

In public relations practice, ethical behaviour relates both to the practitioner and to organisations. Public relations practitioners therefore need to be concerned with their own personal and professional ethics as well as with the institutional ethics of the organisation for which they work.

Seib and Fitzpatrick (1995) talk about the five duties of public relations professionals as being to oneself, the client, the employer, the profession and society. Using this list as a guide, when faced with an ethical dilemma, you first need to look within yourself at your own values. These will guide decisions based on what you truly believe is right or wrong. The client or organisation is generally the next loyalty beyond yourself. As a public relations professional, you are obligated to support your colleagues and to be responsible to your peers. Finally, society is the key component to ethical decisions. Public relations practitioners must serve the public interest. In doing so, the practitioner needs to ask the question: 'Will my decision benefit society, even if I hurt myself, my client, my employer or my profession?'

Ethical dilemmas are not easy; they are perplexing situations involving decisions about what is right or wrong. Often they are situations requiring a choice between equally undesirable alternatives. When an organisation downsizes, public relations practitioners often find themselves in a position of having to develop communications strategies and materials directed at colleagues who will lose their jobs.

Ethical decisions have to be made by the CEO and the board of directors where the corporation could lose business and earnings, but where they accept these as the cost of doing the right thing. Recalling a product from supermarket shelves when an organisation is not legally obliged to do so is one example of this. In 1997, Arnott's took all its products off supermarket shelves at a cost of $35 million during a poison-biscuit scare (Gettler 2003). Making decisions in these types of situations is assisted if the organisation has a pre-determined framework for resolving ethical issues.

Business ethics should therefore be considered not in a vacuum, but rather in a broader context. Professor Ralph Potter of Harvard University says that most individuals make ethical decisions based on four factors: the situation and the person's values, principles and loyalties. He arranges these factors in what has become known as the Potter Box, an analytical tool which is used to resolve conflicts. It is a large square divided into quadrants labelled 'situation', 'values', 'principles' and 'loyalties'. Individuals or small groups fill out these quadrants with as many facts and ideas as possible, resulting in people recognising within themselves and others far more values, principles and loyalties than they would normally consider (McElreath 1993: 58).

Public relations ethics in practice

Consider the following example using the Potter Box technique. A consultant in a public relations consulting firm is considering passing on information to a journalist regarding a competitor's alleged underhand tactics to win a large government contract for a construction company. The consultant was given the information confidentially by a friend, a disgruntled public servant. The consultant believes the activities, which have included an overseas trip and entertainment for public officials, have

have placed her client—another construction company—at a disadvantage in the tender process. In dealing with the dilemma of whether or not to contact the journalist, she uses the Potter Box (McElreath 1993: 328) to help her decide what action to take.

Figure 5.1 The Potter Box

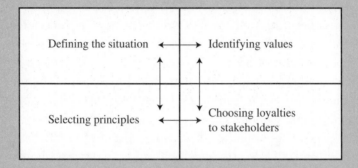

Defining the situation

The issues involved in the situation are whether the consultant obtained the details of the alleged conduct improperly; whether she should breach the confidentiality of the information given to her by her friend; whether the tactics employed by the competitor are legal; whether it is ethical for a consultant to tell the media what a competitor is doing; whether the information should be reported to proper authorities; and whether the actions taken will harm the public.

The parties affected are the consultant, the consulting firm which may 'lose' the tender, the other consulting firm, the public officials and the media.

Identifying values

The values involved are fairness, loyalty, honesty and advocacy.

Selecting principles

Principles that apply include safeguarding confidences; respecting healthy competition amongst competitors; and advancing the flow of accurate and truthful information to serve the public interest.

Choosing loyalties to stakeholders

There are a number of loyalties, including the consultant's friend, who gave her the information confidentially; the consultant's client, who is paying her; the consultant's firm which employs her; the wider public, who would expect public officials to behave more appropriately; and herself—that is, looking after her own career interests.

An ethical decision in this case involves a number of alternatives which can be defended on ethical grounds. She can protect her friend and take no action, or she can act to 'the greatest good for the greatest number of people'. Given the consistent set of values, principles and loyalties that have been identified for protecting the consultant, her firm, her client and the public, it would appear that it would be ethical to talk to the media about the tactics used.

While the Potter Box helps to identify consistent and inconsistent values, principles and loyalties, consistency will not necessarily mean that the most ethical decision will ultimately be made.

There are three basic ethical doctrines—deontology, teleology and Aristotle's Golden Mean (Miyamoto 1996). *Deontology* is the doctrine that ethics is duty-based and relies on moral obligation—for example, truth-telling or promise-keeping—regardless of the consequences. This system depends on the morals and self-discipline of the individual public relations practitioner; however, it will change from person to person, depending on their cultural and traditional biases. *Teleology* is an outcome-based ethics doctrine where 'the ends justify the means'. The rightness of an action is determined by its causes and consequences. This system would apply to public relations techniques used by special-interest groups such as Greenpeace, which in the past have involved civil disobedience. *Aristotle's Golden Mean* is based on what is best for the majority and on actions that represent moderation. This is generally the system used in a democracy where the minority sometimes has to sacrifice something of value if it is best for the country as a whole.

The basis of ethics lies in philosophy. The German philosopher Immanuel Kant (1726–1804) is credited as being a founder of modern ethics. He proposes a three-step ethical process. It is:

1 When in doubt as to whether an act is moral or not, apply the categorical imperative, which is to ask the question: 'What if everyone did this deed?'

2 Always treat all people as ends in themselves and never exploit other humans.
3 Always respect the dignity of human beings. (Pieschek 2002)

Kant's categorical imperative can be applied to questions involving situations such as:

- What if every organisation destroyed records when they knew that the Australian Taxation Office wanted to see them?
- What if every foreign journalist reporting on the Iraq War stole paintings as mementos from Saddam Hussein's palaces?

Moral philosopher Jeremy Bentham (1748–1832) adhered to the theory of utilitarianism in ethics—that is, the belief that judgments should be made on the basis of the greatest good for the greatest number. Utilitarianism maintains that citizens should choose actions that produce the best consequences for all people affected by the action.

This advice springs from two connected theses of critical importance to utilitarianism:

1 that an action or practice is right (when compared with alternative action or practice) if it leads to the greatest possible balance of good consequences or to the least possible balance of bad consequences in the world as a whole; and
2 that the concepts of duty, obligation and right are subordinated to, and determined by, that which maximises the good (Beauchamp 2001: 104).

The role of ethics in public relations

The two acknowledged 'fathers' of public relations, Ivy Lee and Edward E. Bernays, did much to legitimise public relations practice. In 1906, Ivy Lee is said to have issued the following 'declaration of principles', which served as the original maxim for public relations:

> This is not a secret press bureau. All our work is done in the open. We aim to supply news . . . if you think any of our matter ought properly to go to your business office, do not use it. In brief, our plan is frankly and openly, on behalf of business concerns and public constitutions, to supply to the press and the public of the United States prompt and accurate information concerning subjects which it is of value and interest to the public to know about. (Cutlip 1994: 45)

When one of Lee's clients, the Pennsylvania Railroad, experienced a major accident, he insisted that the railroad help the press in covering the story. As a result, the railroad—which for many years had been depicted negatively in the media—was applauded for its openness and its media coverage became more positive.

The role of public relations in today's society is to build bridges and alliances with different publics to create a conducive environment in which businesses, government, voluntary agencies, hospitals and other institutions can operate. To achieve their goals, these institutions need to develop effective relationships with different publics such as employees, members, customers, local communities, shareholders and the public at large.

Best-practice public relations serves the public interest by developing mutual understanding between an organisation and its publics, contributing to informed debate about issues in society and facilitating a dialogue between the organisation and its publics. This assists complex and pluralistic societies to reach decisions and function more effectively, often by bringing private and public policies into harmony.

As ethics is important to organisational excellence on the one hand and to public relations on the other, practitioners should be at the forefront of the movement for ethical organisational conduct.

Because public relations campaigns are often about important community issues, practitioners can be involved in activities that affect the lives of many people—for instance, encouraging drivers to speed less or promoting the wise use of water. This responsibility carries with it significant social accountability.

Depending on whether or not they are part of a dominant coalition (that is, part of the senior management team), public relations practitioners themselves do not always have power (Grunig 1992: 79). However, they work for organisations which do have significant power, and whose actions and messages can have a profound effect on the society around them. Those organisations are judged and their reputations formed by the extent to which their behaviour and messages are in accord with the ethical expectations of their stakeholders.

Empirical evidence shows that practitioners basing their decision-making and recommendations to management on ethical principles are more likely to have a greater role in management decisions and activities (Grunig 1992: 309).

Four major roles played by public relations practitioners have ethical implications. They are the roles of counsellor, advocate, corporate monitor and corporate conscience.

The role of counsellor

Public relations practitioners are increasingly viewing their role as that of a counsellor to senior executives in protecting and building an organisation's corporate reputation. Counselling involves objective observation and analysis of a client's or employer's situation, and the prescription of strategic solutions to management. These solutions may involve changes in corporate policies, organisational behaviour or communications.

Whenever a significant corporate decision needs to be made, the public relations implications of the decision need to be considered, along with the legal, financial and operational impacts on the organisation. To provide this advice, practitioners need to be able to interpret the operating climate of an organisation and how its actions will be perceived and interpreted by various stakeholders.

An organisation seeks public relations counsel on all kinds of strategic matters, ranging from responding to a crisis situation to announcing the appointment of a new chief executive officer.

The public relations counsellor needs to have a broad perspective on an entire industry rather than just their own organisation, and to be able to exercise good judgment regarding various publics' expectations about an organisation's activities.

The role of advocate

It is the practitioner's central role as an advocate that has led to the current debate about public relations ethics. 'Advocacy' is the act of publicly representing an individual, organisation or idea with the object of persuading targeted audiences to look favourably upon, or to accept the point of view of, the individual, the organisation or the idea. In this respect, public relations practitioners share the general nature of their purpose with lawyers.

From this definition, we can deduce that a major objective of advocacy is persuasiveness. O'Keefe (1990) defines persuasiveness as a 'successful intentional effort at influencing another's mental state through communication in a circumstance in which the persuader has some measure of freedom' (1990: 17), thereby distinguishing it from coercion. The key to persuasion is to communicate successfully the reasons why a target audience should accept a particular point of view while acknowledging and refuting the other side of the issue.

Persuasiveness in communication is not inherently wrong. Rhetoric in the art of persuasive communication has a long history as a vital contributor to free debate in a democratic society. It can be argued that the first public relations practitioners were members of ancient Greek society, known as sophists and rhetoricians, who were usually paid to argue causes before the masses in an effort to sway opinion on matters of public interest.

Many of the critics of public relations are also advocates for their own particular position or cause. Special-interest groups associated with environmental causes are known to have released information based on bad science. Greenpeace has been accused of exaggerating environmental problems. Nufarm, a Melbourne-based chemical company, was forced to close temporarily following Greenpeace's alleged discovery of dioxins in the company's discharges into Melbourne's sewer system. A subsequent environmental audit found that the company was not discharging dangerous levels of dioxins (O'Neill 1991).

Public relations advocacy is practised professionally—and hence ethically—if the practitioner conducts his or her role as counsellor first. This means the practitioner applies the objectivity of the counsellor to determine first of all whether a particular client or issue merits their services as advocate—for example, helping a property developer win approval for converting a building with an historical background into office space.

While public relations professionals are advocates for their organisation and have a responsibility to present their organisation in as favourable a light as possible, this should not involve distorting the situation or deceiving the public. Public relations practitioners need to reconcile their roles as advocates for self-interested causes with their roles as facilitators of social communication. Practitioners are simultaneously advocates for a single interest and trustees for the integrity of the public policy process. In practising two-way communication, the practitioner needs to strike a balance between advocacy for an organisation's interests and identification with outside interest groups to ensure their views are communicated to decision-makers.

Scholars such as the Grunigs have begun to eschew the use of persuasion in favour of a more balanced process, popularly called 'two-way symmetric communication' (discussed further in Chapter 3). In the two-way symmetric approach, public relations practitioners act as mediators between organisations and their publics, facilitating what may simplistically be described as one long conversation in which each party continues to further its own interests, but all respect the others' viewpoints and work together to find solutions.

The result of this conversation is that all parties benefit and that no one party attempts to control the perceptions and ideas of the other. The audiences are regarded as ends-in-themselves rather than as mere means towards ends.

This approach, inviting an exchange between equals, is the most ethically desirable. Yet real-life situations often result in public relations practitioners being in a compromise position of guarding an employer's best interests while also furthering a debate that is in the public's interest.

Guidelines for ethical advocacy

Basic guidelines for ethically desirable advocacy are:

- objective evaluation of an organisation's cause before representing it;
- valuing the organisation's interests above those of opposing interests;
- sensitivity to the prospect of 'overmatching' counter advocates—that is, not taking undue advantage of lacking expertise in opposing camps;
- clearly identifying all persuasive messages as originating from the organisation;
- respect for audiences and a willingness to promote dialogue over monologue;
- truthfulness, trustworthiness and absence of deception;
- defensibility of claims against challenges to their validity; and
- mutual consent to the rules of communication—communicating under conditions to which it can be assumed that all parties consent to the communication (Edgett 1998).

Organisations have a genuine right to present images of the world from their own perspectives. This must, however, be done in such a way that acknowledges that the organisations themselves are speaking and that allows publics to respond with opposing points of view.

The role of corporate monitor

The public relations practitioner needs to act as an informed corporate monitor for their organisation. This means they need to interpret and guide an organisation's policies, programs and actions to match public expectations. Corporate public relations departments interpret the operating environment and prescribe how dialogue with an organisation's publics will be carried out. They can affect the extent to which organisations engage in consultation with interest or activist groups and the extent to which communications are truthful and accurate. A practitioner is acting as a corporate monitor when they listen to discussions in Parliament, attend industry seminars, analyse media coverage or conduct research.

Pat Jackson wrote nearly three decades ago: 'Proactive public relations begins in continually investigating the daily routine of the organisation—yes, even if that means getting in the way of line execs . . . practitioners must be the gadflies, assumption deflators, complacency destroyers.' (in *PR Reporter*, 12 August 2002: 1)

Instead of waiting for mistakes to occur, practitioners need to scan both internal and external environments for social, economic and other factors that may impact an organisation's reputation and relationships. This results in identifying publics likely to make issues out of managerial decisions. It can also lead to the development of relationships with those publics. However, in providing advice to management, practitioners need to do more than reflect public opinion: they must be able to interpret the opinion and exercise informed judgment about the actions that should be taken. Public relations contributes to organisational effectiveness when it helps reconcile the organisation's goals with the expectations of its strategic publics. Issues management is discussed further in Chapter 13.

The role of corporate conscience

Another role of the public relations practitioner is as the conscience of the organisation—to serve as the moral keeper for both its communications and actions.

The public relations department controls the flow of good and bad news to employees and the community. Senior public relations managers advise on how transparent and open a company should be during a crisis and also help draft an organisation's mission statement and values. In doing this, a practitioner needs to look at decisions, policies and actions not only through the eyes of stakeholders, but also in terms of whether they are the ethical way of behaving. The boundary-spanning role of public relations means that practitioners are in a position to bring skills and experience as well as external perspectives into an organisation (Grunig 1992: 93).

In addition, the public relations practitioner needs to encourage truth-telling in an organisation—for instance, concerning the correction of mistakes that might occur in published information regarding the accuracy of financial results, the effectiveness of a drug or the safety of a product.

Contemporary society expects organisations to go beyond the pursuit of profitability and demonstrate social responsibility and good corporate citizenship. This requires a focus away from the maximisation of short-term profits to activities that serve the long-term interests of an organisation and all of its stakeholders. Corporate social responsibility involves an organisation's continuing commitment to behaving ethically and contributing to economic development while improving the quality of life for its employees, its community and society. International companies have been criticised for promoting and selling products in foreign countries that have been deemed unsuitable for use in their own countries—for example, pesticides and herbicides. The tobacco industry's promotion of cigarettes in Asia has also been criticised as unethical by some, with others arguing that it is just good business.

Corporate citizenship is the extent to which businesses meet the responsibilities imposed on them by their various stakeholders. Organisations need to balance the cost of their corporate citizenship activities against the cost of manufacturing and marketing their products and services in a responsible manner. Chapter 14 discusses this role in more detail.

Ethical challenges for practitioners

Practitioners face ethical challenges in different aspects of their daily professional lives. While many of these challenges are not socially significant, they call for judgments to be made which have varying degrees of ramifications.

Most ethical challenges in public relations stem from social responsibility issues or from relationship issues with a client or employer, the news media, stakeholders or colleagues. They usually result from poor relationships, inadequate corporate standards and conflicting obligations in certain situations where the values of a client, employer and society may not be easily reconcilable with a practitioner's own values.

An ethical dilemma exists when a practitioner is faced with having to make choices. These may involve alternatives that are equally justified; significant value conflicts amongst differing interests or significant consequences on stakeholders in a particular situation. Ethical dilemmas can occur on a variety of levels. These are:

- interpersonal;
- organisational; or
- stakeholder.

Interpersonal

This involves a dilemma occurring between a practitioner and peers or superiors in the workplace. Have you sat quietly in a meeting while your boss and other senior management discuss corporate responses to a situation that is legally safe but makes you personally feel uncomfortable?

The relationship between two individuals is subject to trust and mutual respect. Trust is maintained if there is honest, accurate information and mutual involvement in key decisions. Especially for new practitioners, it can be difficult to reconcile the commercial pressures of the real world with the ideal approach to resolving an ethical issue—for instance, you may not wish to work for an organisation promoting gambling, but you may feel you are risking your consultancy job by refusing to work on the account. Peer pressure can also be experienced and used as an excuse for making hasty decisions which do not consider the full ethical ramifications of a situation. A boss may place pressure on your department to complete an urgent news release. You are unable to reach the spokesperson and, to avoid embarrassment, your colleague insists you develop quotes based on what the spokesperson has said before.

In any organisation, the CEO needs to set an example in building a corporate culture of integrity.

Organisational

Organisational issues can arise between a practitioner and an organisation's internal policies and protocols. What do you do when your CEO insists that his wife's favourite charity is sponsored, even though the organisation does not meet the criteria set in your corporate sponsorship guidelines?

Ethical challenges can arise from any part of an organisation's operations. They can involve misleading information, discrimination issues, employee working conditions, fair marketing and pricing practices, corporate environmental responsibility, the promotion of inferior products and services, discrimination or gain at the expense of others, the incorrect use of corporate assets and, importantly, compliance with the law.

When the organisation is a public relations consultancy, ethical challenges can arise from the promotion of controversial clients; the solicitation of clients from other consultancies; or being asked to work on a contingency fee basis—that is, being paid only in the case of success; or being asked not to disclose the identity of a client behind the organisation of a coalition of interest groups.

Public relations practitioners, especially in their counselling role, can be provided with confidential information which they promise not to reveal. This can include business strategies, personal employee information or trade secrets. This obligation should only apply to promises that it is morally right to make.

Organisational behaviour which can facilitate ethical decision-making by practitioners includes enhancing the public relations voice in decision-making, promoting transparency and disclosure, improving the clarity of communications and increasing public relations participation in compliance ethics activities. Many organisations have developed specific processes for dealing with ethical dilemmas and these are described later in this chapter.

Stakeholders

Ethical dilemmas can arise between an organisation and publics that have an interest in its actions—for instance, activists and regulators. Has your company established a citizens' consultative committee for the purpose of seeking the community's views about the proposed establishment of a landfill in the local area and then not considered its recommendations?

An organisation's activities have consequences for other people, and for the communities in which they live and work. Dialogues with stakeholders should not be masked attempts to manipulate public debate or to create an image of a socially concerned business. They need to be genuine attempts to understand public expectations and the standards against which the organisation will be judged. Stakeholders' views need to be presented to senior management and feedback provided to stakeholders about their concerns, along with the rationale for any decisions made by the organisation. When there is no open two-way communication, conflict can occur, with publics becoming activist and organising around an issue.

Stakeholders make assessments of organisations based on their perceptions of the organisation's consideration and responsiveness to their needs. Strategically managed public relations is designed to build relationships with the most important stakeholders in an organisation (Grunig 1992: 123).

Ethical challenges can also arise from other stakeholders, such as aggressive competitors who have a win-at-any-cost mentality and who spread malicious rumours about your organisation or its people. They can also involve an organisation's media relations practices, such as providing journalists with expensive gifts, tours to overseas operations or entertainment. These activities can be misconstrued as bribes.

Organisations need to develop and document a process for dealing with ethical dilemmas as they arise. Ideally, they need to be resolved by a group—for example, an ethics committee comprising senior managers.

An ethical framework

The basic ethical framework that practitioners need to follow is to observe their professional association's code and the code of conduct of their workplace.

Professional association codes

The primary obligation of membership to a public relations professional association is the ethical practice of public relations. Each association has a code of ethics which provides guidelines for professional conduct and which also demonstrates what superiors and clients should expect from practitioners. Adherence to a code is a way of ensuring that practitioners meet a minimum standard of practice. They are a valuable safeguard to the community and to clients utilising the services of professional association members. Codes also need to be supported by education programs for association members which provide examples of good and bad practice, so as to better inform members' ethical practices.

However, because membership of communications associations (such as the PRIA and MEAA) is voluntary, codes of ethics cannot be enforced. This is in contrast to professional registration in groups such as the Law Society and the Medical Registration Board. In these examples, not only is membership compulsory in order to practise, but transgressions can be sanctioned by suspension or withdrawal of one's licence to practise.

It is important to recognise that it is difficult for an association to sanction its members without giving rise to libel and restraint of trade issues. Therefore, associations also need to provide education programs to encourage ethical behaviour.

PRIA

The Public Relations Institute of Australia (PRIA) is governed by a fifteen-point Code of Ethics which is supported by a procedure for dealing with alleged breaches. The code operates at three levels:

1 regulating the conduct of public relations professionals in terms of relationships with their client;
2 regulating practitioners' relationships with other members and the profession itself; and finally,
3 imposing obligations on PRIA members vis-à-vis the public (Breit 2000: 70).

The Code is included as an appendix at the end of this book.

Examples of improper conduct under the Code are a member implementing a 'grass roots' campaign on behalf of undisclosed interest groups, a member spreading unfounded and malicious rumours or a member entertaining a government official beyond certain limits.

Investigations of ethical complaints are carried out by representatives of the College of Fellows of the PRIA:

> The PRIA has a nationally uniform procedure for dealing in a professional, rigorous and fair manner with allegations of breaches of the Code of Ethics, with requests for investigation of dubious practices, and, of course, with proven complaints. (PRIA 2003)

MEAA

The Media Entertainment and Arts Alliance (MEAA) operates the Australian Journalists' Association's Code of Ethics, which is the legal umbrella code with which journalists working within the media or in public or private sector organisations need to comply. Media Entertainment and Arts Alliance members engaged in journalism commit themselves to honesty, fairness, independence and respect for the rights of others. This Code sets out fundamental principles of journalism including respect for truth and the public's right to know. It is important for public relations professionals to understand this code because of the interaction between the two professions and also because of overlap between professionals across the communication sphere.

PRSA

The Public Relations Society of America (PRSA) has a code which focuses on universal values that inspire ethical behaviour and performance. Under the Code, there are no enforcement or quasi-judicial bodies to review ethical violations. Instead, the ethics board can comment on a company or PRSA member publicly and point to specific code clauses that the member or firm may have violated. However, the PRSA Board of Directors retains the right to bar from membership or expel from the Society any individual who has been or is sanctioned by a government agency or convicted in a court of law of an action that is a violation of the Code.

IABC

The International Association of Business Communicators (IABC) Code is simple and based on three universal principles of corporate communication that apply throughout the world. They are that professional communication is legal, ethical and in good taste. The articles in the IABC Code cover principles such as fostering the free flow of essential information in the public interest; promptly correcting erroneous communication; being sensitive to cultural values and beliefs; protecting corporate information while complying with corporate disclosure regulations; and not guaranteeing results that are beyond the personal power of the communicator to deliver.

IABC prefers to foster compliance through global ethics education activities, though it will terminate membership of the Association if a member is found guilty of violating laws and public policies governing their professional activities by an appropriate governmental agency or judicial body.

ABA inquiry

The Australian Broadcasting Authority (ABA) inquiry in 1999 into what has become known as 'cash for comment' put the ethics of all communication professionals into the spotlight.

The inquiry concerned the practice of radio broadcasters, including John Laws and Alan Jones, entering into lucrative contracts with large firms to make favourable comments about their products and services, but without disclosing any financial interest in making such comment to their listeners. Because of the potential for misunderstanding between these practices and legitimate public relations practice, the PRIA created a submission for the benefit of the inquiry.

The PRIA submission covered a range of issues relating to the ethics of professional communicators and the Institute's position on unethical behaviour. This included the blending of advertising with editorial, a critical factor in the creation of the inquiry. The PRIA's Code of Ethics stipulates that members have to be prepared to identify the source of funding of any public communications they initiate or for which they act as a conduit. Excerpts from the submission included:

> Our members are subject to a Code of Ethics that requires them to deal fairly and honestly with the communication media and with the general public, as well as with clients and other stakeholders. The Institute's Code does not permit the practice of hidden payment for editorial content.

From the earliest years there was concern to establish ethical standards of practice to improve the reputation of public relations.

This was facilitated to some extent by the existing Institutes joining in 1960 to form a national body, the Public Relations Institute of Australia. Its National Council was able to develop uniform national policies, including the Code of Ethics.

During the past 20 years there has been a great development in the range and diversity of public relations practice. It may seem strange to state in the context of this Inquiry but public relations has moved a long way from merely being concerned with media publicity, important as though that can be. This Inquiry is, of course, evidence of that.

Best practice public relations, as encouraged by the Institute, serves the public interest, developing mutual understanding between on organisation and its publics, contributing to informed debate about issues in society and facilitating a dialogue between organizations and their publics. It helps our complex, pluralistic society to reach decisions and function more effectively, often by bringing private and public policies into harmony. (McCoy 1999)

In 2000, the ABA introduced new requirements that radio presenters would need to read out a full list of their sponsors each day. Presenters have to disclose service contracts over $25 000 which involve promoting a third party's interests or providing consultancy services in respect of publicity or public relations (Davies 2000).

Codes of conduct

Most organisations have a code of conduct to guide the behaviour of their employees and suppliers. Codes of conduct generally provide a statement of company philosophy and commitment to ethical conduct, general guidelines on decision-making, specific rules and definitions. They cover matters such as:

- compliance with laws and regulations;
- prohibition of bribery;
- gifts, gratuities and entertainment;
- confidential and proprietary information;
- conflict of interest;
- proper use of corporate assets;
- political activities and relationships with foreign governments;

- social responsibility of the company;
- accurate financial reporting; and
- relationships with suppliers, customers, competitors and others.

Codes should address the issues that have the greatest impact on the success and public image of a particular organisation. They should give specific guidance to employees who are confronted with a moral dilemma.

In their work, public relations practitioners need to encourage the adoption and enforcement of codes that will stave off the costly and reputation-damaging results of scandals or other charges of misconduct that can come either from within or outside an organisation. The public relations function should be represented in discussions where organisational policies are reviewed and formulated and codes are drafted. It also needs to communicate the existence and significance of a code to employees, suppliers and other publics.

However, all the moral rules and professional ethics guidelines in the world are meaningless if individuals fail to reflect upon, internalise and conduct themselves according to a consistent set of values. Immanuel Kant said that 'no one can make another person virtuous'. The point that he was making was that no amount of force, coercion or incentive can ensure the development of a morally good character.

There are further issues relating to codes of conduct and codes of ethics that should be considered. One problem in the operation of corporate codes is that many are general and do not refer to specific instances.

In addition, practitioners must be aware of their legal obligations and how these relate to their ethical responsibilities. Sometimes the two can come into conflict— for example, clause 3 of the MEAA Code of Ethics, after warning that confidences must be carefully entered into, then requires that 'where confidences are accepted, respect them in all circumstances'. This can lead to a conflict with the law, and journalists have been sent to gaol or fined for not revealing sources when ordered to by a court. Practitioners need legal knowledge, at least to the extent that they appreciate when an issue may involve a question of legality or a conflict between ethics and law.

A guide, however, lies in the adage that 'the law is the floor' and ethics must work above this. There are many situations in everyday public relations practice where one can be unethical and operate within the limits of the law—for instance, withholding information from superiors, fudging on budgets or constantly complaining about colleagues. Similarly, companies can operate at the margin of legal and regulatory compliance and have low ethical standards. Chapter 4 discusses the legal issues relating to practitioners in more detail.

Ethics as a public relations strategy

There will always be some divergence between the interests of the public and the interests of business. Within organisations, there is an inherent conflict between the drive for wealth maximisation for shareholders and the call for social responsibility by the organisation's stakeholders. These can include shareholders, employees, governments, non-governmental organisations and the diverse communities in which they operate.

The past decade has seen increased awareness of ethical issues amongst individuals and organisations. This has led to government legislation for new corporate governance regulations in Australia.

Ethical investment arose from a concern amongst investors that they should make socially responsible investments.

There are a number of ethical and green shareholders' groups in Australia—for example, Paperlinx Ethical Shareholders Group, Wesfarmers Investors and Shareholders for the Environment and BHP Shareholders for Social Responsibility. They provide a network that smaller shareholders can use to air their concerns or raise suggestions regarding the ethical, environmental or social aspects of a company's operations. Typical concerns have included sourcing of raw materials, safety of manufacturing processes, nature of wastes produced and donations to political parties. Sometimes these groups can influence government action, which then influences the actions of companies—for instance, promoting legislation in areas such as provision of recycling services (<www.shares.green.net.au>).

The Australian Shareholders' Association (ASA) is an ethical watchdog whose views are widely sought by companies and commentators. It represents its members mainly from financial and corporate governance viewpoints. Its concerns include matters such as relevant and timely disclosure of information, payment of dividends, multiple directorships, director/executive remuneration, executive options, and consistent and honest financial reporting.

There is a growing sensitivity among consumers about the corporate social performance of companies that they buy from or work in. For example, people increasingly desire a cleaner environment, the preservation of wildlife and their habitats and flexible working hours.

Organisations have realised that they have to pay more attention to these demands and have responded by improving their corporate citizenship, transparency and accountability as foundation stones for building a commercially successful business. Some of the companies who are leaders in this area are those that have been targeted for bad practices in the past.

Shell Oil was criticised for the sinking of an oil platform in the North Atlantic in 1996 and also accused of ecological abuses and supporting a corrupt and autocratic political regime in Nigeria. Following these crises, which resulted in negative media coverage and decreased employee morale, the company realised it 'had lost touch with its environment' (Fombrun and Rindova 2000: 82). Management revisited basic planning and strategy assumptions in the light of public attitudes about the environment and human rights and concluded that a stakeholder outreach program based on open dialogue was needed. A Statement of General Business Principles was developed and promulgated to stakeholders. Shell began issuing social responsibility reports which committed the company to a program of standards development, new management systems, independent monitoring practices and new stakeholder communications. This included a set of systems for institutionalising transparency and responsiveness, including proactively and systematically taking into account the perceptions and evaluations of stakeholders (Fombrun and Rindova 2000: 91).

In Australia, in response to criticism about the size of bank profits, Westpac developed a communications program to ensure all stakeholders were aware of the bank's commitment to maintaining a balance between meeting its social responsibilities and producing a positive financial result. The bank launched 'Being Accountable', Westpac's statement of its business practices and policies which is aimed at ensuring improved work practices and culture. 'Concern Online', a staff feedback mechanism, was also established (*Westpac News*, 10–24 July 2001: 11). The ANZ Bank also responded to change by introducing a new communications strategy, which is discussed as a case study in Chapter 11.

Organisations are adopting a broader, more socially conscious view of their company's responsibilities to employees, customers and the communities in which they operate. *pr reporter* quotes Reginald Jones, former Chairman and CEO of General Electric, as saying:

> Public policy and social issues are no longer adjuncts to business planning and management. They are in the mainstream of it. The concern must be pervasive in companies today, from boardroom to factory floor. Management must be measured for performance in non-economic and economic areas alike. (12 August 2002: 2)

Today's environment is such that the public activities of corporations are being scrutinised more than ever. Hand in hand with this is the trend towards ethical investment, and the growing importance of non-financial indicators in judging a company's success through the quality of the workplace, environmental responsibility and corporate citizenship.

These factors and others have led to a high level of interest by management in building corporate reputation, with the most admired organisations being those which balance commercial objectives with social responsibility.

Corporate governance

An ethical culture is central to good corporate governance. The Organisation for Economic Cooperation and Development (OECD) defines corporate governance as the system by which organisations are directed and controlled (OECD 1999: 7). The structure specifies the rights and responsibilities of various groups within an organisation, such as the Board of Directors, managers, shareholders and other stakeholders, including policies and practices for making decisions. A governance system needs to guide managers at all levels to do the right thing when faced with tough decisions and, through incentives, encourage ethical behaviour by all employees.

It covers a wide range of activities that relate to the way an organisation is directed and governed—for example:

* strategic and business planning;
* board composition;
* risk management;
* performance assessment;
* reward and benefit distribution;
* Chief Executive Officer succession and appointment;
* disclosure and stakeholder reporting;
* corporate values and culture; and
* organisational structure. (Kaye 2001)

A failure of corporate governance was behind the bankruptcy in 2001 of Enron, the energy trader that was once America's seventh largest company. By utilising deceptive accounting practices, Enron was able to maintain a healthy balance sheet. However, the result was a mess of paper shuffling, false reports and insider trading. There were no internal safeguards to protect investors or employees. In addition, external experts such as the company's auditors and stockbroking analysts, on whom the public relied for accurate information, failed in their jobs.

Enron's corporate governance model was too weak to prevent the problems from escalating. Internally, there were five areas in which governance failed (Gopinah 2002). They were:

1   The roles of Chairman and CEO were not separate, except for a brief period. This resulted in dilution of management supervision of the Board.
2   The audit committee failed to bring organisational lapses to the full Board.
3   Several of the external directors suffered from serious conflicts of interest and lack of independence including being paid for external consultancy, being involved in third party-related transactions, and benefiting from substantial donations to non-profit organisations with which they were involved.
4   The flow of information to the Board was not timely or adequate; however, the Directors made no effort to obtain further information.
5   Too many directorships were held by directors, with one director being on the Boards of eleven public companies. (Gopinah 2002)

In Australia, the general insurance company HIH collapsed in March 2001 and lost $5.3 billion of the public's money. At the subsequent royal commission, Justice Neville Owen summed up HIH's corporate culture:

> There was insufficient ability and independence of mind . . . to see what had to be done and what had to be stopped or avoided. Risks were not properly identified and managed. Unpleasant information was hidden, filtered or sanitised. And there was a lack of sceptical questioning and analysis when and where it mattered. (*The Age*, 18–19 April 2003: 10)

How to address ethical issues

Vogl says:

> In today's globalisation era values cannot be split between domestic and foreign interests. Every action by every division of a multinational firm impacts its global reputation, its effectiveness and ultimately its survival. (2002: 3)

Yet, while ethical conduct must be considered in a global context, issues can arise when considering intercultural activity. Special problems exist for public relations practitioners in an intercultural context. These centre around two broad issues.

First, there are different ethical underpinnings to local cultures—for instance, bribery of officials is allowed in some countries and can be claimed as a business expense. Second, an imbalance of power can be created through globalisation and multinational activity in underdeveloped countries. A common criticism is that international investment has altered the physical and social environments of some countries and has utilised exploitative labour practices.

Ethical relativism needs to be applied to acts which are good in some circumstances or cultures but not in others. While there needs to be respect for a cultural diversity, the practitioner needs to consider the social environment in which the standards and actions exist and the consequences of the action.

Global and intercultural issues focus attention on ethical policies and programs at a macro level. Within organisations, an ethical climate prevails when clear barriers are established to limit the opportunity for unethical activities and when ethical behaviours are rewarded. Employees should be able to recognise ethical issues as they arise and be aware of the resources available to help them act ethically and according to organisational culture and policy.

A company's overall performance needs to be assessed against its core values, ethics policy, internal operating practices, management systems and, most importantly, the expectations of its stakeholders—owners, employees, customers and local communities. Stakeholder interests need to be considered in all decisions and actions.

Organisations can manage ethics in their workplaces by establishing an ethics management program which is developed and implemented by a cross-functional team. These programs convey corporate values using codes, policies, procedures and activities to guide decisions and behaviour. It is important that the organisation's Chief Executive is seen to champion the program.

Ethics program components can include:

- an ethics committee at the Board level to oversee the development and operation of the ethics management program;
- an ethics management committee to implement and administer the program, including training and resolving of ethical dilemmas;
- managerial ethics training;
- use of an ombudsman system;
- managers serving as role models;
- standardised training procedures with new employee orientation, annual employee awareness training and interactive workshops using real-life scenario simulations;

- written policies consisting of a statement, a policy manual of practical workplace issues and a code of conduct;
- an ethics audit by an external auditor;
- an ethics hotline to give anonymity; and
- an employee survey to benchmark attitudes and practices.

Vogl (2002) says that, at a minimum, organisations need to consider the following corporate ethics practices:

- ensuring regular review by the board of directors of the corporate code of ethics and how compliance is being assured;
- providing chief ethics officers with the authority to directly discuss key issues with corporate boards of directors;
- ensuring that consideration is given in board compensation committees to ethical perceptions and issues;
- relating compensation of senior managers to their ethical performance; and
- reporting on global corporate social responsibility practices and ethics code performance.

Management systems need to institutionalise transparency and responsiveness. Organisations must be committed to a regular comprehensive policy of publication of agreed performance data and information, as well as operating traditional activities such as help-lines, complaint lines, feedback mechanisms and formal consultative programs.

Other than abiding by corporate and professional codes, how can practitioners make ethics a part of their daily life and an organisation's business strategy? Here are some simple ideas on how public relations practitioners can address ethical issues in their work, within the broad ethical framework already discussed. A practitioner needs to:

1 objectively evaluate the specific issue, client or organisation before determining whether it merits public relations advocacy. This involves recognising any moral dimensions to the task or problem and identifying the parties who will be affected by the decision and their obligations to each. This requires open discussion;
2 respect audiences as individuals with rights to adequate information to make informed choices;
3 consider their cultural values and beliefs;
4 tell stakeholders about the reasons behind decisions;

5 clearly identify all communication on behalf of the client/organisation as originating from that source;
6 act truthfully, without evasion or deception;
7 know the law and public policies; and
8 know themselves and their core principles and how they are reflected in their behaviour.

Conclusion

Ethics in the twenty-first century has to be the responsibility of all decision-makers and has to be part of mainstream management. This necessitates a change in the role of public relations practitioners from merely wielding self-serving influence to being active participants in the development of corporate business strategy, ensuring that commercial objectives are balanced with responsibility to all stakeholders. This will require practitioners to be facilitators of dialogue, and listeners as much as speakers (as well as imitators) of appropriate corporate policies and actions.

Public relations, where practised properly, encourages social responsibility and a greater contribution to society on the part of major institutions. This gives the profession the opportunity to be a leader in ethical practice, not a follower.

Turnbull posits that the most successful organisations in the next decades will be those which build trust by aspiring to authenticity and practising transparency (2003: 1). He says these concepts are rapidly becoming more important as societies react against past excesses and future uncertainties.

The challenge for public relations centres on a need to move toward genuine professionalism. A movement toward genuine professionalism, of course, will not guarantee that answers to the various complex ethical quandaries the practitioner may face will necessarily be provided. However, if more practitioners begin to bring a genuine professional approach to public relations, then the subject-matter of ethics will be the subject-matter of public relations. Ethics will not be something 'out there' with which the practitioner is only abstractly concerned. Instead, public relations practitioners will understand that professional ethics interacts with professional conduct and is part of an overall search for excellence which in no way neglects 'the bottom line', but instead humanises it.

Discussion and exercises

1 What makes an occupation a profession? Discuss this, considering elements such as education levels, accreditation, codes and licensing.

2   An organisation has ethical responsibilities to its various stakeholders. Discuss the types of ethical issues that exist for customers, employees, competitors and shareholders.

3   Based on your understanding of the PRIA code of ethics, discuss the following scenarios:

   (a) *Confidential information*: A colleague confidentially tells you that she is planning to quit the company in two months to start a family. Meanwhile, your boss tells you that you are not able to be given a new opportunity in the company because your fellow employee is next in line for an internal promotion. What do you do?

   (b) *Accurate information*: A marketing manager wants you to write a news release launching an old product as new, without having changed any of its features. What is your advice?

   (c) *Public interest*: A client who owns a shopping centre has received reports of a stalker molesting children there. The client asks you to keep it out of the media because he risks losing business. What is your advice?

   (d) *Honesty*: Your organisation is paying a professor who is a world expert in nutrition to promote its range of breakfast cereals. Should you disclose the fact that he is being remunerated in the media materials that you have prepared?

4   Australian companies conduct business around the world. What cultural issues can arise? Whose ethics should they follow? Is globalisation creating a more standardised view of ethical standards?

5   If a public relations consultancy takes on a controversial client or a client who is engaged in questionable practices, should employees be able to choose whether they will work on the account? Discuss.

Further reading

Bajer, L.W. (1993) *The Credibility Factor: Putting Ethics to Work in Public Relations*, Business One, Illinois.

Botan, C. (1997) 'Ethics in strategic communications campaigns: the case for a new approach to public relations', *Journal of Business Communication*, vol. 34, no. 2, pp. 188–202.

Centre for Media and Democracy, <www.prwatch.org>.

Harrison, S. (1997) 'Earning trust by telling the truth: how should public relations and media professionals behave when a disaster happens?', *Journal of Communication Management*, vol. 1, no. 3, pp. 219–30.

Heath, R.L. (2001) *Handbook of Public Relations*, Sage, Thousand Oaks.

IABC Communication Bank, *Ethics*, International Association of Business Communicators, San Francisco.

L'Etang, J. & Pieczka, M. (eds) (1996) *Critical Perspectives in Public Relations*, International Thomson Business Press, London.

Schwartz, P. & Gibb, B. (1999) *When Good Companies Do Bad Things: Responsibility and Risk in an Age of Globalization*, John Wiley & Sons, New York.

Stark, A. (1993) 'What's the matter with business ethics?', *Harvard Business Review*, May/June, pp. 38–48.

Stauber, J. & Rampton, S. (1995) *Toxic Sludge is Good for You! Lies, Damn Lies and the Public Relations Industry*, Common Courage Press, Maine.

Weintraub, Austin E. & Pinkleton, B.E. (2001) *Strategic Public Relations Management*, Lawrence Erlbaum Associates, Hillsdale, New Jersey.

References

The Age (2003) 'The blind mice who cost us $5.3 billion', editorial, 18–19 April, p. 10.

Beauchamp, T. (2001) *Philosophical Ethics*, 3rd edn, McGraw Hill, Boston, Massachusetts.

Breit, R. (2000) 'Law and ethics', in J. Johnston and C. Zawawi (eds), *Public Relations: Theory and Practice*, Allen & Unwin, Sydney.

Cutlip, S.M. (1994) *The Unseen Power: Public Relations. A History*, Lawrence Erlbaum Associates, Hillsdale, New Jersey.

Davies, A. (2000) 'Tighter reins on 2UE radio presenters', <smh.com.au>, 28 March.

Donaldson, J. (1989) *Key Issues in Business Ethics*, Academic Press, San Diego, California.

Edgett, R. (1998) Toward an Ethic of Advocacy in Public Relation: An Exploratory Study, Unpublished thesis, Syracuse University, New York.

Fombrun, C. & Rindova, V. (2000) 'The road to transparency: reputation management at Royal Dutch Shell', in M. Shultz, M.J. Hatch and M. Holten Larsen (eds), *The Expressive Organisation: Linking Identity, Reputation and the Corporate Brand*, Oxford University Press, Oxford.

Gettler, L. (2003) 'Corporate crisis? Apply lots of light', *The Age*, 3 May.

Gopinah, C. (2002) 'Corporate governance failure at Enron', *Business Line*, 4 March, The Hindu Group of Publications.

Grunig, J.E. (ed.) (1992) *Excellence in Public Relations and Communications Management*, Lawrence Erlbaum Associates, Hillsdale, New Jersey.

Josephson Institute for the Advancement of Ethics, (2003) *Resources: Making Ethical Decisions*, <www.josehpsoninstitute.org>.

Kaye, P. (2001) 'Corporate governance in practice', June, <www.consultgroup.net.au>.

Longstaff, S. (2003) 'Public relations and the corporate conscience', St James Ethics Centre, <www.ethics.org.au>.

McCoy, L. (1999) 'PRIA Submission to ABA Inquiry', National President of Public Relations Institute of Australia, August.

McElreath, M.P. (1993) *Managing Systematic and Ethical Public Relations Campaigns*, Brown & Benchmark Publishers, Dubuque, Iowa.

Miyamoto, C. (1996) 'Public relations ethics 201: challenges we just can't ignore', *Mega Comm 96*, Honolulu, Hawaii.

O'Keefe, D.J. (1990) *Persuasion: Theory and Research*, Sage, Newbury Park, California.

O'Neill, G. (1991) 'Dioxin—Less Deadly After All', *The Age*, 24 September, p. 11.

Organisation for Economic Cooperation and Development (1999) *Principles of Corporate Governance*, OECD Publications, Paris.

Pieschek, M. (2002) 'Ethics: the best PR money can't buy', paper presented at Public Relations Society of America International Conference, San Francisco, California, 19 November.

pr reporter (2002) vol. 45, no. 31, 12 August, Pr Publishing Company, Exeter, New Hampshire.

Public Relations Institute of Australia (PRIA) (2003) 'How the PRIA handles ethics complaints and enquiries', <www.pria.com.au/ethics/complaints.html>.

Seib, P. & Fitzpatrick, K. (1995) *Public Relations Ethics*, Harcourt Brace College Publishers, Orlando, Florida.

Turnbull, N. (2003) 'Trust, authenticity and transparency—a new paradigm in corporate reputation and branding', paper presented at Stakeholder Communications 2003 Conference, 25 February, Sydney.

Vogl, F. (2002) 'The U.S. business scandals: perspectives on ethics and culture at home and abroad', Presentation to Transatlantic Business Ethics Conference, 27 September, Georgetown University, Washington DC.

WestpacNews (2001) 'The right balance', 10–24 July, no. 115.

Wilson, I. (2000) *The New Rules of Corporate Conduct*, Quorum Books, Westport, Connecticut.

PART 3
PROCESS AND APPLICATION

6 RESEARCH AND EVALUATION

Raveena Singh and Leanne Glenny

In this chapter

Introduction

Research is undertaken at all stages of the public relations process. Many issues arise when a practitioner is asked to prepare or evaluate a campaign or program. The solutions to those issues are arrived at through the research process of asking relevant questions and obtaining answers. The information gathered during the initial phases of research provides *input* into the planning of a communication program. Research during the development and implementation stages of a strategy contributes to more effective *outputs*. And research at the end of a communication program provides insight into the *outcomes* of the entire effort. These three types, or phases, of research, how they interconnect and their link to the public relations process are explained in this chapter.

In order to proceed with any research the practitioner must be aware of the range of *methodologies* available and the most appropriate use of these in public relations planning and development. Depending on the skills and resources available and the desired outcomes, researchers can utilise formal techniques to produce scientifically valid results or more informal techniques in order to simply increase their understanding of the situation. The researcher also has a choice between *qualitative* and *quantitative* methodologies, depending on the type of information required.

Within these methodologies, there are many *techniques* available to the public relations researcher. While surveys are commonly used, they can be time-consuming and resource-intensive. A wide range of other research techniques gives the public relations practitioner the ability to select options, taking into consideration the time, money and skills available.

The need for research

Research is an essential task within public relations, used to identify the requirement for a communication program, to assist in establishing that program, to check progress and to evaluate the effectiveness. As such, research needs to be ongoing, throughout all stages of a campaign, although its focus and the research techniques will change throughout. Seitel (2001: 106) identifies the continued importance of instinct and intuition in public relations, but states that 'management requires more [such as] facts and statistics from public relations professionals to show that their efforts contribute not only to overall organisational effectiveness but also to the bottom line'.

Management today is concerned with accountability. Budgets 'invested' in public relations activities must be justified, monitored and accounted for, often with the prospect of achieving funding for future products depending on the cost effectiveness of the previous campaign. In conjunction with the close examination of the resources spent, the relevancy and accuracy of the communication effort are also under scrutiny. In the same way, community groups and not-for-profit organisations must be thrifty in their use of resources. The best way to analyse all of these factors is by thorough research.

In most cases, public relations research focuses on understanding the environment within which the organisation operates. Organisations may require information about the needs or attitudes of their target publics or stakeholders. They may also need to know what the strengths and weaknesses of their competitors are, or more about the environmental or political issues that could affect their success.

The daily work of a public relations practitioner and the requirements of a public relations program or campaign are therefore based on an understanding of the 'current situation'. Knowing what needs to be done to address the situation and what the organisation can afford to do with its available resources puts the practitioner in a position to determine the aims, goals and objectives of a public relations program. In addition, the practitioner should have a clear understanding of the publics that must be addressed and the type of message or messages that must be given to these publics. Where and through what communication medium the publics can be found and targeted must also be explored and determined.

Not surprisingly, the use of research at any stage of public relations practice is the main determinant of whether the practitioner functions as a professional or a technician. Effective strategic management demands informed and sound judgment based on researched findings. The use of research thus positions public relations 'as a purposive, goal-directed, and problem-solving management function' (Broom and Dozier 1990: 12).

Considerations in conducting research

Deciding to undertake research can present challenges for the public relations practitioner. Time, money and the availability of human resources are three of the most difficult obstacles standing in the way of a thorough research program. Research can be a costly part of any program and those allocating the budget do not always understand its value. Although a properly researched program can be more cost effective in the long term, it is often only seen in terms of the short-term expense. In a similar manner, many practitioners work under the pressure of tight deadlines and are tempted to try to remove the more time-consuming elements of a program, such as research. This short-term focus is often to the detriment of the overall program.

Deciding what to research is also another challenge for the public relations practitioner. Care must be taken to ensure a balance between conducting enough research to be useful and conducting too much research—wasting money and time unnecessarily or for little gain. Setting clearly defined goals and objectives for the research during the input and output phases, and measurable communication objectives for the outcome phase, will provide a forum for agreement on the research direction prior to any expenditure of funds. Goal- and objective-setting for both the research tasks and the communication program is a significant part of the planning process and should always take into consideration the research capability of the organisation.

Recognising the level of research skills and knowledge in the organisation can identify further obstacles to the effective conduct of research. Public relations practitioners need to have a good understanding of the principles of research and be able to identify how to acquire additional skills when required. An understanding of terminology and options will give the public relations practitioner the ability to identify what is required, determine what research can be conducted within the organisation and decide on what elements to outsource. This knowledge will also give the practitioner the ability to direct and supervise any outsourced work effectively.

What and when to research

Conceptualising public relations as a process that, once set in motion, is ongoing is extremely important for the public relations professional. In this cyclical view of public relations, which is preferred by the Public Relations Institute of Australia, research contributes to all the functions of planning, action and evaluation. Evaluation is often recognised as being the beginning of a new effort, not just the completion of a previous activity (Baskin and Aronoff, in PRIA 1999: 4).

One of the most effective ways of viewing the research process is in terms of *inputs*, *outputs* and *outcomes* (Pritchitt and Sherman 1994). Inputs determine what goes into the project or program, outputs are the actual elements of the program or campaign (e.g. an event or a newsletter), and outcomes are the result of those outputs on the target public or audience. In order to determine what inputs and outputs should be, and what outcomes actually are, public relations practitioners conduct research.

This input/output/outcome model can be aligned with a cyclical public relations process in order to better understand what needs to be researched and when that research should be undertaken. When those decisions are made the practitioner can then choose the most appropriate research methodologies and techniques to use in the collection of information. These relationships are demonstrated in Figure 6.1.

Figure 6.1 Relationship between a model of a PR process and research

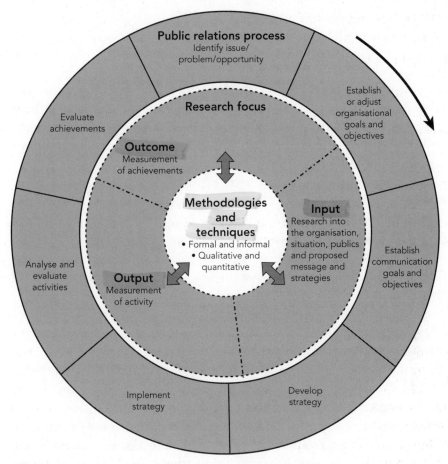

For example, when an issue is first identified, the first step for the public relations practitioner is to obtain a thorough understanding of the situation. Information obtained from the outcome research of previous communication activities can be analysed and used to direct and complement input research into the organisation, situation and/or publics. This new information can then be used to clearly define the issue and to help establish or adjust the organisational and communication goals and objectives.

The public relations process of planning, implementing and evaluating can take several forms. The outer circle shown in Figure 6.1 is a simplistic representation of a generic process, which can be aligned with various phases of research according to the input/output/outcome model, represented in the second circle. At the centre of the circle is the wide range of research techniques that can be used during any or all three of the research phases.

Input research

The results of input research provide the practitioner with a practical road map. They can indicate what problems or opportunities actually exist, what the perceptions and beliefs of the publics are, and what tools or methods of communication would be most effective in helping the organisation achieve its objectives with those publics. Input research thus informs strategy and planning.

Marston (1979) emphasises that the first vital step in research is for the practitioner to clarify the organisation's objectives and the role that public relations can play in achieving these goals. In order to do this, the public relations practitioner needs to gather as much information as possible on the organisation itself. This could include information on the image of the organisation, its status, history, overview of previous campaigns, and a SWOT (strengths, weaknesses, opportunities, threats) analysis.

The second step entails the gathering of all relevant existing information on the situation. This can be done by collecting information on the external environment and the factors that influence the current situation or issue.

The third step is more complex, involving the understanding of the opinions and attitudes currently held by the target group to whom the organisation directs its communication. Before embarking on gathering the target public's opinions and attitudes, it is best practice for the public relations practitioner to examine existing evidence that the organisation has on record from the evaluation of previous programs or campaigns. This will help create a better understanding of the target public/s and the goals and objectives expected of the new campaign. This perusal and analysis of existing information is then used in the planning of the program or campaign. Research into the target public should answer the following, or any other questions that the organisation needs answered:

• Who is the public?
• What are their characteristics?
• Where do we find them?
• Why are they important to us?
• How active or involved is this public relative to our interests?
• What is their hierarchy of importance?

Once the public has been segmented, the public relations practitioner needs to gather information about the organisation from each segment. How will the target public be reached and what are the considerations for the message design? The gathering of such information about the different segments of the target public contributes to the formulation of the goals and objectives of the public relations campaign.

During the initial stages of a program or campaign, different types of input research may be undertaken. These can include what are known as exploratory and development research and benchmarking.

Exploratory research offers details on the situation, and may proffer answers to questions that the practitioner has at this time. Exploratory research may also explain why an issue should be reviewed and which target publics must be addressed. Generally, exploratory research will inform the practitioner about previous research and available data. Research gathered from such existing sources is known as *secondary research*. Exploratory research often reveals gaps in the information at hand and indicates to the practitioner or the organisation what other information is needed. *Primary research*, specifically undertaken to obtain this type of information, may be required.

Once a sound understanding of the issue and current situation has been achieved, other questions may need to be answered. Based on the findings of the exploratory research, other issues may arise that need to be addressed, which may not be immediately possible because of lack of resources, insufficient timing or other priorities. However, once the exploratory research has identified the issues, *development research* can be undertaken, where the priorities of the program or campaign are set. The target publics may comprise a large number of people who cannot all be reached at the same time, at the same place or through the same message. In addition, there may be some clusters of the target group that are more important to the organisation than others. Development research guides the organisation in subdividing and prioritising the target publics identified by the exploratory research. Once these target groups have been identified, the practitioner must research and assess the best time to launch a campaign or program and what the best communication messages to address this issue will be. While responses to all these considerations serve to develop a strategy, the practitioner must also determine the costs involved in implementing the program. Development research addresses this aspect as well.

These initial research efforts indicate what must be done to rectify, improve or maintain the situation. This means that they allow the practitioner to set a starting point to measure what the program will achieve. This is known as *benchmarking*. Benchmarking is used to identify the situation before a program or campaign is implemented and then to measure its success or failure after completion. Bench-marking contributes to the evaluation of public relations campaigns and programs.

Information sought during this input stage of research should provide an adequate background for the design of the campaign. When considering the input, checks need to be made that the research undertaken was in sufficient depth and that the findings of the research were used to guide message content, identify target publics and confirm objectives.

Output research

During the output phase, research can reflect on the delivery of messages, allowing the practitioner to fine-tune, alter or modify the plan as it is implemented, achieving greater success with public relations outcomes. Output research gathers information on the appropriateness of the message and activity content, and the quality of message and activity presentations (Cutlip et al. 1994). This information can then be fed back into the strategy development or implementation phases in order to improve the delivery of the message.

Information sought during the output phase of the research could also include the number of messages sent to the media and the number of activities designed, the messages placed and activities implemented, and who received the messages and participated in the activities (particularly important in countries with multi-cultural populations).

This type of information is useful for measuring activities, but should not be used to justify the effectiveness of a program. It may, to some extent, provide an organisation with data from which to analyse the efficiency of activities and could be used for further analysis with other data collected in the outcome phase. The information may be used to examine the business processes and activities within the public relations department of an organisation. However, it is important not to confuse activity with achievement.

Output evaluation checks that the channels of communication (e.g. radio, television, newspapers, magazines, the internet) and the communication mix (e.g. brochures, pamphlets, workshops, community meetings) were correctly chosen and designed for the particular campaign or program.

Outcome research

Outcome research not only indicates the level of success or failure of the strategy, but can also demonstrate how effective planning and communication have been.

This information can be used in the input phase of the next planning cycle. This is the phase in which achievements are measured and evaluated to determine the success of the campaign. Outcomes should reflect a change in the awareness, understanding, attitude or behaviour of the target publics; therefore, the evaluation should reflect the size and direction of that change from an agreed and pre-determined benchmark. Things that motivate/trigger change in target publics can be difficult to determine, but self-report surveys and indirect observations can be used to determine these. The essence of the effort in evaluation is to find linkages between information, attitude and behaviour: of these, only the last is truly observable (Pritchitt and Sherman 1994).

In order to do this effectively, evaluation criteria must be established at the beginning of the planning stage, prior to implementation of the campaign. All those involved in the campaign or program should be in agreement on the use and purpose of the evaluation. The criteria should be directed by the program's objectives, which must be set in observable, measurable and time-specific terms. This will ensure that the most appropriate techniques to gather information are used and that the research will measure the most important aspects, providing useful and relevant feedback on the success of the program. It is crucial that evaluation findings be used and fed back into the program, as well as reported to management (Cutlip et al. 1994: 412–13). Accurate documentation of the processes and decisions undertaken throughout the campaign will assist in the evaluation of current, and the development of future, campaigns.

Outcome research measures the extent to which the original campaign objectives were met, providing a sound basis from which to begin the planning for future campaigns.

Methodologies

An organisation can obtain the information it seeks through both *formal* and *informal* research, using *qualitative* or *quantitative* methodologies. Additionally, the practitioner may make use of *primary* research, which is original research conducted by or for an organisation; or *secondary* research, which utilises others' findings or material. Within all of these methods, a wide range of techniques can be used by the researcher to gather information. The concepts of formal, informal, primary and secondary methods will be discussed first and then an introduction to some of the techniques will follow.

Figure 6.2 shows the most common relationships between each of these methods and techniques. The table acts as a guide from which students can begin to understand the breadth of techniques available. A research plan will not be limited to one method or technique, but will use a range of tools depending on the desired outcomes and accuracy level, the available time frame and the available budget.

Figure 6.2 Research methods and techniques

		Techniques	Input	Output	Outcome
Formal research	Qualitative	In-depth interviews	•		•
		Focus groups	•	•	•
		Ethnographic studies	•	•	•
		Analysis of existing data	•	•	•
		Organisational culture study	•		•
		Communication audits	•		•
		Analysis of feedback	•		•
		Pre-testing	•		
		Attitude and image studies	•		•
	Quantitative	Surveys	•	•	•
		Content analysis		•	•
		Media monitoring		•	
		Readership studies/statistics on distribution	•	•	
		Readability studies		•	
		Benchmark studies	•	•	•
		Audience analysis		•	•
		Response mechanisms		•	•
		Recording and analysis of incoming phone calls		•	•
		Advertising Value Equivalents (AVE)		•	

Informal research	Case studies	•		
	Environmental monitoring	•		•
	Archives	•		
	Libraries	•		
	Electronic databases	•		•
	Interviewing, unstructured	•	•	•
	Diaries	•	•	•
	Testimonials	•		•
	Expert review	•		•
	Panel discussions	•	•	•

Formal and informal research

In defining research, Leedy maintains it is 'the systematic process of collecting and analyzing information (data) in order to increase our understanding of the phenomenon with which we are concerned or interested' (1997: 3). Broom and Dozier define research as 'the controlled, objective and systematic gathering of information for the purposes of describing and understanding' (1990: 4). In essence, formal research is a scientific approach to answering questions. It is relatively expensive and time consuming, but is objective, credible and reliable. It is also focused, affords insight and depth to issues, and has a high prediction value.

According to Leedy (1997: 5), formal research is characterised by scientific procedures, methodologies and analysis. He adds that formal research begins with a question that requires an answer. Before the research is commissioned or undertaken, goals must be set for what is expected of the research. Formal research is undertaken in a step-by-step method or procedure, working towards answers to a main problem. For accuracy, validity and logistical considerations, the main problem may be broken down into sub-problems, or smaller problems. Each of these is then researched and the data used in planning or evaluation. In essence, formal research is underpinned by a question or hypothesis and is undertaken in a scientific manner. The collection and interpretation of data from all research contributes to the growth of organisational knowledge and expertise.

Informal research has no agreed rules and procedures, and is cheaper and more immediate than formal research. It is also highly subjective and does not offer the prediction value that formal research offers, so is therefore less reliable. Informal research cannot, as a rule, be replicated; however, it serves a purpose, especially in the early stages of exploratory research. Many informal research techniques are used to offer insight into various issues in public relations.

Qualitative and quantitative research

Formal research is undertaken within two main methodologies—qualitative and quantitative. Each has its own characteristics and provides particular types of information and outputs. They can be used individually or combined in a research program.

Caywood describes qualitative research as using 'discovery-based methods' (1997: 43). Qualitative research is normally used to explore new aspects or to delve further into a particular area. This form of research probes deeper and may sample a relatively small group of respondents. Eliot Eisner (in Leedy 1997) characterises qualitative research as that which is interpretive and in-depth. While the researcher has a clear understanding of the purpose of the research project, qualitative research does not necessarily offer answers only to set questions. Often, there are other details important to the organisation which the researcher has not considered. Qualitative research is open to the additional information and new insight. In public relations it may be used as exploratory research, conducted to help plan a campaign. Qualitative research is descriptive and informative, with the emphasis on the analysis and synthesis of information.

Quantitative research, on the other hand, uses 'verification-based methods' (Caywood 1997: 43), meaning that it is used to verify situations that the organisation may already be aware of, but is without any information to substantiate these beliefs, thoughts, feelings or opinions. Quantitative research in public relations is thus generally described as confirmatory research. Larger sample sizes are used in this type of research and the study is often undertaken through the various measuring instruments of surveys. Often the research results in mathematical analysis, as the data gathered are often based on either simple or complex statistical formulae. This type of research must be conducted by professionals who are trained and experienced researchers as question construction and survey sample selection are very important. An important difference between qualitative and quantitative research is that quantitative research can be *replicated*.

According to Leedy (1997), the decision to use a methodology is dictated by the nature of the data required. If the data are numerical, then generally the use of quantitative research is appropriate; if the data are verbal or more descriptive, then generally the methodology is qualitative. It should be noted that these methods can be used together and are merely different methods for solving a problem or answering a question.

Research techniques

Once a general methodology has been selected, the public relations researcher needs to consider which techniques will achieve the agreed research objectives. Despite resource limitations, the range of options available ensures that some level of research is possible. Selection of a technique should therefore take into consideration not only the objectives, but also the time, budget and skills available.

Surveys

One of the most frequently used research techniques in public relations is the survey. Surveys are a convenient way of gathering data about the target public's level of knowledge or information, attitude, opinions and beliefs, and are administered through a questionnaire. Surveys of publics can also enable the practitioner to gain insight into the responses to messages imparted during the campaign. A survey sample will determine whether generalisations may be drawn from the results, or whether they will simply offer insights into attitudes and behaviours.

According to Babbie, 'survey research is perhaps the most frequently used mode of observation in the social sciences' (1995: 256). It is from these scientifically based surveys that statistics are drawn. The main tool used by the survey researcher is the *questionnaire*, and the group that is surveyed is the *sample*. For the public relations practitioner it is essential to understand these basic concepts, but specific skills, necessitating a systematic, precise approach, normally require a professional pollster or research company.

The four main methods of questionnaire delivery are mail, telephone, face-to-face, and internet, each with its own strengths and weaknesses. Other methods include fax or newsletter.

Mail

This method of delivery requires the respondent to complete the questionnaire and return it to the researcher. A letter will usually accompany the questionnaire to explain the objectives of the research. This technique often relies on follow-up mailings to ensure the best possible response rate. Strengths of this method are that many people may be reached at once, in a wide geographic location at a relatively low cost. A major weakness is that the response rate is quite low, as it relies on respondents to initiate their own response. Because of this, it is becoming common to include an 'incentive' in the survey. One researcher stapled a teabag to the survey to encourage recipients to take the time to fill it out.

Telephone

This technique is often acknowledged as including attributes of mailing and face-to-face interviews. A wide range of people may be interviewed, in geographically broad locations. Other strengths are that several interviewers may use one office, and it is easier, safer and less expensive if interviewers are not in face-to-face environments. The major drawback of this technique is that it relies on respondents being listed in the phone book, being home at the time of calling, and being prepared to answer questions and not simply hang up. As a result, the non-response rate can be relatively high. Because of the growth in the telemarketing sector, this technique may offer increasingly limited responses.

Face-to-face

Babbie (1995) puts the response rate of face-to-face interviews at 80–85 per cent. Clearly this high response rate is one of the major strengths of this technique, which also allows for explanation on the part of the interviewer, recording of in-depth responses and probing of responses. The high cost of this labour-intensive technique is seen as a major drawback, as it is costly to train interviewers. Safety factors relating to door knocking unknown residences are also an issue. This technique, used by the Australian Bureau of Statistics and Census collectors, can then form the basis for secondary research.

Internet

The use of the internet (email and electronic questionnaires) as a contact method for surveys has grown over the past ten years. It is generally viewed as more cost effective than other methods; however, as Kotler et al. (2003: 130) indicate, there could be additional costs in the software development. While the speed of response is good, other issues to consider are the technical capability of the audience, the response quality, privacy issues, possibility of viruses and the accuracy of sampling.

In addition to the method of delivery, researchers can employ a number of tactics using surveys. *Pilot questionnaires* allow the practitioner to pretest the content of questions and audience understanding/misunderstanding/confusion over question content. *Focus groups* or *telephone surveys* can be used to conduct pilot questionnaires.

Omnibus (or piggy-back) *surveys* research two or more, normally related, issues in one questionnaire. Two or more organisations may participate in the study, sharing the costs of the research.

Questionnaire design is an important task in survey research as it can impact on the accuracy of the results. The type of information required will dictate the type of questionnaire administered. Questions may be either *closed* or *open-ended*. In closed questions, the respondent is given a list of answers from which to choose. In open-ended questions, the respondent is asked to give a response that requires some comment. For example, a closed question might ask the following to ascertain cinema attendance trends: 'How often do you go to the movies—less than once a year/once a year/several times a year/once a month/once a week/more than once a week?' An open-ended question might elicit more detail if framed: 'What prompts you to go to the movies?' The response might cover everything from 'wet weather' to 'I see every movie with Keanu Reeves in it'. In closed questions, the response list should be as exhaustive as possible, including every response within the boundaries of the answers provided. Whatever style is chosen, only one question should be asked at a time, avoiding what are called 'double-barrelled' questions, such as: 'Would you go to the movies more if you lived closer to the cinema and had more spare time?' Questions should also be free of bias. A biased question would be: 'Would you go to the movies more if the queues weren't so long to get in?'

Scales are a standard part of many questionnaires, allowing respondents to fit their answer into a quantifiable category. Various techniques are used: the Likert scale requires the respondent to select from a range of answers from 'strongly agree' through to 'strongly disagree'; other techniques include the semantic differential, Bogardus, Thurstone and Guttman scales (Babbie 1995).

Sampling procedures must also be considered in the design of survey research. The two main sampling procedures are probability and non-probability. *Probability sampling* requires a sample group to be representative of the population as a whole. Random selection is the most scientific method because it gives equal chance of selection and does not include bias. *Non-probability sampling*, while not so scientific in approach, can be extremely useful in public relations research. There are a number of techniques that are used, providing useful exploratory information; however, non-probability sampling cannot be used as a true reflection of a wider population, as it is not representative.

Example of a questionnaire used in surveys

Dear Students,

The objective of this survey is to establish the satisfaction level of students regarding the services at our university refectory. Please do participate in this survey; your opinion is important to us and the results of this survey could either confirm that our services are of an acceptable standard or it could contribute to improved services for students.

All information is confidential and only aggregated results will be used. Your response is anonymous. Thank you for your contribution. *(Please place a cross in the box provided where relevant.)*

1. **What year of study are you in?**
   1st year   2nd year   3rd year

2. **In which faculty are you studying?**
   Science   Management   Law
   Engineering   Information Sciences   Health Sciences
   Social Sciences   Education   Other

3. **During your semester, do you obtain (buy) your food/snacks/drinks from the university refectory?**
   Yes   No (go to Q. 6)

4. **If yes, how regularly do you buy your food/snacks/drinks from the refectory?**
   Daily
   Twice a week
   Three times a week
   Four times a week

5. **Could you please indicate the times at which you normally buy your food/snacks/drinks.**
   Between 09h00 – 11h00
   Between 11h00 – 14h00
   Between 14h00 – 17h00
   17h00 and later

6. If you do not obtain (buy) your foods from the university refectory, what is your main reason for not obtaining your food at the university refectory?

_____

_____

_____

_____

_____

_____

7. With regard to the variety of food/snacks/drinks that are available in the university refectory, how would you rate the following:
   (1—poor; 5—outstanding)

	1	2	3	4	5
Range of breads and other bread products (e.g. bread rolls)					
Range of sandwich and roll fillings					
Choice of Asian foods					
Choice of vegetarian foods					
Choice of salads					
Range of drinks (fruit drinks, water, sodas, etc.)					
General quality of food/snacks					

8. What other food/snacks would you like to be sold at the refectory?

_____

_____

_____

_____

9. In the refectory, how would you rate the following:
    (1—poor; 5—outstanding)

	1	2	3	4	5
Staff assistance					
Waiting times for service					
Cleanliness					
Furnishings					

10. Do you have any other comment regarding services at the refectory?

_____

_____

_____

_____

_____

11. On the issue of price, how would you rate the prices of food/snacks/drinks in the refectory?
    Affordable   Unaffordable

12. What food products in particular do you find exceptionally high in price?

_____

_____

_____

_____

_____

13. Do you have any other comment/opinion that you believe could contribute to making the refectory a better place for students (affordable food/snacks, comfortable environment, etc.)?

_____

_____

_____

_____

_____

Again, thank you for your time and contribution.

Other research techniques

A range of other qualitative and quantitative research techniques are available to the public relations practitioner. The most commonly used include the following.

In-depth interviews

Conducted with specifically chosen people or samples within the target public, these use questions that are generally pre-tested and asked of all respondents, requiring explanation in responses. In-depth interviews allow the practitioner insight into the respondents' attitudes, beliefs and action as a result of program messages and activities. Personal interviews provide the opportunity to gather a wealth of information. Interviewing large numbers of people at workshops, meetings and conferences can reduce travel costs. When this technique is used in informal research, interviews are free-ranging and not designed to cover specific questions, as in formal research.

Focus groups

This is currently one of the most frequently used techniques in public relations. The focus group is made up of between eight and fifteen people who share similar characteristics. Discussions are led by interviewers or facilitators with the ability to move the group in the necessary direction without imposing their views on the group, avoiding irrelevant discussion and resource wastage. Focus group facilitators are also adept at ensuring that all members of the group are heard, rather than allowing the discussion to be hijacked by a vocal majority. Focus group discussion enables the practitioner to collect preliminary information from the target audience about message comprehension and acceptance. This technique can be used in a pilot study or as a pretest of key messages. It can also be used to measure changes in attitudes or knowledge in the target audience, with emphasis placed on depth of feeling towards key messages.

Ethnographic studies

These are undertaken by observation and involve research on groups in urban, suburban or cultural settings. The researchers are physically in the situation and among the people they are observing. Ethnographic research requires interviews, reviewing records and seeking opinions. It seeks knowledge about the daily routines, habits and predictable aspects of the lives of groups or cultures being studied.

Case studies

These provide factual data recorded from real-life practices and experiences. They may be used to examine issues and events, and allow analysis and evaluation of the positive and negative aspects of events, campaigns or programs. This analysis can then be considered when planning new campaigns. While case studies work on real-life situations, hypothetical case studies are sometimes designed and drawn for student analysis.

Analysis of existing data

An examination of all documentation relating to previous programs or campaigns and other organisational issues helps the practitioner to establish what has been done previously by the organisation and reflect on the strengths and limitations of those actions. It may also uncover useful information that will not need to be collected through primary research techniques.

Organisational culture study

This is used to understand the organisation in terms of its image perception, management style, line functioning, communication and general policies. The information collected in this study can then be used to inform new campaigns.

Feedback analysis

Complaints, compliments and inquiries can be recorded and analysed, providing useful information for future campaigns. Responses from audiences through any medium, such as incoming phone calls, internet or written responses, can systematically be logged for future reference and examination.

Media monitoring

This technique establishes the extent of media coverage, with an emphasis on reach (the total number of target audience exposed to the program) and frequency (the number of times the target audience was exposed to the same message). When two forms of media are used (e.g. radio and newspaper), the gross rating points (GRP) of both media are considered. The formality of this technique can range from detailed (through the use of complex database management techniques) to informal (such as a collection of press clippings).

Content analysis

This technique enables the researcher to analyse themes and trends in transcripts of panel discussions, in-depth interviews and selected media. Practitioners systematically code and quantify pictorial and verbal content of printed or transcribed material.

More specifically, media content analysis focuses on the nature of media coverage. Close attention is given to analysing the content and tone of media clips and reporting of the key messages. The analysis concentrates on what is put out by the media and not on what the target public understands. This type of research can be outsourced or conducted in-house. Research organisations can undertake thorough analysis and reporting. However, companies can also conduct their own analysis with free or purchased software applications or develop their own proprietary systems of analysis.

Benchmark research

This type of research allows the practitioner to identify the existing status of a range of topics, such as target public attitude/opinions, amount of media coverage or readability levels of publications. Conducted before the implementation of a campaign, it can be used following the campaign to assist in determining the level and direction of change.

Statistical analysis

This systematically records reaction/response from the target public, such as the numbers visiting workshops/presentations/exhibitions, buying publications or meeting organisation officials.

Environmental monitoring

At the organisational level, this technique is the initial step in the strategic management process facilitating the identification of problem areas. At the societal level, macro trends are identified that may affect organisations. Such trends are systematically monitored. According to Brody and Stone (1989), the process involves three components:

1 identifying, tracking and analysing trends that may ultimately affect individuals or organisations;
2 interpreting and defining the implications of identified trends and alternative processes; and
3 developing strategies and plans that can best be managed by the organisation.

Scanning and tracking are two processes used in environmental monitoring. Scanning involves ongoing observation of trends in the environment, while tracking is the constant monitoring of opportunities or threats in the environment that affect organisations. This technique is used in the area of issues management and community consultation and is analysed further in Chapter 11.

Communication audits

Communication audits are used to analyse and assess existing channels of communication, messages and the communication ethos of the organisation. This type of audit could be undertaken both internally and externally, using a range of research tools such as surveys, focus groups and analysis of existing data. The emphasis is on evaluating the effectiveness of existing internal and external means of communication used by the organisation. Three methods are commonly used in communication audits: *readership studies*, designed to measure the number of people in the target public who read organisational publications and remember the information read; *content analysis*, designed to measure how the media handle news and other information about the organisation; and *readability studies*, which measure the ease with which the target public reads all written communications from the organisation. Organisational and audience issues are also examined, such as the position and function of public relations in the organisation, target public identification, image and perception studies, the strength and power of the publics and their concerns. The goal of this type of research is to plan future public relations strategies.

Corporate communication archives

Written recordings of an organisation's previous campaigns and data gathered about the target public, as well as minutes of meetings and proceedings, form part of the corporate communication archives.

Testimonials

These are verbal and written statements from satisfied members of the target public.

Expert review

This technique involves the practitioner consulting a person (such as an academic or senior member within the industry) or an organisation with the knowledge or expertise to verify, challenge and help develop the required component of the program or campaign.

Internet monitoring

The content of online newsgroups, chat rooms and web page bulletin boards can be monitored to identify and analyse the views of others, providing further information to inform campaign development or evaluation. This technique can be conducted in-house or it can be outsourced; however, this can be costly in terms of time and human resources. The Institute for Public Relations (2002) refers to this as cyber image analysis, as it measures the image of an organisation on the internet. Holtz (1999: 100) suggests four ways of conducting this type of research:

- reading newsgroups;
- using search engines;
- using software; and
- subscribing to mailing lists.

Measurement of online presence

Holtz (1999: 233) stresses the importance of setting measurable objectives before explaining various ways to measure the impact of a company's online presence. For example, the impact of web activity on an integrated campaign, the public's behaviour and media coverage can all be measured and used to assist in future strategy development.

Advertising value equivalents (AVEs)

This technique involves placing a value on the media coverage obtained by calculating what the space would have cost in advertising terms. This is not generally recognised as an accurate methodology for various reasons: AVEs do not separate positive, neutral or negative coverage and the subsequent estimation of the true value of the coverage is questionable.

Secondary information sources

A range of libraries are available from which data can be gathered. These include personal, public, academic and specialised libraries. With new technology, these libraries offer a range of options to collect data for program and campaign planning. Internet services are also available to gather information from local, national and international sources. There is also an increasing use of online academic databases that are available 24 hours a day (e.g. ERL, ERIC, ComIndex, ComSearch and APAIS). While secondary information can provide useful and relatively low-cost data, the quality of the information should be assessed by considering whether it is current, accurate and objective. Any deviation from these factors could impact on the validity of the research. A range of potential sources of material is provided in Table 6.1.

Table 6.1 Suggested sources of secondary information

Specialist encyclopedias

International Encyclopedia of Marketing
Encyclopedia of Television News
International Encyclopedia of Public Policy and Administration
Companion Encyclopedia of Psychology

Dictionaries

Dictionary of Communication and Media Studies
Dictionary of Statistics for Psychologists
The Collins Australian Dictionary of Political Terms

Almanacs, yearbooks, handbooks

Whitaker's Almanac
B&T Yearbook
Yearbook Australia
The Australian Political Directory
Commonwealth Government Directory
The Statesman's Yearbook
The Europa Yearbook

Information about people

Who's Who in Australia
Who's Who
The Australian Dictionary of Biography
Federal electoral rolls
Newspapers
Familiar quotations
Networking, contact and interviews

Contacting organisations

Government Who's Who of Australia
Directory of Australian Associations
Directory of World Associations
Margaret Gee's Media Guide
Willing's Press Guide
White and Yellow Pages

Government information

Commonwealth Government Entry Point
<www.gov.au>
Commonwealth Government Online Directory
<www.gold.gov.au>

Statistics—online directories

Australian Bureau of Statistics
<www.abs.gov.au>
University of Michigan's Statistical Resources on the web
<www.lib.umich.edu/govdocs/stats.html>
United Nations
<www.un.org/Depts/unsd/mbsreg.htm>

Content

Books
<www.nla.gov.au/libraries/>

Media sources

Newspapers
e.g. <http://global.factiva.com/en/gen/browser.asp>
TV Online
e.g. <www.sbs.com.au>

Industry information

Industry-specific information can generally be accessed through local industry associations and their websites

Ethical considerations in research

The PRIA's Code of Ethics provides the public relations practitioner with the benchmark for sound ethical practice (see also Chapter 5). Within the domain of research and evaluation, it is essential that the practitioner be conscious of coercion, dishonesty, hurtful manner and manipulation of data to meet any other ends than the stated objectives or hypothesis. The following standards provide good guidelines for the practitioner:

- Give full disclosure of the research procedure.
- Make sure results are accurately reported and distributed freely and widely.
- Keep respondent information confidential (or anonymous) as promised.
- Do not promise clients and sponsors what cannot be delivered.
- Do no harm. (McElreath 1997: 240)

Research organisations in Australia

There are many private and public organisations in Australia that undertake research for the public relations and related industries. Some of the most comprehensive information, as a secondary source of information, is available from the Australian Bureau of Statistics (ABS) (at <www.statistics.gov.au>). Research information and reports are readily obtainable on demographics, psychographics, values and lifestyles, and geodemographics. This type of information has already been captured in the Census data, and the relevant information for the practitioner's needs can often be extracted from these. Practitioners thinking of embarking on primary research should first contact the ABS to check whether it has the required information. ABS services include the Social Atlas series, CDATA, Business Register Service, Economic Indicators, Labour Market Analysis, Census Update and Australian Social Trends. Attitudinal studies, the latest geographic data, emerging trends, graphic representation of data, data on population and housing, and the online time series are other effective ways of using and managing organisational resources. Private research organisations in Australia are ACNielsen, AGB McNair, Roy Morgan and Market Attitude Research Services (MARS). The professional body for market and social research is known as the Market Research Society of Australia (MRSA). The Association of Market Research Organisations (AMRO) represents organisations that offer market research services to commerce, industry and government.

Numerous organisations have been established within Australia and on a global basis for the sole purpose of researching and measuring media and internet coverage. A number of companies also offer software that can be used in-house to conduct the research. For example, the MASS Communication Group offers a tool called MASS COMaudit® which gives an organisation the ability to undertake its own planning and evaluation research using media analysis and prepared survey questionnaires. The media analysis tool MASS MEDIAudit® covers both qualitative and quantitative measurement of media coverage, share of voice, audience data and media facts as well as other information. This data can then be presented in easy-to-read charts.

Conclusion

This chapter discusses the application of research in the input, output and outcome stages of a public relations campaign or program. The style of research adopted by an organisation depends upon the system under which it operates, its environment and the requirements of the program being undertaken, including the objectives. Formal and informal research methods can be used to gather information, with the choice of methodology dependent on the levels of reliability needed, the information required and the project's budget. Both input and output research are necessary to plan, monitor and manage successful public relations activities. Measuring achievements through outcomes will help determine the effectiveness of a program at all three stages and provide input into future public relations programs.

Case study 6.1: Australian Bureau of Statistics—2001 Census Communication Campaign

The fourteenth national Census of Population and Housing was held on 7 August 2001, following an extensive communication campaign primarily designed to create awareness of the event. Numerous research activities were undertaken prior to development of the campaign, during its implementation and as part of the evaluation process. This case study examines the research conducted during each of the input, output and outcomes stages.

The Census is conducted every five years, measuring the number of people in Australia, some key characteristics about the people and where they live. While the primary use of the information is to guide the distribution of government funding, it is also used for planning purposes by all levels of government and other private and commercial users.

The support of all Australians is necessary in achieving the highest possible count of Australians on Census night. The overall strategy of the ABS was therefore to 'position the 2001 Census as a friendly, non-threatening exercise with indisputable benefits for all Australians'. From this, the goals and objectives of a communication strategy were established.

The *goal* of the campaign was to support the ABS's corporate aim to ensure that the 2001 Census had the highest possible count of people in Australia on Census night.

The *objectives* were:

- *recruitment*—to recruit most of the 30 000 temporary Census field staff;
- *awareness*—to raise awareness of Census night among people in Australia:
  - to encourage full and accurate completion of the form on Census night; and
  - to inform people of the operational aspects of form distribution and collection;
- *time capsule*—to inform people of the Centenary of Federation Census Time Capsule Project.

Objectives are an important research consideration, as they are used to determine what needs to be measured.

The 2001 Census Communication Campaign comprised paid advertising, issues and crisis management and numerous public relations and information activities aimed at the public, the media, ABS staff and other stakeholders.

Input stage

In order to develop appropriate plans for implementation, the ABS undertook research prior to and during the development of the campaign plan. The results of previous Census communication campaigns, particularly that of 1996, were examined in detail and assisted decision-making in relation to 2001 activities. For example Worthington Di Marzio conducted focus group research into the usability of the 1996 Census advertisements and logo. Outcomes of this research resulted in a new logo for 2001, a new suite of print advertisements, and revamping of the 1996 television advertisements, which had also been used in 1991.

ACNielsen undertook a benchmarking survey in December 2000, in order to understand the public's current level of awareness and understanding of Census issues. The survey particularly focused on informing the first two stated objectives.

Other information was gathered from market research undertaken by Market Attitude Research Services, and from various expert sources on communicating with indigenous, ethnic and visually impaired audiences. Advice was also sought from other government departments and agencies and relationships developed with family history organisations.

Throughout this research, ABS communication staff also spoke with ABS field staff to identify potentially damaging incidents, working with them to implement strategies in order to lessen any negative impacts.

Output stage

A number of tactics were used to measure and track the progress of the campaign's outputs, once the campaign plan was finalised and implemented. To begin with, the ABS engaged Capital Public Affairs Consultants to undertake an independent review of the total strategy, in particular to identify areas that may have been overlooked.

ACNielsen followed its benchmarking survey with three tracking surveys throughout July 2001, measuring changes in the awareness and attitudes towards the Census as a result of the ongoing integrated communication campaign.

As part of the implementation, briefings were conducted for community and other public opinion leaders, in which feedback could also be obtained. Material developed for indigenous audiences was tested in remote and urban communities. Similar testing was also completed on material for multicultural audiences.

The output from the media relations program, which was aimed at encouraging journalists and commentators to cover relevant Census issues in a timely and accurate manner, were measured primarily through media analysis. Rehame undertook this research during the months of July and August 2001. Results indicated that the key messages of the campaign were covered in an overwhelmingly complimentary manner and particularly highlighted the prominence and success of the ABS spokespeople, an important part of the communication campaign. The Rehame research determined that there had been extensive use of ABS-prepared information, and that the media had been an important conduit in promoting the website address, the hotline number and census as a topic of discussion.

The Rehame research also highlighted the fact that, while there was some negative media coverage, particularly through talkback radio, this also indicated that the public were at least aware of the Census. ABS spokespeople were then able to address many of the callers' concerns. The media analysis also revealed the importance of interest groups in keeping the census in the news and enabled the development of appropriate organisational changes and communications responses via the media and one-to-one contact. Criticism by interest groups was taken seriously but formed only a small part of overall coverage.

Three particular promotional tactics within the communication campaign that received positive media coverage were the recruitment campaign, the official launch and the program of issuing newborn babies with t-shirts with the slogan 'I just made the count'.

Outcome stage

An important part of research into outcomes involves determining whether the campaign objectives were met. The ABS research used all of its tools, such as the benchmarking research, the independent media analysis and focus groups, to determine the success of its outcomes. Research illustrated that the corporate aim of achieving the highest possible count was met with a Census count of 97.8 per cent of the Australian population.

The three objectives were also achieved. The objective of recruitment was measured by a quantitative analysis of the inquiries and application for positions. The objective of awareness was measured primarily by the benchmarking survey, showing that 98 per cent of people had heard of the Census and Census advertising and public relations achieved an 82 per cent recognition. The research also demonstrated a statistically significant positive shift in attitude from the 1996 campaign. The objective of informing the public about the Time Capsule Project was measured by the benchmarking survey as well as the Census itself, which could determine the numbers who had marked the appropriate question. The results of the survey showed that approximately 85 per cent of people had made an informed decision regarding their participation in the project.

The ACNielsen research, through the final post-Census survey conducted immediately following the 2001 Census, also provided some recommendations for the next Census in 2006. The research highlighted three areas that could be taken into consideration in the input stage of the next Census communication plan:

- The Census should focus on attitudes, not just awareness.
- The young, the less educated and those from a non-English speaking background should be specifically targeted.
- Privacy issues and the usefulness of the data should be addressed through the key messages.

The success of the ABS 2001 Census communication campaign relied heavily on the thorough research conducted at the input, output and outcome stages of campaign development and implementation. The cyclical nature of the research was evident in its beginnings of examining the 1996 outcomes and in the final recommendations for the 2006 campaign. Many methodologies and tools were used at all stages of research, concluding in research that directly measured the level of success of the campaign in meeting its stated objectives.

Source: Written with the assistance and permission of Stephen Dangaard, Director Media & Public Affairs, Australian Bureau of Statistics.

Discussion and exercises

1   Why is research fundamental to the public relations process? List three different forms of qualitative and quantitative research and discuss the application of these to the public relations process.
2   What is meant by formal and informal research? What are the different characteristics that identify these types of research? Identify some informal techniques used in student research.

3   Consider the differences between input, output and outcome research and when these might be applied during a campaign about:

(a) the use of illicit drugs;
(b) water restrictions; and
(c) an association membership drive.

4   Why is research described as cyclical? Consider existing programs in your community to which this might best apply. Develop lists of research and evaluation for these programs and see where they overlap.

Further reading

Brody, E.W. & Stone, G.C. (1989) *Public Relations Research*, Praeger, New York.
Dozier, D.M. & Ehling, W.P. (1992) 'Evaluation of public relations programs: what the literature tells us about their effects', in J. Grunig (ed.), *Excellence in Public Relations and Communication Management*, Lawrence Erlbaum, New Jersey.
Government Communications Unit (2001) *How to Use Research and Evaluation in Government Communications Campaigns*, <www.gcu.gov.au/code/pdf/RandEBook.pdf>.
Hendrix, J.A. (1998) *Public Relations Cases*, 4th edn, Wadsworth, Belmont.
Institute for Public Relations Research and Education (1999) *Guidelines for Setting Measurable Public Relations Objectives*, Gainesville, Florida.
—— (2003) *Guidelines for Measuring the Effectiveness of PR Programs and Activities*, Gainesville, Florida.
Leedy, P.D. (1997) *Practical Research: Planning and Design*, 6th edn, Prentice Hall, Englewood Cliffs.
Lindenmann, W.K. (2001) *Public Relations Research for Planning and Evaluation*, Institute for Public Relations, Gainesville, Florida.
Moss, D., MacManus, T. & Vercic, D. (1997) *Public Relations Research: An International Perspective*, Thomson Business Press, London.

References

Babbie, E. (1995) *The Practice of Social Research*, 7th edn, Wadsworth, Belmont.
Brody, E.W. & Stone, G.C. (1989) *Public Relations Research*, Praeger, New York.
Broom, G.M. & Dozier, D.M. (1990) *Using Research in Public Relations: Applications to Program Management*, Prentice Hall, Englewood Cliffs.
Caywood, C.L. (ed.) (1997) *The Handbook of Strategic Public Relations and Integrated Communications*, McGraw-Hill, New York.
Cutlip, S.M., Center, A. & Broom, G. (1994) *Effective Public Relations*, 7th edn, Prentice Hall, Englewood Cliffs.

Dozier, D.M. & Ehling, W.P. (1992) 'Evaluation of public relations programs: what the literature tells us about their effects', in J. Grunig (ed.), *Excellence in Public Relations and Communication Management*, Lawrence Erlbaum, New Jersey.

Grunig, J. (ed.) (1992) *Excellence in Public Relations and Communication Management*, Lawrence Erlbaum, New Jersey.

Holtz, S. (1999) *Public Relations on the Net*, AMACOM, New York.

Institute for Public Relations (2002) *Dictionary of Public Relations Measurement and Research*, <www.instituteforpr.com/pdf/Dictionary.pdf>, accessed 20 January 2003.

Kotler, P., Adam, S., Brown, L. & Armstrong, A. (2003) *Principles of Marketing*, 2nd edn, Pearson, Sydney.

Leedy, P.D. (1997) *Practical Research: Planning and Design*, 6th edn, Prentice Hall, Englewood Cliffs.

Littlejohn, S.W. (1999) *Theories of Human Communication*, 6th edn, Wadsworth, Belmont.

McElreath, M.P. (1997) *Managing Systematic and Ethical Public Relations Campaigns*, 2nd edn, Brown & Benchmark, Madison.

Marston, J. (1979) *Modern Public Relations*, McGraw-Hill, New York.

Newsom, D., VanSlyke Turk, J. & Kruckeberg, D. (1996) *This is PR*, Wadsworth, Belmont.

Pritchitt, J. & Sherman, B. (1994) *Public Relations Evaluation: Professional Accountability*, Gold Paper no. 11, International Public Relations Association, Sydney.

Public Relations Institute of Australia (PRIA) (1999) *Position Paper—Evaluation*, PRIA, Sydney.

Seitel, F.P. (2001) *The Practice of Public Relations*, 8th edn, Prentice Hall, Englewood Cliffs.

Tymson C. & Lazar P. (2002) *The Australian and New Zealand Public Relations Manual: 21st Century Edition*, Tymson Communications, Sydney.

Wilcox, D.L., Ault, P.H. & Agee, W.K. (1995) *Public Relations Strategies and Tactics*, HarperCollins, New York.

7 STRATEGY, PLANNING AND SCHEDULING

John Allert and Clara Zawawi

In this chapter

Introduction

This chapter aims to make students aware of the necessity for public relations practitioners to think and practise strategically in order to be relevant in today's organisation. We will explain what a strategy is, how a public relations strategy can and needs to fit into an organisation's overall operational strategy, and how practitioners can organise themselves through planning, budgeting and scheduling to make their strategies effective.

The process from formulating strategy to creating and implementing a strategic plan can be visualised as a funnel. Each stage of the funnel further defines and clarifies the tasks that the practitioner must perform to successfully implement each stage of the public relations process. The stages of the strategic process in public relations are:

- creation of organisational vision and mission statements;
- creation of public relations vision and mission statements;
- establishment of performance indicators;
- budgeting;
- writing of a strategic public relations plan;
- scheduling of public relations plan activities.

Organisational strategy

Historically, *strategy* referred to the role of a military commander and his art and skill. It later came to mean managerial skill in administration, leadership, oration and power, and later still was generalised to include all aspects of coordinating and planning intellectual and physical skills in order to best position oneself, or the organisation, for the long-term purpose at hand. A simple definition of strategy is: a series of planned activities designed and integrated to achieve a stated organisational goal. A more academic definition is:

> strategy is a pattern or plan that integrates an organisation's major goals, policies and action sequences into a cohesive whole. A well formulated strategy helps to marshal and allocate an organisation's resources into a unique and viable posture based on its relative internal competencies and shortcomings, anticipated changes in the environment and contingent moves by an intelligent opponent. (Mintzberg and Quinn 1991: 5)

A public relations strategy is a process by which the leadership of an organis-ation deliberately manages its communications proactively so that they are open, candid and primarily focused on the marketplace and the customer as the first cause (D'Aprix 1996: 5). As Potter says:

> Strategic communication thinking recognises the cause and effect relationship between our communication activities and the achievement of the organis-ation's mission. It means that communication programs support successful completion of the organisation's strategic activity in a measurable way. (1998: 3)

Strategy is not a series of campaign steps or tactics. It is the underlying rationale that guides the selection of these tactics or stages.

The strategic public relations program or campaign, by definition, is a proactive one: it is not driven by the demands of others. In order to achieve its ends, careful planning is necessary to maintain direction and focus. Specific goals and objectives need to be determined and achieved and action plans developed and coordinated if tools such as brochures or newsletters or events such as launches or news confer-ences are to be successful in implementing the strategy. Planning is therefore an extremely important part of managing strategic public relations.

Public relations strategy

Consider this: you are only likely to be as good a public relations practitioner as your CEO will allow you to be. Therefore, the first strategic move often needs to be made internally. This means educating management about the value of strategic public relations—a role for a professional public relations manager rather than a technician. For the public relations function to be carried out with optimum results, the public relations role must operate within the decision-making dominant coalition of the organisation. This means either reporting directly to top management or even being a member of the governing board. This ensures that the public relations manager is influential in the shaping and development of the strategic plan, rather than merely the disseminator of other people's plans. It is important when devising the organisation's strategic plan that it be designed with communication in mind. The public relations practitioner's input into the design influences its ability to be understood by all the organisation's publics. After all, if an organisation's strategy cannot be understood and accepted by publics, it will remain an unworkable document.

From a public relations perspective, strategies must be designed for communication with all target groups, such as employees, government, pressure groups and local community. Strategic decisions also need to be made to define an organisation's corporate image or ethical parameters, in order to determine how the organisation will respond in crises and issues situations. Therefore, corporate culture, ideology, values and beliefs, systems and business processes influence the public relations strategic planning in social, economic and political contexts.

Value of strategic public relations

Strategic public relations as a highly valued organisational function is highlighted in a major study conducted by the International Association of Business Communicators (IABC) in the United States (Grunig 1997: 286–300). The survey of 5000 people in 300 organisations, conducted by Professor James Grunig, found that chief executives saw corporate public relations as a worthwhile investment— in their view, a typical public relations department provided an average 185 per cent return on investment to the organisation. The return was even higher—about 300 per cent on investment—when the chief executive officer (CEO) supported a well-performing public relations department.

The study found that public relations tended to be valued more highly than the typical department in an organisation. One of the main reasons for its high standing was that it helped the organisation deal with major social issues—but only if the head of public relations was in a strategic management role. The study found that the single greatest determinant of communication excellence was strategic manager expertise.

The study further discovered that the top executive and the dominant coalition of senior management understood the strategic role of communication and wanted to involve the communication function in strategic decision-making. However, it appears that the greatest barrier to making this happen is the knowledge level—or what management perceives to be the knowledge level—of the top communicator. The study found that too many senior public relations practitioners still consider themselves to be technicians, or communicators concentrating on the technical rather than the policy aspects of public relations. This greatly reduces their effectiveness, which is why it is imperative that public relations students understand strategy, both from a management perspective and from the communication or public relations perspective.

Though the IABC study concentrated on in-house practitioners, there is no difference when the relationship is that of client and public relations consultant. A survey conducted some years ago (Allert 1992) indicated that public relations consultants were held in fairly high esteem by chief executives as far as skills of communication, media relations and publicity (the technical skills) were concerned, but too many consultants were found not to understand business. This boiled down to a lack of strategic understanding of how a business (as opposed to any other kind of organisation) operates: its aims, its objectives and its reason for existence.

The Grunig study outlined twelve characteristics of excellent communication departments (Grunig 1992). In practical terms, the main five characteristics are summarised by the view that the excellent communication or public relations department:

- is run by managers who make communication policy decisions and accept responsibility for the success or failure of the programs;
- contributes significantly to the organisation's strategic plan and organisational decision-making;
- works with top management to solve organisational problems that involve communication relationships;
- facilitates two-way communication between top management and key stakeholders, helping them understand each other and developing win–win situations;
- uses formal and informal research techniques to understand the environment inside and outside the organisation to identify key issues.

Chief executives set the tone for corporate communication. They spend up to three-quarters of their time on internal and external communication. The head of public relations can be truly effective only with the backing of the CEO, and should have a direct line to that person, if not a formal reporting relationship.

The public relations role within a management structure is to influence the behaviour of people in relation to each other, through two-way communication. Public relations can further be explained as building, consolidating and maintaining relationships, centring the function more on the relationship and on communication as the tool that helps to achieve that relationship. Relationships—which are a valuable resource—should be managed in the same way as other resources (White and Mazur 1995: 35) (other definitions are discussed in Chapter 1). What is important is that you understand what you need to know and do it strategically in order to achieve your public relations goals. Importantly, the organisation itself must be clear about its mission, direction, values and objectives, and must be certain that what it says is consistent with what it actually believes and does.

Strategically managed public relations has a significant role in developing a strong corporate reputation for the organisation, which translates into a stronger presence in the marketplace. A good reputation pays off because well-regarded organisations generally:

- command premium prices for their products;
- recruit better-calibre staff;
- attract greater loyalty from internal and external stakeholders or publics;
- have more stable revenues;
- face fewer risks of crisis;
- are given greater latitude to act by their constituents. (Frombrun 1996: 72)

How to plan a public relations strategy

The first step to take before building the framework of the strategic plan is to ask some basic questions. What business are we in? Why does the business exist? What are our aims? What do we stand for? How do we see ourselves? How do others see us? What values and beliefs do we hold? How can these be made manifest in our business? How do we view our clients? Each of these questions should be considered carefully and answered satisfactorily before progressing in any business direction. Once a pattern emerges that clearly indicates where you should be heading, how you will proceed, why you are heading in your chosen direction and when you need to do what, you are ready to start building the framework of your strategic plan.

Vision and mission statements

The first vital parts of this framework are the vision statement and the mission statement. These are essential components in defining what you are doing and where you are going. The *vision statement* describes the future state of the organisation at a selected time. It is arrived at through a process whereby management determines the best direction for the organisation and its ultimate destination, and succinctly formulates these determinations into a vision statement. It is best kept brief (about two to four sentences), and it should be quantifiable and agreed to by all members of the organisation. Ideally, it is developed through group participation.

Once the vision statement is developed, the organisation usually compares its present position and its ultimate destination and determines ways in which to close the gap between the two. This process is often referred to as 'gap analysis'. Central to this process is the concept of an 'unsatisfactory present' which can be translated into a more perfect future. Management theory indicates that if management sees the organisation as currently being perfect in all its aspects, there is a danger that complacency will set in. Nothing stands still in the evolutionary process of life, including the evolution of an organisation. It either goes forwards or backwards; if it stagnates, it dies. Therefore, it is strategically sensible to acknowledge that the organisation can always do better and that the present is fleeting, with change evident as soon as an attempt is made to document a current situation.

The *mission statement* is formulated to help close the gap between the unsatisfactory present and the more perfect future. Once a future envisioned scenario is forecast through the vision statement, a mission statement is formulated, describing the broad practical steps for reaching the vision. Mission statements are formulated using the same principles used for developing vision statements. The mission statement should be a brief, clear statement of the reasons for the organisation's existence, its purpose/s, the function/s it performs, its primary stakeholders or publics, and the primary methods through which it fulfils its purpose. A mission statement is:

- consistent with and supportive of an organisation's vision;
- the road map that describes how the organisation will move to reach its vision;
- the means of telling people why the organisation is in business;
- the source of strategies that collectively create a business plan.

When an organisation has an agreed vision and mission, it knows where it is going and how to get there.

Public relations mission statements are directly applicable to the public relations aims and objectives of the organisation, and are thus developed from, and directly related to, the organisation's overall vision and mission. An example comes from AlintaGas, a Western Australian government utility whose vision statement reads: 'AlintaGas aims to be Australia's best gas utility, with a focus on excellent customer service. AlintaGas will ensure natural gas is a reliable and cost effective energy source for Western Australian homes, business and industry.' The public relations mission statement follows, as do the public relations strategies that clarify and define that mission (see 'Public affairs mission' box).

Public affairs mission—AlintaGas

The Public Affairs Branch has a loyal and enthusiastic commitment to provide and facilitate effective and clear issues management, public relations activities, environmental management, corporate advertising and communications for AlintaGas employees, external customers and the media through the innovate use of visual, verbal, print and electronic means. The AlintaGas public affairs strategies are divided into seven specific strategy sections that assist in further defining the public affairs mission.

- *Strategy 1—Internal communication.* To establish and maintain a communications program with employees which promotes face-to-face dialogue, together with a well-informed, motivated and productive workforce.

- *Strategy 2—Issues management.* To research, identify, monitor, manage and evaluate issues to minimise any adverse effects and to maximise positive opportunities for AlintaGas; to develop and implement a media liaison program; to manage communications in a crisis.

- *Strategy 3—External communications.* To develop a working relationship and comprehensive program of communications with government, business and industry.

- *Strategy 4—Environmental management.* To coordinate environmental activities through the Environmental Management Committee.

- *Strategy 5—Reputation management.* To enhance the corporate reputation of AlintaGas through the management and coordination of promotional activities and image development.

- *Strategy 6—Community relations.* To develop effective communication and education programs which build a support base within the community and demonstrate good citizenship.

- *Strategy 7—Professional development.* To pursue professional development opportunities and provide communication skills advice to the organisation.

Source: Adapted from Sweet (1998).

Key performance indicators

The vision and the mission will often be associated with a set of corporate values summarising the expected attitudes and behaviour of employees. This brings us to an important and practical part of strategic planning: the development of key performance indicators (KPIs), sometimes called key result areas (KRAs). Most organisations use these as measurable indicators of their progress towards achieving their mission.

KPIs were developed to gauge operational performance between one period and the next, measuring the most important performance results, such as the number of product items manufactured and revenue. Many executive directors, CEOs or their equivalents are people with a quantitative background—people with MBAs and from the sciences. They, and their financial directors, look for percentages and statistics through what is known as the positivist methodology of research and evaluation. (This is known also as the scientific method, and is discussed further in Chapter 5.) The desire for results of all kinds to be measured in this way has led to KPIs becoming popular as instruments of measurement for public relations as well as other organisational activities.

However, there are strong arguments that KPIs are less well suited to public relations strategies, because the results of public relations work can be intangible in nature and are not often repeated on a regular basis. This makes it difficult to treat them statistically. As a result, the public relations practitioner can be obliged to nominate KPIs that measure only the more quantifiable areas of public relations. This may also mean that inputs and outputs are measured rather than the more important outcomes, because they are easier to quantify (it is easier to measure how many press releases were sent out and how much coverage was achieved than the effects such coverage had on the target audience or public).

It may be necessary for the public relations manager to strategically resist the use of KPIs, proposing instead some of the more qualitative evaluation techniques. As can be seen in Chapter 5, much public relations work is measured using qualitative methodologies, where units of meaning and understanding of the largely human factors of business are needed. Fortunately for public relations practitioners, the bias towards positivism is slowly changing as the importance of human values of interaction and the global necessity of building international alliances are recognised. Management's increasing reliance on controlling global reputation is another reason for the acknowledgment of the public relations practitioner's qualitative skills. However, the public relations professional should understand both types of research methodology, so mutual understanding and constructive dissertations can be achieved.

Strategic planning

Public relations strategic plans are often created in a similar format to business or marketing plans, as management is familiar with and readily relates to these. One such format is that of Lester Potter's (1997) 'ten-step strategic communication plan'. This can cover situations ranging from an annual plan through to a specific or single issue over a shorter time frame. The ten-point structure of the communication plan, which has been proven to meet the needs of many types of organisations, is as follows:

1 Executive summary
2 The communication process
3 Background
4 Situation analysis
5 Main message statement
6 Stakeholders
7 Messages for key stakeholders
8 Implementation
9 Budget
10 Monitoring and evaluation.

Alternative plan formats that deal more specifically with public relations aims and objectives have also been developed (see 'The Zawawi–Johnston strategic public relations plan' box below).

The writer of an effective *strategic communication plan* must always remain conscious of the principles of effective communication, by:

- being *open and honest*—there needs to be a willingness on behalf of the communicator to share information freely, unless it is legitimately sensitive/confidential, in which case this should be made clear to the listener;
- being *two-way and responsive*—communication works best if it is two-way, because people are more likely to listen to us if we listen to them;
- being *receiver-oriented*—it is not what our message does to the listener but what the listener does with our message that determines our success as communicators;
- being *timely*—people are more likely to support a change that affects them if they are consulted before the change is made;

- being *clear and consistent*—communication should be based on clear, consistent messages that are keyed to the success intent of the strategy;
- being *comprehensive*—make sure that everyone who has an interest in the project is included in the communication, and ensure that communication flows upwards, downwards and laterally.

The Zawawi–Johnston strategic public relations plan

1 *Executive summary*. This plan-at-a-glance needs to summarise concisely the situation that led to the need for the plan; the research that was carried out to guide the plan; the goals and objectives of the plan; what tactics will be required to implement the plan; the time frame required; and how the plan will be evaluated. The executive summary should always be written after all other sections have been completed, providing an overview for the reader of the contents that follow.

2 *Vision and mission*. These guiding statements for the plan need to be detailed.

3 *Background and situation analysis*. This needs to detail and analyse the problems or opportunities that led to the formation of the plan. An analysis of the strengths, weaknesses, opportunities and threats (SWOT) of the situation needs to be prepared, with all these areas being listed separately. The organisation's goals in the situation should be clearly identified.

4 *Define strategy*. This needs to answer the following questions: What is the relationship between the situation and the organisation's mission? What are the public relations goals and what objectives need to be achieved in order to reach those goals? What is the underlying rationale for tactic selection?

5 *Define publics*. With whom is it necessary to communicate in order to achieve the aims of the strategy? Are publics internal or external, active or passive, antagonistic or friendly? The more accurately these questions can be answered, the more relevant the messages and tactics ultimately chosen will be.

6 *Define main message*. What main message is required by the strategy, and how should it be altered to communicate with the various publics, if necessary?

7 *Select tactics and communication methods.* Choose and provide detail of the various tactics and show how the use of these particular tools will help achieve the strategic aims of the plan.

8 *Implementation and scheduling.* Demonstrate how the plan will be implemented and provide relevant calendarisation, checklists, Gantt charts or other scheduling documentation that illustrates the critical path and timeline for tactics implementation.

9 *Monitoring and evaluation.* Demonstrate how the effectiveness or otherwise of chosen tactics will be monitored and what tools will be used to evaluate this. Detail at what stages of the plan the monitoring and evaluation will occur and what steps will be available to correct or alter the elements of the plan resulting from these findings.

10 *Budget.* Last but never least! The cost of each activity or element of the plan needs to be carefully detailed. And while the executive summary, which comes at the beginning, is written after the rest of the plan, the budget, which traditionally comes at the end, needs to have its parameters established at the very beginning of the planning process. Each planned activity or item can then be carefully costed to establish their feasibility for inclusion in the plan, and the budget can be refined as the plan progresses.

Budgeting

No plan, no matter how strategic, can succeed without successful and efficient budgeting. Budgeting is all about the direction, monitoring and control of organisational resources. Competition for these resources is often fierce between departments of an organisation, and the public relations manager may need to negotiate for their slice. Effective public relations management depends on a successful combination of all of these elements.

According to McElreath (1997: 158), 'A budget is a plan for coordinating resources and expenses over a period of time by assigning costs (either estimates or actual costs) to goals and objectives for specific activities.' Organisations usually operate under two different types of budgets. The first are *financial budgets*, which give detailed estimates of income and expenditure for the entire organisation in a given period of time, usually a financial year. The second are *operating budgets*, which estimate the costs of the goods and services that the organisation will use for specific purposes, in terms of both actual costs and physical quantities. As Baskin et al. (1997) point out, public relations managers are typically responsible only for preparing their own operational budgets, but an understanding of the entire process makes them more strategically effective (1997: 142).

Typical public relations budgets include salaries and on-costs (superannuation, sick leave, holiday leave); production costs; supplier costs; travel; out-of-pocket expenses; phone, fax, postage and courier fees; overheads; contingencies; and profit. These costs can be broken down into two categories of expenditure: administrative costs and program costs. Administrative costs are salaries, on-costs and fringe -benefits (motor vehicles, subsidised canteens, company gymnasiums) for full- and part-time employees. Program costs include everything else required, from photography to printing, catering, travel, gifts, production, room hire, accommodation, phone and fax transmissions, website creation and maintenance, and so on. Overheads (office space, electricity, equipment leasing, etc.) and profit also need to be factored into budgets. A contingency amount (usually 10 per cent) is factored into most budgets, allowing for unplanned expenditure. The way in which all these items are handled differs according to whether they are prepared by an in-house public relations department or by a consultancy (discussed in detail below). Because budgets are basically forecast estimates of the amounts to be spent on each item, they need to be revisited regularly to check how actual expenditure is matching up to the forecasts. A skilled budgeter will accurately estimate costs at the start, 'bringing in' most items right on the forecast amount rather than over or even under budget.

Budgets for public relations consultancies

Public relations consultancies are businesses which make their income and profit from the advice and expertise that their consultants give their clients. Like lawyers and doctors, they do this by charging for their time—mostly at an hourly rate. The hourly rate varies according to the experience and expertise of the consultant. Secretarial time is also charged out, at a lesser rate. The charge-out rate must not only accommodate the consultant's salary, but also cover overheads and profit for the consultancy. Consultants, particularly at senior level, can be under considerable pressure to maintain their 'billable hours' in order to justify a high salary.

The necessity to charge for time spent working for a particular client means that it is important for consultants to forecast accurately how much time any particular task will take. The consultancy fee, which incorporates the consultants' hourly fees, is a main budget item.

Consultancies also need to recover all costs, including those incurred in routine office work—photocopying, phone and fax transmission, printing and so on. These costs are allocated to clients through the use of often-sophisticated systems. For example, it is not uncommon for consultancies to have photocopiers that require a job number to be entered for cost allocation of the copies to be made before any copying can take place. The data are collected at the end of each month and each client is accurately billed for copies made on their behalf. Similar computerised telephone systems automatically track and charge calls.

Revenue is also raised through the addition of percentage loadings (this will vary from consultancy to consultancy, but lies somewhere in the vicinity of 10 per cent) to the fees of other professionals, such as photographers, or to costs such as printing or video production. A program or campaign budget for a consultancy needs to reflect all these elements accurately in order for the business to be profitable. Consultancies need to be *income centres*.

Budgets for in-house public relations departments

By contrast, in-house public relations departments are characterised as *expense centres*. They do not need to generate revenue directly for the organisation (Stoner 1978, in Baskin et al. 1997: 142). Profit is made from whatever line of business the organisation is in, such as mining, banking or entertainment. The work of the public relations department supports the organisation in achieving profit, but does not achieve it for and by itself. Even though some organisations expect in-house public relations departments to treat other departments as their 'clients', they are not expected to make a profit from the work they do on behalf of these 'clients'. The public relations department, however, may be expected to justify its yearly budget by 'billing' back to other departments for work carried out on their behalf.

The lack of a profit imperative means that some in-house public relations program or campaign budgets do not include administrative components at all, but simply list the program costs. This can undermine the effectiveness of the budget, as little consideration is given to what human resources are in fact available to do the job. Generally speaking, in-house public relations budgets need to cover the same ground as consultancy budgets, with hours allocated and expenses accounted for, without adding premiums to the actual costs.

Scheduling

Once a comprehensive strategy plan has been written, problems and opportunities defined, goals and objectives set, messages, methods and timing determined, and the budget established, the plan needs to be implemented. And no plan—no matter how carefully researched and prepared—can be implemented effectively without thorough scheduling. As McElreath (1997) points out, the major value of planning is that it helps to allocate organisational resources efficiently by identifying and emphasising appropriate administrative controls. Lists of activities can be prepared which allow detailed staffing arrangements to be made, budgets to be prepared and deadlines to be discussed and established (1997: 244). The planning process also allows the practitioner to select or discard various tactics that may or may not fit into budget or schedule. Without careful planning, it is impossible to ensure that tactics are implemented in the right order and at the right time, which greatly reduces the effectiveness of the campaign.

Many organisations, such as Alcoa Australia, integrate scheduling into their strategy document, which is maintained digitally on the company intranet. Through the use of hyperlinks, Alcoa's public relations personnel can jump straight from reading the section on corporate newsletters to the part of the document that details the scheduling this newsletter requires in order to get it out each month.

Scheduling not only helps to identify a manageable set of activities, it helps to get jobs done on time. In some cases, scheduling consists of a simple list of things to do. In other cases, it is used to establish a timeline or even a project flowchart. These may be found in Case study 7.1 at the end of the chapter.

Lists

Making lists allows the practitioner to pull the public relations process apart and look at it systematically. Lists allow the cataloguing of every step of the public relations process, keeping order and providing organisation and follow-up (Johnston 1999). Lists prevent the possibility of something slipping through the cracks, being forgotten or not being started until it is too late. Though lists are used as an everyday tool by all public relations professionals, they are most useful to the new practitioner in the organisation, as they not only provide an immediate orientation for that person but ensure that existing organisational procedures are followed closely. This assists enormously in maintaining and strengthening organisational culture.

Basic checklists should be prepared (and constantly updated and maintained) for all routine events regularly undertaken by the public relations practitioner. Newsletters, media conferences, special events, product launches—even the procedures for sending out press releases or briefing photographers—should have checklists that detail all the steps required and information necessary to complete the job. Following are two examples of checklists: one is used by Hamilton Island public relations to ensure that all media 'famils' run according to plan; the other is an evaluation checklist designed to supply feedback after an event.

Hamilton Island Media 'famil' checklist

All media famils to Hamilton Island must use this checklist.

Famil name: _____ Host: _____

Arrival date: _____ Departure: _____

- ☐ Complete media evaluation form
- ☐ Book accommodation
- ☐ Book flights/transfers
- ☐ Confirm all details in writing to journalist
- ☐ Ascertain story needs and preferred angles
- ☐ Arrange interviews
- ☐ Book photographer
- ☐ Prepare itinerary
- ☐ Fax itinerary and confirmation letter of arrangements
- ☐ Phone day prior to arrival to confirm details
- ☐ Prepare media kit tailored for the particular journo
- ☐ Check room is ready for arrival
- ☐ Guest expression (relevant gift in room)
- ☐ Pick-up from airport
- ☐ Site inspection
- ☐ Meet to discuss itinerary and story needs
- ☐ Brief interviewees

☐ Brief photographer

☐ Prepare transportation to interviews, do introductions, etc.

☐ Make dinner reservations, child care arrangements, etc.

☐ Host at least one meal during stay (more if solo traveller)

☐ Daily follow-up (informal meeting while here)

☐ Informal meeting day prior to or morning of departure to ensure all story needs are covered and seek feedback on their stay

☐ Complete evaluation form for end of month report inclusion

☐ Welcome home/thank you letter/fax/call after departure

☐ Include clipping, tape or evaluation in relevant monthly report

☐ Send thank you letter to journalist upon publication

☐ Include contact details on database for newsletter mailouts and future information

Events checklist: Evaluation

Please return this section of the form to the Public Relations Branch on completion of the event.

Branch requesting event organisation: _____

PR staff member organising event: _____

Please rate the success of this event:

    Highly successful   ☐

    Moderately successful   ☐

    Unsuccessful   ☐

Please rate your perception of the event organisation:

Very well organised ☐

Reasonably well organised ☐

Needed better organisation ☐

Which areas do you believe needed more attention to detail?

_____

_____

Overall, how would you rate the performance of the PR Branch, and in particular the staff member organising the event:

_____

_____

Name: _____ Signature: _____

Date: _____

Flowcharts

More complex activities can benefit from being placed in a flowchart, so that the practitioner can see at a glance what elements of an activity need to be given priority over others or to be completed first. Such a flowchart can also assist the practitioner should things not flow smoothly, by demonstrating what needs to be done in a variety of circumstances. A good example of a flow chart can be seen in the Alcoa case study at the end of the chapter.

Calendars and Gantt charts

The scheduling process not only allows the practitioner to avoid making mistakes by overlooking material, it also helps to establish timelines and deadlines. These are then commonly 'calendarised'—a process of listing activities to be performed in order of calendar dates and times (deadlines) by which they need to be performed. However, there are sometimes problems in determining exactly what these dates should be, and simple calendarisation does not tell the practitioner what to do if the dates are not met—or what other activities may be affected.

Figure 7.1 Gantt chart

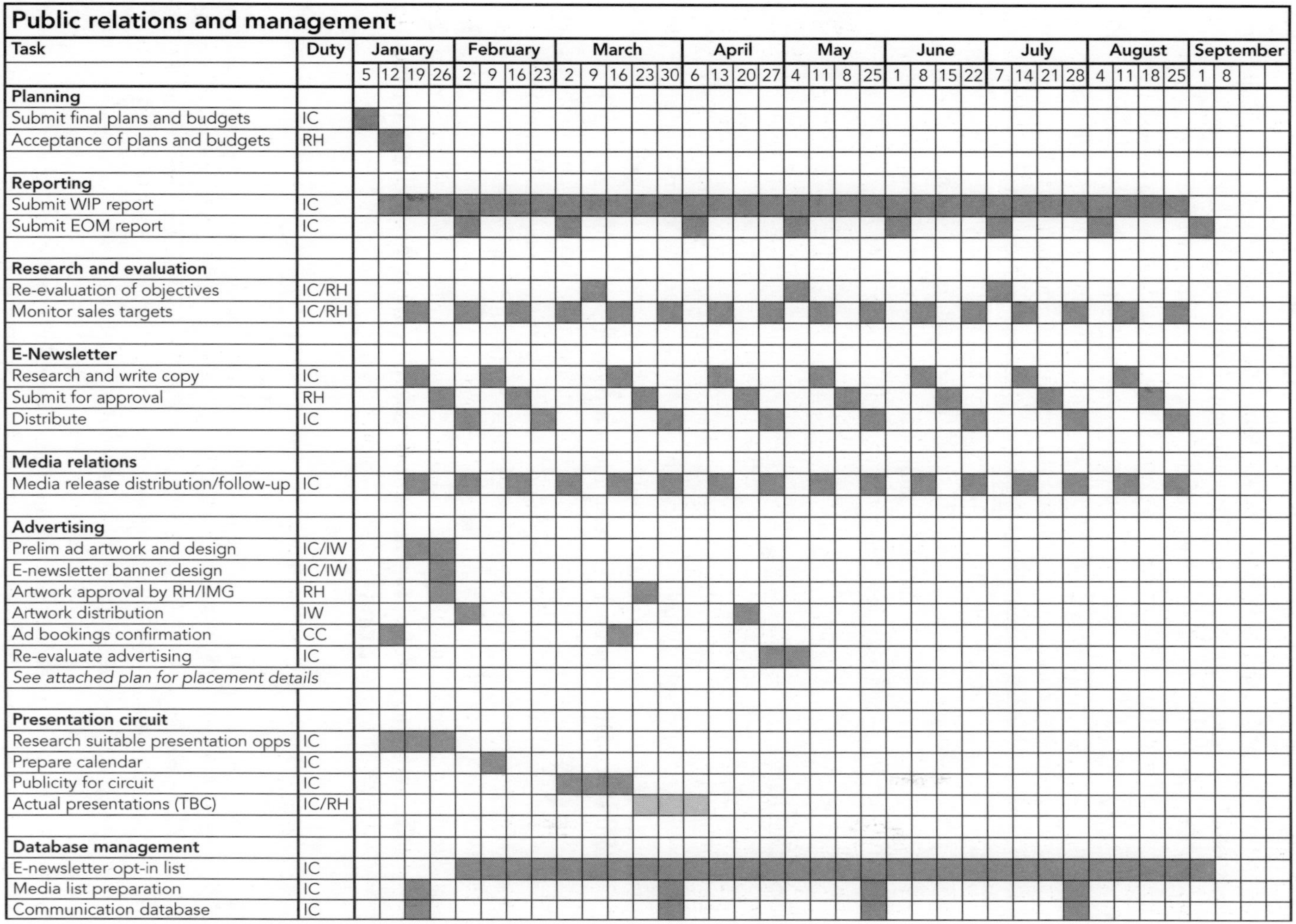

Public relations and management

Task	Duty	January (5 12 19 26)	February (2 9 16 23)	March (2 9 16 23 30)	April (6 13 20 27)	May (4 11 18 25)	June (1 8 15 22)	July (7 14 21 28)	August (4 11 18 25)	September (1 8)
Planning										
Submit final plans and budgets	IC									
Acceptance of plans and budgets	RH									
Reporting										
Submit WIP report	IC									
Submit EOM report	IC									
Research and evaluation										
Re-evaluation of objectives	IC/RH									
Monitor sales targets	IC/RH									
E-Newsletter										
Research and write copy	IC									
Submit for approval	RH									
Distribute	IC									
Media relations										
Media release distribution/follow-up	IC									
Advertising										
Prelim ad artwork and design	IC/IW									
E-newsletter banner design	IC/IW									
Artwork approval by RH/IMG	RH									
Artwork distribution	IW									
Ad bookings confirmation	CC									
Re-evaluate advertising	IC									
See attached plan for placement details										
Presentation circuit										
Research suitable presentation opps	IC									
Prepare calendar	IC									
Publicity for circuit	IC									
Actual presentations (TBC)	IC/RH									
Database management										
E-newsletter opt-in list	IC									
Media list preparation	IC									
Communication database	IC									

A more sophisticated approach is a Gantt chart (McElreath 1997: 248). This requires the practitioner to make a list of things to do (activities), placing them in chronological order. A grid is created by listing the things to do down the left-hand side of the page with the first activity at the top. The bottom of the page is marked across with units of time, which may be hours, days, weeks or even years, depending on the program or campaign being planned for. A line is drawn for each activity, indicating when it will begin and end. This line will allow the practitioner to see exactly not only when each activity should begin and end, but how long it should take. If the activity does not finish on time, the practitioner can see what other activities will be affected. Naturally, many activities will overlap because they are being performed at the same time. This tells practitioners the amount of time and resources needing to be allocated to each activity on what days, allowing them to plan time and resources to devote to each activity (see Figure 7.1).

Conclusion

This chapter has covered a wide-ranging but critical area of public relations practice. The strategic and systematic design of public relations plans is vital to the effective identification, implementation and management of the public relations goals and objectives that complement and support organisational goals and objectives. From the effective framework of a strategic public relations plan, budgets can be firmly established, tactics selected and implementation monitored and evaluated against clearly set and relevant public relations goals and objectives.

Case study 7.1: Newsletter production and distribution work instructions

Public relations will research, write, edit, publish and distribute regular location newsletters. The content will vary to answer the needs of different location management, while the style will conform to agreed overall guidelines. Newsletters will be aimed at providing the general information needs of all Alcoa employees, while specialist newsletters may be published to meet the needs of specific employee groups.

The objectives in publishing internal newsletters are to:

- provide a reliable and authoritative medium that has the acceptance of employees and the confidence of management;

- establish common goals and identity within each location;
- assist in communication and focus attention on location changes and events, workforce changes, safety, productivity and efficiency, and performance achievement.

Flowchart steps

1 *Develop round.* Identify a person within each major location area or workgroup who can be relied on to provide news of events, activities, achievements etc. that could be of interest to the newsletter's audience.

2 *Program time.* Allocate and diarise time on a regular basis to research, interview, write and produce stories and photographs for the newsletter. Give this programmed time a high priority. Do not accept other appointments or tasks in its place unless the time is rescheduled. Strong stories and good production are impossible to achieve if attempted at the last minute. As a general guide, it will take at least a full day of elapsed time to produce a four-page newsletter.

3 *Contact correspondents.* Check each person in the 'round' for each edition. Most correspondents will not volunteer stories on a regular basis, but can discuss what is happening in their departments, from which will come the news lead. The more often they are contacted, the more likely they are to start volunteering story ideas and perhaps undertaking some research and writing. Use the contact process to comment on (recognise) the publication of that correspondent's latest story.

4 *Obtain story leads.* Apart from correspondents, there are many potential sources for stories. Personnel appointments, management meetings, authorised projects, news items from other locations, etc. will all provide leads for stories. Surveys show employees are particularly interested in personal and corporate achievements, in health and safety issues, and in information about new starters. People stories are always more widely read and remembered than impersonal accounts. Newsletter content should include material from the location's social club and provide space for employee classifieds.

5 *Research or interview.* Research may involve contacting external sources, using the company library, developing an understanding of complex processes, or simply verifying material from established data. Good research avoids the need for subsequent corrections to stories. Journalists use six standard questions to cover each story, which are particularly important for interviews:

- Who did it?
- What did they do?
- How did they do it?
- Where did it happen?
- When did it happen?
- Why did they do it?

Always check spellings—specifically the correct spelling of a person's name and their job title. Ask the person themselves—do not rely on secondary sources. During the interview, ask questions that require more than a 'yes' or 'no' answer. Give the interviewee time to relax and feel comfortable about discussing the topic. Many people need to talk about an issue for some time before they get to the bottom line. Some people are nervous about talking 'on the record'. Always offer to check the story back with the interviewee, so that they will feel they retain control over the information. Interview in their office or workplace, so they feel 'at home' (also because often they will need to access a document).

6 *Commission stories.* At times someone else might want or need to write a newsletter story, because they have an important personal message, for example, or because they have technical expertise in the area. The newsletter editor needs to give correspondents help and guidelines about content, style and expression, and should always edit these contributions to ensure their readability. In many cases the stories will need to be subbed back to a suitable length, which will require some diplomacy with the contributor.

7 *Write stories.* The beginning of an article—the 'lead'—is as important as the whole story. The lead acts as a hook, enticing readers to read the rest of the piece. The lead must tell the reader what the story is about. Many people skim publications, and read only the first one or two sentences unless they are involved in the topic.

Newsletter articles follow the same rules as a news story. Follow the pyramid rule, where information in the story is told in order of importance— the most important first and the least important last. The bottom line must be the top line.

Quotations are always important. They keep the reader interested and bring a human aspect to the story. Good quotes add credibility and immediacy to the article.

Short sentences are important. Each paragraph should contain a maximum of two sentences. Try setting an upper limit of 20 words per sentence, and ruthlessly break up longer sentences. As in the preceding sentence, learn to spot connective words such as 'and'.

Alcoa Alumina newsletter flowchart

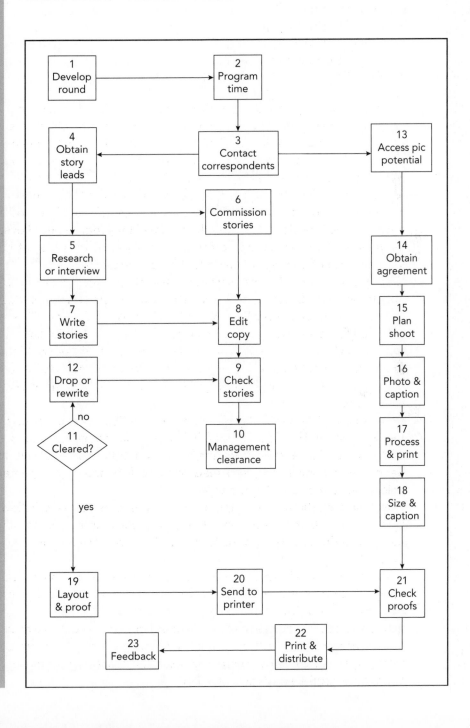

The writing style should be friendly and informal, without being folksy, using easily comprehensible language. Avoid technical words and jargon. Spell out acronyms in the first reference.

8   *Edit copy.* Editing should produce a newsletter within the standard style. This style has been approved by senior management, and the PR group has agreed that proposed style changes will be referred to that group for endorsement. Elements of this style are:

Masthead:	'Location' newsletter (e.g. Pinjarra Newsletter).
Frequency:	Once a month.
Content:	News items will target one or more of the PR enablers. News items will have a specific communication objective. Emphasise safety, quality improvement, environment. Advertising can be included for Alcoa-supported events, non-commercial community groups and non-commercial employee classifieds (except 'work wanted'). Social club notes go as provided by the clubs. Discounts or services to members should be news references only—not advertisements—with no commercial logos. A standard box on the back page will include the address, editor's name and Australian Company Number (ACN). Content must not include production costs, raw production data (some indexed data is OK), political comment, items protected by copyright.
Typeface:	Body copy—12pt Times New Roman. Pic captions—12pt Times New Roman italic. Headings—Times New Roman, covering the copy.
Paragraphs:	No indent, flush left, ragged right.
Colour:	One plus black.
Size:	A4 portrait, minimum 4 pages (numbered), no maximum.

Source: Adapted from Wills-Johnson, Alcoa Alumina Limited (1999).

Case study 7.2: Hostile company takeover bid for Aliquot Asset Management Limited

Brisbane-based investment company Equitilink eLink Limited (EKL), as the second largest shareholder in Western Australian property management company Aliquot Asset Management Limited (AQT), launched a hostile takeover campaign when its board became highly dissatisfied with the way in which directors were operating the public listed entity. The company was running at a substantial loss, with related party transactions to the directors and their associated entities being by far the largest expenditure items. Cash at bank had fallen dramatically from $2.96 million in September 2002 to $1.75 million by December 2002. With a relatively minor 20 per cent stakeholding in the company, Equitilink eLink chairman Paul Crowther launched a campaign to gain sufficient proxies to overthrow the current Board at an Extraordinary General Meeting which was scheduled for 18 February 2003.

The primary strategy behind the campaign was to convey the detailed and complicated information necessary to enable shareholders to make an informed decision while maintaining total control of the message. An external public relations consultancy, with offices in Brisbane and Perth, was retained and briefed to implement the strategy. Issues relating to corporate regulation and legislation would control this implementation. A very close relationship between the legal team and the public relations team was required. The extensive vetting of materials by the legal team meant that responses by the public relations team took longer to formulate.

Strategically, the media would be used both to reinforce the message to shareholders as well as serving to embarrass the directors of Aliquot, who were high-profile members of the Western Australian business community.

Accordingly, tactics chosen were aggressive direct mail (to shareholders) as well as a highly targeted media campaign aimed at the weekly West Australian publication *WA Business News*, the business pages of the *West Australian* and the *Australian Financial Review*. The first direct mail issued was a letter to shareholders detailing the Equitilink eLink directors' concerns, referring to information contained in Aliquot's Annual Report and drawing their attention to matters as they currently stood in contrast to the position reported in the Annual Report. This initial mailout was also forwarded to the media, with interviews provided by Paul Crowther of Equitilink eLink. It took Aliquot two weeks to respond with its own direct mail to shareholders, allowing Equitilink the opportunity to respond once again, providing further information as well as copies of the media coverage to date, which had been highly critical of Aliquot. A third mailout allowed Equitilink to thank those who had already provided their proxies as requested, while allowing a final reminder and call for provision of proxies from those who had not yet done so. The final *coup de grace* for Aliquot was delivered in Trevor Sykes's influential Pierpont column in the *Australian Financial Review* on Friday, 14 February 2003—four days prior to the EGM.

Aliquot's board also defended the loss of $1.2 million last financial year, saying that success did not come overnight and the company had to spend money to make money. It's certainly making some money for Michael and Peter and their associates (the Aliquot board members) . . . The treasurer of the ASA's WA branch, Gerry Pauley, attended last year's annual meeting of Aliquot but could not ask questions about the related-party transactions because Michael closed the meeting. Michael later said he had left early to go to the first day's play in the England–Australia Test at the WACA . . . (if Gerry) has enough proxies, Michael could be watching cricket all summer.

Sykes, Trevor (2003) 'The watchdog just may catch the car', *Australian Financial Review*, Friday, 14 February

The result of the campaign was that a gain of more than 40 per cent of the proxy vote was secured before the EGM. This resulted in an offer just prior to the enactment of the EGM itself that saw all three Equitilink eLink directors appointed to the Aliquot Board and allowing all to provide a framework not only for good corporate governance but the ability to trade successfully into the future.

Discussion and exercises

1   It is said that a public relations strategist is only as good as the CEO will allow them to be. Give examples of how a public relations department or consultancy can quantifiably prove its worth and contribution to the organisation's bottom line.
2   The vision and mission statements are seen as the central building blocks of and focus for the organisation's reason for being. Demonstrate several of the components that must be evidenced in the vision and mission statements to make them workable documents.
3   What is the difference between a financial and an operating budget? Describe the elements of a typical public relations budget.
4   Careful scheduling is vital to the effective management of public relations practitioners' time and resources. Describe a range of scheduling tools discussed in this chapter and discuss how each can be used in a relevant situation.

Further reading

Baskin, O., Aronoff, C. & Lattimore, D. (1997) *Public Relations: The Profession and the Practice*, 4th edn, Brown & Benchmark, Madison.

Brody, E.W. (1988) *Public Relations Programming and Production*, Praeger, New York.

Grunig, J. (ed.) (1992) *Excellence in Public Relations and Communication Management*, Lawrence Erlbaum, New Jersey.

Heath, R.L. (1997) *Strategic Issues Management: Organisations and Public Policy Challenges*, Sage, Thousand Oaks, California.

Mintzberg, H. & Quinn, J.B. (1991) *The Strategy Process: Concepts, Contexts, Cases*, 2nd edn, Prentice Hall, Englewood Cliffs.

Potter, L. (1997) *The Communication Plan: The Heart of Strategic Communication*, IABC Strategic Communicator Series, IABC, San Francisco.

References

Allert, J. (1992) 'A Delphi Study on Chief Executive's Attitudes to Public Relations' Practitioners' Competencies', unpublished survey.

Baskin, O., Aronoff, C. & Lattimore, D. (1997) *Public Relations: The Profession and the Practice*, 4th edn, Brown & Benchmark, Madison.

D'Aprix, R. (1996) *Communicating for Change: Connecting the Workplace with the Marketplace*, Jossey-Bass, San Francisco.

Frombrun, C.J. (1996) *Reputation: Realizing Value from the Corporate Image*, Harvard Business School Press, Boston.

Grunig, J. (ed.) (1992) *Excellence in Public Relations and Communication Management*, Lawrence Erlbaum, New Jersey.

Grunig, L. (1997) 'Excellence in public relations', in C.L. Caywood (ed.), *The Handbook of Strategic Public Relations and Integrated Communications*, McGraw-Hill, New York.

Harrison, K. (1996) 'Developing a public relations strategy', cited in *Public Relations 300* lecture, Curtin University of Technology, Perth.

Johnston, J. (1999) *The Art of Lists*, course material notes, ART 2510, Griffith University, Gold Coast.

McElreath, M.P. (1997) *Managing Strategic and Ethical Public Relations*, 2nd edn, Brown & Benchmark, Madison.

Mintzberg, H. & Quinn, J.B. (1991) *The Strategy Process: Concepts, Contexts, Cases*, 2nd edn, Prentice Hall, Englewood Cliffs.

Potter, L. (1997) *The Communication Plan: The Heart of Strategic Communication*, IABC Strategic Communicator Series, IABC, San Francisco.

—— (1998) 'Strategic communication: dead or in demand as never before?', *Communication World*, special edn, September.

Sinclair, M. (1998) *Change Communication Plan for the Public Affairs Branch of the Ministry of Justice*, Rowland Company, Perth.

Sullivan, S. (1999) *The Hamilton Island Communication Plan*.

Sweet, D. (1998) Public Affairs Manager, AlintaGas, 'Public affairs management', presented at a Curtin University *Public Relations 300* lecture, Perth, August.

Sykes, T. (2003) 'The watchdog just may catch the car', *Australian Financial Review*, 14 February.

White, J. & Mazur, L. (1995) *Strategic Communications Management: Making Public Relations Work*, EIU Addison Wesley, Wokingham.

Wills-Johnson, B. (1999) *Strategic Planning in Public Relations*, Alcoa of Australia, internal document.

8 TACTICS

Marian Hudson

In this chapter

Introduction

Students often use the terms 'strategy' and 'tactics' interchangeably; however, while the two are inextricably linked, it is important to understand the differences and how they fit together. Strategy is the overarching plan that allows a public relations practitioner to help ensure that organisational goals and objectives are achieved. This strategy will determine the campaigns that may be necessary and the choice of tactics can then be made. Every tactic must relate directly back to its defined purpose: achieving the strategic outcome.

A huge range of tactics is available to the public relations professional. They include publicity, newsletters, direct mail, advertising, corporate publications, functions, speaking opportunities, internet sites, information kits, media relations, brochures, competitions, videos, lobbying, meetings, competitions and so on. While many public relations campaigns utilise a range of different tactics, successful public relations does not necessarily require use of multiple tactics. It is also useful to remember that, while most tactics are visible and easily identifiable, many campaigns owe their success to the use of tactics that are not overt—such as keeping *out* of the media spotlight.

As society becomes more complex, so too does the choice of tactics. Where communities were once easily defined, with distinct target audiences receiving information from easily identifiable communication channels, people in modern Western societies suffer information overload, and target groups are blurred and often unreceptive to unsolicited information. The sheer numbers of messages aimed at audiences of all kinds has led to a tendency to turn off, or even react through 'culture jamming'—responding negatively to marketing advertisements through defacing public sites (Klein 2000).

Spurred by a growing distrust of major corporations and other organisations, society no longer accepts information at face value. This trend is often expressed as a move from 'trust me' to 'tell me' to 'show me' to 'include me'. This has manifested in changed consumer and/or target audience behaviour, seen through an increasing propensity of target audiences or individuals to rally together to publicly oppose projects or comment on issues, even taking high-profile public action if they feel aggrieved enough. The fact that the media like to portray stories in the context of conflict, with television current affairs shows or talkback radio hosts choosing to adopt the tone of the 'man in the street' (Alan Jones constantly describes his listeners as being on 'Struggle Street') means that corporations in particular are often positioned immediately as being 'guilty'.

Adding further complexity has been the consolidation of issues of global concern—the environment, security, unemployment, breakdown of family traditions—which are changing the primary factors driving organisational reputation. Where tangibles such as performance, products, services and price were once primary considerations, the emotional drivers that address these global concerns are now emerging as equally or more important. Add to that the internet as a means of immediate worldwide transmission, enabling stories to flash around the world in seconds, and we start to get some idea of the complex environment in which the choice of tactics must be made. Additionally, public relations professionals need to be aware of operating in a world in which high-level regulation, lawsuits, watchdogs and corporate governance influence the choice of tactics, their content and how they are implemented.

Controlled versus uncontrolled communication

Tactics can be broken up into two major groups: controlled and uncontrolled. Controlled tactics are those over which the public relations practitioner maintains control of every aspect of the process—from message creation and crafting to final distribution. Examples of controlled tactics would be advertising, annual reports, brochures, posters, direct mail and advertorial. In all of these cases, the practitioner crafts the message, selects exactly how it will be produced, what visuals may be utilised, and what kinds of colours, typefaces, fonts and papers may be chosen, then determines exactly where and when the information may appear or to whom the printed materials will be distributed.

Conversely, uncontrolled tactics are those that can be altered or even blocked completely. The most obvious uncontrolled tactic is media relations, where the practitioner can provide a media release and train a spokesperson. However, the decision as to whether the material is used at all, in its original or in an altered form, lies solely with a news gatekeeper—a journalist or an editor. Another example of an uncontrolled tactic would be a public meeting, which could be boycotted or hijacked by a vocal minority.

Considering that it is difficult enough at the best of times to ensure the communication of a single strong message, as each audience and individual will interpret it in the context of their own personal experience and views, careful consideration needs to be given to the choice and mix of controlled and uncontrolled tactics. The impact of a piece of editorial through the uncontrolled tactic of media relations may be far higher than that of an advertisement in the same publication, gaining the third-party endorsement of the publication itself. However, the intended message may be diluted or changed completely. It is therefore likely that the practitioner would choose a balance between controlled and uncontrolled tactics to ensure that the desired message is actually communicated. For example, a few years ago, when the Australian federal government introduced its new tax system, which included GST, it generated a lot of media debate that sent mixed messages to the public. The government used a range of controlled tactics such as advertisements and brochures to explain the intricacies of the system.

Methods of delivery

Along with the selection of the most suitable tactic and mix of tactics, the chosen method of delivery of an item of communication to the recipient plays a critical role in determining its impact and effectiveness. While sometimes it is difficult to be flexible because of distance or timing, each of the following options has advantages and disadvantages that should be considered.

- *Mail* in an electronic age is comparatively slow, but it has the advantage of delivering information to a specified recipient, either at home or work, depending on where they will be more receptive to it. While it can be expensive for mass distribution, particularly of larger items, mail does allow for bulkier items such as product samples to be distributed, as long as guaranteed delivery time is not critical. The Australian Taxation Office uses the mail system to distribute information to taxpayers about updates or changes to the taxation system.
- *Faxes* offer instantaneous communication, and are ideal where a short written message needs to be delivered, such as to alert media of an event, confirm a conversation or send maps for directions. Faxes are also useful as they offer a printed record that the information was actually sent. If using faxes to send information, however, it is important to remember they can be lost at the receiving end, or buried in the myriad of other information pouring through the fax machine, particularly at media organisations.
- *News distribution agencies* such as PR-Net send media releases on behalf of organisations to various media outlets in a very similar fashion to the news wire services such as AAP. The material is usually grouped in pre-arranged categories such as metropolitan business press, regional radio or fashion editors to ensure targeted delivery.

- *Email* is instantaneous and good for short sharp messages delivered directly to the addressee. However, with people receiving hundreds of messages continuously it may be considered spam (junk mail) and become an annoyance that is easily deleted. Email has the advantage of being cost effective and it can include text attachments or graphics, such as JPEGs, TIFFs or PDF files, that better illustrate a point. For example, a JPEG or TIFF file can transmit photographs or graphic design while a PDF file is ideal for documents that the sender does not want changed, such as an invoice or a proposal.

- *CD-ROMs* are an easy-to-deliver information package. As they are durable they are less likely to be thrown instantly into the bin than paper-based communication. They can be used for anything from company profiles through to catalogues of products or services and, because they are small, can be distributed economically to a widespread audience.

- *Couriers* lend themselves to situations where larger amounts of information need to be delivered urgently, often to a deadline, to a smaller target audience or when an item is too large to post or fax. Couriers can be used to deliver annual reports simultaneously to media or to send samples or invitations.

- *Videos* are ideal for delivery of information that needs to be visually portrayed in situations where location, time or budget prohibits personal visits. For example, a video can show the calibre of overseas performers at an upcoming festival or the highlights of a travel destination.

- *Video-conferencing* enables remote or off-site audiences to simultaneously and economically participate in events or meetings. Its other increasingly frequent use is to deliver instructions to remote audiences such as city-based medical specialists instructing doctors in remote areas on medical procedures in real time.

- *Personal delivery*, while effective because of its 'human' nature, is often restricted by cost, time and the availability of key people. However, it is critical where relationships need to be built, where feedback is required—such as in pitching for new business—or where the credibility of individuals is required, such as the CEO at a shareholders' meeting.

- *Websites* enable copious amounts of information to be dispersed globally, including vision, text and audio. They are ideal where information is dynamic, such as stock prices, or where an audience chooses to access information at times convenient to them. Banks often use websites to provide financial information and banking services, and the Department of Foreign Affairs and Trade uses a website to provide information on travel destinations.

New technology and message delivery

Newer technologies have huge advantages in message delivery. The internet is an extremely effective tool when the subject-matter is of high interest to an audience which will actively seek out information at a time when you want to communicate it. This has the added advantage of encouraging users to explore other parts of an organisation's website, achieving greater exposure to an organisation's broader activities. It can also provide instant access, at a time convenient to the user, to information on organisations, their activities, philosophies and products and services.

In other cases, the internet is best used in tandem with other communication vehicles to provide further, or more detailed, information on a topic after other, more directly targeted, vehicles reach an audience. For example, an advertisement may provide scant information on a particular community initiative, with the website providing more in-depth details, site maps, 3D visuals, contact details, Q&As, chat rooms, feedback forms and so on. In this case, the website may even develop rapport with a target audience, allowing vital feedback and data to be collected (the latter taking privacy laws into account).

Paradoxically, the internet also can be a public relations practitioner's ultimate nightmare, as it is now often used by adversaries to spread their negative messages far and wide instantly. Unfortunately, these often damaging and even misleading messages sometimes have more appeal than those being portrayed by the public relations professional. Further, their sources are often hard to trace and there is little that can be done to control or balance them, or to remove them from the internet.

One of the greatest mistakes on websites has been the tendency to post information that is not tailored to the medium, such as 'brochure ware'. The internet requires short, sharp information that is user friendly, interactive and engaging. Ultimately, the web is a 'live' tool with the most successful sites being dynamic and evolving almost daily to suit the needs of their target audiences.

Perhaps the greatest technological advances benefiting the public relations profession have come with the development of technology that drives a range of existing tactics. For example, printing technology now reduces expense and time, while PDFs mean that information placed on the website cannot be altered and that graphic designers can send concepts electronically.

Tactic selection

While it is clear that the range of tactics is only limited by the practitioner's imagination and the limitations of the strategic direction of the campaign, it is useful to discuss some of the more commonly used tactics in greater detail. Many of the following tactics are discussed further in other chapters.

Research

Research is sometimes best known as a tool for forming and evaluating campaigns, but it can also be used extremely effectively as a tactic in its own right. For example, the Reserve Bank of Australia issues an annual survey of bank fee income, which can generate a frenzy of bank bashing. However, to defuse the situation, the Australian Bankers' Association commissions its own study through PriceWaterhouseCoopers (PWC) to demonstrate the gains that consumers may have made, regardless of the amount they may have paid in fees. In the April 2003 study, PWC was able to demonstrate that retail banking customers paid $17.9 billion less per annum through lower interest rates in 2002 than they did a decade earlier. This, when offset against the fees income to banks of $7.8 billion, meant that consumers were $10 billion better off (Bartholomeusz 2003).

Media relations

Media relations is a complex tactic which requires careful consideration. Outcomes cannot be controlled or guaranteed, as the agenda of the media outlet will always be paramount. If the news generated by the public relations practitioner is of high interest—either because it is controversial or popular—the media can provide an ideal and cost-effective vehicle to rapidly reach a mass audience. However, if the message is of minimal interest, trying to attract coverage may be counter-productive, and may even damage the reputation of the practitioner with the media. The key considerations in choosing the media as a tactic include the following:

- If guaranteed delivery of a message, its timing and control of content are critical, the media may be a poor choice, as they are under no obligation to report any news.
- If a media statement has the potential to turn negative, through the media seeking comment from adversaries, this may change the whole focus of the story and end up being detrimental to the public relations campaign.
- If the story is not particularly newsworthy, it may fail to get placement as it must compete against literally hundreds or thousands of other stories. This is

particularly pertinent when other issues such as world events or election campaigns are dominating the news. Gimmicks or stunts may increase a story's appeal, but on a busy news day even the most elaborate event will not gain coverage over more newsworthy items.

- Complex messages are not well conveyed through the media. Newspaper or magazine articles and current affairs shows are the only vehicles which may offer the space necessary to convey the detail of an issue. With their extremely short story times and even shorter 'grabs', television and radio news programs offer only the most superficial coverage of an issue or event. Further, a practitioner trying to leverage television news could easily have their message upstaged by an outrageous act that is highly televisual—such as a pie in the face.
- Media releases are an invitation for further comment by the organisation. Without an adept spokesperson, attempts to gain publicity can backfire badly. Before approaching the media, the spokesperson may require training or, at minimum, rigorous briefing, to stand up to the pressure and stick to key messages.
- Does the organisation have the ability to provide adequate responses to any negatives associated with news to gain the upper hand and avoid keeping the story going for several more days if necessary?

Printed materials: brochures, leaflets and flyers

Brochures, leaflets, flyers and other printed materials are some of the most commonly used tactics. They serve an important purpose in a broad range of campaigns, often employed in tandem with other tactics, particularly where detail, persuasion or a lasting reference document is required. However, in an era when mail boxes and in-trays are overflowing, their effectiveness relies on skilful execution of all aspects of their production from the graphic design and quality of paper through to content tailored to compel a target audience to actually pick them up and read them. There are many considerations in selecting the correct printed material, based on the suitability of the message to the medium.

Paper sizes

- DL publications are standard envelope size (attained by folding a standard A4 sheet of paper into thirds) and are ideal when postage or cost considerations are paramount. A DL publication can consist of larger paper sizes folded down to

DL size, such as A4 folded twice to give six pages or it can be a two-sided single page leaflet.

- A5 publications are larger (attained by folding a standard A4 sheet of paper in half), allowing for multiple pages in booklet form. However, A5 is a less conventional size for publications and will require special matching envelopes if they are to be posted.
- A4 publications are commonly used when a larger amount of information is required, particularly when a page needs to be large enough to include illustrations or photos with accompanying text.
- A3 publications (sheets twice the size of a standard A4 sheet of paper) are less common and are usually used for posters or if large-scale information, such as a detailed map, needs to fit on a single page.

Publications are often displayed in special stands and care needs to be taken that they fit the stand size.

Colours and embossing

- Single-colour publications are much cheaper than multiple colours and may be suitable when the publication is small, when the message can be conveyed without eye-catching colourful visuals or if it has a short shelf-life. A good example of this would be a site map for a trade show or to indicate walking tracks in a recreation area.
- Two-colour publications are a cost-effective option between three- and four- or single-colour documents. They are more visually appealing, have more impact and allow greater flexibility than single-colour publications. In some cases, their conservatism is also a bonus. For example, used by a not-for-profit organisation, they would demonstrate restraint in costs.
- Three-, four- and five-colour publications allow the greatest flexibility and, when photographs or a high degree of visual impact or prestige are required, they are ideal. For example, real estate brochures for prestige properties or car brochures are usually at least four colours.
- Embossing and gold or silver foiling can add a degree of status, but will significantly increase the cost of publication.

Paper stock

There are many paper stocks from which to choose, ranging from matt to semi-gloss and gloss stocks, and their selection impacts significantly on price. They should be chosen to match the message being portrayed. For example, unbleached stocks demonstrate care for the environment whereas gloss stocks are suitable for high-end documents such as sophisticated fashion brochures.

Stocks can also be coated or uncoated. Coated stocks can be matt, satin or gloss finished and should be used when photographs are to be included as uncoated stocks will always have a matt appearance and they soak up ink, making photographs dull and lifeless.

There are also speciality stocks such as translucent and textured paper, as well as a range of colours that add interest.

Binding

The choice of binding depends on the size and use of a document. Saddle stitching, which staples the document in the fold or 'gutter', can be used for larger documents, generally up to about 48 pages. However, publications over this size are usually too bulky for this method. They need to be *burst bound* or *perfect bound* where sections are glued into a spine in a magazine-style. However, if the document is likely to be used frequently, there is a risk with this method that the pages will fall out over time. In this case, *wiro binding*, where the pages are hole-punched and bound with wire, is ideal. Wiro binding can also be used for small documents and it has the advantage of allowing flexibility as the document will lie flat when it is opened and pages can be turned back on themselves. It is often used for workbook-style publications.

Common to all publications is matching the suitability of the message to the medium, along with its style:

- The amount of detail or information required, along with the number of photographs or illustrations, will dictate the size of a publication.
- A small budget will restrict a publication in terms of size, colours and photographs, as all these elements increase cost.
- The method of delivery also needs to be taken into account. If it is to be posted to hundreds of people, this starts to become a significant cost as opposed to a publication that will be part of an information pack or be distributed at a function.
- Production time for publications ranges from two to three weeks for a simple one-colour DL brochure to up to six weeks or more for a high-quality, multi-coloured publication, particularly if photographs are included.
- Desktop publishing is quick and cheap, but it is probably not suitable if high quality is desirable.

- Serious messages usually dictate a formal and serious style of writing and presentation, whereas communication for more community-based purposes can be more relaxed or even comical. Straight text is suitable where the publication's purpose is to communicate a simple message or extensive information, while a question and answer format is more suited in communicating a complex message that raises multiple questions, such as the introduction of a new tax or health system.
- Words that attract the attention of the target audience can give a lasting impression.
- Devices such as fridge magnets or CD-ROMs add extra appeal and can increase the life of a message. For example, many service industries such as plumbers use magnets to encourage retention of their telephone number in a handy place.

Many printed materials are produced in consultation with professional graphic designers and printers. There is often an advantage in appointing a graphic design firm to oversee printing, as they have the required expertise in print production. However, it may entail an additional charge. Graphic designers and printers should be selected on the basis of the style of work they do and their capabilities. It is usually advisable to obtain three quotes to compare costs. Quotes should include some flexibility for corrections and other contingencies such as the use of additional photographs or multiple copy changes.

A brief should include:

- the document's purpose;
- the target audience;
- the quantity to be printed (it is useful to get comparisons in costs for different quantities, such as 500, 1000 and 2000, as there is often little difference in price over a certain print run);
- the desired image including the type of design;
- the number and type of visual images;
- the expected number of pages (dictated by the amount of text and number of images);
- the paper stock;
- the number of colours to be used;
- the preferred size (e.g. DL, A4);
- special considerations, such as use of company colours, logo, stock which can be used by machines to insert it into other documents, compliance with Australia Post mailing requirements;
- the required delivery date.

Initially the designers and/or printers will provide a quote that can sometimes be revised to suit a budget through changing the number of colours or photographs or paper stock. Following approval of the quote, a production timetable should be drawn up, allowing additional time prior to the deadline as invariably there are delays with copy checking or sourcing material. Following this, there will be numerous stages to approve initial design concepts, layout, photographs, printing proofs, and so on. Importantly, prior to printing, the document should be thoroughly proofread, carefully checking spelling, names, titles of photographs, dates, phone numbers, websites and other addresses. Not only do mistakes look unprofessional, they can be extremely costly to correct at a late stage.

Annual reports

Annual reports record the highlights and challenges experienced by an organisation, including financial details, for the financial year (usually from 1 July to 30 June). These are legally required of public companies and some other organisations. They usually comprise two sections: the editorial or 'marketing' copy at the front; and the financial and statutory obligations in a section at the back. Sometimes, organisations produce these sections separately to save money, as not all recipients want or need both sections. While some organisations choose to meet their legal or statutory obligations with a basic photocopied document, the annual report is often the organisation's most critical communication vehicle, as it provides an in-depth overview of how the organisation is developing. It will also be current for at least a year and often forms the basis of other corporate activity such as financial and business relations, marketing and general corporate information. In the case of public companies, the annual report—along with any half-yearly report—is probably considered the most credible communication tool, as it is legally required to meet certain reporting criteria, including audited financial figures.

The role of the public relations practitioner in annual report production varies greatly. Some may serve a design and editing role, while others may produce it from the ground up, deciding on the graphics, content and central theme. The manner in which information is presented is also diverse. Some organisations report against their corporate key result areas (KRAs) and key performance indicators (KPIs), as well as their strategic direction. Some companies also report along divisional or operational lines. It is now also common to place an abridged version of the annual report on a company website or CD-ROM. Some companies also produce a smaller version for internal communication. Whatever the approach, it is vital that it is produced professionally, with strict attention to detail. Public relations practitioners should work in concert with relevant experts such as lawyers, the Company Secretary or Chief Financial Officer to ensure all legal and statutory reporting requirements are met.

For practitioners who need to confirm or clarify the specific terminologies of the finance sector, it can be useful to consult a financial reference such as that found at <http://au.docs.yahoo.com/finance/glossary/>.

Australia Post uses its annual report as an information tool to advise the community and business customers of its activities and results, as well as treating it as a marketing and branding tool targeting its business customers. The report also meets Australia Post's accountability objectives, outlining its performance to its shareholder (the federal government) as well as the reporting requirements of the Australian Postal Corporation Act. To do this, it produces three annual reports: an A4 full-colour report which is also the basis of an online report; a B5 black-and-white report which meets Parliamentary tabling requirements; and an employee report for all Australia Post employees. The 2001/02 full-colour report demonstrates Australia Post's focus on customers by providing real-life examples of products, services, relationships and partnerships with the content and design built around the theme 'Taking it Further'. The design and colours reflect the contemporary nature of the organisation's new services with the addition of silver metallic throughout reflecting change and technology. It uses different paper stock, style and colours to separate the editorial section at the front from the financial and statutory reporting sections at the back.

The staff annual report was produced as a special edition of *Post Journal*, the monthly magazine sent to the homes of Australia Post staff, but it retained some of the overall feel of the larger report through similar design elements and case studies. As the majority of staff are mail officers, posties and retail counter staff, it was more informal and tailored specifically to them in style and language. It aimed to communicate the organisation's achievements and results, promote staff ownership of, and involvement in, the results, and to provide a sense of forward direction through provision of information on Australia Post's strategy (Australia Post 2001/02).

Newsletters

Newsletters have many similarities to other printed materials. Their major difference is that they are ongoing communication, usually aimed at building long-term rapport with a target audience. This includes their ability to facilitate two-way communication through competitions, feedback or opinion polls, which can also provide valuable information on the profile and needs of recipients. One of the major critical success factors is their ability to engage their audience, as they are competing against a myriad of other messages. The basic considerations for all printed material (outlined above) should be taken into account in newsletter production, with particular emphasis on the style of writing. Conversational style newsletters with a heavy emphasis on topics that address recipients' primary needs tend to be the most widely and thoroughly read. For example, newsletters initiated by health insurance funds typically cover health-related topics, while they subtly weave in the advantages of the particular fund being promoted.

Newsletters can be categorised into two types: vertical and horizontal (Bivins 1995). A vertical newsletter is usually distributed *within* an organisation, from the floor staff to the senior executives. As the name implies, it is aimed at all levels of staff. This type of newsletter is often used as an organisational tool, to inform staff about what is going on within the organisation. They are especially useful in an organisation that is geographically diverse, such as Australia Post, which has staff all over the country. Horizontal publications are aimed at a readership with a more narrowly defined common interest, often with technical knowledge or a special interest connecting them. Such audiences would range from plumbers to dairy farmers and localised community action groups.

Inclusion of a column from the CEO, Chairman or key figure can provide a direct line of communication from/with that person. However, it is critical that the message content is in line with the rest of the newsletter and is not 'top-down' communication. Most newsletters will have a name (usually tying into a theme or organisational name) and a masthead which will include the date and issue number. Other items may include a table of contents, a range of newsy articles, a calendar of forthcoming events, announcements and sometimes external advertising, if the newsletter needs to be self-funding.

Direct mail

Direct mail differs from brochures, leaflets and flyers as it is directed at a specific targeted audience and demographic group, such as a geographic area, income bracket, or those with particular hobbies or education level. It is usually personally addressed and is effective when more personalised communication is required, such as soliciting donations, selling products or promoting candidates during election campaigns. In some instances it is used to generate a direct response, while in others it can be used to create awareness to support a broader campaign. The response rate depends on numerous factors, from the nature of the offer or information to the accuracy of the mailing list. Generally, a campaign will generate a 2–5 per cent response rate unless it is directed to an audience already familiar with the offer—this could increase it to between 5 and 10 per cent (Horoowitz 2003). A direct mail campaign can consist of a single letter or a series of letters, the latter often used for high-quality prospects. A key success factor is the integrity of the mailing list that can either be generated in-house from customer or community data or purchased. Purchased or rented lists should be guaranteed at least 95 per cent accurate.

However, federal Privacy Act amendments passed in 2000 now regulate how personal data can be obtained and used, so it has also become more difficult to obtain and use targeted mailing lists. Practitioners need to be up to date with legal restrictions or be prepared to seek legal advice when using such lists, with specific care taken in areas such as collection of data, disclosure, data security and sensitive information. The range of material covered by this amendment is far-reaching. Details may be found at <www.privacy.gov.au/act/privacyact/index.html>.

Successful direct mail relies on:

- grabbing the reader's attention through design or a clever message that can include a 'teaser' on the envelope such as 'your chance to win a car' or 'discount card enclosed'. Postcards can be extremely effective as are 'handwritten' personal messages, as they stand out from regular mail;
- gaining the reader's interest through a short, sharp compelling first sentence that can come before the salutation. This should be coupled with other tactics that involve the reader, such as a survey, information of high personal interest, or inclusion of a gimmick like a puzzle or free brochure offer. The use of a typeface that looks like the letter was personally typed is also more attractive, along with a legible handwritten signature. A powerful neatly handwritten PS is also effective;
- ensuring the message or offer is clear including any price, terms, conditions and the action readers are required to take, such as calling a number or subscribing to a service. Layout is a critical part of this and direct mail should be a single page with copy on one side only, which should be folded with the copy side out. It should also be laid out so that it is easy to read through indented short first sentences of short paragraphs that vary in length, ragged right-side margins, underlining or bolding of key words and lots of white space;
- repeating the offer, guarantees, etc. throughout the direct mail piece;

- compelling people to take action through emotive words or powerful images, a free demonstration, once only opportunity, discount, etc. This includes removing any doubts about the legitimacy of the offer by including warranties, money-back or other guarantees and service charters; and
- ensuring a response is made easy, through the provision of a reply paid envelope, free-call 24-hour telephone number, fax-back response, email address, collection of samples for testing, and so on.

While there might appear to be no reduction in direct mail to the average household, one study undertaken by a Sydney postgraduate student (Johnson 1998) has indicated that this form of communication, as used by the not-for-profit sector in particular, has lost ground to the internet: 'Where once telephone, direct mail, radio or even television may have been used to communicate to current or prospective donors, the Internet may now offer a more effective medium to retain or attract donors, volunteers and corporate supporters.'

Design and production: bringing it all together

Best-practice communication relies on consistency, and this needs to extend beyond key messages to design and production, as it too sends impressions—particularly relating to the professionalism of an organisation. This applies to uniformity in all documents produced by an organisation—internal and external. However, it does not mean that the basis of a central design cannot be varied for specific purposes, such as differentiating product brochures from corporate brochures. Ultimately, all communication vehicles should be able to be placed beside each other and look like a 'family', while any variations adapted for different purposes should at least look like 'cousins' to the central family.

To maintain the consistency of documents:

- *Colours* selected should be of the same shade across all documents. While some degree of variation may occur because of different paper stocks (gloss versus matt) and the type of colour being used, the public relations practitioner needs to liaise with the graphic designer and/or printer to specify what variation is acceptable. Further, the application of colours needs to be constant—for example, all headings and dot points may be green while body text is always black.
- *Typeface* and *size* should be consistent across all publications, including specifications for headlines, headings, sub-headings and text. For example, all

headings may be 14 point Helvetica and bold, sub-headings 12 point Helvetica and bold with body text being 11 point Arial. If this is not possible because space is limited, then at least the relationship between headings, sub-headings, etc. should be consistent.

- *Dot points* need to be of a consistent style across all documents—for example, either round or square.
- *Layouts* for all documents should generally be uniform. This includes the number of columns, alignment of paragraphs and text (e.g. as flush left or centred) and where and whether typeface is reversed. A decision needs to be made about whether bold or underlining is to be used, how illustrations or gimmicks are incorporated and where regular columns or sections sit.
- *Photographs* can be framed or unframed and the quality of shots, the perspective of them (close up or distant), backgrounds, captions and so on must be consistent.
- The *style of writing* and overall *graphic design layout* should be dictated by the target audience, with a casual style more suited to an audience that needs to be communicated with in open, friendly terms. Conversely, a corporate audience will require a more formal style of text and design. A first-person form of address is generally more friendly and suitable where a close rapport with the target audience is desired, whereas third-person communication tends to be more formal and is often applied to business applications.
- *Grammar* needs to be consistent, with a decision made on whether colons or semi-colons, etc. are used and whether US or English spelling will be adopted.
- *Icons* and *graphic design features* can be great detractors from otherwise professional productions unless they are developed specifically for the particular production so they are relevant and 'match' other elements.

It is advisable for public relations practitioners to undertake regular audits of all communication vehicles to assess any aberrations and corrective action that needs to be taken. This is done by taking a sample of all communication vehicles and comparing their content from language to design and application of logos or slogans. It is also often astute to use the same graphic designer, or at least a limited number, for all design work to maintain consistency of style.

Branding and consistency

These days, branding is acknowledged as a very specific skill, often developed by experts in the field; however, the need for image consistency also extends to the public relations process. Public relations cannot work in isolation from the brand. Strategies, campaigns and tactics must all align to ensure that brand integrity and positioning are maintained.

A brand defines how a company wants to be perceived, as communicated through a range of public and internal activities such as its slogan, logo, communication style, company behaviour, culture, products or service pricing. For example, two companies selling insurance may position themselves totally differently through their brand and slogan—one as 'affordable' and the other as 'flexible'.

Slogans are essentially a written positioning statement, usually adding more depth or description to a logo, or used as part of a distinct campaign or intended image by an organisation.

Company behaviour, products/services and actions, including selection of tactics, must then be consistent with the image being portrayed by a brand and/or a slogan. If a brand depicts a company as being funky and new age, then communication vehicles must also portray this same image so that marketing and public affairs campaigns are entirely complementary.

Obviously, organisations aim for immediate recognition of their logo and/or slogan by their primary audiences. This is undeniably the case with the 'Golden Arches' of McDonald's fast food outlets. So effective has this logo become that, according to one source, the big 'M' is now more widely recognised worldwide than the Christian Cross ('McLibel' 2000). In Australia, many 'home-grown' organisations are also recognisable by their logos. Some include the Wool Corporation's Woolmark, Billabong surfwear's parallel waves, the ABC's infinity symbol and the Qantas flying kangaroo.

A decision to re-brand an organisation may occur when a market position is desired. This will then mean simultaneously changing all organisational material including letterhead, business cards, signage and website to align with the new brand strategy.

Videos, DVDs and CD-ROMs

With the evolution of other multimedia applications such as the web and email, corporate videos are no longer the sole solution for all communication requiring 3D or animated visuals. Fundamental to their success is their use in situations where visuals will give the message extra impact, or where it requires movement, sound or a multi-dimensional approach. This includes showing a production line process, graphs, comparative data or an organisation's 'personality'. For example, a corporate video (also produced in DVD format) can be used as a supporting tool to outline a company's services or operations, its corporate direction or to graphically demonstrate a company's improved financial position during a shareholders' meeting. Corporate videos can also be used to provide detailed instructions for a new appliance, to show how to administer first aid or to educate an audience on the visible signs of a health problem such as skin cancer. Qantas uses a video to demonstrate its safety procedures on board aircraft; Krupps provides a video on the use of its espresso coffee machines; and Fisher & Paykel offers the same service with its whitegoods.

Videos are also useful where a more personal message needs to be delivered to multiple sites, or when personal visits are neither cost effective nor practical. For example, a CEO may want or need to deliver a message simultaneously to staff in geographically spread offices. Videos are also useful to convey the beauty or excitement of a location. One created to attract delegates to the World Energy Congress in Sydney in 2004 used images of Sydney, the Australian lifestyle, energy infrastructure, nightlife, food and shopping. As its target audience was international, the video had no voice-over but relied on images, music and a few captions to break through language barriers. Other applications for videos include showing tourist destinations or the lifestyle benefits of certain products, such as cars or gym equipment.

Corporate videos must be professionally produced to ensure their quality and credibility. This includes the use of expert talent or presenters, camera operators, sound recordists and editors. Further, care needs to be taken that planned images or messages won't be outdated within months, as shooting and editing in new vision and sound can be expensive.

A tool that utilises similar techniques to video is the CD-ROM, which also can be expensive to make but, given the base technology, is relatively cheap to update, reproduce and disseminate. However, they rely on the target audience having the right computer technology on which to play the CD, and can lose impact through being played on computer screens with relatively poor sound systems. Often, CD-ROMs are viewed in an office environment; however they have also found a niche in the home. For example, house paint companies sometimes produce CD-ROMs to show available colour ranges and how they would look when applied to a style of houses. Three-dimensional presentations created in programs such as ArchiCad and CADD are now being used frequently, and are particularly useful when demonstrating what a particular concept—such as a proposed development—will look like from multiple perspectives. The important thing is to ensure compatible computer systems between the CD-ROM provider and the audience.

Photography

Photographs are extremely effective, as they are a visual medium. Essentially, they are viewed as a tactic that 'doesn't lie', though there is an enormous amount of debate over the proper and improper use of digitally altered photographs in the news media.

In many cases, the subject and location of the photograph required, along with budgetary considerations, will dictate its source. The most important consider-ations are quality and consistency with the image of the project. Often existing photographs may be out of date or taken in a style which detracts from an other-wise high-quality product. For example, in a corporate profile, headshots of executives that are inconsistent in style, background, lighting or scale may contradict the image being portrayed by the text and design.

The advantage of taking new photographs is that they can be tailored to suit the application and other existing material. However, it is vital to source a photographer with a solid track record in the relevant type of work, such as fash-ion, industrial, food or corporate projects, and brief them thoroughly on matters such as:

- *end use* of photographs (e.g. annual report or display). This will largely dictate the format to be used (see below);
- *format* (digital, transparencies, prints, large format, etc.). Generally digital photographs are more limited than transparencies in their use, as they may not retain their quality if they are required to be used on a larger scale than the original specifications—for example, for a poster or display. This means the photog-rapher must be advised of the largest size required for the photograph's end use. Transparencies in medium and large format are generally more flexible and are suitable for anything from a postage stamp size application to a billboard. Both formats can be manipulated to remove undesirable elements such as com-mercial signs or to enhance features;
- dimensions of the final use (e.g. a horizontal image 50cm x 20cm). For example, vertical shots for a PowerPoint presentation are unsuitable as there would be a lot of white background;
- style (e.g. formal, casual);
- black and white, colour, sepia, and so on;
- props such as products or the use of talent (models or other people). If talent is used, they should sign a talent release form, assigning you (or the photographer) the rights to use their image in the desired applications;

- whether makeup, wardrobe or other experts need to attend; and
- location, including travel required (which can impact on budget). Sometimes a photographer will visit the location of the shoot prior to the project to produce a shot list including potential angles, lighting, ideal times of day and props required. It is a good idea to attend this.

Commercial photographers hold copyright on their photographs. The practitioner needs to consider and negotiate the duration of use of the photographs, the applications covered by the permissions agreement and any other special conditions.

After the shoot, the photographer will provide either transparencies, an electronic file of the photographs via a JPEG, TIFF, or other format file, or the electronic (digital) images burned onto a CD-ROM. TIFFs are preferred for quality printing, as they are uncompressed, high-resolution files. JPEGs are a compressed file which can be transferred quickly via modem to any part of the world. They are widely used in all web and PowerPoint presentations, but don't have the resolution to be utilised in printing—the images will appear pixellated or grainy.

Photographic libraries offer a wide variety of shots on different subjects and their prices vary depending on a range of factors. These include the number of copies in which the photograph will be used, the nature of the use such as extensive advertising versus a foyer display or domestic versus international, along with any ongoing expenses for talent and so on. Libraries are an excellent source of photographs when a generic shot is required or if the nature of the photograph means it is either too expensive or too difficult to take. On the other hand, it may be difficult to source material that is consistent with the desired style and the organisation's image. They can also be used by anyone, including your competitors, which could be embarrassing—particularly if they are placed in the same publication. Further, there is a risk that a photograph sourced interstate or internationally may depict practices, buildings, flora or fauna that, to a well-informed audience, are obviously not local, drawing criticism and reducing the credibility of the message. Other photographs may be too staged or outdated. Organisations that require the ongoing use of photographs often have their own library, which can be a worthwhile investment over time.

Speeches

Writing compelling speeches is a real skill, relying on interesting content and the speaking talents of the presenter to command the attention of an audience.

Speeches can be used to communicate to a large audience, at formal functions such as the opening of premises, to make announcements or statements, or to impart knowledge on a particular topic. Politicians are generally the masters of giving speeches and have often become very polished in their content and delivery from years of practice.

Good speeches are short and to the point. They take into account the audience's level of knowledge, receptiveness to the content of the speech and expectations. Importantly, in trying to relay a message, it is vital to tap into factors that motivate, or are relevant to, the audience. Humanising speeches and/or making them entertaining, if this is consistent with the presenter's style, will also make them more impacting. Like all effective communication, it is imperative to establish key messages, attract the audience's attention and then tell them what you are going to say—then tell them again! As Humes puts it:

> Think back to school days. Remember when the instructor marked in the margin on your report 'redundant' when you were repetitious. Well, if being repetitious is a *vice* in an article, it is a *device* in a speech. (1991: 29)

Messages should be supported with facts, figures, case studies, examples and evidence, dispelling any issues or concerns throughout. Creating word pictures, and using specifics rather than generalisations, will help to keep your audience's attention. Good speeches should always conclude on a strong point, as this is what the audience will hear last and hence remember.

Speeches must be written to suit the style and competence of the speaker. Some people are natural presenters and require only dot points which they can embellish; others read speeches, so they need to be written in a conversational manner. If the speaker is a formal type of person, they will need a speech which is conservative and prescribed. However, if they are casual and relaxed, then the speech should be written in that same style, using language that is not too formal. In some instances, the subject will also dictate the style: a serious subject such as a government minister announcing new safety legislation will require a sombre approach, while a sports icon announcing a fundraising campaign for breast cancer will require a more empathetic and warm approach.

Writing for the spoken word is markedly different to writing for an audience of readers, and it is a good idea to read the speech out loud to ensure the nuances and tone reflect the speech's intention and that it runs to the exact allocated time. Humes (1991) points out that speeches should be clear and defined: 'That is why a talk should have more the bold lines of a cartoon caricature drawing than the detail of a photograph.' (1991: 29)

Presentation training—or at least several rehearsals—is also a good idea, particularly as speeches are now often videoed or videoconferenced. While the content can be first rate, poor delivery is often the reason speeches fail to grab the audience's attention.

Prior to the commitment of Australian forces to join America and Britain in the war against Iraq in March 2003, Australian Prime Minister John Howard sombrely addressed the nation, sending three key messages that highlighted the need for security. First, he described the threats Australia faced if no action was taken, using the terrorist attack on Bali as an example. Second, facing criticism because of Australia's alignment with the United States, he outlined why the relationship was critical to Australia's future security and that it was legal. Finally, he made the point that the war was not against Islam, but against 'a dictatorship of a particularly horrific kind'.

Presentations

Presentations allow for multiple communication tactics to be used through the incorporation of visual and other props that add impact to the key messages. They are used where a concept or idea needs to be actively demonstrated (usually visually) or to impart knowledge (for instance, at conferences). Organisations also use them to present financial or operational reports, to support sales pitches, to address community meetings or to sell the advantages of a service or product. They are, however, limited in scope as the audience must be close enough to the presenter or a screen to see the content.

The principles used in speechwriting also apply to presentations but, while the use of visual aids such as PowerPoint displays or videos can make a presentation more compelling, sometimes technical issues thwart their use and a back-up presentation of overhead transparencies is good forward planning. It is essential to keep visuals clean, and to include succinct summaries of the presentation content, making sure they are legible to an audience that may be many metres from the screen. Be wary of clip art or sound effects that are now outdated and overused. Organisations that do a lot of presentations are now choosing to develop their own tailor-made icons.

Using celebrities and spokespeople

The use of celebrities and spokespeople can have enormous benefits. Celebrities can bring great value through their high public profile, which can often cut through communication noise and command immediate attention. Their status also offers implied endorsement of a message so they are often used to spearhead social campaigns such as medical research or to endorse products from alcohol to cars.

Pharmaceutical company AstraZeneca has used a variety of celebrities to draw attention to significant community health issues, as part of its social responsibility charter. In 2003 the company embarked on a program to highlight the importance of effective cholesterol management using high profile golfers. This campaign, dubbed 'Break Par, Beat Cholesterol', featured golfers Craig Parry, Peter O'Malley, Stephen Leaney and Nick O'Hern. Designed to put cholesterol back on the health agenda by reaching the target audience who primarily experience this problem (many of whom are golfers!), the program saw AstraZeneca pledge $750 to the Heart Institute every time one of the four golfers scored a birdie or an eagle at the ANZ Championships. Not only did this raise $57 750 for research over four days, but the program opened up access to sports pages that would not normally carry a health message.

Celebrity endorsements raise three issues, according to McGrath (in Brook 2002). These are:

1   'brand fit'—does the celebrity suit the product, organisation or campaign?;
2   the possibility of celebrities detracting from the product and taking the focus on to themselves; and
3   the credibility of the celebrity making a statement about the brand.

The benefits of celebrity endorsement can be massive: 'You can gain recognition very quickly with celebrities and that's their power . . . you can revitalise a brand by attaching a celebrity to it. A celebrity gives a brand an instant personality.' (McGrath in Brook 2002: 5)

However, it is widely known that celebrities and some spokespeople attract significant fees, leading to cynicism and diminishing the credibility of a message. As David Ogilvy notes: 'Viewers guess the celebrity has been bought, and they are right.' (in Brook 2002: 4) Further, there is no guarantee that a celebrity or spokesperson's past or future behaviour will not bring him or her into disrepute or create controversy, thus significantly damaging a campaign. There have been numerous cases where either bad personal behaviour or the use of drugs or alcohol has caused the termination of sponsor contracts. When dealing with celebrities, it must be remembered that the boundary between public and private life is blurred—even nonexistent.

It is therefore absolutely critical that a celebrity or spokesperson is carefully selected and vetted and that particular attention is paid to ensure that their portfolio of endorsements or activities aligns with the type of campaign being undertaken. Their credibility in their particular field of expertise also needs to be considered. For example, a recognised consumer rights advocate could be more appropriate to endorse a financial services product than a sportsperson, though a sports celebrity could make an excellent representative for an anti-perspirant. Bonner et al. (1999) conducted a survey of Australian daily television, newspapers and magazines in 1997 and found the majority of celebrity stories were about international celebrities (including Australian-born, but now internationally famous, celebrities such as Nicole Kidman), with entertainment celebrities recording far more coverage than sporting stars. Royalty stories were surprisingly low, below stories on 'ordinary citizens' and just above those on business celebrities.

Celebrities and spokespeople are usually available through their agents, professional associations, businesses or professional speaking agencies. Their role should be explained fully, with their participation scripted or approved by the public relations professional.

Events

Events take many forms, from functions to introduce a new CEO or promote products through to tours of factory facilities, and briefings to prove points or dispel negative impressions. In some cases, they are used to attract media attention—either through the use of a gimmick or by providing access to a key figure.

Their advantages are that they usually involve personal interaction and facilitate in-depth discussion on a topic. Done well, they can be memorable, sending an impacting message and leaving a lasting impression. They are most successful when the topic or key figure is of great interest to the target audience (or this interest can be stimulated), as this guarantees a high participation rate from invitees and media.

A good example is Bacardi's Latino Festival in Sydney. One of the few free events of the Sydney Festival, the Bacardi Latino Festival at Darling Harbour sees the surrounding bars, clubs and restaurants take on a Latino feel for the nine nights of the Festival. Entertainment on the main aquashell stage includes international and local talent and free salsa lessons every evening. Bacardi has sponsored the Sydney Festival for sixteen years as a way to leverage its Cuban heritage and brand quality, and position itself as a supporter of the premier Latino event of the year. Attended by 120 000 people every year, the Bacardi Latino Festival has been instrumental in reviving the brand's image in Australia.

The downside of events is the enormous amount of detailed preparation involved, which makes them time-consuming and sometimes expensive. An event which lasts one hour may take months to arrange. Planning must consider logistical issues such as venue selection, guest lists, catering, clean up, seating facilities, parking, audio visual requirements, guest check in, security and so on. In addition, arrangements need to be made for support material such as invitations, information kits, speeches, running sheets, briefing notes, giveaways, displays, models, brochures and other printed material. All these need to be professionally executed, otherwise they may detract from the key purpose of the event. It is also critical, in the decision-making stages, to ensure that the date does not clash with any other major events and establish whether or not it will be commandeered or undermined by 'anti' groups or individuals.

Community meetings

Community meetings are also events, but they deserve special consideration as they need to be strictly controlled to be successful, particularly in controversial circumstances. They can be used in relatively positive situations, such as to outline a new community beautification program to rally community support. As part of a consultation process, they also serve as a valuable litmus test of public sentiment and issues that need to be addressed. However, their use in controversial circumstances—such as to address opposition to developments—is more risky. Serious thought needs to be given to whether a meeting will merely provide a platform for opponents to rally more support, reinforced by the media who may be difficult to exclude either because they are entitled to attend or because omitting them may send a very negative message. In these instances, it is often more effective to meet people individually or through a representative nominated by the community. In any circumstances, it is essential to have a clear agenda and control it, including audience interjections and questions which may be best addressed individually outside the meeting. It is also critical to ensure that presenters do not respond negatively to an aggressive audience and are well briefed to answer a range of queries. This is where the support of a technical or other experts is useful.

Materials such as a PowerPoint presentation, displays and documents should also be used to graphically illustrate points.

Advertising

Once seen as the exclusive domain of marketing, advertising is an extremely effective tactic for public relations campaigns. While it can be expensive, it is one of the most powerful forms of controlled communication, as it uses persuasive messages which can serve as a central pillar for a campaign, reinforced by other activities such as brochures, web information, posters, direct mail, etc. In an era suffering from communication overload, the downside is the ability of an audience to 'switch off'—sometimes literally—from the bombarding messages. However, other forms of communication are also subject to the same factors, and at least advertising can be extremely targeted and compelling.

Generally television is considered the most powerful form of advertising, as it has the ability to leverage emotional triggers through impacting visual images and sound. It can also reach a broad audience quickly and 'prove' the central message by demonstrating it. Radio can also have a major impact, and is probably best suited to messages that have some emotional appeal, as radio 'talks' in pictures. It is also good for disseminating information quickly and has the advantage of cheaper production costs. However, both television and radio are restricted in the amount of information that can be portrayed in fifteen or 30 seconds, or sometimes up to one minute, if the budget allows. Unless the message is of high personal interest to the audience—such as changes to a health system—or the message is portrayed using a very clever creative approach, print media generally tend to work best in tandem with radio and television to provide more detailed information. Magazines are particularly useful in reaching a very well-defined target audience such as women or car enthusiasts. Billboards, bus sides, bus shelters, taxi backs and so on are good for short, sharp messages which require little explanation or as part of a broader campaign. Successful advertising campaigns usually use a mixture of mediums.

While some public relations practitioners develop advertisements, the usually substantial investment really calls for the exacting talents of advertising agencies or experts. Some agencies have relationships with media buying services that specialise in recommending the most suitable mediums to reach target audiences, and ideally they should work in conjunction with each other from the beginning. An advertising/media-buying agency brief should include:

- the ultimate aim or objective of the advertising—for example, 'to reduce the number of deaths or injuries from road accidents in rural areas';
- key messages (outcomes expected from the advertising);
- full details of materials to be produced—for example, radio advertisement, stickers, inserts, including quantities, size, colour/black and white;
- target audiences and any research data on them, such as current perceptions;
- timing;
- budget (production and media);
- any other specific requirements, such as synergy with existing advertisements, legal considerations, tone;
- measures of success, such as awareness of the advertisement or recognition of key messages.

Community service announcements

Many radio and television stations provide an avenue for free community service announcements. However, as they are inundated with requests, they usually require adherence to strict guidelines, such as the work being non-commercial and/or for community-driven purposes. Space is usually also restricted and organisations will generally not guarantee placement or frequency. This means their use is ad hoc, with them often being placed as 'fillers' in late-night television and radio programs when the majority of the target audience may be asleep. The most successful community service announcements are usually those with wide appeal to a mass market or those linked to paid advertising. In the latter example, the relevant media outlet may also produce the advertisement or a scripted announcement for a nominal fee. In all cases, it is critical to ensure that the quality is of the same standard as fully funded advertisements.

The recent community program 'Bush to Beach', a Rotary initiative that was supported by McDonald's Australia, saw 500 children from drought-stricken areas of Queensland brought to the Gold Coast for four days of fun and activities. The program was also supported by media partner Channel 10, who ran a series of community service announcements to support the project.

Sponsorship

While a well-chosen and effectively managed sponsorship can deliver excellent returns for an organisation, there are serious issues that need to be considered before deciding to choose sponsorship as a tactic. These include:

- the identification of common goals and objectives between the sponsored organisation and the public relations objectives of the sponsoring organisation;
- synergy of the sponsored event or activity with the organisation sponsoring it and/or with the project;
- a sponsorship structure that allows for adequate guaranteed exposure to the target audience or association with the event or project; and
- evaluation criteria that are measurable and determine the success of the sponsorship against the original objectives.

Sponsorships may provide either funds or 'in-kind' support, or both. An example of such sponsorship is the Bayer Solar and Advanced-Technology Boat Race, an international boating event open to any craft that travels on water and is driven by non-polluting fuel sources (excluding wind power), held in Canberra each year. The race is considered the boating equivalent of the internationally recognised World Solar Challenge for cars, and encourages innovation which might then be adopted by industry and the wider community to help protect Australia's waterways. Bayer's sponsorship package provided promotional and operational elements in addition to $25 000 per year for three years. Support included artwork for a new race logo, construction and scaffolding for the event, 500 jackets and hats for participants and organisers and access to Bayer's PR consultancy. Media coverage of the event included print, radio and television, across national, metropolitan, suburban, regional and trade media. This coverage reached more than 7.6 million people, with representation in all states.

Conclusion

There is no guaranteed correct set of tactics that will ensure successful implementation of a public relations campaign. Rather, success relies on the analytical and creative skills of the public relations practitioner to consider tactics in the light of a complex range of impacting factors. First and foremost, tactics must relate back to strategy—they are the link between how it is executed or delivered to target audiences. Second, they must be selected with regard to target audiences, their appropriateness as a vehicle for the message, their advantages and disadvantages as well as the available budget.

Case study 8.1: Gaining public support for the ENERGEX Community Rescue Helicopter Service

Situation analysis

As an energy distributor and retailer whose operations potentially impact on more than 1.1 million customers in southeast Queensland ENERGEX needs to position itself as a socially responsible organisation. In 1994 ENERGEX began sponsoring the Sunshine Coast Helicopter Rescue Service, a non-profit organisation that undertakes vital rescue, medical and search missions. It branded the service ENERGEX Community Rescue and raised funds by urging its customers to donate $2 or more with their quarterly electricity accounts, raising approximately $540 000 annually from about 102 500 donors. While the sponsorship was successful, there was an opportunity to better leverage the initiative to raise the profile of the service and increase donations.

Campaign objectives

1   Increase the number of donors by 40 per cent (and hence raise more money).
2   Demonstrate ENERGEX is a community-minded corporation.

Research

- donor trends, including retention;
- previous fundraising activities and their success—for example, direct mail versus telemarketing;
- inquiries to the ENERGEX Contact Centre and the conversion rate of potential donors;
- media hits, including correct labelling of the service.

Target audiences

- ENERGEX customers;
- southeast Queensland community;
- media;
- ENERGEX staff;
- businesses within ENERGEX's southeast Queensland distribution area.

Helicopter cliff-top rescue helped by crewman, Sunshine Coast, 1999.
(Photo courtesy ENERGEX)

Strategy

- Create widespread awareness of ENERGEX Community Rescue and its operations by communicating dramatic rescues.
- Position the service as a worthy recipient of limited community funds through emotive communication of human interest stories.
- Maximise the potential of existing fundraising channels through the provision of incentives.
- Introduce new fundraising channels.
- Leverage the existing goodwill of 3000 ENERGEX staff towards the service to attract them as advocates and donors.

Tactics

- Branding of all stationery, including letterhead, media releases, newsletters, envelopes, with ENERGEX Community Rescue.
- Development of emotional rescue stories that were the foundation of many communication tactics outlined below.

- Utilisation of human-interest stories of survival or heroism to depict the necessity for the service.
- Inclusion of information in all promotional material that all donations go directly to the service and are tax deductible.
- Achievement of press, radio and television publicity that included the ENERGEX Contact Centre telephone number for donations.
- Story placed in ENERGEX's customer newsletter with a mail-in coupon to sign up for donations, along with notices on electricity accounts and envelopes. These were mailed to approximately 860 000 households in southeast Queensland.
- Production of a brochure with a tear off donation coupon which utilised the same theme as the customer newsletter and was placed at the ENERGEX stand at the Brisbane Exhibition and other strategic locations.
- Development of a distinct web page on the service within the ENERGEX website that included a downloadable donation form.
- Development and placement of emotional television, radio and news-paper advertisements, matched by some media with community service announcements spots.
- Establishment of prompts for Contact Centre staff to ask customers if they wanted to contribute to the service.
- Implementation of an 'on hold' telephone message about the service for customers calling the Contact Centre.
- Implementation of a Contact Centre promotion to engender support for promoting the service, including incentives, posters, fact sheets and moti-vational targets.
- Direct mail campaign to 2500 businesses to promote the service and sol-icit donations, including incentives for donations of more than $250.
- Placement of information on the service, including rescue stories and requests for donations on the ENERGEX intranet and staff newsletter, as well as the incentive of a helicopter ride for staff who donated.
- Implementation of a payroll deduction scheme.

Budget

Considerations and expenses included:

- production of TV, radio and press advertisements;
- media (advertising) placement;
- business direct mail (printing and mailing);
- support to Contact Centre (posters, on hold message, etc.);
- brochure production;

- photography;
- placement of article in customer newsletter and on bills;
- website development.

Results

The first objective of the campaign was to increase the number of donors by 40 per cent (and raise more money). The results were:

- The average number of donors increased by 50 per cent.
- Donations increased to approximately $750 000 per year.

The second objective was to demonstrate that ENERGEX is a community-minded corporation. The results were:

- Market research in 2002 showed that there was 91 per cent awareness of the service, 80 per cent awareness of ENERGEX as the sponsor and 97 per cent support for ENERGEX's sponsorship of the service.
- ENERGEX's Community Regard Index, which measures community perceptions, has improved from its 1998 base line and now continues to outstrip its interstate competitors on the relevant 'sub measure' with market research showing that the service is a major contributor to this.

Evaluation

The campaign was successful and exceeded its objectives. Success factors included the use of emotive angles and the ability to achieve mass coverage through the tactics selected. The direct mail activity to businesses was not as successful as anticipated, and more research was undertaken to ascertain target audience receptiveness and motivators.

Source: Material supplied by ENERGEX

Discussion and exercises

1   Having read both Chapter 7 and this chapter, write down your own definitions of strategy and tactics. Think of a local public relations campaign—perhaps one carried out by your local council or sporting body—and formulate an appropriate strategy and list of tactics for this campaign.

2 What different tactics could be used to reach active and passive publics? Consider controlled and uncontrolled tactics in the mix. On a whiteboard or piece of paper, write these two lists next to each other and compare the end results.

3 Develop a draft of a newsletter or a brochure for an organisation or a community group. For the newsletter, consider what items you would include. For the brochure, what are your key messages? Using information from this chapter, think about the format, the target readership and the distribution of your chosen tactic.

4 Imagine you have been asked to write and send media releases about the following issues/events:

- A new building is being opened at your university by the premier next month.
- A power line is down in the CBD.
- A major road closure is planned for next week.
- A free immunisation campaign in your state is being launched tomorrow.
- A media conference is being held to announce the closure of a local factory which employs 150 people.

Consider the best method/s of delivery for each of these media releases and, using information from Chapter 10, on Media relations, develop a local media distribution list for each release.

Further reading

Bivins, T. (1995) *Handbook for Public Relations Writing*, NTC Business Books, Illinois.

Commonwealth of Australia (1994) *Style Manual for Authors, Editors and Printers*, 5th edn, National Office for the Information Economy, <www.noie.gov.au/projects/egovernment/Better_Information/style_manual.html> (note: 6th edn is also available in hard copy, published by John Wiley and Sons).

Grunig, J. & Hunt, T. (1994) *Public Relations Techniques*, Harcourt Brace College, Fort Worth.

Klein, N. (2000), *No Logo*, Picador, New York.

References

Australia Post (2001/02), 2001/2002 Annual Report.

Bartholomeusz, S. (2003) 'Face the fact: bank fees are better for you', *Sydney Morning Herald*, 18–20 April.

Bivins, T. (1995) *Handbook for Public Relations Writing*, NTC Business Books, Illinois.

Bonner, F., Farley, R., Marshal, D. & Turner, G. (1999) 'Celebrity and the media', *Australian Journal of Communication*, vol. 26, no. 1, pp. 55–70.

Brook, S. (2002) 'Does fame lead to fortune?', *The Australian*, media insert, 1–7 August.

Horoowitz, S. (2003) *Direct Mail Strategies: Low-cost, High Return Approach*, Frugal Marketing.com, <www.frugalmarketing.com/directmail.shtml>.

Humes, J.C. (1991), *The Language of Leadership*, The Business Library, Melbourne.

Johnson, M. (1998) *Nonprofit Organisations and the Internet*, OpenConsult, Inc., <www. openconsult.com>.

Klein, N. (2000), *No Logo*, Picador, New York.

'McLibel' (2000), SBS Television, 22 February.

9 INFORMATION AND COMMUNICATION TECHNOLOGIES

Jeffrey E. Brand and Severin Roald

In this chapter

Mobile phones, email, intranets and extranets, Wi-Fi enabled PDAs . . . all these are in the toolkit of today's increasingly mobile professional. It's easy to think that simply using these communications technologies will enable better and more efficient communications, but time and again experience demonstrates that this is not the case. While communications technologies are essential to the function of public relations, they do not provide the solution to every problem. As other parts of this book have demonstrated, effective public relations practice requires that practitioners strategise and plan their work; while technology tools should be part of this planning, it is important to understand that they will not provide solutions on their own.

This chapter demonstrates that technology should follow rather than drive good public relations practice. In it, the concepts and selected theories that provide a context for communication technologies as tools are explored. Then the practical applications and tools that are at the centre of the current pro-technology buzz in public relations are developed. Along the way, 'secrets of the sages' are suggested, in the form of tools, techniques and concrete steps. Finally, two case studies illustrate the key theme point: technology in public relations . . . not for its own sake.

Concepts and theoretical perspectives for ICTs

In general, the notion of communication suggests a process of message and meaning exchange. Of course, this process of communication often occurs through technologies. Technologies are the tools, devices or artifacts—and even many of the practices—developed and used by a complex industrial culture; the book you are reading now is both an example of a communication technology and of the complex culture which developed and uses it. When technologies are used specifically for communication, they are the devices or artifacts, and the practices that go along with these, to facilitate the exchange of meaning between and among people. Sometimes the technologies that are clustered behind what appears to be a single technology, like email, are tools for data, rather than human, transmission. These are often referred to as information (rather than communication) technologies.

The acronym ICTs (which stands for information communication technologies) is used throughout this chapter to refer to all those tools and practices combined to facilitate information and communication exchange in public relations. Hearn, Mandeville and Anthony (1998) use this acronym to encompass both information and communication technologies and to acknowledge that convergence of telecommunications and computer technologies has necessarily involved the blending of technology clusters that serve both information and communication functions.

Traditionally, public relations practitioners have used ICTs for outbound communication flows—sending messages out from the organisation to target publics, or 'get the word out'. To a lesser extent, they have used ICTs to communicate across part or all of the organisation to 'spread the word' inside. Increasingly, however, public relations specialists are using ICTs for inbound communication from their publics. Indeed, management increasingly sees communication as an exchange rather than a delivery, consistent with Grunig's theory of two-way communication, which was discussed in Chapter 3. This is a fundamental shift in public relations 'flows' because publics now have the capacity to initiate communications directly with employees at all levels of the organisation with the help of ICTs.

This 'flow' change has required public relations professionals to reinvent their profession and find innovative new ways of using ICTs. Implicit in this process is a theoretical and philosophical debate about the role and power of technology in society. Briefly, this debate is encapsulated in the notions of the public sphere, technoculture, technological determinism, appropriation and interactivity.

Communication technology and the public sphere

If the public sphere shifted from the court to the town in the eighteenth and nineteenth centuries and from town to the mass media in the nineteenth and twentieth centuries, as Habermas (1995) has suggested, then it is shifting again from the mass media to ICTs in the twenty-first century. The question of whether this is a good thing for the public sphere is predicated on the fear that ICTs such as email and mobile phones may not emancipate public debate from the control of powerful elites.

The importance of elites in the transitions of the public sphere has been debated (c.f. Boyd-Barrett and Newbold 1995). However, it is widely accepted that, over the past three centuries, elites and therefore 'governors' of the public sphere have progressed from royalty to aristocracy, from aristocracy to industrialists and so on. It is also accepted that, as the public sphere has evolved and changed venues (as from courts of state to coffee houses to television to the internet), participation has become increasingly mixed, with elites, academics and the educated working class engaged in discourse on matters of importance to the civil society. While Habermas lamented the decline of a vibrant public sphere as a function of the commodification of the media (1989), and others have suggested that consumer society more broadly has deteriorated the quality of the public sphere (Elliott 1995), some believe that ICTs may be reinvigorating it (Fernback, cited in Green 2002). The argument is that ICTs provide a forum for free speech, unfettered by (although certainly including) state and business interests.

In a public relations context, libertarian ICTs present both promise and peril. A responsible and informed public, including both private individuals and public and private corporate participants, engaged in debate (carried through ICTs, for example) about a wide range of social, political and economic issues presumably features all the robustness of a healthy self-correcting system—promise for organisations and their public relations professionals. However, the freedoms of unregulated, libertarian exchange with their attendant absence of responsibilities and guidelines may imperil the quality of the public sphere, ensure a 'conflict paradigm' for its existence and, while increasing communication volume, destroy communication function. Inherent in this point, then, is the argument that public relations professionals have a special obligation to elevate rather than exploit the public sphere with the ICTs at their disposal. One way to achieve this is to understand the concept of 'technoculture'.

Public relations and technoculture

Lelia Green (2002) says that technoculture is a special word with too powerful a degree of usefulness to define generally. She explains: 'The concept of techno-culture should be reserved for communications technologies use in the mediated construction of culture. To be technocultural, the technology concerned must facilitate cultural communication across space and/or time and should, in some way, raise issues of place.' (2002: xxviii) Technoculture, then, is the use of communication technologies for the transmission of cultural products within a physical locale or psychological space.

Public relations practitioners are part of the cultural transmission industry. They create, innovate and disseminate ideas to their publics. In doing so, the way they communicate using new ICTs may be as powerful or as weak as the meanings they create inside their messages. Many would argue, however, that technologies used by professional communicators will *change* the profession, its messages and its effectiveness. While we can argue that modern culture (and the public relations profession within it) is facilitated by technocultural tools, we may not be able to conclude that modern culture is *caused* by them. This point raises questions about the notions of technological determinism and socio-culturalism.

Technological determinism versus socio-culturalism

Views about the influence of technology on society fall into two general classes. The first is that technology is responsible for shaping and changing the individual, social, economic and political landscape. This view is called *technological determinism*.

The second is that societies make of technology what they want, and use technology to serve particular needs. Several perspectives are consistent with this view, the most common being *socio-culturalism*.

Deterministic theories are arguments that one thing is responsible for (or determines) outcomes (Chandler 1996). Technological determinists believe that technologies produce social and behavioural changes independent of other influences. They would argue that the internet, for example, will radically change people. In public relations, a technological determinist would claim that newer media will improve the practice.

Socio-culturalism is the notion that societies determine how technologies are developed and used. In this view, the causal relationship is the reverse of that expressed in technological determinism. Instead of technology affecting society, socio-culturalists argue that society moulds technologies, finds uses for them, and rejects those that work badly or offer little benefit. The public relations profession has its share of socio-culturalists as well as technological determinists (see the first exercise at the end of this chapter for an example).

Appropriation

> Technology is often thought of as simply equipment or technique, but this level of understanding misses its most important elements. Embedded within technology is a system of know-how that disposes of former knowledge and introduces a new set of rules and opportunities. (Sussman 1997: 19)

Appropriation is the process by which equipment and technique are blended by rules and patterns of behaviour. When public relations practitioners choose, modify and set rules and patterns for their technocultural tools and ICTs, they appropriate them. Much of what we discuss in the technology section below is appropriation. Rules for effective use of email and patterns for the innovative use of channels like SMS are appropriations of these technologies. Naturally, the appropriation of ICTs in a field like public relations is about productivity and efficiency. It is important to note that the reasons for technology use as a professional communicator may be different from those as an individual citizen or consumer. While the former is always looking for more productive and efficient means to exchange messages, publics may have different needs—among them, the need to feel important and personally addressed. This is where interactivity becomes vital to the professional communicator.

Interactivity

Many years ago, media designers decided that, in order to create interactive media experiences, media channels needed to simulate face-to-face communication by covering the senses and by creating a sense of social presence (that is, being present in the same physical place as a social other) while creating the illusion of an unmediated environment (Durlak 1987). To create an illusion of an unmediated environment, they claimed that interactive media needed to be transparent or easily overlooked by the users and to be personalised by allowing the media channel to facilitate seemingly personalised communication. In many ways, newer channels of communication now used by public relations practitioners achieve these general rules.

However, Rafaeli (1988) suggested that interactivity is more a human function than a machine function, regardless of the machines that are used. He noted: 'for full interactivity to occur, communication roles need to be interchangeable . . .' (1988: 113). This argument reinforces the importance of the earlier point: public relations professionals are irreplaceable and communication tools are only tools, not wholesale solutions to communication problems.

Yet many tools used today are called 'interactive'. Jensen (1999) suggests that interactivity can take on different forms and conceptualised four degrees including:

- transmissional—a system user has choice in a one-way system, such as using the remote control on the television;
- consultational—a system user has choices in a two-way system, such as the web or a phone menu;
- conversational—allows a user to input communication such as speech or text; and
- registrational—the system adapts to a user's needs and actions, including those that are non-verbal and para-linguistic, such as facial expressions and tone of voice.

So far, this discussion about interactivity has blurred the roles of and relationship between the technical system and the user or communication participant. In in-depth interviews with multimedia professionals, Downes and McMillan (2000) found that the people who design interactive media messages divided interactivity into three technology-based and three user-based dimensions. In other words, they found that communication interactivity depends not only on the technology, but on the people. They concluded that the dimensions of interactivity included the following:

- technology-based dimensions:
  - *direction of communication* (the technology must support two-way message exchange);
  - *time flexibility* (the technology must allow for both synchronous or real-time message exchange and asynchronous or delayed message exchange); and
  - *sense of place* (the technology must create a sense of place or presence for the participants . . . it needs to create the illusion of either transporting one to the other or both communicators to a common 'place').
- user-based dimensions:
  - *level of control* (the user should be able to exercise a degree of control over the flow and content of communication exchanged);
  - *responsiveness* (the user should be required to react to and input communication for the exchange); and
  - *perceived goals of communication* (the user should be able to at least exchange information with and at most persuade a communicator at the other end).

The concept of interactivity is a muddy one (Heeter 2000), although its discussion here highlights its importance both to a discussion of new communication technologies in public relations practice and to an understanding of the role of people in interactive tools. For the tools to be interactive, people must—at some point along the communication exchange—be on both ends of the channel. In other words, interactive and newer media tools are not a replacement for good communication by professionals.

Newer channels of communication in public relations

For the successful practitioner, a comprehensive public relations strategy is no longer just a case of targeting audiences through traditional media like print, television and radio. To carry out their roles effectively, public relations professionals must now understand and address new channels—including WAP delivery, online forums, SMS and MMS. New technologies may speed up response times and give public relations practitioners opportunities to communicate directly with stakeholders without the mediation of journalists. Two groups of ICTs have dominated media, industry and academic discourse over the past twenty years: telecommunications and computers. Public relations practitioners increasingly use these groups of ICTs to communicate with their stakeholders. New channels (and a few that are now more commonplace but remain popular) include SMS, MMS, WAP, email and the internet, which will now be discussed in some detail.

SMS

Short message service (SMS) is a wireless service available on digital mobile phone networks. SMS enables the transmission of text messages between mobile phones and other systems such as electronic mail, paging and voice mail. Up to 160 characters (about 35 words) can be sent and received through the network operator's message system to the mobile phone. Organisations and businesses increasingly run SMS campaigns in order to inform their publics, as SMS offers a reach that is unprecedented in the digital realm. With mobile phone penetration up from 61 per cent in 2000 to 68 per cent of the Australian population in February 2003, with a predicted rise to 80 per cent in coming years driven mainly by the explosion of messaging, SMS has become not only a truly mass-market phenomenon, but also a viable communication tool for public relations practitioners (Sainsbury 2003). The advantages of SMS are its impulsive and pervasive nature and its immediacy. SMS is an extremely cost-effective method of communication, making it a communication tool that appeals to youth—an audience which can be difficult to target through traditional mass media channels. Two case studies exemplify how SMS can be applied to engage and inform targeted publics. Yet SMS also has its disadvantages.

Case study 9.1: Amnesty International

Amnesty International, the worldwide campaigning movement that works to promote internationally recognised human rights, has been running SMS campaigns since 2000. Amnesty offers notices of urgent cases sent to subscribers' mobile telephones using SMS text messages. People interested in taking part in the campaign will register on the website <www.stoptorture.org> or sign up by sending an SMS message or email to Amnesty International (often there are appeals for people to do this using advertisements on buses, trains, posters and so on). They will then receive either an SMS or an email each time someone is taken captive—which happens about once a week according to Amnesty International estimates. In order to register their protest, users need only to reply to the message with the case number. Such a message was recently distributed reading: 'Danger of execution. Hanan M. Rashid was sentenced to death in March for killing her husband. Send: appeal <your name> to the President of Egypt'. Amnesty International aims to generate 'virtual petitions' by collecting thousands of text messages of support from mobile phone users to lobby governments and to alert them to the strength of feeling about particular human rights violations. From experience, Amnesty International argues that the risk to a person's life can be reduced dramatically if action is taken within 48 hours and perpetrators realise the wider world knows they are holding someone captive.

Case study 9.2: The Hong Kong government and SARs

SMS messages are also being used as a crisis communication tool (Wong 2003). When an internet story that Hong Kong was designated as an 'infected city' sent new fears about Asia's mystery illness (Sudden Acute Respiratory Syndrome, or SARS) through the area, authorities used a fast and simple way to quell the rumour—they sent a blanket text message to about six million mobile phones. The Hong Kong government used the text message after the 'infected city' hoax report appeared online, prompting panic among some residents who thought the territory would be shut down. Some rushed out to stock up on food and supplies. The government text response said: 'Director of Health announced at 3 p.m. today there is no plan to declare Hong Kong as an infected area'. The hoax story was allegedly posted by a fourteen-year-old boy who copied the website design of popular Chinese-language *Ming Pao* newspaper. He was arrested and subsequently quoted as saying he did it for fun, and didn't think anybody would believe the story.

SMS has opened the door to a more time-sensitive, interactive and cost-effective dialogue between organisations and their publics. Yet SMS has several disadvantages as a public relations tool. In the Hong Kong SARS case, some people didn't get their text for about six hours due to network traffic—an unsatisfactory delay when time and speed are crucial.

SMS messages also have the capability to create more confusion than they resolve, as they give the sender little scope for the provision of context such as scene setting or background in only 160 characters. Moreover, recipients may not always know that the SMS itself is genuine and not a hoax. For these reasons, SMS campaigns should be combined with faster, richer and more trustworthy media such as printed material, radio and television. Essential to the success of SMS campaigns is the fact that SMS messages can be sent across all networks in Australia, so that—regardless of whether senders and receivers use Vodafone, Telstra, Optus, Hutchinson, or are PPTT subscribers—anyone can participate.

MMS

Multimedia messaging service (MMS) is a service enabling users to deliver rich multimedia experiences. Users can combine text, pictures, photos, animations, speech and audio for rich and detailed messaging experiences across different technology platforms like mobile phones, hand-held computers and PCs. A multimedia message can, for example, be a photo or picture postcard annotated with text and/or an audio clip, a synchronised playback of audio, text, photo or, in the near future, a video emulating a free-running presentation or a video clip. It can also simply be a drawing combined with text.

MMS makes it possible for mobile users to send these multimedia messages from MMS-enabled handsets to other mobile users and to email users. It also makes it possible for mobile users to receive multimedia messages from other mobile users, email users and from multimedia-enabled applications. Colour and rich-media text messaging have begun appearing on mobile devices throughout Australia and will likely be adopted widely by public relations practitioners, enabling them to send detailed messages to their stakeholders' phones.

WAP

The delivery of internet information to mobile phones through WAP (wireless application protocol) is another channel available for public relations professionals. At present, WAP is suffering from disappointing performance because of poor GSM (Global System for Mobile Communications—the dominant digital network system used for mobile phones in Australia) networks and a lack of support from operators, which has led to consumer dissatisfaction. It has also experienced a lack of financial support as businesses are more skeptical about m-commerce (mobile phone-based e-commerce) than they were of e-commerce. Many WAP sites are still in an embryonic phase, meaning high-value content is limited. Yet many public relations consultancies did embrace the WAP technology when it was introduced. August.One Communication was one of the first consultancies in the world to introduce a mobile phone internet service. The agency launched a WAP service to make information accessible to clients, staff and press, any time and anywhere in the world. It was launched on 1 August 1999 in Sydney, London and Paris. Information is immediately accessible to users through a WAP site while they are on the move, without a landline or a PC.

WAP service provides clients, journalists and staff with announcements, documents and contact details. WAP is generally designed to complement existing websites rather than replace them. By using WAP, stakeholders will have immediate access to information and then, for further background details, pictures or audio clips, they can access an organisation's website or other communications.

Email

Electronic mail messaging has been used in Australian public relations now for more than a decade. Yet it is remarkable how many practitioners fail to recognise the unique characteristics of email that require specialised uses. The bottom line is that professionals who fail to understand how to use email properly will experience resistance and rejection from their stakeholders. Every communication professional should learn standard etiquette for email sent to publics, especially the media. Often email is preferred to faxes, phone calls or mailed news releases.

Guidelines for effective email

- Use a descriptive subject line.
- Keep your message short and to the point. More information should be accessible in the attachment or at a website.
- Sign your message. Public relations consultants should also make it clear exactly whom they are representing.
- Reply promptly to messages you receive that warrant a reply.
- Quote the part of a previous message to which you are responding, so that readers of the email know what you are talking about.
- Do not put all the journalists in the 'to-field' when you distribute press releases to several journalists . . . apart from alerting them to the fact that your message is being broadcast widely, it also makes it possible for one journalist to reply to all the others. One common solution is to put the addresses on the 'Bcc' line.
- Use common formats when you send attachments.
- Pictures, backgrounders, and so on should be accessible on the web. Do not distribute large files such as high-resolution pictures by email without the permission of journalists.
- Do not spam journalists. Ensure that you have researched your media list thoroughly. Targeting of messages is as important online as offline.

The biggest challenge facing professional communicators who want to use email is unsolicited bulk email (UBE), also known as 'spam'. The challenge isn't so much in creating and sending email messages, but in not doing so. According to the Coalition Against Unsolicited Bulk Email, Australia (CAUBE.AU 2003), spam is increasing exponentially. In its routine survey of email spam, CAUBE has found that the volume of unsolicited messages to email accounts doubles every four and a half months, or by a factor of nearly six each year.

Why is this happening? CAUBE claims simple economics are to blame:

> Spam . . . a unique form of advertising which has no incremental cost to the sender, imposes real and measurable costs on the recipients, and has the potential to destroy the value of electronic mail. Advertising that has no incremental cost to the sender . . . is the one feature of UBE which leads to all the consequences which make UBE uniquely destructive to the medium it uses—electronic mail. (CAUBE.AU 2003: online)

The message here is quite simple: spam might be very cheap for the sender, but it is costly (especially in time) to the receiver; for this reason, it is a very poor way to communicate with valued publics.

The internet

User friendly, cost effective and flexible, the internet is an efficient tool to generate publicity and establish ongoing media relations. Indeed, the internet is particularly effective for establishing *dialogic relationships*—a term developed in the mid-1990s by Michael L. Kent and Maureen Taylor (Cooley 1999). This concept is used to describe the emerging model for interactive communication among an organisation and its publics:

> A dialogic relationship exists when all parties involved in the communication process are contributing equally and involved in a dialogue that is geared towards building relationships. (Cooley 1999: 41)

However, a survey by Jupiter Communications, an American research institution, revealed that 'some 42% of top-ranked sites took longer than five days to respond to e-mails sent to their site. Retail sites did better, but still only 54% responded within a day.' (Sumner 2000) A survey of 100 Fortune 500 companies revealed that only 9 per cent of websites had discussion groups (Cooley 1999). What these studies suggest is that many organisations are not taking advantage of their websites. This may be a function of not understanding that communication on the web is indeed dialogic: information not only goes out, but also comes in. It is useful therefore to discuss the web in terms of information out and information in.

Information out

Web pages can be used for providing detailed information to a seeking, motivated public. However—and this is the key—the site must be desirable to the public of interest, because internet users who 'surf the web' or browse through several pages in one session must sort through a trail of pages. Even advanced search tools can bury an organisation's website. Therefore, although a public relations practitioner may use the web to publish media releases (for example), these are effective only when used in conjunction with email or other ICTs that let the target publics know where to look for them. Several public relations strategies are available on the web that can increase the effectiveness of the organisation's website, including online media rooms, online press conferences, online campaigns, crisis management opportunities, online resource centres and e-influencers.

Online press room

Dynamic media rooms dedicated to journalists are a highly effective communication tool. With media releases, photo library, various materials (white papers, backgrounders and media folders), videos to download, financial information and contact information all online, journalists are able to find relevant material about an organisation in seconds. When shaping an online media room, it is important to think about the sort of information journalists on tight deadlines will need and make it easy for them to find it. This includes access to spokespersons, good quality photographs that are easy to download, media releases and simple-to-navigate background information. The online media room might also present success stories, historical information, information on sponsoring, relevant topics, partnerships and research. A mailing list where journalists can sign up to receive material as soon as it is issued is often a popular service among specialist journalists. Online media rooms come with a few rules, however:

- Content must be easily accessible even with old software.
- Respond ASAP if you receive an email from a journalist. Do not let them wait. At least let them know when they can expect to receive an answer.

- Be discriminating about the type of information you load on to the site. Prioritise.
- Product information, financial information, media releases, pictures and contact information can all be important.
- Journalists are interested in a range of topics. Consider whether the site can be organised by topic.
- A wide selection of pictures that the media can use should be accessible, both high- and low-resolution images.

Online media conferences

The web is an ideal space for media conferences, especially when targeting technology-savvy audiences such as IT journalists. Numerous organisations world-wide have adopted this technology and launched new products and services, made important announcements and presented their stand on an issue live and online. Those who 'attend' these conferences are often invited by email and find this alternative very practical and efficient. It negates the need for travel and unnecessary time out of the office; the conference can be followed in real time online; and all the media materials such as backgrounders, media releases, fact sheets and pictures can be downloaded immediately. Journalists can also ask questions by email or alternatively in person by using their own web camera. The slow introduction of broadband services such as ADSL (asynchronous digital subscriber line), which carry data faster than standard modems, has constrained the audience so far. Yet in the near future this problem is likely to be solved and public relations professionals will be able to reach an even wider group of people online.

Online communication campaigns

A campaign website can be a powerful communications channel where stakeholders can be reached at a relatively small cost. Web campaigns have proven to be highly successful as long as they are tailor-made to stakeholders. Running promotions on the internet is similar to running offline promotions. It is important not to rely on the web alone and to offer alternative paths to web-based information. The web is part of a diverse and complex communications environment, and public relations professionals must embrace both new and old channels in order to communicate effectively and generate online traffic. A campaign website is useless without visitors.

Crisis management

The web is an ideal tool for information delivery in a crisis, as information can be published electronically and be produced, updated and made public in a very short time. Companies that are enmeshed in a crisis can counter media bias by providing open and complete information from their point of view. For example, consultancy group Edelman Worldwide has a crisis preparation and response system that uses the web and internet technologies. Among its features are an internet 'crisis channel' capable of containing complete (compared with tightly edited) independent videotaped interviews of company personnel, third-party testimonies favourable to the company and information pages to educate or explain the crisis.

Online resource centres

Public relations practitioners can publish written content in various online resource centres. According to Nemec (2000: 34): 'Journalists need only register to tap into the resources, which have been developed by organisations seeking to tell their stories online as they have traditionally done through . . . other electronic distribution services.' However, not all online resource centres are automatically successful. A lot of the content on many resource centre sites is available to many journalists, and this makes it difficult to create a unique story.

Reach and inform online influencers

As information exchange on the internet continues to grow, relationships, spheres of influence and communications channels will become increasingly mediated. The influential movers and shakers who have mastered these relationships and communication channels have been identified by global public relations consultancy Burson-Marsteller as 'e-fluentials'. E-fluentials, who comprise 10 per cent of the US online adult population, were among the first to explore the internet frontier. They remain the most prominent online trailblazers. Compared with the average internet user, they are far more active users of email, newsgroups and other online vehicles when conveying their messages. While extremely influential online, e-fluentials spread their opinions in the offline world as well. Civic-minded e-fluentials are more likely to vote, attend public meetings, serve on local committees and make speeches. According to Burson-Marsteller, their families and peers regularly approach them for information, opinions and advice on a wide range of subjects, from business and politics to entertainment and health/lifestyle issues (Burson-Marsteller 2003). If e-fluentials are indeed as influential as they appear to be, organisations need to identify and create relationships with the e-fluentials that can be found in their relevant publics. They also need to win their favour by offering incentives, high-quality products or services, support and easy-to-use websites. If successful, these organisations will not only win the loyalty of the e-fluential community, but also the loyalty of existing and potential customers within the social networks of e-fluentials.

Information in

While the internet is a powerful and now standard tool for getting the word out, it may be even more useful to the public relations professional for collecting information. This feature of the internet makes it an unparalleled communication technology. Among the 'information in' uses of the internet are media monitoring, issues research and observing competitors' activities.

The internet hosts electronic versions of Australia's national and capital city newspapers, international news magazines, and many local or regional publications. Moreover, all Australian broadcasters such as the major TV networks have websites. These media sites are usually archived, and some of the archives can be searched at little or no cost.

One use of this ready access to media sources is issues research. It is critical that public relations professionals keep track of emerging issues to anticipate both developments that relate directly to the organisation and media inquiries about these issues. Moreover, as more companies appear online, it will become easier for key publics to find the organisations they are looking for. This means it will become increasingly easy for the public relations practitioner in one organisation to look for and observe the competition's communication activities and strategies. The following internet-monitoring strategies are often used by professional communicators who are collecting badly needed information (Kassel 2000).

Search engines

Search engines and directories are the most evident tool for monitoring the internet. However, competing search engines and directories like AlltheWeb, Yahoo!, Lycos, InfoSeek, Go, Google and Northern Light monitor only a fraction of the web. An often cited 1998 study in *Science* by Lawrence and Giles of the NEC Research Institute concludes that only 40 per cent of the web was available when using a combination of some of the known search engines of the day. The same authors published a survey in 1999 for *Nature* in which they maintain that 'search engine coverage had decreased 16 per cent' (Kassel 2000). Moreover, search engines do not sort out new documents and rarely search the daily media.

Database information aggregators

Established information aggregators such as Dialog (<www.dialog.com>), Factiva (<www.factiva.com>) and Lexis-Nexis (<www.lexis-nexis.com>) offer electronic monitoring and clipping service by subscription. These companies have served an extraordinary purpose for years. However, they have significant disadvantages for current news and information monitoring. Many of the publications incorporated into these databases are not included for between one and six weeks following publication. In addition, the databases fail to monitor the web and they are expensive considering the fact that much of the information is available free via other sources.

Electronic news services

Internet-based customised news services such as NewsEdge (<www.individual.com>), MyYahoo (<my.yahoo.com>), MyLycos (<my.lycos.com>) and Moreover.com deliver tailor-made material from publishers to their customers. Each day, the online service automatically delivers to the user the top ten or so articles to the viewer's selected topic. These services have become popular among many corporations, which have made them available to their employees on the desktop or through the company's intranet. The content is often delivered free or at low cost. However, their shortcomings include the limited number of news sources, the limited number of stories that are delivered automatically, and the limited scope of articles. Moreover, automatic deliveries are confined to news; the services rarely deliver editorials or other pieces such as product reviews, and stories in regional publications never make it into the internet-based news services.

Internet monitoring and clipping services

Internet monitoring and clipping services are highly automated services designed to provide comprehensive and timely 'clips' on customised topics. They capture the most current information from web publications, electronic bulletin boards, websites and news sources. Companies can employ these services to track mentions of company activities, brands and trade marks, as well as those of competitors. It is possible to monitor daily any subject of consequence, such as key topics that centre on trends, regulations, legal issues and thought leaders (Kassel 2000).

Chat (IRC)

Chat, or internet relay chat (IRC), is a real-time, text-based messaging system through which two or more participants may communicate over the internet. It looks and works like email except that, rather than sending a message to a particular address, you log on to an internet location called a 'chat room' and begin to see the written comments of participants accumulate on the screen. Thousands of chat rooms have been dedicated around the world to ongoing public discussions about major corporations, governments and organisations and their actions, products, services, management and so on. According to a 2001 study by Middleberg Euro RSCG and Columbia University, nearly a quarter of 4000 journalists surveyed in an American nationwide study said they would consider reporting rumours obtained via web chat rooms or online news groups—even without verification from an outside source ('25% of journalists' 2001). It is critical that public relations professionals monitor, if not participate in, relevant chats from time to time, in order to gauge emerging public sentiment and/or emerging crises.

'Netizens', or net citizens, are those people who spend enormous amounts of time online. They have a strongly democratic view of the internet, fighting for it to return to its commercial-free status of many years ago. These purists argue that corporate monitoring (called lurking) of internet chat rooms is insulting. Be that as it may, public relations monitoring of these internet sites is increasingly necessary to protect an organisation's reputation. Many professional communicators have discovered that chat rooms and other public discussion areas of the internet serve as inexpensive, reliable and quick forums in which to research public sentiments in a manner somewhat like focus groups. Because chat is thought of as a safe haven for netizens, announcing one's presence as a company representative is a delicate matter. One practitioner suggests that the best way to enter a chat room is to write something like: 'I hear you've been talking about my product. This is my URL address; if you want more information, e-mail me.' (Rapaport 1997: S103) According to Maddox and Blankenhorn (1998: 208), 'the advice here is to keep your message short, keep it to the point of the group, and (if you can) point to a web site for more information'.

Newsgroups

Newsgroups are another internet text-based messaging system. These discussion groups work like email except that messages are posted to a public place where others can read them. They are like chat in that they present public messages, but differ from chat in that messages are delayed. Messages may be posted about something that is not currently being discussed in a newsgroup, or may be written in response to one or many other existing messages. Newsgroups cater for both experts and novices debating topics of mutual interest. Indeed, a distinguishing feature of newsgroups is that they are organised by topic and they are a public-posting free-for-all—almost. Newsgroup topics span the interests of humanity and vary in their intended audience and geographical relevance. Newsgroups are created and discontinued daily.

What is being said about a company in newsgroups can have a severe impact on public perception of brands, products and services. The fact that newsgroup 'posts', or messages posted on the newsgroup, tend to be available for days—if not weeks—means the messages may be seen by many people over extended periods. Negative messages may cause damage to an organisation's reputation, a company's stock value and its sales revenues.

Newsgroups give professional communicators a ready resource for monitoring public sentiment and conducting issues research in much the same way as chat does. Newsgroups lend themselves particularly well to opinion (rather than factual or knowledge) research because the quality of information provided by participants is often poor and usually cannot be verified, but opinions are readily available. Because specific newsgroups are created by people motivated by and interested in a particular topic, and because they are operated on a host computer that may be located within a company, public relations practitioners are beginning to create their own newsgroups, where clients, customers and employees can debate issues related to the organisation.

One provocative use for newsgroups is as an online forum for employees in large organisations. A large medical company with thousands of employees has created a newsgroup that its founder calls an 'electronic water cooler', whereby employees and managers can exchange ideas, rumours, recipes and anything else that can be communicated to improve employee morale and the flow of information in the organisation (Rapaport 1997: S104).

Internet misinformation and rogue websites

Some practitioners tend to think of the internet in traditional media terms—as a one-way communication channel with which they can send information to target publics. However, as easily as public relations professionals can publish on the web, disgruntled consumers or corporate saboteurs can publish web pages that disparage organisations.

These are called 'rogue' websites and newsgroups, and are dedicated to defaming organisations and people. Rogue sites contain complaints, parodies, fraudulent claims, and myths or rumours about an organisation, product or service. They are created by grassroots organisations, activists, consumer groups and individuals. Transnational companies are particularly susceptible to these threats—in part because their reach is geographically very wide and in part because their visibility makes them a more valuable target of angry netizens. Examples of these include 'I Hate McDonald's', 'Toys R Us Sucks', 'Linux Sucks', 'Chase Bank Sucks', 'I Hate Microsoft', 'I Hate Apple' and 'No More AOL CDs.com'. Before the internet emerged as a popular medium, disgruntled customers would tell ten others about their discontent; today the number of people within reach of all internet users is in the millions. Many companies and practitioners who have succeeded in protecting their reputations in traditional media have failed to do so on the internet. Even the competent communication professional struggles with just the right response to damaging impostor web pages. The biggest mistake is to over-react to misinformation. Actions like press releases or suing for misuse of brand can draw more attention to a site than it would ever attract on its own. Some sites have no traffic at all and can be ignored. Boyd Neil at Hill & KnowIton Canada has prepared a list on how to handle attack sites (Neil 2000):

- Prepare rebuttal pages for your own website that directly answer charges on the spoof or attack sites.
- Offer to discuss—or attempt to resolve—the underlying cause of the dissatisfaction with the web originator, especially if he or she is an angry ex-employee or dissatisfied customer.
- Register all possible domain names, especially ones that lend themselves to negative connotations.
- Consider legal action. For example, if a website copies your logo, it may infringe your copyright.
- Attempt to persuade the ISP to shut the site down if it is making defamatory or questionable accusations.

The means by which organisations choose to handle corporate attacks can be detrimental for company public relations. According to Neil (2000), a company's public or corporate affairs department should have a specific program in place to deal with internet rumours. The program should include:

- identifying and monitoring any websites which could take an interest in the company's products and services, especially websites of disgruntled employees or advocacy and special interest groups;

- monitoring online news services and renegade newsletters; and
- an action plan which includes a means of responding quickly and authoritatively with clear and open messages and factual information about the subject of any web-based rumour; together with steps to line up your allies so that you can challenge rumours on your turf; and the use of your website to clarify rumours and ensure that employees are kept informed about your efforts to challenge them.

As other authors in this book have demonstrated, successful public relations is as much about monitoring one's business and reputation among diverse publics as it is about creating and disseminating the organisation's news. It becomes clear that ICTs like the web can both improve the communication between an organisation and its publics, and introduce dangers by giving equal power and reach to disaffected members of these publics. The internet is different from traditional mass media in that it is inexpensive, provides rapid access to publics, and creates a forum for exchange between the organisation and its publics. Moreover, it combines the expedience of interpersonal communication with the reach and impact of mass communication. Therefore, the interactive and cost-effective characteristics of the internet make it an ideal playing field for other communicators as well. The challenge for contemporary professional communicators is to send and receive messages with skill in this new environment.

Conclusion

This chapter has defined concepts related to ICTs. It has reviewed communication tools commonly used by public relations professionals, and in doing so has introduced some promises and pitfalls. New ICTs are enabling the professional communicator to publish electronically and use telecommunications tools to communicate with target groups at any location and at almost any time. It seems that a new channel for communication is being introduced every year, and that this proliferation of technologies introduces difficulties as well as advantages to the practitioner.

The difficulties include loss of control over communication programs, technology failure, user incompetence and adoption of technology by a competitor. Yet the difficulties should not overtake the professional communicator; it is vital that public relations professionals look at ICTs as tools for communication rather than the focal point of communication. Furthermore, they must recognise that no one tool stands alone in any communication program. Many of the ICTs discussed in this chapter bypass the traditional media and enable the professional communicator to target influential publics directly. This ability undoubtedly requires additional writing, design and editorial skills in order to be effective.

As with any communication strategy, professional communicators must consider the objectives, audience, desired results, likelihood of the results using the ICT, and how the strategy fits into the total communication program. ICTs are only the vehicle: their ability to get one from point A to point B depends on the competence of the driver.

Discussion and exercises

1   Read the following paragraphs. Which one sounds like technological determinism and which socio-culturalism?

(a) We are witnessing amazing technological advances in the communication field—faster modems, Internet, video conferencing, cellular technology and e-mail, just to mention a few. These are all designed to improve the speed and effectiveness of communication . . . All these advances are great. However, there is no guarantee that throwing money and advanced technology at a problem will solve it. We need to remember one very important point—humans dictate the successful use of this technology. (Cole 1997: 49)

(b) Public relations is a very hands-on relationship business. Previously, practitioners might have been concerned that technology diminishes this. These days, however, they're beginning to realize that technology can only aid, not replace, the potency of the human mind. (Wiesendanger 1994: 23)

2   Investigate the following related industry websites. How many address the emergence of the web as a public relations tool? What characteristics of the web make it a medium distinctive from more traditional media?

<www.recognition.com.au>

<www.prsa.org>

<www.edelman.com>

<www.hooked.net/iabc.com/welcome.html>

<www.portnernovelli.com>

<www.energex.com.au>

3   Enter a newsgroup related to one of your favourite brand names from your campus 'news' server. Follow the thread for a couple of days. Is there any evidence that the company behind the brand is monitoring? If so, what is this evidence and how effective is the company in using this channel? If not, how do you know, and does this seem to have an adverse effect on the reputation of the brand?

4   Visit the websites of at least five major Australian or New Zealand corporations. Which site appears to apply the principles of effective public communication espoused throughout this textbook? Which ones are using the web effectively? Do any of the sites provide opportunities for public comment, exchange or debate? Should they? Why or why not?

Further reading

CAUBE.AU (2003) Coalition Against Unsolicited Bulk Email, *Australia: The Problem*, <www.caube.org.au/problem.htm>.

Elliott, P. (1995) 'Intellectuals, the "information society" and the disappearance of the public sphere', in O. Boyd-Barrett & C. Newbold (eds.) (1995) *Approaches to Media: A Reader*, Arnold, Sydney.

Jensen, J. (1999) ' "Interactivity"—tracking a new concept in media and communication studies', in P.A. Mayer (ed.), *Computer Media and Communication*, Oxford University Press, Oxford, pp. 160–88.

Rafaeli, S. (1988) 'Interactivity: from new media to communication', in S. Hawkins, J.M. Wiemann & R.P. Pingree (eds), *Advancing Communication Science*, Sage, London, pp. 110–34.

References

'25% of journalists use unchecked chatroom gossip as news source' (2001) *PR Week*, available online by subscription: <www.prweek.com>.

Boyd-Barrett, O. & Newbold, C. (eds) (1995) *Approaches to Media: A Reader*, Arnold, Sydney.

Burson-Marsteller (2003) 'The power of online influencers', <www.e-fluentials.com>.

CAUBE.AU (2003) Coalition Against Unsolicited Bulk Email, 'Australia: the problem', <www.caube.org.au/problem.htm>.

Chandler, D. (1996) *Shaping and Being Shaped*, <http://users.aber.ac.uk/dgc/determ.html>.

Cole, L. (1997) 'To see communication it has to be measured', *Communication World*, vol. 14, no. 8, pp. 49–51.

Cooley, T. (1999) 'Interactive communication—public relations on the web', *Public Relations Quarterly*, vol. 44, no. 2.

Downes, E.J. & McMillan, S.J. (2000) 'Defining interactivity: A qualitative identification of key dimensions', *New Media & Society*, vol. 2, no. 2, pp. 157–79.

Durlak, J.T. (1987) 'A typology for interactive media', in M. McLaughlin (ed.), *Communication Yearbook 10*, Sage, London.

Elliott, P. (1995) 'Intellectuals, the "information society" and the disappearance of the public sphere', in O. Boyd-Barrett & C. Newbold (eds), *Approaches to Media: A Reader*, Arnold, Sydney.

Ericsson, *Share the Good Times*, <www.ericsson.com/mms/>.

—— Short Message Service, online <www.ericsson.com/technology/SMS.shtml>.

Flytxt, 'Charities can now text their way to a great result', <www.flytxt.com/press/press_CharityWeek_04_09_02.html>.

Green, L. (2002) *Technoculture: From Alphabet to Cybersex*, Allen & Unwin, Sydney.

Habermas, J. (1995) 'Institutions of the public sphere', in O. Boyd-Barrett & C. Newbold (eds), *Approaches to Media: A Reader*, Arnold, Sydney.

—— (1989) *The Structural Transformation of the Public Sphere*, MIT Press, Cambridge MA.

Hearn, G., Mandeville, T. & Anthony, D. (1998) *The Communication Superhighway: Social and Economic Change in the Digital Age*, Allen & Unwin, Sydney.

Heeter, C. (2000) 'Interactivity in the context of designed experiences', *Journal of Interactive Advertising*, vol. 1, no. 1, <www.jiad.org/>.

Holz, S. (1999) *Public Relations on the Net*, Amacom, New York.

'The importance of monitoring and using new channels', *PR Profile*, <www.profilepr.co.uk/forum/prtips/prtips11.html>.

Jensen, J. (1999) '"Interactivity"—tracking a new concept in media and communication studies', in P.A. Mayer (ed.), *Computer Media and Communication*, Oxford University Press, Oxford, pp. 160–88.

Kassel, A. (2000) 'A guide to internet monitoring', *PR Central*, <www.prcentral.com>.

Maddox, K. & Blankenhorn, D. (1998), *Web Commerce: Building a Digital Business*, John Wiley & Sons, New York.

Magic Four (2000) 'Magic four aids Amnesty International', <www.magic4.com/about_us/pr/2000/world-091000.html>.

Marken, A. (1998) 'The internet and the web: the two-way public relations highway', *Public Relations Quarterly*, vol. 43, no. 1.

Neil, B. (2000) 'Crisis management and the internet', *Ivey Business Journal*, January.

Nemec, R. (2000) 'How to avoid a cybercrisis', *Communication World*, vol. 17, no. 6, p. 34.

'One claims first in WAP information site', *PR Week*, August, <www.prweek.com>.

Rafaeli, S. (1988) 'Interactivity: from new media to communication', in S. Hawkins, J.M. Wiemann & R.P. Pingree (eds), *Advancing Communication Science*, Sage, London, pp. 110–34.

Rapaport, R. (1997) 'PR finds a cool new tool: internet helps corporations deal with public-relations disasters', *Forbes*, 160, 6 October, pp. S100–106.

Romeike, Services and Solutions, <www.romeike.com/>.

Sainsbury, M. (2003) 'Telstra pins its hopes on mobiles', *The Australian*, 25 February, p. 18.

Sumner, I. (2000) 'Web site novelties can bring PR opportunities', *Marketing*, 17 June, p. 42.

Sussman, G. (1997) *Communication, Technology, and Politics in the Information Age*, Sage, London.

Wiesendanger, B. (1994) 'Plug into a world of information', *Public Relations Journal*, vol. 50, no. 2, pp. 20–23.

Wong, M. (2003) 'Mass SMS quells HK SARS rumour', *The Australian*, 'IT' section, 4 April.

PART 4
PUBLIC RELATIONS
IN ACTION

10 MEDIA RELATIONS

Jane Johnston

In this chapter

Introduction

When asked to define what public relations practitioners do for a living, most people will give you a response that includes dealing with the media. Media relations is one of the best-known elements of public relations because the work is *seen* to be done—that is, we can see the outcomes every day in the media.

The term *media relations* is often used synonymously with *publicity*. As noted in

Chapter 1, publicity is an important function of public relations, and Chapter 2 has shown it to be one of the key phases in the historic development of the profession. But the role of media relations today is far broader and more complex than that of publicist or press agent. Other chapters show how media relations can be at the centre of a wide range of activities. For instance, when dealing with crisis management, interaction with the media is crucial. Community relations will often require contact with the media, and special events and sponsorships usually hinge on the media bringing a message, a story or an image to various publics. And what political campaign is not fought on a media platform? Sometimes media relations means dealing with a few select contacts on a regular basis; alternatively, it may mean managing hundreds of media personnel at a national event (as in the case study at the end of this chapter). At any level, dealing with the media is an integral part of much public relations activity, and its impact and power should never be under-estimated.

This power of the media—in particular, of talkback radio—came under the spotlight with the public outcry over the Sydney Organising Committee for the Olympic Games' (SOCOG) plan to use predominantly overseas marching bands in the official ceremonies of the 2000 Olympics. SOCOG's decision to review the band format followed overwhelming public opinion, led by talkback radio, after the story first broke in the *Sydney Morning Herald*. The media was called a 'powerful tool' in the decision by SOCOG to restructure the band format in favour of Australian members (Jonathan Gatt, on *Media Report* 1999: 3). As one media commentator put it: 'This is a story of how decisions, with major public impact, can be driven by a small number of people using the media.' (Bolton, on *Media Report* 1999: 1)

The media are big business

The Australian media are characterised by controlling monopolies. In the late 1970s, author, academic and social commentator Humphrey McQueen wrote *Australia's Media Monopolies* (1978), which focused on the 'big three' in Australia's media ownership. His chapters were titled: 'Fairfax and great grand sons', 'Murdoch Junior' and 'Packer and sons'. A generation later, we can see that the names have stayed the same.

Of the twelve daily metropolitan and national newspapers in the country, Rupert Murdoch's News Corporation owns six (*Daily Telegraph*, *Herald Sun*, *Advertiser*, *Mercury*, *Northern Territory News*, *Australian*); Queensland Press (also owned by Murdoch) owns the *Courier-Mail*; three are owned by the Fairfax group (*Sydney Morning Herald*, *Age*, *Financial Review*); one by Western Australian Newspaper Holdings (also part owned by News Ltd) (*West Australian*) and one by Rural Press (*Canberra Times*). Ownership of Sunday papers is also dominated by News Ltd. Kerry Packer's Publishing and Broadcasting Ltd (PBL), on the other hand, holds the lion's share of Australian magazines, with fourteen of the top 30 titles, including *The Australian Women's Weekly*, *Woman's Day*, *Cleo* and *Cosmopolitan*, in its stable. Also significant is News Ltd and Fairfax's dominant shareholding in Australian Associated Press (AAP), the news or 'wire' service that supplies news stories to media subscribers (*Communications Update* 2002).

Debate about media monopolies has focused on the issue of cross-media ownership—the ownership of different mediums in the one location by the same company—and foreign ownership—the percentage of ownership allowed by non-Australian citizens. But just how much media is too much when controlled by a single organisation? And how much foreign ownership should be allowed into the equation? Key issues in this long-standing debate include those of diversity, plurality, regulation and, most recently, technological convergence.

In 2002 the Broadcasting Services Amendment (Media Ownership) Bill was tabled in Parliament, proposing a reduction on cross-media ownership restrictions. The changes proposed that operators could seek a special Media Exemption Certificate from the Australian Broadcasting Authority (ABA) to hold both a commercial television and radio licence and own a newspaper in the same location, provided editorial separation was maintained between the media organisations and the levels of local content was also maintained (*Communications Update* 2002: 1). Proposed changes to cross-media ownership invariably result in polarised opinions: existing media outlets are generally in favour of loosening of restrictions while others, such as the Media Entertainment and Arts Alliance (MEAA), the union and professional body that represents journalists, believe arguments to reduce restrictions are flawed because the major mediums are so inherently different. Proposals represent both an ongoing and complex debate, which continues to pose significant stumbling blocks to reform. Indeed, one commentator noted in April 2003 that the proposal was 'the government's latest, and perhaps last, attempt to change the media ownership rules' (Westfield 2003: 39).

However, many proponents argue that changes to media laws are inevitable, just as the industry itself has undergone major change in the past few decades. One of the biggest changes has been the convergence of media industries. Convergence in media platforms has the benefit of enabling them to reach wider and more varied audiences with the same message. It also allows the reader, viewer or listener to seek out the item in their own time. This might mean tracing a missed newspaper story on the internet or reading an internet transcript of a radio story that you tuned into halfway through. It also means that, whatever your preferred medium, you can still get the story. In late 2000, the ABC ran a live broadcast simultaneously on television, radio, the internet and on cable Sky News on the landmark 'stolen generation' case of *Cubillo v Commonwealth of Australia*. The judgment summary, read by Justice Maurice O'Loughlin of the Federal Court, was the first judgment ever delivered live and broadcast simultaneously on all three mediums: 'The judge agreed to the broadcast because of the great public interest and because it gave people the opportunity to hear directly and immediately about the reasons for his decision.' (Phillips 2001)

Despite the relatively few players in the major media environment, there are segments of the media that continue to grow and flourish. The growth of community and alternative press and broadcasters, as well as the trade press, represent different types of media. The print media include publications targeted at minority or special-interest groups, like left- and right-wing newspapers, indigenous, ethnic and gay press, as well as independents like the *Big Issue*, which deals with a variety of serious news and features. The community media are extremely well represented on the internet and community radio is also on the increase, as recent studies have shown.

> The community radio sector has shown phenomenal growth in the past decade, with the number of community radio stations now surpassing the number of commercial broadcasters. In 2002, the Australian Broadcasting Authority listed 236 community broadcasters and 104 active aspirant stations working toward a full licence (Forde, Meadows and Foxwell 2002: 1).

Trade newspapers and magazines (fondly called 'the trades') also represent a major market, with publications servicing just about every profession and occupation from Aviation to Zoology; these publications are usually available on a subscription basis. The very nature of 'the trades' means that the readership is very narrowly defined. Public relations writers can usually be optimistic about this sector of the media using their stories.

The relationship between the media and public relations

But what does all this mean for the public relations practitioner? For trade, alternative and community media, operation largely by volunteers or small staff often means a reliance on information from public relations outlets. So, while audiences may not be as widespread or large as most mainstream media, they can provide avenues of publicity that should not be overlooked. Similarly, media outlets that represent minority groups, such as gay or ethnic radio stations, should be considered for their specific target audiences.

In mainstream media, greater concentration means fewer major outlets. With the exception of Sydney and Melbourne, each capital city in Australia has only one daily newspaper. This has resulted from either the full closure of papers or the amalgamation of two papers into one, and follows the demise of all afternoon newspapers. With this contraction of daily print media has arisen a reliance on syndicated work, press agencies and news subsidies—material generated by organisations and channelled through public relations practitioners. Complexity of news issues and the reliance on smaller staffing numbers to fill news space also make it easier for public relations to gain access to the media.

In his analysis of the rise of public relations in the early 1900s, Habermas noted how the demands of the press enhanced the growth of the public relations industry (1989). Analysts have continued to note this trend: 'PR has become one of the most important external influences on journalism as it is now practised' (Marshall and Kingsbury 1996: 127). Studies on the impact of public relations on the media reinforce the role of public relations work. One study showed that 30 per cent of 2500 newspaper articles tracked were wholly or partially based on press releases. Of these, 20 per cent were used verbatim or with only minor changes (Macnamara, in *Choice* 1998: 29).

But while public relations practitioners may rightly see their role as vital to the media, it is not a one-way relationship. Just as public relations provide information to the media, so too does the media provide information to the public relations profession. This is done through the simple task of media monitoring: reading, watching and listening to the media every day—a simple, yet vital, form of research. Media monitoring is about being up to date with issues, events and changes that occur in your town or industry, as well as nationally and globally. The practitioner will use the media in their role of issues manager, monitoring trends, government policy and legislation, debates and opinion. In daily monitoring of the news media, a range of areas should be covered to gauge public opinion and trends. These include the news and feature pages, the editorial or leader, columns, letters to the editor, talkback radio and television panel and review programs.

Due to the range and reach of media stories that can be generated by a single organisation, especially at times of heightened public interest, organisations increasingly hire a professional media monitoring company (or clippings service) to collect and file stories for them. Organisations like Media Monitors and Rehame will clip print stories and monitor broadcast stories on behalf of their client. The client pays a retainer to the monitoring company to receive a daily 'clippings file', which includes all (or as many as possible) stories that feature the name of the organisation. Clippings files provide a useful record of the media coverage of organisations, events or issues and can be important for research if carefully archived.

What makes news?

Clippings services will collate news stories once they appear in the news media, but how do public relations practitioners know whether their event, product, organisation or profile is newsworthy in the first place? What judgment is used by media gatekeepers to determine what is in and what is out? In trying to define just what is worth printing or broadcasting, the value of the news must be determined. Conley lists eight news values: impact, conflict, timeliness, proximity, prominence, currency, human interest, the unusual (2002: 42). Granato also includes sex, disaster, money, drugs and animals (1991: 34). In addition, news values might also include 'underdog' and 'fair go' stories (as characterised in the SOCOG marching band example).

An examination of any daily newspaper or news program will find these news values coupled together. Take the news values of an everyday story, such as the announcement of a new shopping centre development. It may include:

- *impact*—because it will have an effect on the shopping public, other shopping centres, and the local economy;
- *conflict*—if there is any opposition to the development;
- *timeliness*—when the development was announced, construction begun and trading commenced (outside these occasions, the time factor would be an unlikely news value);
- *proximity*—to those living nearby: a development in inner Brisbane would have no relevance to the media outside that city but would certainly be of news value to the Brisbane media;
- *prominence*—tends to refer to people of high public profile, so unless the development was associated with a well-known identity, this would be unlikely to apply; alternatively, if the development were to take place in a prominent site known for something else, such as Anzac Square in Brisbane's CBD (or a similar landmark in any capital city), it would apply;
- *currency*—if the type of story was already topical: if stories on shopping centres,

the location, the developer or another key factor were already in the news, this value would apply;

- *human interest*—depending on many aspects of the development: the location may have historic significance, the people behind the scenes may have a story to tell; this news value generally includes the people factor of a story;
- the *unusual*—depending on what different stories could be located: perhaps the building incorporates new technology or architecture? It is unlikely that this would apply to the development itself, but this factor could be developed in follow-up or feature stories;
- *money*—would form a significant news value, with such an announcement likely to be published in the financial as well as mainstream and community media. If it is combined with the unusual, perhaps costing a record amount, it will be even more newsworthy.

Know your media

Deadlines

Just as it is important to know what makes news, it is important to know the deadlines of the newsrooms. Media outlets run to strict and inflexible deadlines and these vary with the type of medium, the complexity, location and regularity of production. For example, most evening news services have their news line-ups in place by 5.00 p.m. Only a major news story, such as a challenge to a political party leadership role, would be likely to gain placement after this time. Most glossy magazines have a lead time of one to two months, so feature placements in these need careful forward planning. The news sections of morning newspapers are 'put to bed' before midnight each day, but most stories will be written by late afternoon. This allows the sub-editing process to take place.

The most flexible of all deadlines is in radio news updates. Because radio newspeople are constantly putting together news bulletins—either hourly or half-hourly—they can receive news as close as ten minutes before deadline. They also rely on people to phone, fax or courier news items to keep the news updated. For this reason, radio is an important news outlet for breaking news stories or providing updates on crisis situations such as blackouts or road closures. Because of the immediacy of radio, newsreaders often 'rip-and-read' stories—meaning they will grab a news story and read it as it comes off the fax machine.

It is therefore essential that practitioners who deal with different media become familiar with all styles and deadlines and work well within them. This will mean they not only assist the media as information providers but also maximise the chances of gaining exposure for their organisation.

Who's who in the newsroom

Once deadlines have been established, the public relations practitioner must learn who makes the decisions and who writes the news. Two things are important here. First, it is important to understand the personnel make-up of a newsroom. Second, it is critical to know the names and roles of the journalists within the newsrooms in your target area. Figure 10.1 shows a simple diagram of the newspaper newsroom hierarchy, with television titles in brackets.

Figure 10.1 Newsroom hierarchy

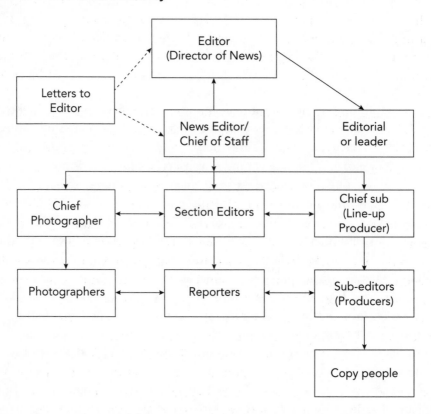

Most newsrooms are characterised by a basic hierarchy. At the top of a newspaper newsroom, with the final word on editorial decisions, is the editor. Next in line is the news editor, who takes day-to-day control of what news is covered. On a parallel to the news editor is the chief of staff, who allocates news and monitors the staff. (Sometimes, especially on smaller publications, the news editor and chief of staff are one and the same.) Then there are section heads, who look after specific sections within the paper (such as entertainment, sport and arts); the chief sub-editor, who oversees all the sub-editors that fit the stories to the paper and write headlines; and the journalists. Roundspeople are located within this last group. Copy people are at the bottom of the hierarchy, performing the tasks of moving and gathering material as required by senior personnel.

Newsrooms in radio and television stations have some similarities but there are differences. Of particular importance is the role of the producer, who arranges material for news broadcasts as well as material for radio talkback shows. Often students think it is best to go 'straight to the top' with their news stories—suggesting the editor as the best person to approach with their story idea, fax or email. In reality, the people who will decide on the daily story rundown will be either a news editor or chief of staff, who will allocate stories to specific rounds-people. Roundspeople also work alone to source stories, so it is at these two levels that public relations practitioners should look to establish daily working relationships.

It is essential for public relations practitioners to have a sound understanding of the role of the roundsperson, because this is an integral part of most news outlets, especially in newspapers. Rounds include politics, courts, local government, education, health, aviation, environment, particular sports such as Rugby League, and general news. On an average-sized daily newspaper with perhaps twenty or more editorial staff members, more than half may have a specific round. However, on a small community paper, in a radio station or on a country TV station, staffing levels may be as low as two or three people. This means reporters will be expected to cover everything, from the local fete to a change of government, and it is unlikely that specific rounds will be allocated. Knowing the needs of individuals will assist in getting the right story to the right person at the right time.

After establishing the various roles in the newsroom, a key factor in successful media relations is getting to know the journalists by name whenever possible. Everyone likes to be referred to by name, and journalists are no exception. In day-to-day dealings, it is imperative to think of members of the media as individuals. This is easier to do at a local level, where the public relations practitioner can talk and meet with journalists personally and professional relationships can be based on an understanding of each other's roles. Fostering positive working relationships will help to eradicate negative stereotypes which can perpetuate what has often been an uneasy relationship between these two professions.

Getting to know the media is also a useful starting point in keeping negative publicity to a minimum. That is not to say journalists will drop a story simply because you know them—they too have a job to do. However, in times of crisis, of embargoed stories, or when a negative story may be balanced by a clearly thought-out response, it is critical to have the respect and trust of the media.

Differences in media styles

The term 'the media' can be very misleading in the context of public relations work. The media should not be thought of as one amorphous mass; rather it must be considered as a complex and multi-layered part of society. Different mediums have specific requirements, offering different opportunities. Even within one medium—say television—requirements are vastly different for a lifestyle show than they are for a current affairs program. The public relations practitioner should be aware of some key differences between these various media.

In supplying material to each medium, the practitioner should always consider the medium's particular needs. Newspapers and magazines may rely on photographs to fully utilise and develop a story. This is often best achieved by supplying the content for a photograph and allowing the print photographer to take it according to their own creative style and specifications. For example, print photographers will often take close-ups to minimise excess space. While some photographs are expected to be supplied, such as headshots of key personnel, some newspapers find the supply of photographs annoying. It is best, when dealing with particular newspapers on an ongoing basis, to check on their policy. These checks should include whether black-and-white photographs or colour transparencies are preferred, or digital photographs sent by email (this is discussed further in Chapter 8).

Similarly, when supplying material to TV news outlets it is wise to consider specific local needs. In general, television relies on vision, and only the strongest of stories will run without it. Stories may run that are weak in news content but strong visually. Supply of written press releases is an acceptable mode, despite this being a broadcast medium. Television journalists are trained to rewrite to broadcast style. In addition, visual material is often accepted and even requested when covering issues or events not easily accessible to camera crews. For instance, footage of mining scenes or outback rail scenes may be supplied to TV newsrooms because of the impracticability of accessing the material quickly. Such visuals, also known as 'wilds' or 'B-rolls', are likely to become 'stock footage' or 'file tape', which is used when visuals are needed for future stories. Studies have shown a reliance on such stock footage: Putnis (1994) found that the same visual material was used repeatedly, with over 50 per cent of domestic commercial news stories in Brisbane using file footage (1994: 2).

Stock footage or file tape should not be confused with the use of video news releases (VNRs), which are fully packaged public relations-generated stories—like a press release in video form, complete with vision, interview grab and scripted story. However, these items are not widely used as finished packages in Australia. Moreover, journalists are generally critical of them, seeing them as far too promotional and as threatening the jobs of working journalists. The key here is to avoid being too promotional while providing useful visual material that allows journalistic input, especially in the areas of the voice-over and script. Practitioners can thus effectively service their client organisation while still assisting the media in its needs. Essentially, the information becomes the raw material for the media to use, just as news releases are used in this way.

Targeting your audience

The primary purpose of media selection is getting a message to a specific audience. In reality, newspapers will only be interested in stories if their readers are interested in that story. Sometimes deciding on which media to inform about a story will be a simple task. It may be clearly defined by the subject-matter or purpose of the story. The announcement of a share float of a public company would need to be sent to financial editors of all major newspapers. The target audiences? Current and potential stockholders plus members of finance industries. A release about a school fete in a country town would be sent to the local newspaper, TV and radio station. The target audience? The local community that lives in, or around, the country town.

Selecting the best media for the message is extremely important. When options are not as clearcut as in the above scenarios, the practitioner must be selective. Different media target different publics, and it is thus essential that public relations practitioners know precisely who they want to get their message across to. The media has become increasingly specialised in the past decade, with newspapers, magazines, TV and radio programs offering a vast range of options from which to choose. Much of the material generated in public relations therefore is directed at a specific media niche. This means finding a particular slot in which to access publicity. The breadth of media opportunities also means a lot of work for the practitioner, in staying up to date with trends and available options. Television choice has diversified to cover just about every topic—from lifestyle programs about gardening and pets to handling money and going on holidays. Panel programs which focus on current events and sports, often in humorous discussions, provide ample opportunities for publicity. Radio programs are just as diverse—from retirement and politics to real-life drama and travel. These issues may be taken up on news or magazine programs or on popular talkback radio—which has been called 'dial-in democracy' because of its capacity to give just about everybody a say. Newspapers too have developed new, consumer-driven sections such as automobile, computer and personnel pages to complement the traditional news and features pages. Of course, the internet provides opportunities to reach audiences who do not even access traditional mediums. However, this should be considered in the media mix and not necessarily as the easy or cheap alternative. As one source notes:

> Circulation and audience reach data show newspapers and television remain the dominant media through which people gain virtually all their information on political, social and economic life in Australia. The Internet, pay TV and global satellite services may one day assume a greater influence in our society, but the lack of broadband access and a base of PCs capable of efficiently distributing on-line multi media products is a fraction of the reach of traditional media. (MEAA 2002: 5)

An idea of the demographic make-up of an audience can be gained by becoming familiar with the content and design of the program or format. In television, for example, the language used, the presenter's age and demeanour, time slot and overall presentation will give an indication of the target market of the show. In magazines, price, layout, the pictures used, headlines (and other language) and point of sale will serve as indicators. Information about audiences and readership can be found on a variety of websites, such as the Australian Bureau of Statistics (<www.statistics.gov.au>) and professional polling companies such as the Gallup Organisation (<www. gallup.com>), as well as news organisations that offer information about their audience make-up, such as SBS (<www.sbs.com.au>).

Media tools

A wide range of communications tools are available to the public relations practitioner for dealing with the media. The most common are the media release, media kit and media conferences.

Media releases

The best-known communication tool is the media release, also called a press release or news release. Media alerts or media announcements are usually shorter forms. However, while a mountain of material has been written on how to write a media release, the reality is that many efforts end up in the garbage bin. A quick analysis of some of these releases will show why. They include long, wordy and clumsy introductions; poorly written and ungrammatical text; nonsensical words; ridiculously long position titles in the lead; and no indication that the communication is in fact a news release. Indeed, a close look at some of these rejects can make for a good exercise in what not to write and how not to write it.

News style

The central rule of writing news releases is to write, where possible, in news style. This means analysing how the print media use stories and how broadcast media air stories. There are many similarities. News stories strive to answer the six basic news questions: Who? What? Where? When? Why? and How? Ideally, most of these will be covered in the first few paragraphs.

Print news is generally written in a style called the inverted pyramid, which can be pictured as an upside-down triangle. This style dictates that the key points are used in the first part of the story, with information following in descending order of importance. The logic with this style is that the newsworthiness of the story can be detected early on, and if necessary the story can be cut from the bottom without losing crucial elements. From a public relations perspective, it also means that a well-written release may be run verbatim but cut off part-way through if space does not allow it to be run in its entirety. In other words, the key elements of the story will still be used. There is scope, however, to break away from the inverted pyramid with a story that is quirky or has a particular point of interest, by using an unusual statement or 'teaser' to tweak the reader's interest in the lead. Whether using the inverted pyramid style or a more narrative approach, all releases should be succinctly written, avoiding waffly, loose or wordy styles.

While releases may sometimes be used verbatim, this should not be expected. The reality is that once a release leaves a public relations office, it is out of the practitioner's control and in the hands of the gatekeeper. (This uncontrolled aspect of the media is also discussed in Chapter 7.) The best any public relations practitioner can hope for is careful and considered attention from the journalist allocated to your story. All practitioners can do is make sure they maximise their chances of getting a run. It is essential that the release be well written, the content newsworthy and that it reach the right media person at the right time. Factors, such as a limited space or news hole, and other events of the day, will also have a bearing on whether your release is used.

Bivins (1995) points out that editors take 30 seconds to peruse media releases. The first three criteria by which they are judged are: (a) who you are; (b) the head-line; and (c) the lead. Stylistics of news should always be considered. In the print media, for instance, numbers are spelt out up to nine, with digits used from 10 upwards. A particular style for dates (1 January 2001), the limited use of titles and capitals, use of active verbs rather than passive, and the almost exclusive use of the verb 'said' all represent preferred media style. Media organisations all use style guides and these can be a valuable reference tool.

The process of sending news releases is similar to the process of sending invitations to news conferences (which is dealt with later in this chapter). In general, though, faxing or emailing news releases are the most popular methods of dissemination.

Media kits

Media kits are made up of a variety of items to make the journalist's job easier. The best-known item is the media release (see above). Often several releases will be included, each covering different newsworthy aspects. Other items in the kit will vary to cover a wide variety of information. There are no set rules of what to include, but a media kit should be updated regularly so it does not become stale or outdated. Items may include: a fact sheet; a backgrounder; a feature article; a newsletter; a biography or profile; a brochure; a map; a calendar of events; a list of key personnel; an annual report; key newspaper clippings; a poster; a keyring; a business card; a media pass; even a t-shirt or cap. Not all of these items will be prepared specifically for the media. Some, such as annual reports, are created primarily for shareholders, staff members or potential investors (these are dealt with in Chapters 8 and 14). While there is a wealth of information that may be used in a media kit, care should be taken not to overdo its contents, as the media may simply find it too complicated or weighty and file it in the garbage.

Fact sheets

These are easy reference guides which list key attributes of an organisation or event. A hotel's fact sheet, for instance, may record key personnel, facilities, historical detail, conference capabilities, room numbers and configurations, other hotels in the same chain and so on. A fact sheet for an event such as a carnival day might utilise the Who, What, Where, When and Why of the event as subheads, listing the times for the event, the venue, who will be appearing and whether the event is linked with a charity. A fact sheet should be uncluttered and easy to read.

Backgrounders

These provide the background to an event or organisation. Unlike the media release, which lists the information in order of importance, a backgrounder is usually a factual account, which may be written in a chronological or narrative fashion. By providing the background, it allows the news angles to be used in media releases; thus they are not 'clogged up' by background information. It is particularly useful in providing historical information about the establishment of an organisation or event. For example, the history of the Commonwealth Games may include interesting points, but a media release each year providing this history would become tedious; hence the history may be included as a backgrounder.

Feature articles

There are two ways for public relations practitioners to provide these: a feature article may be written in full, or a feature idea may be developed and passed on to a journalist. A well-written feature may be used as provided, but features require specific skills and should be written for a specific market. In reality, providing feature ideas is the most effective way. In news value terms, a feature tends to look to the novel, human interest and unusual items, or may develop a current affairs story through a behind-the-scenes approach. Features are usually more relaxed, and often less formal, than news stories. For the public relations practitioner, they often represent stories that are 'holdable' and will not date, or stories that are quirky and may not warrant space in the news pages but make for an interesting story with a twist somewhere further into the paper or on another day. That is not to say features are not strong stories. They often do not have the same urgency as news, but can be used effectively as follow-up stories.

Profiles or 'biogs'

These provide a comprehensive background on an individual or a company. They will usually include the most up-to-date information first—for instance, in profiling an actor appearing in a theatrical production, the actor's most recent achievements will be listed before any earlier credits or training. If, however, an industry award is the key feature of the profile, this will almost certainly be listed first. Company profiles are often written for the benefit of consumers and shareholders, but may be included in a media kit if they include information the media might find useful.

Other items

The inclusion of a business card is essential in a media kit. By distributing a media kit the practitioner is saying to the journalist: 'Call me to confirm or elaborate on any information here'. It is vital that the journalist knows how and where to contact the practitioner who distributed the kit, both during and after office hours.

Media passes may be required by journalists, photographers and camera people at major events. Such passes will allow the media access to an event that might otherwise give limited access to the public or media in general. (The case study later in this chapter illustrates this.) Passes should clearly identify the event, the dates of entry and the person or organisation they have been distributed to.

Maps can be included in cases where directions are necessary. These should be illustrated and clearly laid out.

Posters will usually carry the same message as a brochure or media release, but in a highly visual form. These are a valuable form of public communication, and the media may find them useful for reference purposes.

T-shirts, keyrings and caps offer a catchy way to get a message across for a continued period of time. Catchy slogans and clear pictures work well for these items, which do not lend themselves to clutter or complicated words.

Newsletters, brochures and annual reports are all-important items that may be included in the media kit (these have been described further in Chapter 8).

A calendar of events can be useful when providing the media with a list of dates and events that are planned to take place over a period of time. Sometimes a grid-style or Gantt chart is used to allow a time–event reference to be easily identified.

While the content of all these items will vary with the event, organisation, product or person, the design and style of each press kit should be uniform and consistent. Key phrases and slogans, consistency in letterhead, typeface, presentation and style should mean the media kit is presented as a whole. Not only will it look better, but messages will be clearer. In political campaigning, for example, the media kit should remain consistent with other key communication, such as

TV and newspaper advertising, direct mail and billboard advertising, to keep the message clear and focused.

The media conference

Media conferences, or news or press conferences, are called for a wide variety of reasons. And, while they are not part of the day-to-day life of all practitioners, there is nevertheless a need to have a basic understanding of why they are held, when and where to hold them, and who to invite.

Why hold a media conference?

In general, media conferences are held:

- to allow for a wide dissemination of a story;
- to give all media access to the news at once;
- to allow journalists to ask follow-up questions.

Ideally, the public relations practitioner will be in a position to proactively arrange a media conference, with plenty of time to plan, prepare and check that everything is in place. Sometimes, however, a news conference will be called in haste—for instance, to explain a disaster or crisis. Wilcox and Nolte (1995: 46) identify six main scenarios as appropriate for a media conference:

- when an announcement of considerable importance to a large number of people in the community is to be made (e.g. an election date);
- when a matter of public concern needs to be explained (e.g. a food recall);
- where reporters have requested access to a key individual and it is important to give all media equal access to that person (e.g. a visiting celebrity);
- if a new product or an invention in the public interest is to be unveiled, demonstrated or explained to the media (e.g. a solar-powered vehicle);
- when a person of importance is coming to town and there are many media requests for interviews (e.g. the Prime Minister); and
- when a complex issue or situation is to be announced and the media need access to someone who can answer their questions (e.g. a company merger).

Once the reason for the conference has been established, other key questions should be considered.

When to hold the media conference

The most important consideration here is to find a time that is most convenient to journalists. The primary daily news requirements relate to morning newspapers and evening TV news. Morning conferences, held at around 10.00 a.m., suit most media best. When possible, avoid weekends because the media often have fewer staff rostered on the weekend. However, there is also greater competition during the week for news space from businesses and government departments. Avoid clashes with other media conferences and planned events where possible. Early in the week is generally considered to be quieter than the end of the week.

Who to invite

Obviously all media conferences are different, so there is no set list of who should, or should not, be invited. When preparing the invitation list, the following questions need to be asked: Who would be interested in covering this event? Which media outlets reach which publics? The organiser must have a clear idea of who the message should reach and consider the best media available to reach that market. A media conference announcing a national election will need a different media list from a conference announcing a factory closure, mine disaster or race sponsorship. It is important to keep up-to-date lists, usually on a computer database, to allow easy access to the appropriate media details. Local media lists are a good start. More specific lists should be kept on separate computer databases for specialised media. For example, a boating manufacturer would keep lists of boating media, technical and trade publications, lifestyle and leisure publications and financial media. Such use of databases is simply good management, allowing an assistant or colleague to access information in the absence of the practitioner and to update them regularly.

As well as the mainstream media, there are more specific media, less readily accessed, servicing specific target audiences. Such media include the trade press, ethnic, community, public or alternative media outlets. Media guides will provide the information to compile these lists. Among the most popular is *Margaret Gee's Australian Media Guide*, which is updated quarterly with new names, addresses and publications. It is essential, however, to keep personal lists updated to ensure that invitations or press releases are not duplicated or omitted, or sent to the wrong person.

How to invite them

An invitation to a media conference may be faxed, couriered, emailed or posted, depending on the time available. Email has become a common tool for sending invitations; however, its prolific use can mean an invitation may be overlooked. Once the invitation has been sent, it is usually followed up by a phone call on the morning of the conference to check on attendance. Invitations vary in style from standard invitations to the 'teaser', which gives an idea that a newsworthy announcement will be made. Usually the full story will not be sent out in a release/invitation, because this would obviate the reason for holding the conference in the first place. However, if the conference is designed to give the media visual coverage of an event—say, a touring celebrity—it may be necessary to provide enough detail in the announcement to ensure that the right media attend. A lighthearted function such as a celebrity carnival day will allow the organiser some scope in using a fun-style invitation, whereas the announcement of a food poisoning scare will require an appropriately serious tone.

Media response also depends on the event. If the event is high on the news value list, it is likely to be well attended. If a more pressing news event occurs when the media conference is planned, there could be a disappointing turnout. In news terms, a passenger ferry capsizing in rough waters is a bigger news story than the announcement of a refurbished shopping centre. In general terms, the media will steer towards the less commercial event, knowing they will pick the other up by phone or news release, or a visit later in the day. Many media representatives will not RSVP at all. While it is considered appropriate to call the media to ascertain a rough idea of numbers, most journalists find badgering highly annoying. In most cases, too many phone calls will only make the organiser sound desperate and virtually guarantee 'no shows'.

Where to hold the media conference

There are several key factors that must be considered in arranging a venue for a media conference. The first is whether the venue is central and easily accessed. Venues used for media conferences include large hotels, conference centres, town halls or large offices within corporate headquarters. These work well because they are equipped to cope with parking requirements, phone and fax facilities, and electrical outlets for lighting. They also have the facilities in place for setting up the conference, such as microphones, lecterns, tables and chairs. If a media conference is held at corporate headquarters or within the building occupied by the organisation requiring the conference—such as in a council chambers or a political party headquarters—the conference organiser will need to set up the space for the media—perhaps a boardroom or a small lecture theatre. While there are certainly advantages to holding conferences on site, the organiser needs to consider whether the venue can cope with parking and other media requirements. Alternatively, there will be occasions when it is appropriate to hold a media conference outside, as with on-site inspections of building developments in progress or at a crime scene. Media needs should be carefully considered, as outside catering and cartage may be required.

Set-up and other considerations

The set-up for a media conference will always include a basic list of needs, and a diligent organiser will have a checklist to make sure all aspects are covered. A basic checklist includes:

- a table at the arrival door complete with a media kit or a media release;
- someone to hand these to the media and be available to assist with media needs;
- a floor plan with both sufficient chairs and floor space to cater to print and broad-cast media needs;
- a front table for dignitaries and speakers;
- water for speakers;
- a lectern;
- a microphone;
- a corporate banner or signage to identify your organisation;
- facilities for speakers who may need overheads, charts, internet access or a computer;
- power availability for most indoor venues (most television crews need to use lighting);
- signage in the foyer or at the central arrival point to direct media;
- refreshments for media; and
- a space outside the conference room for one-on-one or television interviews to take place.

Additional items might include name badges or telephone access for the media (especially if mobile service is an issue). Remember, at a media conference no one will notice the things that go right, but they will notice and remember things that go wrong. This includes any omissions or mistakes. So it is essential to physically check the requirements, which means turning up well in advance to make sure everything, right down to the microphone, is connected and in place.

Remember that a large percentage of media need visuals to make their story worth running. Visuals can mean the difference between a four-paragraph story on page five or a front-page story featuring a dominant photograph.

If a media monitoring service is already on retainer for the organisation, it will need to be advised of the conference so it can monitor media coverage of the event. Keep lists at all times. These should include a list of costs for billing purposes. All media releases associated with the conference should be compiled and kept together for future reference. Note which media attended the conference and how you might improve it next time. After the conference, contact the media who did not attend and offer to courier or fax a press kit to them immediately. Similarly, if the media have advised you in advance that they cannot attend but would be able to use sound or vision of the event, plan for this and have it couriered immediately.

Conclusion

Dealing with the media is a critical part of the public relations practitioner's profession. It incorporates both technical aspects, in writing media releases and compiling media kits, and the manager's role, in advising senior personnel about working with the media. Media relations calls on the key attributes of writing, organisation and planning, as well as keen interpersonal skills and up-to-the-minute knowledge of news and current events. It also calls for an understanding of the specific nature of the media environment. Despite an often uneasy alliance between the media and the public relations profession, there is a growing interdependence in the two industries. This can be developed and enhanced through mutual understanding of, and respect for, each other's roles and responsibilities. Only through this clear understanding will effective, strong communication be achieved.

Case study 10.1: Manchester 2002 Commonwealth Games Information News Service

The Information News Service (INS) at the 2002 Manchester Commonwealth Games was responsible for providing Games-time news and information to accredited personnel, primarily the 4000 accredited media.

While it was the internal news agency for the Games, and the official vehicle for all Games news, the INS did not aim to rival national and international news agencies (the Press Association, Reuters, etc.). Its mission was to provide concise, accurate and timely Games coverage for use by the accredited media to augment their stories/reports.

Information News Service personnel had unprecedented and often exclusive access to many areas that both rights-holders—those news organis-ations which had paid handsomely for broadcast and print rights—and other accredited media did not.

The news items generated by INS were available to the news media and other members of the Games family (e.g. athletes and officials) on the Games-time intranet system, the Games family Information System (GFIS).

Modelled on a similar system developed for the Sydney 2000 Olympic Games, GFIS also contained other information essential for the media, includ-ing competition schedules and results, medals, records, biographies, historical results, transportation and weather.

GFIS terminals were located in the tribunes (the computer news desks overlooking the playing arenas) of all the seventeen sports venues, the Athletes' Village and the 1000-seat Main Press Centre (MPC) in central Manchester.

The size of the team varied from venue to venue but was made up of an Information Editor with a number of Information Assistants—usually two or three and mainly local university students—reporting to him or her. The Information Editor was ultimately responsible for the news generated from the venue.

The primary role of the Information Assistants was to assist the Information Editor in producing the news items required to be published on the system each day.

A five-person Main Press Centre editorial team was ultimately responsible for the sub-editing and quality control of information emanating from the venues, as well as the smooth running of the INS operation overall.

News at Games time

Two of the key aims for the Information News Service were consistency and simplicity. For these reasons, news items produced by the INS teams across *all* venues fell into one of six categories:

1   previews: sport preview, daily preview, session preview or event preview;
2   reviews: daily review, session review or event review;
3   flash quotes;

4   press conference quotes;
5   advisories; and
6   news.

Previews

The *sport preview* was an overview of the competition format for each sport, its events/phases and athletes. It was a high-level news item no more than ten paragraphs in length which aimed to provide the media with an understanding of the competition, how it should progress and the athletes/teams to watch.

The *daily preview* outlined the next day's competition. It highlighted the 'blue-ribbon' events for the day, possible outcomes and athletes/teams to watch. It was no longer than eight paragraphs and had to be generated the evening before each day's competition.

The *session previews* were similar to daily previews in that they needed to preview more than one event, but these events would only be in one 'session' for the day. There may be one, two or no session previews required each day, depending on the sport. They were no longer than eight paragraphs and needed to be produced as soon as possible after the previous session was complete.

The *event preview* was a generic title and, depending on the sport, was used for categories (e.g. weightlifting), matches (team sports) and bouts (boxing). The event preview contained event-specific information, a summary of the athletes competing and what they were expected to achieve.

Event previews were not provided for every event. For example, in Table Tennis there was no need to preview each and every match, but a preview was written for each phase of each event. In Hockey, there was no need to preview every match in the preliminary round, but a preview was produced for each match in the semi-finals and finals.

For each of the previews, reporting staff and editors considered:

* *which* events were on for the day/session and which events/athletes/teams were the 'ones to watch';
* *why* they had identified certain events/athletes/teams as the 'ones to watch'. They had to be informative. Was an athlete a reigning world champion? Was a team a defending Commonwealth champion?
* *when* and *where* the events previewed would take place;
* *what* the possible outcomes for the day/session/event were. Was it a qualifying round that would lead into the next day's finals? Was this the final phase that would determine the medallists? How would the results of the day/session/event influence the next day's competition?

The Information News Service provided fast and factual media releases 24 hours a day during the 2002 Commonwealth Games. (Courtesy Manchester 2002 Commonwealth Games)

Reviews

As the name suggests, this category was a review, or a 'wrap', of a day, session or event within a certain sport. An *event review* was no longer than six paragraphs long and had to be produced within twenty minutes of the event. Each *session review* and *daily review* was wrapped up within eight paragraphs and 30 minutes.

When writing Reviews, reporting staff and editors considered:

- *who* the big winners and losers of the event/session/day were, and *what* the scores/times, etc. were. Did any one athlete/team seem to be dominating?;
- *what* phase of the competition it was (preliminary round, final round);
- anything significant that had occurred in the event/session/day;
- what may happen next in the competition and how does the overall tournament now stand; and
- *when* and *where* the event/session/day took place.

Flash quotes

One of the most important roles for the Information Assistants was to gather flash quotes. These were quotes from selected athletes as they left the field of play via the 'mixed zone', which was a dedicated area where media were able to have short interviews with athletes. In order to take flash quotes, Information Assistants were positioned in the mixed zone before the end of competition in preparation for a quick (or 'flash') interview with an athlete or coach.

Quotes were entered as soon as possible. They were an urgent news item. The idea was to get the flash quote published on to GFIS and delivered to the media at the venues for inclusion in their event reportage as soon as possible.

Press conference quotes

Press conferences were held daily at the Main Press Centre, the Athletes' Village and at the venues.

With sponsor backdrops, tables, chairs and dedicated rooms, the press conferences were called by both the Manchester 2002 organisers to make announcements of whole-of-Games importance and by the teams themselves to make country-specific announcements.

On two occasions, the World Anti-doping Agency (WADA) also called press conferences at the Main Press Centre to update the media on emergent athlete drug issues.

Conferences were held daily by several national teams in the Athletes' Village for rights-holding media only (the only media allowed into the Village) and were often followed up by briefings for non-rights-holding accredited media outside the compound gates. Again, by virtue of the monies spent on broadcast and print rights, it was important the rights-holders had first 'bite of the cherry' regarding any announcements or interviews.

The press conferences were coordinated by the Manchester 2002 media team in conjunction with INS personnel. The team press conferences were coordinated by the various team press officers.

Another important role for the INS Information Assistants was to gather quotes from press conferences. They were asked to produce a summary of a press conference, including a selection of its most significant quotes.

Press conference quotes were filed as soon as possible after the press conference, no later than 20 minutes. The format and style was presented in the same manner as flash quotes, including a one-line preamble to put the quote in context.

Advisories and general news

Advisories listed matters of interest to the media that were not necessarily newsworthy, such as any practical or logistical information that may affect their day.

A typical advisory may list the date, time and location of a press conference, or the access rules for photographers on the field of play, or a change to the opening hours of the Venue Press Centre.

General news items provided the opportunity for the reporting team to list newsworthy items that did not fall into any of the above sport-specific categories. In practice, the news category was used to update the media about injuries to star athletes, or to list other 'fast facts' about the sports. They also took the form of general news items about interesting athletes, arrivals, departures and other happenings.

Case study supplied by INS, Manchester 2002.

Discussion and exercises

1   Consider the cases for and against greater control of media ownership. Discuss this issue, referring to technological convergence, ownership monopolies and foreign ownership. Why do you think changes have been on the agenda for so long without resolution?

2   Locate some discarded news releases from your local media outlet and analyse them for style and content, identifying ways in which the releases could be improved. Once you have done this, use the facts in one release to draft your own version.

3   Become familiar with news values by analysing the front-page stories of today's paper. Many of the stories will include a range of news values. List these in order of importance and discuss why some news values are more common than others. Repeat the exercise on a number of occasions during the semester and see whether news values change.

4   Plan a media conference to announce a major research breakthrough at your educational institution. Break into groups and allocate roles of print media, television media, radio media and science media, as well as the panel who will be interviewed. Prepare questions and responses to 'act out' the media conference.

5   Divide the evening television news bulletins among class groups and monitor these for a week. Log stories which you believe rate low on news content but high on vision. In class, compare your lists and see if any patterns emerge.

Further reading

Bivins, T. (1993) *The Handbook of Public Relations*, NTC Business Books, Illinois.
Communications Update (2002), Media Ownership Update, no. 164, April, Communications Law Centre, UNSW, Sydney.
Conley, D. (1997) *The Daily Miracle*, Oxford University Press, Melbourne.
Hudson, M. (1994) *The Media Game*, Longman, Melbourne.
Wilcox, D. & Nolte, L. (1995) *Public Relations: Writing and Media Techniques*, 2nd edn, HarperCollins, New York.

References

Bivins, T. (1995) *The Handbook of Public Relations*, NTC Business Books, Illinois.
Callaghan, G. (1999), 'Sultans of spin', *Weekend Australian*, 24–25 July, p. 26.
Choice (1998) 'Tainted information', July, pp. 26–31.
Communications Update (2002), Media Ownership Update, no. 164, April, Communications Law Centre, UNSW, Sydney.
Conley, D. (2002) *The Daily Miracle*, 2nd edn, Oxford University Press, Melbourne.
Forde, S., Meadows, M. & Foxwell, K. (2002) *Culture, Commitment, Community: The Australian community radio sector*, Griffith University, Brisbane.
Gilchrist, M. & Burke, F. (1999) 'Time to break the media ties', *Australian*, 23–24 October, p. 1.
Granato, L. (1991) *Reporting and Writing News*, Prentice-Hall, Melbourne.
Habermas, J. (1989) *The Structural Transformation of the Public Sphere*, Polity Press, Cambridge.
Henderson, I. (1999) 'Mediators', *The Australian* (media insert), 10 June, pp. 1–3.
McQueen, H. (1978) *Australia's Media Monopolies*, Visa, Melbourne.
Marshall, I. & Kingsbury, D. (1996) *Media Realities*, Longman, Melbourne.
Media, Entertainment & Arts Alliance (MEAA) (2002) 'Submission to the Senate Environment, Communications, Information Technology and the Arts Legislation Committee, The Senate, on Media Ownership Bill', April, <www.aph.gov.au/senate/committee/ecita_ctte/media_ownership/submissions/sublist>.
Media Report (1999) 'The use of the media by people eager to blow their own trumpet at the Olympics', 8 July, pp. 1–11.
Phillips, B (2001) email communication, Federal Court of Australia, Melbourne.

Putnis, P. (1994) *Displaced, Re-cut and Recycled*, Centre for Journalism Research and Education, Bond University, Gold Coast.

Westfield, M. (2003) 'Hard pressed', *Australian*, 5–6 April, p. 39.

Wilcox, D. & Nolte, L. (1995) *Public Relations: Writing and Media Techniques*, 2nd edn, HarperCollins, New York.

11

INTERNAL AND COMMUNITY RELATIONS

Marianne Sison

In this chapter

Introduction
Internal public relations
Community relations
Conclusion
Case study 11.1: Breakout and cultural transformation at ANZ
Case study 11.2: The Moreland City Council consultation framework

---

Introduction

Trust, honesty and community—these are the values that organisations and public relations need to embrace. In 2002, scandals affecting former company heavy-weights Enron and Worldcom in the United States, as well as HIH and OneTel in Australia, not only brought their downfall but also raised major questions of trust. Even global consulting firm Andersen, a pillar in the accounting industry world-wide, failed to escape the onslaught on its reputation. These recent events have provided the impetus towards corporate governance which began in the late 1990s.

Two areas of public relations practice that are increasingly highly valued by business leaders are those of *internal public relations* and *community relations*. Both international and local practitioners have consistently emphasised that internal and community relations should be the first and second priority respectively in public relations practice.

Why is this so? The 1990s saw dramatic changes in the traditional organisation.

Where people used to work for a company for life, employees now work on short-term contracts. The standard now is a basic, leaner workforce, streamlined by restructuring, downsizing and re-engineering. Employees who stay are valued for their multi-skilled abilities because there are fewer people doing more work. Outsourcing of work has gained in popularity. Companies tend to invest more in their existing employees, however, because it is more expensive to keep on training new employees. And part of their investment is in maintaining staff morale and goodwill.

In addition, several studies have revealed the relationship between employee communication and job satisfaction and productivity. Senior managers are now recognising that one unhappy employee has the potential to damage a company's polished image in the community. There have been examples in the past of disgruntled employees allegedly being involved in product-tampering cases. What might start as a relatively simple employee relations issue could easily become a crisis of major proportions. In some instances, while the damage to the company may not be so extreme, it could result in a tarnished reputation. And goodwill is a very important asset for businesses.

Having employees as goodwill ambassadors of the company is a concept that has often been under-estimated. Imagine that a company has 2000 employees, and say 90 per cent of them are happy and loyal, thanks to a strategic employee relations program; we then have 1800 individuals saying good things about that company. Multiply that to include two to five family members who are recipients of that goodwill, and we get up to 10 000 ambassadors promoting the company's good citizenship.

In the same manner, goodwill within the community in which a business operates is now being given top priority by senior management. Again, with the rise of advocacy and community groups, good positive relationships with stakeholders in the community are a key element for the continued operation of a business.

These values of trust, honesty and community are more important than ever for public relations practitioners. Ethical practice (which is discussed in Chapter 5) is high on the agenda of Australian public relations practitioners. Public relations is increasingly taking the role of the company's social conscience.

It is interesting to note how much importance is being placed by companies on the two-way symmetric communication model proposed by Grunig and Hunt (1984), which is discussed in Chapter 3. In addition, Pat Jackson's (1998) total relationship management model identifies employee relations and community relations as the first two vital steps in achieving positive relations with key stake-holders. The importance of these two areas of public relations practice was emphasised by Dickson (1984), who pointed out that the principal factor in the suc-cess of the case studies in community relations is employee relations.

Interestingly, Grunig et al.'s Excellence study (2002: 9) identifies a symmetrical system of internal communication as a key characteristic of excellent public re-lations programs. The same study supports the idea that companies who engage with their activist publics practise excellent public relations (2002: 476).

In this era of turmoil—which has seen protests, empowerment, freedom of speech and information, media access and the threat of trial by media—businesses can no longer remain arrogant, uncaring and selfish. It makes good business sense to start caring. However, it is not enough for businesses just to show they care: they must *genuinely* care for the people who make their businesses work. After all, it is people who make businesses successful.

Internal public relations

Overview

William Scott defines an organisation as 'a system of coordinated activities of a group of people working cooperatively toward a common goal under authority and leadership' (in Goldhaber 1990: 38). What this definition means is that the people performing different functions make up the organisation. Without them, an organisation will have no culture. And, without a strong and distinct culture, the organisation may have difficulty running its operations smoothly. That is why, even when outsourcing or hiring casual workers is a cost-effective proposition, organisations still depend on a group of permanent full-time employees to give the organisation its identity.

Unlike the company premises, cash reserves, equipment and other tangible assets of an organisation, it is human resources which make all the other resources work. Machines are not enough to make a business work because people and their skills are needed to operate those machines. That is why modern management literature focuses on the value of intellectual capital and how organisations should maximise the knowledge base within their organisations.

Who are our internal publics?

Internal publics comprise two main groups: an *organisation's employees*, and an *association's members*. Within the organisation, the employees are all the people working for the organisation, from the Chairman of the Board to the junior in the mailroom. Employee publics refer not only to the full-time permanent staff, but also to part-time and casual employees, contractors and volunteers. On the other hand, association members such as members of the PRIA usually join the association out of a special or professional interest. They become members by paying a joining fee and membership dues and sometimes by going through strict selection criteria. While most of the discussion will relate to both groups, this chapter concentrates on employee publics.

Why is it important to maintain employee goodwill?

Senior managers' awareness of the importance of employees is not really new. However, because of traditional linear and hierarchical organisational structures, it has been difficult to access the people at the top. Modern management texts have popularised flat organisational structures, which have facilitated communication access between the higher, middle and junior levels.

There are a number of reasons why maintaining employee goodwill makes good business sense. In a company with twenty employees, an incident where one employee is unfairly treated will be known to the rest of the staff through word of mouth or the grapevine, and this could result in not one, but five, ten or twenty unhappy employees. The same is true for much larger organisations. And studies of rumour show that we can stop it spreading by closing the knowledge gap—that is, providing more information (Goldhaber 1990; Tedeschi et al. 1985).

Rumour has been defined as information passed on through the grapevine, with its impact determined by the anxiety level of those who hear it (Vaughan and Hogg 1998). In 1947, Allport and Postman cited the importance and ambiguity of information as factors defining the intensity of rumour (in Goldhaber 1990: 163; Tedeschi et al. 1985: 134). To allay the anxiety created by rumour among those affected by its spread, it is best that a credible organisational source provide the facts. So, where an employee is rumoured to have been treated unfairly, and this information has not been confirmed or denied by anyone, it is likely that this lack of information will lead to anxiety among the employees. Whether or not the information is true, it will cause some morale problems among staff. It is therefore appropriate for the head of the organisation or the department to provide the facts to the employees immediately.

Furthermore, the notion of *goodwill* has been often underrated, when in fact most public relations practice is based on the goodwill emerging from relationships with publics. Ferguson (cited in Ledingham and Bruning 2000) identified this concept in 1984 and has often been quoted in the recent uptake of this notion in public relations literature. A whole new body of knowledge is emerging in relationship management (see Ledingham and Bruning 2000). In accounting literature, goodwill resulting from public relations activities is valued as a company asset, albeit an intangible one (Elmer 2001). However, most public relations practitioners seem to focus on goodwill created with external publics. Very little research seems to focus on goodwill with internal publics.

A rather fresh and yet radical approach to internal communication is Holtzhausen and Voto's (2002) notion of *organisational activists*. Drawing from postmodernist theory, Holtzhausen and Voto suggest that:

> The practitioner as organizational activist will serve as a conscience in the organization by resisting dominant power structures, particularly when these structures are not inclusive, will preference employees' and external publics' discourse over that of management, will make the most humane decision in a particular situation and will promote new ways of thinking and problem solving through dissension and conflict. (2002: 64)

In their study of Florida practitioners, they discovered that public relations practitioners found themselves to be advocating employees' concerns to management (2002: 71–73).

In Australia, the unions need to be considered in any employee relations program. To develop positive employee relations, it is important to open and maintain communication links with union leaders and representatives. Traditional management thinking seems to resist discussion with union leaders because it is thought that sharing the discussion table will diminish management's power. However, developing an open communication policy with representatives of the organised workforce can prove a more efficient and productive management strategy. One case where communication broke down between management and the unions was that of the Maritime Union of Australia and Patrick Stevedores. The case started in early 1998 as an industrial relations dispute, after Patrick's management illegally sacked 2000 employees in the interests of waterfront reform. Due to several complex factors, this action generated a lot of media attention and thus evolved as a crisis management problem for Patrick, as well as for the federal government. What this example showed was that the company and the federal government underestimated the power of unions, not just in Australia but at an international level.

When BHP's Newcastle Steelworks announced its closure in 1997, it worked hand in hand with the unions, developing a package for its employees before the actual plant closure. BHP developed a financial and personal assistance support package for employees affected by the closure. This package was 'developed with unions and the Transition Steering Team—which included a representative team of employees and staff to help every employee prepare a personal action plan' (Cameron 1997). The agreement included a completion bonus of 40 per cent of severance pay for employees who remained until closure, and a special attendance bonus of up to $2500.

It is in a company's interests to keep its staff happy, loyal and safe. Keeping them informed, communicating with them, consulting with them and developing relationships with them are some of the ways that show the organisation respects them not just as 'workers', but as 'thinking individuals'. Employee loyalty and satisfaction result from deriving a healthy relationship with an employer. Research by the Gallup Organisation (Onsman 1999) has revealed that the nature of work-place relationships with colleagues, bosses and friends provides the basis for a happy and loyal employee. Research by US department store chain Sears Roebuck has also proved the link between profitability, employee satisfaction and customer satisfaction (James 1999). One can build a positive working relationship only if there is trust and a belief in the individuals in the relationship. Therefore, it is important for management to engender a culture of trust so that its communication with staff will be received with credibility and confidence.

A Good Reputation Index published in the *Age/Sydney Morning Herald* (2002) revealed that, based on employee satisfaction and financial performance, Australia Post had the best reputation. The previous year, Hewlett Packard had enjoyed this title.

How can employees believe in and feel confident about their management? One way is by keeping them in the loop—keeping them informed about what is happening in the company. If employees understand the big picture and their role in it, they are more likely to support the organisation's goals. Another way is to include them in the decision-making process. This 'buy-in' concept, sometimes referred to as participative decision-making (Goldhaber 1990: 85–86), relates to the process whereby employees participate in the development, planning and imple-mentation of a new policy and therefore develop ownership of the policy. Having been part of the process, employees find it easier to 'sell' the idea to their fellow employees and thus become 'ambassadors' of the company.

While the trend in employee relations has followed the path of general public relations practice—from the one-way information dissemination to the two-way symmetric form—companies now combine traditional methods with more modern and technology-based tools.

Tools and channels of communication

The introduction of new technology has added new dimensions to communicating with employees, especially in terms of time and distance. But research (Cutlip et al. 1994; Kopec 1996) has continually shown face-to-face communication to be the most effective way of communicating with employees. However, other tools are used as well.

Newsletters and company newspapers

These are publications that follow the format of the mainstream newspaper or news magazine, but cater to a specialised audience: employees. The basic difference between a newsletter and a company newspaper is the timeliness of its content and the size. Usually newsletters are printed on A4-sized sheets or on a folded A3 to come up with four pages of news. They are published on a regular basis—usually fortnightly or monthly—to give employees updates on what is going on in their organisation. Desktop publishing software programs such as PageMaker and Quark-Xpress have made it easy for in-house public relations staff to create newsletters. The circulation or quantity of copies printed will determine the quality required of the printer. Some newsletters that require smaller print runs and are intended for internal staff members may be produced on a laser printer. Bigger print runs are more cost effective if handled by a professional printer.

What goes into newsletters? Usually the public relations staff work with human resources (personnel) staff to ensure that staffing issues and policies are communicated to employees. There are instances when contributions are requested from different departments or even individual employees. This practice gives the employee some form of recognition and a chance to be involved in company-level activity.

The purposes of newsletters vary. Unlike the days when the popular management form was top-down and communication was one-way, the more common purpose of newsletters these days is to provide a channel of expression for the company's employees. It is important to think of newsletters not as a means of publishing the 'management line', but rather as a joint medium for management and staff to share information about the company. New staff policies are disseminated, but contributions and even letters to the editor are also encouraged. Photographs of company events are other regular features of newsletters. They are important in keeping everyone in the company as part of the loop mentioned earlier.

The content of newsletters will also vary, but as a rule it is important to include information about the organisation (local, national or international news); employee information (benefits, new policies, appointments and promotions); information about community or other external environment news; and some personal or social news items. Photographs are important to gain and maintain readers' interest. (Newsletters are discussed further in Chapters 7 and 8.)

Noticeboards

These boards, also called bulletin boards, can easily be taken for granted, as they seem to be part of the office furniture. The key to getting information on notice-boards attended to is to change it regularly. Maintaining the noticeboard—getting rid of old notices, and keeping it neat and tidy—is a tedious task. But it has to be updated continually to be effective. A newer version of this tool is the electronic bulletin board, which really is another version of email via intranets (discussed in Chapter 9). Location is another key factor in the success of noticeboards. It is important to position them where there is a high flow of traffic (for example, near lifts or by walls near toilets) or where staff congregate (for example, the staff/tea room). Notices should be brief and preferably have catchy graphics to gain people's attention. Some items put on noticeboards are new policies, new appointments, or personal notices (for example, birthday greetings, or congratulatory notes for new parents).

Memos

A memorandum is a form of business communication between staff members. Memos are brief letters that are exchanged by staff on a particular issue. They can be presented in bullet-point form and are preferably not more than two pages in length. Memos can be used to impart confidential information about new policies, new procedures, a reprimand, or a congratulatory note. If this last letter comes with a signature of the CEO, it becomes a good motivational tool for the employee.

Awards

Employees value being recognised for their performance, and awards are one way of doing so and motivating other employees to do the same. Awards come in different forms. In a sales department, there would be awards for top-performing salespeople—someone who has surpassed his/her sales target. The award could be a certificate, a cash bonus, gift, or sometimes even travel packages. Employees are also rewarded for their loyalty to the organisation. Awards are given to employees with long-service records of ten years, twenty years, and so on. Awards to employees with exemplary service records are usually handed out in a ceremony or company event. As an example, every McDonald's outlet proudly displays a plaque of its crew member of the month in store. This award acknowledges the excellent performance of the employee and provides an incentive for other employees.

Events

'All work and no play makes Jack a dull boy', or so the saying goes. Employees do look forward to socialising with the people they work with. Company events have been known to improve *ésprit de corps*. These can range from the TGIF (Thank God It's Friday) drinks to the Christmas picnic or more lavish corporate anniversary dinners. Whatever they are, events aim to develop *camaraderie* among employees, and are recognition that employees are not machines but people who have families and enjoy a social life. Hosting a family event is the company's way of saying 'thank you' to employees and their families for the services provided to the company.

Events also encourage participation and involvement among employees. Examples of corporate events include sports days (tennis, golf, netball, football), picnics or barbecues, anniversary dinners, Christmas lunch/dinners, awards nights, and charity involvements. Examples of company-based charity activities include staff wearing denim jeans on 'Jeans for Genes Day' and forming corporate bike teams for the Smith Family's 'Ride around the Bay in a Day' bike ride. One of the more recent innovations in employee relations strategy is maximising corporate sponsorship of athletes. For example, a company that is sponsoring a sports personality will request the celebrity to attend a company function to boost employees' attendance. In addition, it will use the athlete's image to personify the company and eventually serve as a role model for the employees.

Intranets

Sometimes referred to as local area networks (LANs), intranets are composed of a network of computers within an organisation. The employees linked through a global email address receive only messages transmitted on the intranet. This new technology has allowed instant dissemination of text-based information about the organisation. Because they are immediate and avoid the lead time required by printing, intranets are becoming a popular means of communication from management. The email access provides the facility for feedback. Again, just like the memo, an email can prove a morale booster to an employee who feels he/she is getting a personal email from the corporate boss.

Intranets also provide employees with regular information about what is happening in the organisation. At RMIT University in Victoria, for example, each staff member's email is on a global address, and each week staff receive an email from the corporate affairs office. The content can range from human resources information—such as changes in the payroll system—to events occurring on campus—such as a research and training seminar for female academics. While the weekly email comes from the corporate affairs office, staff contributions are also welcome. Again, depending on the company's culture and size, company executives may or may not respond direct to emails from all employees. Bill Gates has been reported to say that he answers all his emails personally. However, many executives divert emails to another person or department for a response.

Interpersonal communication

Studies continue to show that interpersonal or face-to-face communication rates highest in effective communication techniques. Several studies (Tower et al., in Cutlip et al. 1994; International Association of Business Communicators' Communication World, in Dilenschneider 1996) have found that employees prefer to get information from their immediate supervisor.

Research (Whitworth 2002) has also found that interpersonal communication or face-to-face communication is still the preferred and most credible option because of the opportunity to observe non-verbal cues, such as tone of voice and facial expression, as well as the opportunity for immediate feedback.

When the number of subordinates or their geographic location make it difficult for a superior to visit them face to face, organisations resort to tools such as video-conferencing. While this is one step better than teleconferencing, it has some limits. However, videoconferencing is more cost efficient than paying airfares and hotel accommodations, and physically moving staff for every meeting. A more recent innovation is e-conferencing, which involves either text or voice messages being transmitted in real time through a computer network linking workstations located at different points in the world. Someone in Melbourne can have an e-conference with someone in Tokyo, New York, London and Sao Paolo, and none of the conference members needs to leave their own office desk. While this technological innovation allows cost-efficient communication, staff meetings still provide the most effective communication.

Staff meetings are a form of interpersonal communication that allow team members to keep each other up to date. The two-way communication means participants can provide immediate feedback, with meaningful additions in the form of non-verbal cues such as facial gestures, posture and body language. Also, employees can discuss any issues that need clarification at length, rather than be constrained by time, money or distance.

While acknowledging that time is a premium commodity, it is extremely important for organisations to allocate time to regular staff meetings. Whether it is an annual general meeting, where the company directors meet the hundreds of shareholders face-to-face, or the weekly team meeting, where each team member provides progress reports, the value of meetings cannot be over-emphasised. Aside from sharing valuable information, meetings provide an opportunity for sharing experiences. And it is these moments of shared experiences—which become part of what Deal and Kennedy (1982) refer to as corporate rituals—that strengthen the cultural bonds within an organisation.

Community relations

The importance of community relations

> It is no accident that the resurgence of interest in values and morality coincides with the desire to recreate a sense of community within Australian society. The rising level of concern about standards of ethics—in private life, in business, in politics and government—is directly related to concern about fragmentation of traditional Australian tribal groupings. (Mackay 1993)

Hugh Mackay, in his book *Reinventing Australia*, from which the above passage is drawn, argues that the changes in societal structure such as individualism and the breakdown of extended to nuclear families have led people to be lonely. To address this loneliness, Mackay suggests that people tend to develop relationships with anyone they encounter, including those they meet for commercial purposes (such as banks, retail outlets).

Australian consumers are saying they want every encounter with service providers to have some of the character of an ordinary encounter with another human being:

> If you expect me to maintain a relationship with you or your organisation, then act as if we have a relationship: even though we know the basis of this relationship is commercial, we should still treat each other like human beings. (Mackay 1993: 288)

The above quote may reflect the reaction of members of the community who resist technology, seeing it as a way of depersonalising human relationships. For example, older people have been forced to use automatic tellers in lieu of their customary visits to the banks—not only for banking activities, but for a social chat with the teller. The increasingly impersonal relationship between banks and their customers has been offset in recent years by the emergence of call centres. Before call centres became popular, people calling a bank would be put on hold for several minutes while radio ads or music were played. This annoyed many people—not only because of the long waiting time, but because they were made captive listeners to commercials on the phone! With call centres, waiting time has been somewhat reduced and there is a human and live voice on the other end of the line.

A return to personalising the corporate image seems to be the premise on which most organisations are basing their community relations programs. In the interests of extending their relationships beyond the boundaries of their offices and factories, organisations are communicating with people living within the immediate vicinity of the organisation's physical location. Apart from residents, community relations programs also target schools, churches, local businesses and groups of people who share an interest in a specialised area such as art, music or sports.

The rise in consumer advocacy and community action groups has worked to trigger the importance of community relations programs. People (not only existing consumers) who are affected by the activities of companies—also referred to interchangeably as stakeholders or publics—are now saying that they should be considered and consulted. Companies have no choice but to listen. To proceed with a project without appropriate consultation with community members may be akin to corporate suicide. There seems to be no place for big business to be arrogant or selfish.

Some companies have come to understand—rather painfully—that two-way communication is important not only to the company's image, but also to the financial bottom line. One *unsuccessful* action that nevertheless generated high-profile publicity was the 'Save Albert Park' campaign in Melbourne. The local community aimed to move the staging of the Formula One Grand Prix from Albert Park because it believed that the three-day event was posing environmental, aesthetic and health risks for the Melbourne suburb. The community group organised rallies, tied yellow ribbons around trees in the park, used articulate spokespersons and even went to London to demand a meeting with Formula One boss Bernie Ecclestone. While this campaign did not achieve its purpose—of moving the event outside Albert Park—it showed that an active and well-organised group of community residents could generate local and international awareness and make a dent in an organisation's operations. Community action groups are discussed further in Chapter 16.

Increasingly, companies need to consider seriously the community on which their businesses will have an impact. But corporate enterprises and community groups have become media-savvy. It is in the interests of both groups not to have their confrontations displayed on the media, but rather to become aware of each other by listening, respecting and perhaps developing partnerships.

Corporations are slowly realising the need to engage with their communities. The question is whether the companies are doing so out of a genuine concern for the community or out of compliance. The introduction of triple bottom line reporting—which refers to a framework for 'measuring and reporting corporate performance based on economic, social and environmental factors'—is a helpful start. Perhaps this kind of reporting may counter the threat that Starck and Kruckeberg (2001) suggest exists in global corporations' increased power and lack of accountability.

Approaches to community relations

What these lessons tell us is that it is extremely important for companies to show that they *actually care* and value the relationships with their communities. How can companies include 'caring' in their business strategy?

Consultation

Community consultation refers to developing a two-way relationship between the members of the community and the company. It involves asking community leaders to participate in the planning and decision-making process, and allows the company to tackle potential problems and engage the different members in developing solutions to these problems. Consultation can also take the form of organising information nights or town meetings. During these meetings, organisational representatives can present their case, provide the facts, and ask the community to respond and give feedback. Critical to this tactic, however, is how well the organisation integrates the feedback in the development of the project. Again, the stakeholders should see that their comments have been incorporated and that they are recognised for their contribution.

For example, when Hobart City Council decided to improve road access to Mount Wellington (Walker 1998), part of the brief to its consultancy, Corporate Communications, was to conduct an extensive public consultation program. The outcome was a set of recommendations which was endorsed by the local residents and the Fern Tree Community Association. Aside from a positive result, the community representatives praised the consultative process.

Grunig and Hunt's (1984) two-way symmetric model provides a good basis for developing a community relations plan. It posits that two groups should at least meet, even if they do not come to an agreement. The 'meeting' provides an opportunity for the company and the community to air their ideas and to know where each stands. It is, of course, in the interests of both groups to come to a consensus. But this does not always happen. How the discussion develops will depend on how much each party is willing to compromise. Sometimes neither is willing or able to do so. In any case, enabling each side to have its say can help clear the air.

Scanning the environment

Part of a company's public relations activities is the area of issues management (discussed in Chapter 12). In community relations, companies need to know what their stakeholders in the community are thinking, feeling and doing. One way companies can get this information is by formal research (discussed in Chapter 6). Surveys or focus groups can be conducted with key publics. Companies such as Roy Morgan or ACNielsen offer research services. Another way is through issues tracking, which involves listening to and monitoring what the key publics are saying publicly and privately. To monitor community sentiment, it is important to listen to the media via talkback radio, watch TV news and current affairs programs, and read the newspapers and magazines, particularly the opinion and editorial pages. The 'letters to the editor' section, like talkback radio, provides some indication of how different sectors of the community feel about a certain issue. While we must acknowledge that these letters pass through some gatekeeping function by the editor, and that the average letter-writer is not necessarily representative of the average community member, they can provide interesting insights on issues which companies should take seriously.

Aside from monitoring the mainstream media, it is possible to get valuable information through the grapevine and informal conversations with individual members of the community. While the letters to the editor section is useful, there are members of the community who do not write letters. But it is still important to listen to them and find out what people on the street are saying. Let's say your company is thinking of developing a multi-storey carpark in one of the nearby shopping centres. To gauge the community sentiment, it would help to go to the milkbar, the newsagent, the schoolyard, the church and the shops and talk to the local people. Ask your neighbours and friends how they feel about the proposed development. This way, you can develop a grass roots feel for the issue and incorporate their views in your considerations.

Filling the gaps

We know from research into rumour that people tend to speculate if they do not have enough information on a subject (Allport, in Goldhaber 1990). This ambiguity is one of the key features of rumour. Therefore it is important for companies to provide as much information as possible to their stakeholders. We all know how fast rumours can spread, and also how inaccurate and detrimental they can be. And in the community, where people get together—in church, in school, in shops—rumours can get out of hand and lead to problems for the organisation.

What companies can do is develop a comprehensive information strategy. This strategy could include sending out fliers and brochures, establishing an information hotline, a door-to-door campaign, meetings with key community leaders, and setting up an information booth at the local shopping centre.

Collaborations with community groups

Communication theory suggests that one of the most effective techniques is to involve publics in key communications. When used during a speech, the technique is called *audience participation*. In the same manner, as part of the community relations strategy, organisations should include their publics in their activities. But the key to developing a positive relationship is to include them from the planning stage right through to the implementation and evaluation stages. Once the organisation has identified its key publics through research, inviting representatives of its active publics to join a taskforce or a working party can be a useful strategy. This collaborative technique aims to involve representatives of all parties concerned. To some groups this may be seen as risky, because of the amount of confidential information that may become available to corporate outsiders. The advantage, however, is that involving active groups in the planning allows potentially volatile issues to be resolved earlier. In addition, the members of the taskforce will have ownership of the decisions made by the group. They can then become spokespersons for the group.

Collaborative community projects seem to be a reasonable investment these days, as resources get scarcer. Four key groups would be appropriate partners in any project: the local community council; local business; community special-interest organisations (such as Friends of the Museum); and residents. Organisations that have an interest in and a commitment to keeping the local community happy would be wise to include a budget for collaborative projects. And interest groups that want organisations to listen to them should approach them with a positive project that the organisation can sponsor. This minimises the likelihood of conflicts that can prove detrimental to the purposes of all parties.

Negotiation

In reality, however, peaceful collaborations can be difficult to implement. There will be interest groups that do not want any kind of involvement with an 'errant' organisation. When two-way communication stops and a dispute arises, another strategy should be explored. This is what Susskind and Field (1996) refer to as the mutual gains approach.

The *mutual gains approach* is a strategy that involves the values of respect, humility, trust and commitment to a joint solution to an issue. Susskind and Field (1996) contend that it will take a mature and wise organisation to consider this approach. The mutual gains approach to resolving disputes involves six principles:

- acknowledging the concerns of the other side;
- encouraging joint fact-finding;
- offering contingent commitments to minimise impacts if they do occur, and promising to compensate knowable but unintended impacts;
- accepting responsibility, admitting mistakes and sharing power;
- acting in a trustworthy fashion at all times; and
- focusing on building long-term relationships.

In addition, Susskind and Field (1996: 13) offer a set of prescriptions that focus on building trust and credibility through information-sharing, being honest, identifying an articulate spokesperson who 'is not condescending to the public', and finding an advocate who can stand for the company's credibility.

Conclusion

When Burson defined the four functions of public relations (see Chapter 1), he emphasised the importance of public relations' role as corporate conscience. Taking the role of the social conscience of the organisation, public relations through its corporate social responsibility activities should be genuine, and not just for show. A look at the websites of three Australian companies—Comalco, Lion Nathan and North (listed in the References)—reveal statements on corporate social responsibility which include sponsorships, funding for research and educational programs, and partnerships in areas of youth education and the environment. The dilemma for companies occurs when these values conflict with profitability. However, top management of major Australian companies is now beginning to understand that genuine concern for the community will always be more profitable in the long term, if not in the short term. Similar principles apply to the corporate need to look inward, at one of its most important publics: its internal publics. Strong internal relations will serve to enhance the organisation's overall operations and outcomes.

Case study 11.1: Breakout and cultural transformation at ANZ

In October 2000, the Australia and New Zealand Banking Group Limited (ANZ)—one of Australia's leading banking and financial services groups employing 23 000 people—set itself the goal of becoming a high-performing organisation as benchmarked internationally by McKinsey and Co. A detailed diagnostic on all aspects of ANZ, including its corporate culture, was undertaken and a strategy to build a high-performing organisation was developed. Called 'Perform, Grow and Breakout', the strategy was three-pronged: ANZ would continue to build upon its recent strong financial performance while also investing in new, high-growth opportunities. However, it was the third aspect of the strategy—Breakout—that would truly differentiate ANZ.

Breakout was ANZ's strategy to transform its culture into one where an agreed set of ANZ-wide values were used as a reference point for decision-making; where interaction was open and trusting and new ways of thinking encouraged; and where staff had many and varied opportunities.

Breakout was to be more than a change program. Because organisations are collections of people, a shift in the organisation required the personal commitment of everyone at ANZ to transform themselves and the way they worked.

Crucial to the development of a Breakout culture was the group-wide adoption of the five ANZ values of:

- putting customers first;
- creating shareholder value;
- leading and inspiring each other;
- earning the trust of the community; and
- being bold and having the courage to be different.

These values were derived from the personal values of staff as revealed through a survey conducted late in 2000.

The challenge that fell to ANZ's Communication and Change team was to create the energy, excitement and understanding to drive Breakout and to encourage staff to use the ANZ values as principles for working and decision-making. Both hearts and minds needed to be engaged.

Communicating Breakout and the ANZ Values would also need to be consistent with ANZ's communication policy of:

- informing staff first;
- leading with actions;

- communicating openly and honestly;
- talking straight, with no spin; and
- respecting feedback.

A strategy was developed by the Communication and Change team that involved three major phases:

- generating awareness;
- creating meaning; and
- having people live Breakout (see Figure 11.1).

Figure 11.1 Breakout strategy

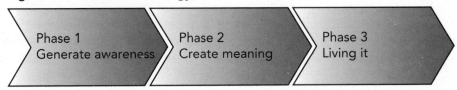

Phase 1
Generate awareness

Phase 2
Create meaning

Phase 3
Living it

Early in 2001, one of the major Breakout initiatives—Breakout workshops—commenced and were open to the most senior 1000 people within ANZ. The workshops were designed to encourage participants to examine the thoughts and values that drive behaviour and impact on interactions in the workplace, and therefore the culture. Most participants emerged from a workshop awakened to the Breakout way of thinking and willing advocates of the ANZ values. The communication strategy was to utilise these workshop participants as 'change leaders' to build widespread commitment to Breakout and the ANZ values through their living example. This served to draw people's interest in Breakout rather than Breakout being 'pushed' on to people.

To support the messages being lived by the change leaders, subtle use was made of all formal communication channels across ANZ such as the intranet, staff magazine and display boards. These channels were used to introduce the 'brand' Breakout and explain the context for the transformation. The Communication and Change team initially avoided using any informal communication tools such as coffee cups and mouse pads to embed messages, preferring to firmly position the ANZ values in the context of the strategic 'big picture' via face-to-face communication from the CEO and the change leaders.

Within a few months, a number of ANZ-wide Breakout initiatives—in addition to the Breakout workshops—got underway. These initiatives were called Breakout Charters and were designed to address the process and system issues within the culture that detracted from ANZ's ability to be a truly high-performing organisation. The communication strategy moved into its second phase, building on a strong level of awareness of Breakout workshops to answer the universal staff question: 'What does Breakout mean to me?'

To create meaning around Breakout and the ANZ values, the Communication and Change team painted a picture of ANZ in the future. The Breakout Charters were launched across the organisation and positioned as steps in the long-term transformation of the organisation. This provided a type of road map for the Breakout journey. An electronic learning tool called the Strategy Map was introduced on to the ANZ intranet to visually convey ANZ's past, present and its future aspirations with the values depicted as the guideposts. The values were further reinforced in all aspects of management, including performance reviews, reward programs and ANZ policies. A mascot of a duck breaking out of a shell was introduced as a fun and appealing symbol of Breakout. The 'Breakout duck' represented irreversible change—transformation—and proved very popular with individuals and small teams who incorporated the symbol into their local Breakout activities and communication, not only to inform but also to celebrate.

The momentum of Breakout continued to build, and by February 2002 ANZ management committed to extending the Breakout workshop program to an additional 6000 staff. A snapshot of the culture had been taken in November 2001—a year since the Perform Grow and Breakout strategy was devised. The results showed a positive shift in the attitudes and behaviours of the top 1000 team. It was now time to address the third phase of the communication strategy: living it.

By this stage, ANZ audiences were at varying levels of awareness through to action due to the staggered rollout of the workshop program and the various takeup of Breakout activities across business units. Communication activities became very targeted, addressing change leaders such as senior management, past workshop participants and the 100-plus volunteer Breakout Champions from across ANZ as a key stakeholder group. Support for this group came mostly in the form of communication tools. A two-way communication channel between key stakeholders and the team managing the Breakout program was established.

Meanwhile, broader communication to staff continued to focus on building understanding and commitment to Breakout action and values-led behaviour. Examples of where Breakout had positively impacted ANZ's business were sought out and shared across the organisation.

Throughout the second and third phase of the Breakout communication strategy, messages were continually reinforced through all formal communication channels.

The communication strategy succeeded in introducing Breakout and the ANZ values to a very large and diverse organisation. The results of ANZ's 2002

Staff Survey showed that over 80 per cent of staff knew about ANZ's values. A further study conducted in November 2002 showed that ANZ was performing at or above the Australian average on all aspects of high performance (McKinsey and Co Performance Ethic Survey, November 2002).

Because Breakout is a journey for ANZ, the communication strategy must remain fluid and flexible in preparation for what is sure to be an undulating course with numerous paths. Communication priorities will be reviewed and revised regularly to build upon existing momentum for cultural transformation and to continually engage those starting out on the journey.

Through the Breakout program, ANZ is encouraging its staff to challenge the mindsets and behaviours that impact corporate culture. (Photo courtesy ANZ)

Case study 11.2: The Moreland City Council consultation framework

Community consultation is a key and difficult challenge for any form of government. Some communities complain about not being consulted on a range of issues, or that consultation had been inadequate. In some local government cases, poor consultation has led to sharp and bitter debates on issues such as road closures and the behaviour of dogs in parks. Some communities equate consultation with 'a deal already done' or 'a snow job'.

Moreland City Council in Victoria faced all of these challenges. And in 2000, it took the step of actually going out to the community to ask how it wanted to be consulted.

Moreland City, comprising the suburbs of Brunswick, Coburg and southern Broadmeadows, sits on the edge of Melbourne. Its population of 137 000 residents includes a large component of people from non-English speaking groups. With an inner-city housing boom and state government pressure for urban consolidation, the council faces a huge variety of high-pressure developmental issues.

Moreland City Council had an ambitious range of community projects across a broad range of fields. However, the projects were increasingly being bogged down by community protests during consultation processes. Furthermore, the state government has called for sound consultation practices with communities to determine the best—not necessarily the cheapest—service for the community.

Because the Moreland City Council has a strong commitment to consultation—undertaking about 2000 public consultations each year on a huge variety of issues—developing a consultation framework was critical for its ability to implement a range of initiatives. Council believes that sound and clear consultation with the community can lead to more efficient implementation of council decisions. Previous poor consultation practices had led to several angry meetings and heated exchanges between councillors and the community. The lack of agreed and clear consultation procedures meant that council officers were confused about the right level of consultation.

A consultation framework agreeable to the community, council officers and councillors was needed to address this situation.

Goals

The consultation process aimed to gain the widest possible spread of community views and ideas on consultation to develop an effective and responsive document. The council needed to understand *what* the community wanted to be consulted on and *how*. It also aimed to ensure that the framework enjoyed a high level of support from council staff.

Research

The preliminary research involved a review of current consultation processes, as well as a review of existing consultation frameworks and protocols of similar organisations. The preliminary research established that there was no general or systematic approach to consultation among local or state governments.

Four focus groups were held with council staff to look at current procedures and to determine the best methods to approach consultation over a wide spread of issues. The groups discussed the best way to involve the community in the decision-making process.

A public meeting was then held to hear from any interested groups or individuals on the subject of consultation, with an independent facilitator to discuss drafting the framework. This was advertised in the local newspapers and on radio. Established community leaders were invited to the event. From this research, a draft community consultation framework was established. Target publics were identified and individual campaigns were developed.

Council staff

Indoor
Internal staff were selected at random across a broad range of groups for a series of focus groups. Briefings were held for citizens' services along with corporate management and senior management.

Outdoor
External staff were selected at random across a broad range of groups for a series of focus groups to learn from their experiences.

Planning
The planning section handles the bulk of the community consultation. A focus group comprising the entire branch was held to ensure they had proper input into the development of the process.

General staff
All staff were surveyed following the development of the consultation matrix in the focus groups. This was done through *The Insider*—the staff newsletter.

Councillors

Councillors were kept informed of the progress of the consultation framework through regular briefings.

External publics

Residents, businesses and ratepayers

These groups were identified by existing databases and targeted through the communication tools of direct mail, the *Moreland City News*, 'Community News' features, and the website. They comprised:

- community associations;
- sporting/recreational and leisure groups;
- ethnic communities leaders;
- businesses/traders' groups;
- community associations; and
- church groups.

The following publics were targeted by direct mail and by the survey with strict minimum quotas for each group.

NESB groups

The non-English-speaking-background (NESB) group was targeted in the survey and, having failed to meet the initial quota, was rung directly. In one instance, an interpreter was arranged to conduct the survey.

VLGA/other local governments

The Victorian Local Governance Association was regularly briefed and acted as a conduit to other local governments.

Communications

The general approach was to distribute the draft Community Consultation Framework widely throughout the community by every available communication means as listed above. This approach gave people an opportunity to tell the council whether they supported the overall approach and what level of consultation they felt was appropriate for council when it was considering an issue or project. It also provided the widest possible variety of means for the community and staff to comment on the framework.

Implementation plan

Several communications methods were used to deliver the key messages to target audiences. The key messages were to ensure that every part of the community felt that it had the opportunity to have its say on issues, that they were listened to as a part of the process and that actions were put in place to address their concerns. The most important key message was that consultation was not participatory democracy and that, at the end of the day, the council— as an elected government—would make the decisions.

Internal implementation

Staff newsletter

The staff newsletter—*The Insider*—devoted one issue to the consultation framework and included a survey on consultation.

PowerPoint presentation

A PowerPoint presentation was used to brief senior staff and councillors and to inform interested groups, such as the government of Thailand.

External implementation

Community survey

A summary of the framework was presented with a simple survey form. It provided the opportunity for respondents to cast a simple vote. On the first page, they could give a 'yes' or 'no' answer to the question: 'Generally, do you support this consultation framework?' Those being surveyed were also asked for feedback on the individual proposals. Written responses were encouraged from people who did not want to give a response to the survey. People were also encouraged to phone the Council if they did not wish to write anything. The survey was distributed by the following means.

- *Direct mail:* The framework and the survey were mailed to target community groups and leaders listed in the community directory. A letter from the Mayor, an explanation leaflet and the survey were included. Recorded messages were developed for Language Link along with short translations in nine languages. A reply paid envelope was provided to increase the chance of return.
- *Advertising:* The content of the framework and the survey was advertised on the Moreland page of the local papers. Residents were encouraged to contact council to get their own copy.

- *Internet:* A copy of the survey was provided on the web page, with the option of emailing responses.
- *Personal collection:* Copies of the framework and survey were made available on the counters of citizens' service centres and in libraries.

Media

Information was available to the media through two media briefings. Coverage was minimal, as the story had no controversial aspects. The consultation framework attracted minor positive coverage.

Response line

The letters and the editorial on the Moreland page provided a phone number for people to record their responses by phone. Specific multilingual numbers were also established.

Community radio

The consultation framework was discussed on council's community radio program—Radio Moreland.

Conclusion

The Moreland community consultation framework attempted to create a realistic solution to the difficult issue of community consultation. Handling high community expectations was a key challenge in the process. The key finding of the framework was that people were generally not interested in the big-picture issues, but were deeply interested in specific local changes such as traffic management or waste collection times. This makes the challenge of consultation quite difficult, as a local government may believe it has sold a broad strategy for a wide range of changes, but when coming to implement it may find that there is widespread community opposition to specific actions. Another key finding was that people wanted to be consulted on immediate issues rather than grand strategies. Consultation also had to be personalised rather than general.

The framework had overwhelming support in the community, with more than 90 per cent of respondents in favour of it. Ongoing monitoring of the framework through an annual survey of 600 residents has shown a slow but sustained improvement in satisfaction with consultation across Moreland from 67 per cent in 2000 to 70 per cent in 2003, with particularly strong improvements in satisfaction with listening to the community from 61 per cent to 72 per cent. The framework remains under constant review.

The matrix developed in focus groups by council staff provided a realistic framework to meet this challenge (available at <www.moreland.vic.gov.au/publications/1downloadpolicy-fr.htm>). More importantly, the framework was developed directly by staff. Staff owned it, and they were therefore responsible for making it work. The focus groups represented all tiers of Moreland council and the shared pool of experience provided a viable solution to a complex problem.

The framework offered a plan for consulting at various levels throughout the community from wide-ranging strategies through to local developments such as speed humps. The framework was successful. It was taken up first by the Department of Infrastructure and then further developed by the Victorian Local Governance Association as a model for consultation. The governments of Indonesia and Thailand have also examined the model, as have local governments in Canada and the United Kingdom. The matrix provides a simple and workable framework for consultation and sent a clear message to the community that Moreland was committed to proper and thorough consultation.

Source: Kevin Brianton, Manager Public Relations and Citizens Services, Moreland City Council.

Discussion and exercises

1   Why should employees learn about changes to the company before the media do? Consider what methods of communication would be most effective to inform employees about:
    (a) a merger with another company;
    (b) a decision to close a suburban branch office.
2   For organisations with diverse employees, in scattered locations around the country, what kind of employee communications would be most appropriate?
3   Look at the websites for Comalco, Lion Nathan and North (as listed in the References) and consider how each company has approached its corporate social responsibility.
4   For communities with a large multicultural population, what kind of community-based programs would be most appropriate?

Further reading

Baskin, O. & Aronoff, C. (1988) *Public Relations: The Profession and the Practice*, 2nd edn, W.C. Brown, Iowa.

D'Aprix, R. (1996) *Communicating for Change: Connecting the Workplace with the Marketplace*, Jossey-Bass, New York.

Larkin, S. (contributor) & Larkin, T.J. (1994) *Communicating Change: How to Win Employee Support for New Business Directions*, McGraw-Hill, New York.

McIntosh, M. et al. (1998) *Corporate Citizenship: Successful Strategies for Responsible Companies*, Financial Times Professional Limited, London.

White, J. (1991) *How to Understand and Manage Public Relations*, Business Books, London.

Wilcox, D., Ault, P. & Agee, W. (1992) *Public Relations Strategies and Tactics*, 2nd edn, HarperCollins, New York.

References

'Australian community: Lion Nathan Australia', <www.lion-nathan.com.au/about+us/community/Ina+community.htm>.

Cameron, G. (1997) 'Newcastle steelworkers support closure benefits package', <www.bhp.com.au>.

'Community and environment', <www.north.com.au/community/default.asp>.

Cutlip, S., Center, A. & Broom, G. (1994) *Effective Public Relations*, 7th edn, Prentice Hall, Englewood Cliffs, pp. 260–79.

Deal, T. & Kennedy, A. (1982) *Corporate Cultures: The Rites and Rituals of Corporate Life*, Addison-Wesley, New York.

Dickson, D. (1984) *Business and its Publics*, John Wiley & Sons, New York, pp. 54–60.

Dilenschneider, R. (ed.) (1996) *Dartnell's Public Relations Handbook*, 4th edn, Dartnell Corporation, Chicago.

Elmer, Paul (2001) 'Accounting for public relations: exploring radical alternatives', *Corporate Communications*, vol. 6, no. 1, pp. 12–17.

'Environment, safety, health and community relations', <www.comalco.com.au/03_community/ 00_index.htm>.

Goldhaber, G. (1990) *Organizational Communication*, 5th edn, W.C. Brown, Dubuque, Iowa.

Grunig, J. (1994) 'Symmetrical systems of internal communication', in J. Grunig, L. Grunig & D. Dozier (eds), *Excellence in Public Relations and Communication Management*, Lawrence Erlbaum, New Jersey, pp. 531–75.

Grunig, J. & Hunt, T. (1984) *Managing Public Relations*, CBS College Publishing, New York.

Grunig, L., Grunig, J. and Dozier, D. (2002) *Excellent Public Relations and Effective Organizations: A Study of Communication Management in Three Countries*, Lawrence Erlbaum, New Jersey.

Holtzhausen, D. and Voto, R. (2002) 'Resistance from the margins: the postmodern public relations practitioner as organizational activist', *Journal of Public Relations Research*, vol. 14, no. 1, pp. 57–84.

Jackson, P. (1998) speech delivered at Public Relations Institute of Australia National Convention, Gold Coast, Queensland.

James, D. (1999) 'In touch at the top', *Business Review Weekly*, vol. 21, no. 22, pp. 104–7.

Kopec, J. (1996) 'Keeping employees informed', in R. Dilenschneider (ed.), *Dartnell's Public Relations Handbook*, 4th edn, Dartnell Corporation, Chicago, pp. 170–205.

Ledingham, J. & Bruning, S. (2000) *Public Relations as Relationship Management: A Relational Approach to the Study and Practice of Public Relations*, Lawrence Erlbaum, New Jersey.

Mackay, H. (1993) *Reinventing Australia*, HarperCollins, Sydney.

Onsman, H. (1999) 'The secret of a happy office', *Business Review Weekly*, vol. 21, no. 22, pp. 46–47.

Starck, K. & Kruckeberg, D. (2001) 'Public relations and community: a reconstructed theory revisited', in Robert Heath (ed.), *Handbook of Public Relations*, Sage, Thousand Oaks, pp. 51–60.

Susskind, L. & Field, P. (1996) *Dealing with an Angry Public: The Mutual Gains Approach to Resolving Disputes*, Free Press, New York.

Tedeschi, J., Lindskold, S. & Rosenfeld, P. (1985) *Introduction to Social Psychology*, West Publishing, Minnesota.

Vaughan, G. & Hogg, M. (1998) *Introduction to Social Psychology*, Prentice Hall, Melbourne.

Walker, G. (1998) *Public Relations Institute of Australia Golden Target Awards Collection*, University of Technology, Sydney.

Whitworth, B. (2002) 'The strongest link', IABC Seminar, 9 June, San Francisco.

12

CRISIS AND
ISSUES MANAGEMENT

Steve Mackey

In this chapter
Introduction
Crisis management
Recognising a crisis
Planning for a crisis
Principles of crisis preparation
Crisis management tactics
Media management in a crisis
After the crisis
Crisis examples
Terrorism and crisis planning
Issues management
Planning issues management
Conclusion
Case study 12.1: Breaking the complaint cycle at Stockland, Townsville

Introduction

This chapter deals with two of the most challenging areas of public relations practice—crisis and issues management. Crisis management can be intense and stressful. A crisis can mean that a name, place or date is linked to a disaster for decades—September 11 or 9/11 now has terrible connotations, Bali is struggling to regain an image as a peaceful tourist destination, and the *Exxon Valdez* has become a benchmark for environmental disaster. Crises can occur at different levels. For organisations, they may be the sudden events that disrupt normal business while at the same time focusing considerable attention on them from the media and other important publics. They can range from a factory closure or strike which produces a demonstration or picket line to an allegation of corporate misconduct which draws the attention of the regulatory authorities and affects share prices, a fire or natural disaster, or an allegation of sexual misconduct or harassment.

Terrorism has emerged as one of the greatest potential causes of crisis for organisations, governments, industries and individuals. While not new, even in the Western world—bomb blasts in London were not uncommon in the 1970s and 1980s—the scale and reach is now greater than it has ever been, making this a truly global threat. Tourism in particular has been affected at all levels, from increased security (with the associated costs for travellers) on airlines to diplomatic conflicts over the issuing of travel warnings around the world. Movement internationally has become more restricted, which has had a negative flow-on effect for business and trade.

Issues are far harder to define and are often only recognised when they impact in a concrete way upon our daily lives. For example, the issue of human equality has led to the development of policies and legislation such as paid parental leave and debate over the ethics of detention of illegal immigrants. The issue of technological development has led to banks closing branches in country towns, resulting in public outcry.

Ideas and attitudes sometimes develop so slowly in a society that they are hard to notice until their effects bite. Unlike crises, which have a beginning and an end, issues may never achieve resolution. If they do, it can be through government regulation, legal intervention or shifts in societal values. In the case of native title, several of the above have come into play. The *Wik* and *Mabo* High Court decisions recognised prior traditional ownership in the land, while changes in societal values can be seen through the songs of Midnight Oil, Paul Kelly, Yothu Yindi, Christine Anu and others. On the other hand, global issues such as terrorism and war, which are based on strong underlying ideologies, may never be settled. Such global issues cannot rely on universal laws or values, thus increasing their scale and complexity.

Crisis management

Crises which suddenly overwhelm an organisation or industry can spring from many causes. For instance, they can be caused by:

- a takeover bid;
- product tampering;

- flood, fire, storm or drought;
- faulty products;
- challenges or changes to leadership;
- industrial disputes; or
- a terrorist act.

How the organisation or industry is seen to deal with a crisis can be vital to its continued success. Important publics can lose faith in an organisation overnight if it is the target of worrying media attention. There are usually plenty of other organisations which people can go to for the same product or service, and which do not have negative media coverage attached to them. Good public relations crisis management can work as an insurance policy against these negative effects. According to one sector most affected by global crises in recent years, the international airline industry, this insurance is essential:

> It is sobering to reflect that 80 per cent of the corporations which have experienced a disaster, without prior planning to deal with crisis, have found themselves out of business within five years. Crisis Communications is clearly not an expensive luxury. It should be regarded as part of a company's liability insurance.
> (IATA, 2003)

Crisis management begins with public relations practitioners looking months or years ahead to predict what can go wrong with an organisation to cause damage to its reputation. Managers and policy-makers need to be alerted to possible crisis scenarios and their consequences. They need to work proactively with all departments in areas as diverse as manufacturing processes, financial strategy, employee relations, customer image and so on to identify potential hazards. Next, communication procedures are put into place to minimise confusion and negative publicity if a foreseeable crisis breaks out despite risk minimisation strategies. Procedures for regaining public confidence after a crisis also need to be considered. The best crisis preparation even goes on to suggest how the organisation can use a crisis to improve its public standing. This is because a magnificent effort to overcome adversity, which was clearly accidental, can become a public relations opportunity when the full circumstances are communicated expertly.

Recognising a crisis

Dozens of different types of crisis can face an organisation, from death and injury to financial swindle or the poisoning of products on the supermarket shelf. But in every case the basic symptoms of a public relations crisis are the same. The main feature is the sudden, searing searchlight of public attention, which immediately points at the organisation. It is a well-known fact of public relations life that a few minutes after something goes *bang*—metaphorically or actually—the news media will be there. Normally they will get there not long after the rescuers. On some embarrassing occasions, they will even get there first. The types and numbers of journalists that turn up will depend on the type and magnitude of the bang. If it was a financial or a stock market bang, the financial journalists will be on the phone or staking out the corporate headquarters. If it was a sacking of a top executive, the business correspondents will be clamouring for an interview. If it was an actual bang, like the 1998 fatal explosion at the Esso natural gas plant at Longford, Victoria, or the 2002 shooting of students at Monash University, all sorts of reporters, photographers and TV crews will be on their way to the stricken site. Some may be in helicopters.

Almost immediately in the case of radio and television, or the next morning in the case of newspapers, the whole world hears, sees or reads a glaring representation of what is going on in the afflicted organisation. The public relations practitioner is concerned about what the most important publics, both internal and external, are going to feel, think and consequently do in these circumstances. Are shareholders going to dump their shares, decimating the value of the company and making it prone to takeover? Will politicians demand inquiries, which could result in punitive restrictions and regulations that might cause bankruptcy? Will customers or clients flock to other suppliers of the same products or services? Will outraged local residents or grief-stricken relatives queue up for TV interviews to pillory management as incompetent and uncaring? Will star employees start making career plans that do not involve the stricken organisation?

Afterwards, the fire might be put out. The top executive who was under a cloud may have resigned. The poisoned pickle jars might be replaced with jars of the most delicious pickles. Floods of money might be diverted into the company to put it back on its feet. But often it is what goes on in the minds of the important publics that decides whether, in the longer term, the organisation is going to recover and flourish—or will wither, or even die, from the effects of crisis.

Do people now see a robust organisation rising to the challenge, acting caringly, expertly, cohesively, wisely, ethically and assertively as it gets back on to its feet and resumes normal business? Or do they see a shambles, with its leaders unable to respond to justifiable criticisms or issuing unbelievable denials as the company slides beneath the waves of public credibility? Crisis planning must be geared to make sure that a crisis has the minimum negative effect on the senti-ments of important publics. These publics may experience a jolt, but a shakeup in the way people view things is not always bad. It may be possible to use the extra publicity to demonstrate what an important job the organisation does, barring an unfortunate occurrence that was not its fault.

Increasingly, organisational crises can end up in court. This will occur if crimi-nal charges or civil actions are brought against one or more parties. If a death occurs as the result of a crisis, a coronial inquiry will be held to determine the cause of death. This occurred following the gas explosion at the Esso plant in Longford, Victoria in 1998. Two Esso employers were killed, others were injured, and gas to most of the state was cut off for two weeks. The Longford Royal Commission and a coronial inquiry followed. Esso was fined $2 million and ordered to pay compen-sation to the families of blast victims. The Esso explosion also resulted in Australia's largest ever class action (Button 1999; Hawes 1999).

It follows, then, that not all crises offer obvious ways of showing the organis-ation in a positive or sympathetic light. However, the good crisis planner will always be trying to think further than just turning around the immediate crisis. They will be looking ahead to consider how the organisation's post-crisis reflection and eval-uation can be harnessed to improve the organisation. One improvement may in fact be that crisis management planning is now taken more seriously.

Planning for a crisis

Emergency and official services in Australia maintain manuals and carry out train-ing to rehearse their responses to natural disasters such as bushfires, floods and earthquakes. Increasingly, these authorities are having to consider preparation to deal with the effects of terrorism. These rehearsals often include the fire services, police, ambulance, hospitals, State Emergency Services, national park officers, and state and local governments. However, too many private and public organisations still do not make adequate preparation for the many types of emergencies and busi-ness shocks which can affect them. This means public relations firms are often called in to assist after the crisis has struck, with no crisis management planning in place to deal with it. Such a lack of anticipation and preparation makes it harder for public relations people to turn around negative perceptions. So one of the first jobs of a public relations adviser may be to persuade their organisation to take crisis preparation seriously.

Principles of crisis preparation

* *Ensure that the organisation's practices are legally compliant.* Most organisations have to conform to health and safety legislation. They have legal responsibilities to take precautions against fire, dangerous machinery, toxic materials and so on. They may have to regulate working hours that are too long in hazardous occupations, such as truck-driving. There are laws governing financial aspects of organisations and regulations to do with the safety and quality of products. If your organisation is offending in any of these spheres, it is your job to make top management fully aware of the public perception risk it is running if negligence causes an accident or some kind of dispute. If you are the company spokesperson, you will have a strong motivation to make sure things are as they should be. In this role, it will be hard to dissociate yourself from the organisation's shoddy, illegal or dangerous practices. Reputable organisations concerned about their public profile make sure they are conforming with, or exceeding, all the required standards for their operations.

* *Brainstorm, or carry out a risk audit.* The public relations practitioner will need to identify anything that may go wrong in an emergency so that any harm can be minimised. For instance, if your client is a coalmine or an airline, a bank or a large manufacturer employing thousands of unionised workers, some crisis risks should be obvious. Just about every organisation also faces financial risks, risks from natural disasters and, unfortunately increasingly, risks from deliberate negative actions such as product tampering or terrorism. There may be a need to set up brainstorming sessions with specialists inside the organisation to discover what crises the organisation is vulnerable to and what the possible orders of severity and likelihood are. But beware: an organisation's managers or employees are not always sensitised to the seriousness of potential outcry if something goes wrong. Alternatively, they may refuse to cooperate if they feel the outcome will make them look bad, or because of interdepartmental rivalries. It is important for public relations practitioners to make their own judgments about the importance to crisis management of matters that may be very close to some organisations' managers and employees. Many organisations now formalise the process of identifying potential crises through risk audits. The result of these audits can feed straight into crisis planning.

- *Build a trust bank.* Make sure your organisation already has good, ongoing media relations and public relations programs in place with its important publics. If people know and trust the organisation, it will be far easier for you to maintain that trust in difficult times.

- *Create a crisis management team.* Build up a team of suitably qualified people who are the most appropriate to handle a crisis. Besides public relations people, these will include senior managers and specialists—the people who know the organisation inside out and who have the skills and authority to give good direction and advice in a challenging situation. Include a lawyer who understands public relations matters. A lawyer who doesn't understand the importance of communication will constantly advise you to say nothing to journalists. This is not helpful in a crisis situation. For the more serious level of crisis, the CEO or equivalent may be part of the team. Public relations consultants who have specialist expertise in crisis management are often used as extra backup.

- *Designate a crisis control centre.* Make sure the crisis team and the public relations department have instant access to designated personnel and to necessary office space and equipment for a crisis breaking at any time of the day or night, on any day of the year. Plan a telephone call-out chain that makes sure the right people notify the right people in sequence. The office space should be suitable for a temporary crisis control centre to be easily set up—perhaps by converting an office or the boardroom in the corporate headquarters. Consider the availability of telephones, mobile telephones, computers, fax machines, TVs, radios, videotape recorders, photocopiers and office furniture. Think about all the details that are necessary for these arrangements: Is the team assigned to shifts if it has to work around the clock? Can catering and security service these shifts? Are we liaising with emergency services, local government and other organisations that we may have to work with closely in a crisis?

- *Create a procedure/protocol.* With advice from the team, devise the appropriate procedures for dealing with the imagined crises. Try to imagine a few unimaginable crises to be on the safe side. Code the crises in a few steps from the least serious to the most serious. For instance, if it is 'level A', we know only a few people need to be notified and the CEO doesn't even need to be told this week. If it is 'level E', we know the CEO has to be brought back from London and the state Premier has to be woken up even if it is in the middle of the night!

- *Practise, practise, practise.* Get the team to rehearse their roles by springing worst-case scenarios on them at least once a year, like unexpected fire drills. If possible, surprise the team by introducing people who are playing cunning and difficult journalists. Have the 'journalists' catch team members out if they talk inappropriately 'off the record' to cameras or microphones believed to be turned off.
- *Team up with other organisations.* It may be possible to coordinate your drill with emergency services which occasionally run very realistic-looking mock disaster exercises.
- *Designate a spokesperson/people.* A vital member of the team will be the spokesperson through whom all information should be channelled for consistency and cohesion. In a large crisis, media from all over the world may be ringing, literally around the clock. A single spokesperson may not be able to handle this barrage alone and may need backup. Other members of the organisation and related organisations should know not to speak to the media or say anything during the crisis period that could affect the consistent message.
- *Keep the CEO in reserve.* It is advisable that the regular spokesperson is not the head of the organisation. This is because of the volume of relatively straightforward communication and because it is useful to keep the CEO in reserve to make any special announcements, corrections or political rebuttals with emphasised authority.
- *Ensure adequate media training.* All potential spokespeople should have training and regular refresher courses on giving television and radio interviews.

Crisis management tactics

Many of the tactics that will be employed in a crisis will already be in place and routinely used by an organisation. For example, websites will already exist, and media conference schedules and media fax lists will be part of the day-to-day running of most public relations offices. In a crisis, the key is to utilise all these communication tactics to manage the event. Keeping up to date and in control can help make the difference between a successfully managed crisis and an organisational disaster. A comprehensive list of tactics is covered in Chapter 8.

The physical location of a crisis will have a major bearing on the response, remembering that the media will immediately want access to the crisis scene. With a physical disaster, the crisis or accident scene will be cordoned off by emergency services to avoid further disruption from media and other visitors. It might be reasonable to take a limited number of journalists or television crews on a supervised site visit. Sometimes one television crew or photographer is taken on condition that they pool their pictures with competing media organisations. The spokesperson may need to be at the corporate headquarters or a similar location rather than the crisis site. In some cases, this may be more convenient for the news media and will help reduce distractions at the site.

Web pages about the organisation—its products, locations, number of employees, what it brings to the local or national economy, the awards it has won and so on—should be kept current. These pages should be revised quarterly or more often so that background information, including financial and numerical data and the correct spellings and positions of personnel, products and locations can be made available easily without more strain on already stretched resources. News releases, including crisis news releases, can quickly be made available as web pages.

All media, including relevant internet websites, should be monitored to see what people are saying about the crisis. Help might be sought from commercial media-monitoring organisations, which will analyse the content of relevant stories in addition to collecting them. VHS and audio recorders with TVs and radios, along with internet-capable computers, should be available in the temporarily set-up crisis control centre. The spokesperson should be regularly apprised of the media reports. The crisis team should also receive news releases of other organisations commenting on the crisis. They should make sure cooperating organisations get media releases at least as soon as journalists do. A file should be kept of all news releases the organisation issues.

News conferences, commercial electronic news release distribution channels such as Australian Associated Press (AAP) and the organisation's website can be used to distribute information if there are, or are likely to be, many queries on the same subject. Making releases available through a variety of methods will mean different mediums are catered to. This will ensure the organisation is seen as both cooperative and proactive.

If specific detail is not getting out to some of the key publics—for instance, employees now at home or shareholders—or large numbers of customers, it may be appropriate to write to them or to take out newspaper advertisements. This may be the only way to apologise, to instruct, to reassure, or to thank large numbers of people for their patience during or after the disruption. If you plan to run crisis advertisements, put out a news release to tell journalists you are going to do this and your reasons for it. This should stop journalists thinking you are trying to contradict their stories. The release may get you neutral or even positive coverage on the editorial pages which summarises what you say in the advertisement and which draws attention to it. News stories are more credible and more widely read than advertisements, so although a news story about the response may be small, it may effectively offer far greater exposure for your message. Working with the media is discussed in Chapter 10.

Media management in a crisis

The operations of substantial organisations can affect people's lives in many ways. These effects can range from public safety to financial or job security, and even to their staff being exemplars of social propriety. As such, these organisations have an ethical responsibility to be candid about their operations—particularly when something goes wrong. In a democratic country, news media are the legitimate channels for accurate and timely information on these matters. The performance of the organisation's spokesperson is critical in effective crisis management. Sometimes news media can spread important, urgently needed information efficiently and, if the crisis-struck organisation gives out reliable, accurate, relevant information fast, it is likely that the organisation will be used as the main source by journalists. A lack of information, or slow or inaccurate information, will cause journalists to look elsewhere. They may go to people who give them ill-informed comments or to critics of the organisation. They will also be more likely to speculate and rumours may result.

The main principles that should guide the spokesperson include the following:

- Candid information given promptly will emphasise the organisation's integrity and ethical standards.
- It is legitimate to withhold some information, such as the names of deceased persons or information that may prejudice a court case or an inquiry.
- News is news only for a very short period. It is vital to respond to journalists' queries as fast as possible. Volunteer relevant newsworthy information as it comes to light, provided there are no legal or personal impediments, such as when relatives have not yet been informed about bereavement.
- Spokespeople should not speculate if the facts are not available. If the speculations are wrong, the credibility of the whole media relations effort can be ruined.

- The spokesperson should not say anything 'off the record' which the organisation would not mind seeing in front page headlines the next day.
- All journalists' phone queries to the spokesperson should be taken by assistants and carefully logged, showing who asked what question. The spokesperson must phone the journalist back soon after the call has been made. This removes the requirement for the spokesperson to think on their feet. The email address, fax or phone number of the caller on the log sheet may be invaluable if a mistake has been made or the situation changes after the initial reply.

If part of the problem is public confidence in the organisation, what is said to journalists and the professionalism with which the message is delivered may be central to resolving the situation. The advice of the chief public relations person to the management group about what should be said and how it should be said may be crucial.

After the crisis

There may be other, more direct ways of thanking people after a crisis has passed. It may be appropriate for senior personnel to visit those affected, or their families. It may be necessary to make speeches or give interviews which outline the organisation's considered assessment of what went wrong and what measures it is taking as a result. A severe crisis may provide just the incentive an organisation needs to genuinely reflect on its structure, policies and mission. A round of thank you speeches to outside and internal audiences can provide a useful opportunity to announce plans for future improvement. During the crisis, the public relations team should have kept a good record of its part in limiting the damage to the organisation's reputation. This record, together with a draft public relations plan for rebuilding a range of relationships, will be valuable in the evaluation phase of the crisis. This will ensure best practice is maintained and improvements are in place for the update of the organisation's new crisis management plan.

Crisis examples

Tylenol and *Exxon Valdez*

The United States provides some of the world's benchmark cases in crisis management. The 1989 *Exxon Valdez* oil tanker disaster in Alaska and the Tylenol pain relief capsule poisoning tragedies of 1982 and 1986 are among the most extensively analysed public relations crisis management examples.

Johnson & Johnson was praised by many commentators for its openness to the media and the public when initially six people were killed by cyanide that had been placed in Tylenol capsules. A copycat strychnine poisoning occurred five days later, and there was another reported death from poisoned Tylenol four years after that. The company's approach was one of social responsibility towards its 100 million customers. Johnson & Johnson exhibited its concern for customers by withdrawing capsules from sale throughout America on both occasions, although the poisonings were confined to Chicago and California in 1982 and New York in 1986. This recall cost the firm a total of US$250 million. At the same time, there was the utmost cooperation with the news media in order to keep the public fully informed. The result was an enhanced reputation and continued customer loyalty. Johnson & Johnson was praised for living up to its company credo as stated on its website: <www.jnj.com/our_company/our_credo/>.

By contrast, giant oil corporation Exxon (also known as Esso in many parts of the world) was criticised for its response to a disastrous oil spill in 1989. Critics suggest that in the earliest phase of the crisis, when its tanker ran aground, Exxon did not express enough concern about the environmental damage caused. In particular, it is suggested that the chief executive should have visited the scene immediately and media facilities should have been set up elsewhere in the United States, not just at the scene (Seitel 1992: 1822). The remote location of the initial crisis information centre delayed communication and made it hard for many media organisations to gather news. Early reporting of the incident featured Exxon's attempts to turn the blame. These factors have made the *Exxon Valdez* disaster a *cause celêbre* in the world of crisis public relations. It is a benchmark against which oil tanker disasters are now compared—such as the sinking of the *Prestige* oil tanker off Spain in 2002.

In December 2002, Exxon—now merged with Mobil Oil as Exxon Mobil Corp, the world's biggest publicly traded oil company—was still making headlines appealing against multibillion dollar compensation judgments for oil damage to the Alaskan coastline. This acts as a reminder that a crisis can continue many years after the initial event occurs. Not surprisingly, organisations are usually shy about their difficulties and keen for them to slip from public memory. There are, however, still many current websites with pictures and information about this crisis, including that of the US Environmental Protection Agency: <www.epa.gov/oilspill/exxon.htm>.

Panadol

In 2000, two pharmaceutical manufacturers in Australia were targeted by extortionists. The first incident was in March, against Brisbane-based Herron Paracetamol; in May, the makers of Panadol, SmithKline Beecham (SKB) (now GlaxoSmithKline), also received an extortion threat.

On 31 May, SKB's Sydney office received a poisoning threat from an extortionist asking for $70 000. SKB immediately contacted the police, the Therapeutic Goods Administration (TGA) and public relations firm Burson Marsteller. Working closely with police, SKB did not announce the threat to its products and did not withdraw them from shops until a week later—6 June. By that time, Burson Marsteller had helped organise a textbook crisis management response. SKB's crisis preparedness manual had been reviewed; similar extortions and product regulation guidelines had been analysed; market research had been examined; publics had been delineated; and the best communication channels to those publics had been earmarked. The main target publics were: consumers, stockists, government departments, industry regulators, industry associations, healthcare professionals and employees of the company. A massive call centre was set up to deal with queries. Within 24 hours of the announcement, it had 180 operators taking calls in English as well as others taking calls in other languages. Letters and other materials were distributed to a range of publics. There were memos to employees; senior SKB officials spoke directly to politicians and other senior government officials; and briefing notes and question-and-answer documents were made available to the sales teams, the CEO Alan Schaefer and to other managers. Schaefer and his Director of Business Development undertook media training, with Schaefer always leading the media response.

The company went public about the extortion and recall of Panadol capsules with a statement at 10.30 a.m. on Tuesday, 6 June. The announcement was followed by a midday media conference which was attended by representatives from the police and the TGA to demonstrate official support. That evening a wire story claimed Panadol only went public after the previous day's bungled police sting attempt to catch the extortionist. Within an hour, SKB put out a statement responding to this claim while the New South Wales police put out their own statement at 6.30 p.m. saying: 'The decision to inform the public was made yesterday by company executives in consultation with senior police, as part of the ongoing operational strategy. Media reports that Police only went public "after a failed operation" are totally incorrect.' (NSW police news statement 6/6/00) A TGA news release on the same day said: 'SmithKline Beecham Pty Ltd, in consultation with the Therapeutic Goods Administration, NSW Police and NSW Health is urgently recalling to consumer level all batches of the above Paracetamol Capsules. These products are being recalled because SmithKline Beecham Pty Ltd has received an extortion threat.'

Later in the week, the media were invited to film Panadol being withdrawn from supermarket shelves and destroyed. Panadol products were put back on the shelves in tamper-resistant packaging in August, but after another threat in October the TGA recommended that all paracetamol products were to be kept behind the counter. The crisis ended with a raid on a house in Brisbane in December 2000 and the subsequent arrest of a suspect who hanged himself in his Brisbane remand cell in May 2001 before facing trial (Mathewson 2001; Chulov 2001).

The CEO of GlaxoSmithKline (formerly SKB), Alan Schaefer, talked about his personal experiences during the crisis:

> A crisis is an emotional rollercoaster. Every day you reach the peaks of jubilation and the depths of despair . . . The first days and weeks of the crisis . . . can be brutal. You don't sleep well and you're exhausted at the end of each day . . . You need to be very clear about who the core team is. You want one or two people making decisions in the earliest hours or so of the crisis . . . Our experience was that if you get the objectives for managing the crisis clearly understood, everyone finds it easier to make their daily decisions. (2001: online)

Newspaper reports put the financial damage of the Panadol recall at $100 million (*Australian Financial Review*, 18 May 2001). In 2002, the SKB case study won Burson Marsteller an award in the 'Emergency/Crisis Communication' category in the International Public Relations Association (IPRA) Golden World Awards, and this provides a comprehensive summary for analysis of this case study (see the IPRA website: <www.ipranet.org/cat6.2.doc>).

Arnott's Biscuits

A sensational round of media coverage erupted in February 1997 when packets of poisoned biscuits were sent to media organisations, police and justice officials with letters demanding that some police officers connected with an unrelated investigation take lie detector tests. The company's reaction was compared with that of the much-praised Johnson & Johnson action in the Tylenol situation (Macey 1997: 9).

Arnott's ordered a massive withdrawal and destruction of biscuits at a multimillion-dollar cost to the company, while it was not known whether the threat to put poisoned biscuits on supermarket shelves would actually be carried out. Arnott's cooperated fully with the police, who arranged with news media for a ten-day delay to publication in an attempt to catch the perpetrators. After that, managing director Chris Roberts placed himself at the disposal of the news media and published an open letter as an advertisement in newspapers. The letter explained that Arnott's was an innocent victim and gave information phone numbers for customers and retailers. Roberts used the letter to stress that customers' safety was paramount in the decision to withdraw the stock: 'Our proud name has been built on the strong bond we share with our customers. We will do whatever we can to protect that bond.' (Saunders and Harris 1997: 1) The threat to put poisoned biscuits on the shelves was not carried out, and shelves were restocked at the end of the month. Arnott's suffered financially, but maintained its valuable relationship with customers for the future.

Sydney Water

The massive publicity over cryptosporidium and giardia bugs in Sydney Water Corporation's supply in 1998 had newspapers using expressions such as 'six weeks that made the city a global laughing stock and sparked concern over tourism and the 2000 Olympic Games' (Walker 1998: 2). Another headline was: 'No, it's not Calcutta, it's Sydney' (Dale 1998: 1). Millions of residents in 152 Sydney suburbs were told to boil their drinking water. Public relations officials involved at the time confirm that public warnings about the crisis were not handled well initially. New South Wales Health's associate director of media issues management, Shari Armistead, broke the news to media organisations at 10.45 p.m. on 29 July. She had been waiting, as agreed, for the separate organisation, Sydney Water, to make the announcement. Under protocols, Sydney Water had the say over what should be announced. But Armistead, whose responsibility involved the health of millions of Sydneysiders, decided the delay had lasted too long. After Armistead's warning, Sydney Water phoned Australian Associated Press at 11.00 p.m. asking for the story to be put on hold (Doherty and Ryle 1998: 2), but 40 minutes later confirmed that there was a water emergency. A Sydney Water spokesperson said part of the difficulty was the complicated relationship between Sydney Water, the New South Wales state Health Department, and the two ministers involved. A few days into the crisis, after an initial inquiry, protocols were worked out to speed official lines of communication. By this time, New South Wales Health's role had been recognised because of the public health nature of the emergency. For much of the six-week emergency, daily news briefings for journalists were held at 1.30 p.m. at the New South Wales Health offices in North Sydney. From the initial uncoordinated welter of official comment, Armistead and her team sorted out which politicians, which medical and which administrative experts should front these regular briefings on which days. Good coordination was arranged with Sydney Water, which sometimes sent representatives. New South Wales Health representatives also attended news conferences at Sydney Water and both organisations cooperated on site visits by journalists to reservoirs and water processing plants. Armistead said her department's work became largely a health education program, helping Sydneysiders to cope with the unusual circumstances until the water was declared safe again.

Mercury Energy

The long-term electrical power outage to hundreds of businesses and thousands of residents in the centre of Auckland which started on 20 February 1998 highlighted the need for risk anticipation. The July 1998 New Zealand government inquiry into electrical retailer Mercury Energy Ltd's responsibility said in part: 'Mercury Energy should review its risk management processes so that all risk is managed within one systematic process to a defined standard.' The Mercury crisis also raised the spectre of both legal liabilities of companies to their customers and the legal implications of what is said during a crisis (Elias 1998: 6; AAP 1998: 9). Melbourne law firm Slater & Gordon offered to represent people affected by the power crisis, as it later represented people affected by the Sydney Water and Victorian Esso gas explosion crises. However, Mercury was able to put in place direct arrangements with its affected customers, making Slater & Gordon's involvement unnecessary. Its public relations people said that fast and fair compensation was the most effective way of resolving the situation. However, the prevalence of lawyers at emergencies, where millions of dollars of losses are in question, means that organisational spokespeople must be careful with what they say. Incorrect statements made at the time may come back to haunt an organisation when money is being considered.

Terrorism and crisis planning

Terrorism is the biggest crisis wild card of this century. It is almost trite to refer to the destruction of the World Trade Center twin towers in New York on 11 September 2001 as an event that changed the world, as we see the aftermath continue to reverberate around the globe. But, certainly in terms of the way that organisations think of crisis management, that action and the Bali bombing the following year have thrown up new and disturbing considerations. Crisis managers rely on being able to think the unthinkable—but these terrorist actions demonstrated that in no case did we seem to be able to imagine that level of chaos, crisis, destruction and tragedy in what were ostensibly low-risk workplaces.

The 'loss of innocence' that was vaunted in the media in the days immediately following September 11 has a particularly harsh and ominous message for the crisis management planner. Suddenly questions were being faced that had rarely been contemplated before, like what would happen if most of an entire major office was wiped out. Not just the office itself, with its records, file and computer hard disks—that might happen in a major fire—but the whole office itself . . . people, CEOs, top management structure . . . all of the intellectual capital of an organisation, not just its records. This is exactly what happened to merchant banker Salomon Smith Barney, whose global headquarters, amongst others, were in the World Trade Center.

And what if no planes can fly to or in the largest market in the world? As aircraft were grounded completely across the United States of America for days following the bombing, wildflower growers in Western Australia were faced with massive losses—they couldn't ship their highly perishable, highly desirable blooms to carefully developed markets in the United States. The same story was being repeated amongst lobster fishermen in Tasmania and oyster farmers in New Zealand. While crisis planning pre-September 11 may have taken into account the grounding or crashing of a single aircraft, the degree to which global air trade was disrupted was itself almost unimaginable, resulting in crises for many businesses, large and small—in many cases, far away from the United States.

Another lesson to be gained from September 11 was the degree to which governmental (local, state or federal) resources and private organisations may need to work together and what crises may occur well after the initial attack. Coffee chain Starbucks found itself in the middle of just such a crisis when, some weeks after September 11, it emerged that one of its outlets had charged firemen for bottles of drinking water . . . interestingly, the crisis itself was provoked not by this fact, but by Starbucks' denial that this could have happened. Almost overnight, a company that had spent a lot of time and energy building a trust bank on its support for remote rural communities in the Third World found itself under attack for being uncaring and unfeeling. Conversely, after the Bali bombing, the management of Channel 7 received a great deal of kudos for making its executive jet, which happened to be in Perth, available to the Air Force to evacuate the injured back to Australia—and not publicising its actions (which were only reported on the ABC).

The ripple effect of major crises cannot be under-estimated, and it is clear that, while many organisations look internally to identify and create crisis management plans, external, global or national events which may seem too far away to cause concern can have a devastating effect on organisations 'downstream' of them. Most poignantly, September 11 and the Bali bombing demonstrated that terrorist activity which results from underlying political, historical and religious or philosophical differences can affect anyone, anywhere. One crisis can lead to another, as the ultimate result of these terrorism attacks was the war on terrorism, which of course has impacted on all corners of the world.

Event managers have to contend with hugely increased security costs, businesses are thinking of diversification of markets, and internal planning needs to take account of the fact that the primary place of business may become completely unavailable with no advance warning. After an attack, would everyone know where to report for work and/or could business be conducted remotely? Are alternative worksites/markets already identified and contingency plans established? Is this even possible? Would you have contact information for *all* your key audiences— internal and external—available quickly even if you were never to occupy your primary place of business ever again?

For some industries, like the travel industry, September 11 marked the first of several major blows. The International Air Transport Association (IATA) reported in 2003:

> Two years of unprecedented airline industry losses have stretched our industry to the limit. In recent weeks, the crisis has been worsened by two new concerns—the conflict in Iraq and the outbreak of Severe Acute Respiratory Syndrome (SARS) . . . SARS has severely affected travel and tourism in the Asia Pacific region. IATA is closely cooperating with the World Health Organisation (WHO) and relaying WHO information to member airlines, who are working closely with their national health authorities. (IATA CEO Bisignani, 2003)

Planning for crisis is clearly a priority for IATA, as its Crisis Communications consultancy shows: 'In 1998 IATA launched a number of initiatives to help airlines, and other related organisations, to plan and manage their public responses to crisis situations. Since then, IATA Crisis Communications has worked directly with over 50 airlines, related companies as well as non-aviation corporations.' (IATA 2003)

The Crisis Communications consultancy service assists companies in preparing to deal with the demands of the news media in times of crisis. The range of services includes:

- audits of crisis management preparedness;
- assistance with the development of plans and procedures;
- exercises for crisis management team members;
- skills training for emergency responders and crisis managers;
- crisis communication audits;
- crisis communication manuals;
- design and organisation of crisis management centres;
- crisis communication training; and
- A Global Crisis Response Advisory Service.

IATA organises regional and global Crisis Communications workshops for airlines, airports and related companies. Global workshops were held in Cape Town, South Africa, in 1996; in Phoenix, Arizona, in 1998; and in Munich, Germany, in May 2000, bringing together aviation public relations professionals from around the world (IATA, 2003).

Issues management

While issues and crises are linked in the sense that many crises do indeed arise out of issues, it is tempting to think of issues and crises in only a negative sense. In many ways, the resolution of issues or the way in which they are played out depends on which side of the fence you occupy. For example, a parental leave case that is played out in the courts could be a crisis for the employing organisation, but a huge win for the union.

Some issues, such as terrorism, are global in nature and require global or national approaches and solutions. While it may be impossible to resolve the issue of terrorism on an individual organisational level, it is certainly possible—having identified the issue—to plan for management of the threat. The Bali bombing demonstrated the ability of major issues to explode into major crises, and showed how, in such major crises, cross-organisational planning and cooperation are necessary to manage both the crisis and its underlying issue. For example, not only the Australian Air Force but Qantas mobilised flights in and out of Bali; all major Australian civilian hospitals, private and public, were organised to accept victims; Australian Federal Police investigators and legal advisers joined the Indonesian police force; and individual travel companies worked to advise and inform their customers, changing plans and helping them to leave Bali if necessary. This was all aided by the media, which broadcast hotline numbers, and was accompanied by a concerted diplomatic effort between the Australian and Indonesian governments to find and bring to justice the perpetrators and their leaders.

The inevitable result of the Bali bombing was to demonstrate to Australians that the issue of terrorism had come home to roost with a vengeance. Its results have been far-reaching in terms of ongoing planning—hospitals have revised their crisis management plans in case such an event takes place in an Australian city, the government has extensively tightened security for major events, such as the 2002 New Year's Eve fireworks on Sydney Harbour, and the removal of rubbish bins from outside airports around the country.

Issues and organisations

At an organisational or industry level, issues management is about maintaining the viability and reputation of the organisation or industry by anticipating, under-standing and keeping in touch with significant currents of thought in society. It may involve advising an organisation/industry to change its activities or policies in order to maintain its relevance to the contemporary world, or advising an organisation/industry to intervene in public debates to counteract opponents' views or to try to head off looming disadvantageous government legislation or regulations. The advice may be to change internal policies or oppose external actions. Advisers have to consider carefully whether intervention in public debates can create the nega-tive impression of a powerful organisation throwing its weight around, particularly if this stance is unpopular with important publics.

Issues often centre on policy debates and public opinion, so they give rise to a range of conflicting perspectives. The object of issues management is to identify the issue far enough back down the 'timestream' to allow the organisation to position itself to deal with the issue in the way that best suits it. For example, organisations that implemented equality of employment opportunities before they were forced to by legislation probably found that they had a better staffing profile than if they were suddenly forced to employ less qualified people simply to meet an externally determined profile. One aim of good issues management is to solve problems before they become crises. Much issues management therefore lies in the successful anticipation of a problem or change. As with the corporate sector, governments at all levels are constantly alert to issues as they position themselves in public favour. For example, local governments around Australia must closely monitor water supplies and usage during ongoing periods of drought conditions to ensure continued supplies. This has resulted in criticisms that some councils should have better anticipated growth rates and expanded water needs. It has certainly resulted in a range of campaigns aimed at reducing water consumption.

The first step in managing issues is to watch for and attempt to understand the life cycle of constantly emerging and evolving legitimate demands of individuals and representative groups. Management may need to be advised on how to tackle conflicts within contemporary public expectations or physical constraints, before the matter becomes a major problem. If criticism is not detected and tackled early on, effective lobbying groups—such as professional associations, political parties, environmental groups and authorities, consumer advocates, local councils, regional interest groups, academic institutions, business associations, trade unions and ethnic minority representative groups—may become involved in public opinion campaigns that carry the issue through to the end of its life cycle with changes to government policy, regulations and laws.

Issues which have become important in Australia over recent years, and which may develop over the next few years, include:

- terrorism and war;
- the dropping fertility rate in Australia and the linked subject of employees' paid parental leave;
- the number of overweight children, which has been linked to the marketing of fast food;
- illegal immigration and detention centres, in particular the detaining of children in detention;
- the privatisation of organisations such as Telstra;
- medical insurance blow-outs and the flow-on effect to doctors and patients; and
- insurance liability hikes and the resulting impact on some industries and groups.

Issues become most potent when they are taken up by community, activist groups and political groups, or when there is already a broader public sentiment for the mooted change. Failure to respond appropriately to issues which are now firmly on the public agenda may affect the organisation's reputation, or influence the finances or profitability of an organisation. This is dealt with in more detail in Chapters 14 and 16.

Like crises, issues can raise court-related problems. Increased litigation of doctors, and the resulting blow-out of medical insurance, have seen some areas of the country now under-serviced by some specialist areas and the federal government having to top up medical indemnity payments. In 2002, the country saw one of the major medical insurance providers, United Medical Protection (UMP), go into receivership, leaving the majority of Australian doctors confused and concerned over their insurance status. In some states the medical indemnity 'crisis' resulted in general practitioners withdrawing labour for up to one day due to a stalemate with the federal government over tort law reform of medical negligence.

Planning issues management

Scanning for and identifying issues

Some major global corporations rely on dedicated issues managers and may hire issues management consultants. But for many organisations, efficient scanning and identification of important issues is part of general management practice. Management at all levels needs to talk and listen to its stakeholders. It has to trust in the intelligence of its personnel and take their views and concerns seriously. Gathering information from staff to feed into issues management planning need not be complicated. Top managers may go to business meetings with other business and community leaders and attend conferences and training courses. They probably also read the relevant business press and journals. They may consult politicians and political lobbyists, commission commercial research, and take advice from academics and leading authorities in particular fields. The marketing and salespeople are out there talking to customers. Human resources staff are talking to unions. Professional specialists such as lawyers, accountants, engineers and the waste disposal people are hearing from peers in their trades and professions. Public relations staff are monitoring media coverage and talking to all sorts of stakeholders. All of these contacts, if dealt with systematically and taken seriously, help in scanning for and identifying issues.

A great deal of issues management is carried out by industry associations on behalf of their members. For instance, Australian banks may be assisted and represented by the Australian Bankers' Association on issues of joint concern. The National Farmers' Federation does the same job on behalf of its members and The Minerals Council of Australia represents mining firms. There are often sectional and regional groups represented by smaller, specialist associations or state divisions within, or in addition to, these national bodies. Small organisations are represented by many other industry associations such as the Pharmacy Guild of Australia, the Australian Newsagents' Federation, the Australian Medical Association and the Australian Dental Association. The public relations industry has the Public Relations Institute of Australia. Universities have associations. Students have student associations. In fact, most significant types of businesses, trades and professions have representative bodies, part of whose responsibility is to discover, monitor and respond to publicly expressed views and issues. If issues move beyond unstructured controversy, they may enter the province of public affairs. Here, association responses may involve lobbying government and devising publicity in order to influence the outcome of legislation.

All organisations, whether corporate, government or NGOs, also rely increasingly on monitoring world events through the mass media. The daily news media, including newspapers, television, radio and the internet, can act as predictors as specialist writers analyse changes, events and problems at an international level. Analysis of a global media can also allow the public relations practitioner to consider a local issue on a wider scale. For example, the issue of paid parental leave has been identified in this chapter as an emerging one. In some countries, this is not a new issue and those with an interest in it in Australia can piece together information from a range of media in Asia, Europe and America. In a similar way, advisers can monitor progress in government debate and foreshadow changes to legislation which may affect their organisation. Monitoring the news media is not suggested as an alternative to sourcing primary documents, but in many cases this may be the best—or simplest—way to access a range of perspectives or facts.

Issues analysis and prioritising

Of course, not all concerns raised by issues scanning are fundamentally important or can be dealt with by an organisation that has finite resources. At the issues analysis stage, senior managers—including those carrying out the public relations role—have to weigh up the damage or potential advantage involved in facing up to or ignoring certain widespread or strongly put opinions. These opinions (or predicted opinions) may impinge on the organisation's current activities or have implications for operations in the future. Careful calculations may have to be made about the ability or otherwise of certain public opinions to gain enough momentum to pose a genuine problem. It might be possible to take a robust view and brush off some concerns. However, powerful organisations also have to weigh the ethical implications of ignoring weak voices that perhaps have a valid point. Priorities need to be set and reviews need to be undertaken periodically into how the organisation is intervening in the public debate over some matters and perhaps changing its thinking and internal practices to do with other matters.

Implementing issues management strategies

Public relations practitioners use a range of strategies to manage issues. A government relations program may be necessary if the organisation is seeking to influence the outcome of legislative change—think about how the National Farmers' Federation has lobbied the National Party and Liberal Party over native title. A media relations campaign may be what is required—think about what Greenpeace does to gain publicity for its protests, whether against Japanese whaling or against the continuing use of the Lucas Heights Nuclear Reactor in suburban Sydney. Engaging in philanthropy may be the answer—think about McDonald's setting up Ronald McDonald Houses in association with children's hospitals around the world. Issues managers may go further, to the extent of counselling management about the modification or cessation of certain practices and processes—tourists, for instance, are discouraged from climbing Uluru in response to indigenous people's concerns. The crucial element to success in issues management lies in being far enough back up the time stream—identifying the issues early enough—to defuse or control what might be an ugly dispute. This may be by changing policy or by creating an effective, proactive strategy for success before the issue becomes an uncontrolled public controversy which might spoil the organisation's reputation or result in adverse legislation.

Conclusion

This chapter has described how effective crisis and issues management is crucial to the well-being of an organisation and how the public relations arm of the organisation should be constantly mindful of possible scenarios. Crisis management means being on the lookout for what might go wrong, dealing with it and, if possible, turning the situation into a win for the organisation in terms of image management. No one wants to see a crisis within, or affecting, an organisation. However, anticipating worst-case scenarios is a very real function for public relations practitioners and, as such, should be handled systematically and professionally. Issues management, on the other hand—because of its less obvious nature—can creep up on an organisation. This is why it is so important for public relations professionals to be alert to current trends and future decisions in business, government, the law and other sectors determining public agendas. More than ever, these two areas of public relations require a close working relationship with senior levels of management in the organisation.

Case study 12.1: Breaking the complaint cycle at Stockland, Townsville

The Stockland Trust operates a major suburban shopping complex in Townsville, North Queensland, surrounded on three sides by established residential areas. The closest homes are only two lanes of traffic from the centre's doors.

Stockland employed a major national development company to undertake a multimillion-dollar refurbishment of the centre, and wanted to minimise disruption to shoppers and economic impact on tenants. Because they were unable economically to close even part of the centre during trading hours, the project was conducted between 9:00 p.m. and 6:00 a.m. every night, with all equipment removed to storage each morning to ensure shopper safety and amenity.

The project's seven-night-per-week schedule caused great concern amongst the approximately 100 local residents, who were particularly upset about construction noise and heavy vehicle movement. To compound this, developers had not sought to communicate with either neighbours or the Queensland Environmental Protection Agency (EPA), and residents found it impossible to address complaints to the developer during overnight operations—gates were locked and phones went unanswered.

Residents believed not enough was being done to reduce the noise, disruption and inconvenience they were experiencing, and in the absence of any easy way to contact the developers, neighbours made repeated formal complaints direct to the EPA.

Within three weeks of project commencement the situation had escalated to the degree that the EPA issued the developers with a warning that if they did not take immediate action to resolve the issues, they faced potential revocation of their permit to operate.

Stockland Trust sought professional communication support to manage the issue before it spiralled into a full-blown crisis. Initial assessment noted five fundamental areas requiring urgent attention:

1   operational change to remedy the causes of resident complaints, in particular the reduction of construction noise, vehicle operations in residential streets and disruption to parking and access;
2   policies and procedures to reduce the need for complaint;
3   mechanisms to allow residents and regulators to make immediate contact with the developer at all times, day and night;
4   clear and effective channels of communication with neighbours to reduce

antipathy towards the project and maintain an ongoing communications flow to engage residents in the refurbishment, keeping them informed in advance of major phases and potential disruptions; and

5   demonstration that the developer was serious about responding to and reducing community concern.

This issue provided an opportunity to defuse a highly volatile situation with the potential to close a multimillion-dollar project, engage sensitised residents and encourage their acceptance and 'ownership' of the development. The project goal was *to reduce the level of community complaint and allow the project to proceed without threat of closure*.

The situation's obvious urgency and critical nature required immediate and focused research, which took the form of a consultant visiting each neighbouring residence personally and asking people to clarify their situation, explain the nature and magnitude of their complaints and seek their input into immediate solutions.

This direct first-person approach also helped to establish resident's perception of, attitude to and level of knowledge about the Stockland project— hinting that residents were also reacting to being kept out of the process in their neighbourhood. This information formed the basis of the strategy to maintain constant contact with neighbours and mitigate their concerns.

Research found:

- ninety-two residents were directly affected by the refurbishment project (50 from four streets fronting Stockland and 42 from surrounding streets);
- issues sensitising residents included noise from after-hours construction work, bright lights, heavy vehicle movement and parking (including music from radios), blocked driveways and limited avenues for complaint;
- no consultation had been undertaken with residents who, as a result, knew little about the refurbishment and were therefore largely hostile to its progress; and
- no measures had been implemented to soundproof the site and residents identified a number of possible basic improvements that could succeed in reducing the noise.

The communications strategy developed was simple and effective, involving:

- the introduction of basic operational policies and modifications to the site area to safeguard residents against the effects of heavy construction;
- the development of a single, clear line of communication between developers and residents to ensure immediate resolution of any other operational problems;

- ongoing communication with residents and the EPA to advise them of upcoming potential disruptions;
- the development of a strategy to encourage residents to accept and 'own' the project; and
- ongoing monitoring and evaluation.

Based on this strategic framework, a number of basic tools were developed:

- *Complaints 'Hotline'*: a 24-hour, seven-days-a-week complaints line supervised personally by the site manager. A dedicated mobile phone was purchased and carried at all times by the site manager. The Hotline number was provided to all residents, who were encouraged to use it at any time as the primary point of contact. Calls to this mobile took priority over all other work for the site manager.
- *Complaints log*: the complaints log was reviewed and developed into a complete contact management tool including information from face-to-face research, records of all calls from stakeholders and details regarding the resolutions to these calls. This log allowed the team to better understand and identify patterns in complaints and resolutions. It was made available to regulators on request.
- *Zero noise tolerance policy*: the policy was implemented to ensure neighbours would not be subjected to significant noise without prior warning. Any complaint made was dealt with within five minutes and the offending action immediately stopped. Residents and regulators were repeatedly reminded of this policy.
- *Letters to residents*: helped open communication between residents, developers and Stockland Management. The series of personalised letters initially apologised for the disruptions to date, and reassured residents of the developer's commitment to rectifying the situation and providing access to complaint procedures. Later letters discussed ongoing issues, pre-informed neighbours of potential disturbances and invited them to attend events and activities within the centre.
- *Media relations*: although local media were aware of the issues, the small scale and rapid resolution of the issues meant no negative media coverage was generated. Responses to possible media queries were developed and the media were issued with project updates to help inform local residents.

Implementation of the strategy was relatively clear cut and defined. All components were put into operation immediately to diffuse the critical nature of the situation and provide the structure for its ongoing maintenance.

Once the two major problems—operational inconveniences and communication shortfalls between developers and residents—had been addressed, strong opposition to the refurbishment dissolved quickly.

Two other peripheral issues arose which had the potential to impact on the success of the project. Both were resolved using the strategy and tools developed for the broader project:

- A large crane was contracted to install a skylight over the shopping complex's centre stage. The 150-tonne crane—the largest in North Queensland—had previously been dubbed 'the death crane' by local media following its role in a fatality elsewhere. Subsequently, briefings were provided to local media on the crane's role in the project, and site tours and photo opportunities were arranged.
- With the issue of noise already a major concern for local residents, a free concert being staged by a retailer in the complex carpark had the potential to cause further alarm. All residents were notified of the concert in writing a week in advance and were personally invited to attend. They were also sent a sample of a new product the retailer was introducing to thank them for their patience.

Although the overall budget for the public relations operation was less than A\$4000 in total, the results were impressive:

- Operational measures to resolve noise and traffic problems were implemented quickly and effectively.
- Contact with residents (both personal and written) directly addressed their expressed concerns.
- Contact with other stakeholders conveyed concern for the issues and a readiness to resolve problems.
- The flow of information to the media maintained a positive and balanced perception of the project.
- The level of community complaint quickly dropped to almost nil.
- The developers retained their licence to operate the project and the refurbishment continued with no interruptions or delays caused by resident or regulator concerns.
- Residents' hostility towards the project was dissipated and replaced with greater knowledge, positive perception and a degree of 'ownership'.
- The few complaints received were directed to the developer rather than regulators and were quickly dealt with using simple procedures.

The size and speed of the project meant evaluation was limited to follow-up contact with key stakeholders (Stockland, developers, EPA and selected residents) to confirm that the situation had been resolved and no additional issues had developed.

This project, undertaken by David Donohue of QCCN (regional Queensland's largest corporate communications firm), received a Gold Award in the Community Communication category of the 2001 PRIA Queensland Awards for Excellence.

Discussion and exercises

1   Discuss the differences between crises and issues and the different ways the public relations practitioner could best prepare for each.
2   List some contemporary public issues—for instance, falling birth rates and parental leave rights; concerns about children's consumption of fast food; increasing reliance on poker machines by community and sports clubs; the rising cost of university education. Add some of your own issues from this week's newspapers. Under each issue, write how the issue might impinge on your life over the next ten years; how it might affect your employer over the next ten years; how it might affect any family member over the next ten years.
3   Small crises occur regularly in some organisations. For example, there are often local power outages after storms. Traffic is sometimes disrupted or diverted during roadworks. There are sometimes significant train or plane delays. New car models are sometimes recalled. Occasionally, theatre or music festivals are cancelled or experience the withdrawal of headline artists. What communication tactics and channels would best be utilised for ongoing or regular occurrences such as these by the organisations involved?
4   Using the principles outlined in this chapter, set up a mock crisis in class— perhaps a food poisoning, a factory fire or a bomb scare. How would you handle the crisis? What tactics would you use? How would you involve the media?

Further reading

Heath, R.L. (1997) *Strategic Issues Management: Organisations and Public Policy Challenges*, Sage, London.
Irvine, R.B. & Millar, D.P. (1998) *Crisis Management and Communication: How to gain and maintain control*, International Association of Business Communicators, San Francisco.
Lerbinger, O. (1997) *The Crisis Manager: Facing Risk and Responsibility*, Lawrence Erlbaum, New Jersey.

Spinney Press (2000) Issues in Society Newsletter, Sydney.
Xavier, R. (2001) 'The tampering trilogy: exploring ethical considerations in crisis planning and response', *Asia Pacific Public Relations Journal*, vol. 3, no. 1.

References

AAP (1998) 'A prayer for power', *Age*, 9 March, p. 9.
Bisignani, G. (2003) *Of War and SARS*, IATA, <www.iata.org/pressroom/iata_speaks/2003-4-09-01.htm>.
Button, V. (1999) 'Longford: Esso faces charges', *Age*, 29 June, p. 1.
Chulov, M. (2001) 'Fatal mistake that brought an accused extortionist undone', *The Australian*, 18 May.
Cutlip, S., Center, A. & Broom, G. (1994) *Effective Public Relations*, 7th edn, Prentice Hall, Englewood Cliffs.
Dale, D. (1998) 'No, it's not Calcutta, it's Sydney', *Age*, 31 July, p. 1.
Doherty, L. & Ryle, G. (1998) 'How Sydney was kept in the dark', *Age*, 31 July, p. 2.
Elias, D. (1998) 'Too much power for one, not enough for the rest', *Age*, 25 February, p. 6.
Gardiner, A. (2002) 'Police probe cash offers: pipeline company denies wrong doing', *Herald Sun*, 5 April 2002, p. 10.
Hawes, R. (1999) 'Gas blast Esso's fault', *Australian*, 29 June, p. 1.
International Air Transport Association (IATA) (2003) *Crisis Communications*, <www.iata.org/crisiscomms/index>.
Macey, R. (1997) 'Arnott's dumps loads of stock', *Age*, 22 February, p. 9.
Mathewson, C. (2001) 'Bitter pill to swallow', *Courier Mail*, 18 May.
Murray, D. (2000) 'Victims find themselves in Panadol Searchlight', *Daily Telegraph*, 9 December 2000, p. 1.
Saunders, M. & Harris, T. (1997) 'Extortion bid shatters Arnott's', *Australian*, 15 February.
Schafer, A. (2001) 'Management crisis: how GlaxoSmithKline managed its extortion crisis', CEO forum, <www.ceoforum.com.au/200109_ceodialogue.cfm>.
Seitel, F. (1992) *The Practice of Public Relations*, 5th edn, Macmillan, New York.
Walker, F. (1998) 'Sydney water scare is still a mystery', *Age*, 20 September, p. 2.

13 SPONSORSHIP AND EVENT MANAGEMENT
Susan Boyd

In this chapter

Introduction

This chapter looks at the way in which organisations use the specific tactics of sponsorship and special events to achieve their goals. These range from growing their trust banks to communicating values, developing strategic alliances with key publics and positioning themselves in very specific ways to differentiate themselves from their competitors.

Sponsorship is one of the most expensive tactics which can be chosen by an organisation, but the goodwill delivered by a well-chosen and managed sponsorship can be commensurately large. In recent years, with an increased focus on corporate governance issues, sponsorship has moved from being simplistically regarded to being a visible manifestation of community partnering.

Events, which always include careful planning and timing, can demand the greatest attention to detail of all available tactics. Events can range in size and budget from the Olympics through to Opera in the Vineyards to a business breakfast. The larger the event, the more likely it is to require some form of sponsorship, often requiring these two tactics to be considered in tandem. There is no doubt that a well-managed event can turn a public relations professional into the star of an organisation—at least temporarily. Poorly managed events, on the other hand, can have disastrous career results.

Newspaper editors detest clichéd events such as ribbon-cutting ceremonies, but events are a chance for public relations practitioners to exercise their creative abilities. They must try to stage events that not only fulfil the aims and strategies of the organisation or the sponsor, but also attract the attention of the media.

In 1961, Daniel Boorstin first recognised the creation of the public relations event in his book, *The Image*. Boorstin identifies four characteristics of what he calls the 'pseudo event' to differentiate such happenings from a 'real' news event like a train smash. These are:

1   It is not spontaneous, but has been planned, planted or incited.
2   It is planned primarily for the purpose of being reported or reproduced.
3   It communicates on more than one level and uses ambiguity to create links.
4   It becomes a self-fulfilling prophecy. (1961: 11, 12)

It is important to understand that events which are created to fulfil public relations objectives need to fit well with an overall public relations strategy.

Sponsorship

Sponsorship is the purchase of specific rights and benefits associated with an event, organisation or individual. Sponsorship should not be confused with donations, philanthropy or bequests. Such gifts are made without expectations of a bottom-line return: 'Giving is philanthropy. It's for individuals. You don't expect a return.' (Huxley, in Turner 2003: 2) Sponsorship expects a return.

Turner (2003) says the recent change of terminology to corporate partnerships reflects the sophistication of the sponsorship industry. He points out that the move is an attempt to reflect the growing variety of relationships which do not necessarily focus solely on money. Corporate partnering can be about sharing resources such as expertise and manpower (2003: 2). While sponsorship is, of course, by no means dead as a term, true partnerships are widely seen to be the direction in which the industry is heading.

Sponsorship (by any name) is popular with many organisations because it generates goodwill and provides opportunities to enhance the image and reputation of the organisation by association. Sponsorship also provides a focal point for sales and marketing efforts, offers product brands high visibility to potential customers and generates media coverage for the sponsoring organisation.

Geldard and Sinclair (1996: 7) outline a selection of sponsor benefits as being:

- exclusivity (the ability to lock out competitors);
- image association;
- hospitality for client entertainment;
- product sampling;
- signage rights;
- merchandising;
- networking with people of importance;
- media coverage;
- use of personnel for advertising; and
- promotions and sales opportunities.

Types of sponsorship

Philanthropic sponsorship

Philanthropic sponsorship is as close to a donation as sponsorship can get. In the areas of arts, medicine, education and research, this kind of sponsorship is generally community-based. It does offer measurable benefits in the form of taxation considerations, however, as well as generating community goodwill towards an organisation. Philanthropic sponsorship can also engender goodwill in employees. The Pratt and Myer family foundations are excellent examples of this. Philanthropy is covered in more detail in Chapter 14.

Corporate sponsorship

This is sponsorship of an event or activity not normally linked to the sponsoring company's general business. Examples are the Ford Australian Open Tennis Tournament, the Hahn Premium Race Week and McDonald's Junior Tennis. These sponsorships are entered into in order to link the sponsoring organisation to a popular or high-profile event or activity, and thus to reap the benefits of this positive connection in the minds of the organisation's publics.

Marketing sponsorship

This is the most popular form of sponsorship, and is a common inclusion as a cost-effective sales and marketing strategy. Marketing sponsorship offers cash and goods in return for tangible revenue-oriented results. Geldard and Sinclair (1996) say this form of sponsorship is used primarily to promote products and services to targeted market segments and/or to reinforce a product or brand or promote sales activities (1996: 14).

Marketing sponsorships are taken out by businesses of all sizes for the sole reason that the sponsorship will have a quantifiable effect on the company's bottom line— that is, it will generate profit, usually through increased sales.

Sportswear companies, such as Nike and Adidas, enter into marketing sponsorship agreements with high-profile athletes, who appear on and off the field in clothing that predominantly displays the sponsor's logos. This has an immediate 'spin-off' effect, as people who want to be identified with these sports stars emulate them through wearing the appropriate brands.

Globally, the sponsorship industry is worth an estimated $35–$40 billion. Prices in the Australian sponsorship market have risen nearly 5 per cent in recent times (Lawson, 2002).

Melbourne-based consultancy Sponsorship Solutions specialises in valuing sponsorships in sport. According to its 'Top 40' ranking for 2003, the Australian Open Tennis was the most expensive sporting event to sponsor in Australia, costing its major sponsor $9.8 million.

The second most valuable event was the Australian Grand Prix, with naming rights estimated at $9 million. In third place is an AFL premier partner, with an estimated value of $8 million.

Champion swimmer Ian Thorpe was Australia's most marketable athlete, with annual sponsorships estimated at $480 000, followed by tennis stars Lleyton Hewitt at $430 000 and Pat Rafter at $400 000.

Sprinter Cathy Freeman was worth an estimated $395 000 in the year she officially retired from competition. Car racer Mark Webber managed to increase his sponsorship value from an estimated $300 000 in 2002 to $370 000 in 2003, while estimates of golfing mainstay Greg Norman's sponsorship value dropped from $400 000 in 2002 to $365 000 in 2003. The other sporting stars in Sponsorship Solutions' list of top ten sports sponsorships were cricketers Adam Gilchrist and Steve Waugh, golfer Karrie Webb and swimmer Grant Hackett.

These figures are based on Sponsorship Solutions' estimation of the value of sponsorship packages for individual sporting events and athletes; they are not the actual figures being paid. The criteria for valuing sporting events are: the key characteristics of the event, the nature of the communication platform, level of exposure for a sponsor, the image transferred to a sponsor, rights provided and the presence of other sponsors.

The criteria for valuing athletes are: career achievements, celebrity status, personal characteristics, exposure provided to sponsors and the athlete's image.

Source: Adapted from Sponsorship Solutions (2003)

Writing a sponsorship proposal

Understanding the motives and goals of the target audience is crucial when writing a sponsorship proposal. A generic sponsorship document will not generate support. Before approaching any organisations for sponsorship, ask the following questions:

- What rights and benefits are being offered?

- Will the sponsorship improve image, boost sales, provide a competitive advantage, offer exclusivity, generate publicity, enhance brand or product awareness, involve customers, change customer goodwill, entertain clients, communicate key messages, form business relationships, improve staff morale, or offer cost-effective advertising opportunities?
- What are the objectives of the sponsorship? Are they to raise funds, generate publicity, obtain goods or services, raise awareness, promote a brand, generate revenue, reach a target audience, obtain access to experts or save money on advertising?
- Is the sponsorship being sought for an event—are the event participants/spectators likely to support the sponsorship? Are they from the sponsoring company's target demographic or can their purchasing decisions be influenced? How can this be determined?
- What considerations may give rise to unsuitable sponsors? Are there any conflicts between sponsors? Some sponsors may not be suitable for specific types of sponsorships (e.g. an alcohol company sponsorship would not be appropriate for an event involving children).
- What resources are available to sell and service the sponsorship?

Once this analysis is complete, the public relations practitioner will be in a position to formulate a sponsorship proposal to submit to prospective sponsors.

The decision to involve a particular organisation in a sponsorship may be made by a dedicated sponsorship manager (if the company is large and invests a great deal in sponsorship), a marketing manager or the public relations manager. Very often these people are inundated with requests for sponsorship and it may be difficult to raise them on the telephone, so the first point of contact is generally through a written proposal. The writer will, in most cases, have to identify the specific 'hot keys' of the decision-maker without any prior contact with that person.

Experienced practitioners suggest researching the target organisation thoroughly, by requesting a copy of the annual report, looking at its internet site for information on its other sponsorships (many organisations have direct links to event sites), attending events sponsored by the organisation and researching and examining likely sponsor benefits. Among the questions that should be considered are:

- Is there VIP seating?
- Is there noticeable media coverage?
- What are the signage opportunities?
- How many spectators/participants are there?

When writing the sponsorship proposal, it is sometimes easy to get carried away with the excitement and detail of the event, event schedule and participants. While it is important to include this background information, it needs to be limited to one page. The target audience is more interested in what is actually in it for them in terms of sponsor benefits. On average, a sponsorship proposal—which may have taken hours to compile—will be considered for three minutes by the decision-maker, after which time it will either be filed or actioned. The best advice is to sell the sizzle (rather than the steak) of the sponsorship, keep it short and relevant to the reader and most of all be comprehensive about what the potential sponsor is being offered. A proposal that says: 'We want $20,000 for our great event and we can tailor benefits to anything you want' may sound attractive and flexible to the author, but the reader is probably going to consider it unprofessional and disorganised.

A sponsorship proposal should include a covering letter summarising the content of the proposal; one page of background on the event; one to two pages of sponsor benefits; one to two pages of pictures of past events (to demonstrate signage, entertaining facilities, spectator number, capability of delivering promised benefits); and a specific request for the amount of the sponsorship contribution.

The Australasian Sponsorship Marketing Association recommends linking the sponsor's investment to their return and not to market rates. A premium investment can be requested if there is a unique and perfect 'fit' between sponsor and sponsorship:

> Event organisers should also be prepared to offer quantifiable targets in the proposal and factor bonuses into the sponsorship investment. For example: an event organiser might set targets based on the sponsor's objectives ranging from minimum crowd levels to raising awareness of the sponsorship to a certain level and specify that the additional investment for each target met is $10,000. This not only has the potential to increase the revenue from sponsorship, but also shows the target corporation that the event organiser is conscious of the need to meet the sponsor's objectives and is prepared to be accountable for ensuring that these objectives are met. (Austin 2002)

Many large organisations now have dedicated sponsorship pages on their websites which clearly define the steps and information to be provided to the organisation in order to be considered for sponsorship.

Telstra has an extensive sponsorship section on its website outlining events the company has sponsored as well as the Telstra Awards program. A part of the site gives detailed guidelines on how to apply for sponsorship (see opposite).

Telstra sponsorship page

Key requirements for potential sponsorships

To achieve objectives, Telstra chooses to sponsor organisations or activities that meet certain criteria, including:

- A strategic plan to achieve objectives.
- A defined target audience.
- Clear start and finish points.
- Specific achievable outcomes.
- A comprehensive evaluation and monitoring plan.
- A national focus.
- Strong commercial opportunities to leverage business objectives.
- Innovative elements.

Application requirements

When assessing a submission for sponsorship Telstra will take into account the overall benefits to the Australian community as well as how closely our marketing and business objectives can be met in each target market by utilising the activities within a sponsorship. Outlining the following detail will assist in a speedy evaluation of a submission:

- Objectives of the organisation requesting sponsorship.
- A defined target audience and expected numbers who will participate or form the audience which will be reached by the sponsorship activities.
- Detailed outcome of the project and activity plans.
- Details of the marketing opportunities available for the sponsor.
- Details of why you believe this opportunity will add value to Telstra's marketing objectives.
- Details of the opportunities for product promotion and sales within the sponsorship activities.
- Strategies to launch, publicise and promote the project.
- Start and finish dates of the sponsorship.
- Implementation timelines and list of locations and venues to outline geographical impact.

- Evaluation method for measuring impact and success of sponsorship investment.
- Evaluation method for measuring changes in attitudes and behaviour specifying expected outcomes as a result of the project.
- Performance indicators to demonstrate sponsorship achievements and attaining sponsorship goals.
- Relevant experience and credentials of the applicant.
- Amount sought for the sponsorship including leverage funds.
- Other confirmed sponsors.

Source: Telstra, <www.telstra.com.au/sponsorship/requests.htm?tR=3at>

Ambush marketing

Ambush marketing occurs when a company misrepresents itself as being associated with an event when it has no official, legal or moral rights to do so. It can take the form of a hot-air balloon carrying signage flying low over an event with which the company has no formal connection, gaining TV coverage or simply being seen by a large number of spectators; or it can involve a non-sponsoring company giving away 'freebies' like hats or sunscreen or placing signage outside an event venue.

O'Riordan (2002) quotes two schools of thought when it comes to ambush marketing. The first comprises sporting organisations and sponsorship advocates, who believe it is unethical; the second consists of marketing executives, who argue that it just separates the strong brands from the weak.

Ambush marketing can destroy the concept of sponsorship and the viability of some events. It is also an unpopular marketing move, with Ligerakis (2003) citing a post-2000 Olympics study showing that 62 per cent of people disagree with ambush marketing. Case study 13.4 at the end of the chapter shows how easily such an ambush can take place.

All steps should be taken to protect your sponsorships. Sponsorship proposals should be written in a clear and precise manner so there is no ambiguity about benefits offered and contributions required. Sponsorships should be undertaken only on the basis of clearly defined parameters.

How to prevent an ambush

Following are some guidelines to assist in preventing the dirty tactics used by ambush marketers. However, despite its best actions and intentions, the organisation may still become a victim. Here one should be aware that trade practice laws may have been broken, and it may be possible to pursue legal avenues to protect the sponsorship.

The target audience must know who the real sponsors are. This should be an ongoing activity in servicing the sponsorship (through logo identification on printed materials, newsletter stories, mentions in news releases, and so on). In extreme cases (where an ambush has occurred), organisations have placed advertisements to identify and thank their sponsors.

If more than one sponsoring organisation is involved, each needs to take ownership of its part of the sponsorship and clearly define its rights and benefits. It can be useful to communicate levels of sponsorship undertaken and benefits offered to all sponsors at each level. This will assist in policing ambush marketing from within, as a minor sponsor may represent its level of sponsorship to the detriment of organisations that have made greater contributions.

Integrated marketing should be introduced as a component of the overall sponsorship strategy. Integrated marketing in events encompasses items such as TV rights, advertising during the broadcast, signage and promotions with the standard sponsorship benefits and rights. Integrated marketing reassures sponsors of the minimal risk of an ambush on their sponsorship investment, as well as offering some strong commercial benefits to make the sponsorship more attractive and valuable.

If the sponsorship is for an event, the sponsorship managers need to control all aspects of that event. As pointed out earlier, it is highly unlikely that a public relations professional will be expert in all areas of special event management, and it is common to contract out specific duties to third parties or committees. It is vital to keep communication lines open with everyone involved in event operations.

It is also up to individual sponsors to accept responsibility and deter ambush marketing techniques. Sponsors of Rugby World Cup 2003, including Coca-Cola, Visa, Heineken, Qantas/British Airways, Bundaberg Rum and Telstra, met more than twelve months before the event to determine a strategy to protect their sponsorship investment.

Gotting (2003) reports that Rugby World Cup organisers will have task forces at all venues across Australia in October 2003, helping security to capture any third party that may be trying to get its brand name into an event. They will patrol the areas outside the grounds, as well as inside, although they will have much less power to control what happens at 'live' sites around the city.

The most common avenues for event ambushing are:

• *Advertising in event publications*. Here competitors take an advertisement in the event program. This can easily be overcome by ensuring that responsibility for signing off on program artwork is carried out by someone fully briefed on all objectives of the event.

- *Signage sales.* Many major events contract their signage sales out to an external company, whose goal may be to achieve sales rather than protect sponsor rights. It is important that an event representative accept responsibility for final approval of all signage before signwriting or placement proceeds. Another ploy is the placement of billboard signage (mobile or fixed) outside a major event venue.
- *Sponsorship of an individual or sporting team.* This is a contentious area, where an individual sportsperson or team may be sponsored by an organisation in competition with the sponsor of the event in which they are competing. Accordingly, it is not uncommon for events to restrict the display of conflicting signage or logo identification on uniforms or racing equipment. For example, the conditions of entry for Australia's largest outrigger canoe event, the Coca-Cola Cup on Hamilton Island, restrict participants from wearing uniforms or displaying logos of Pepsi or any other rival soft-drink company. In one instance, a crew had to remove signage from the side of their canoe before they were permitted to compete.

Kendall and Curthoys (2001) examine some other ambush marketing methods used in the Sydney 2000 Olympic Games. These were:

- sponsoring the broadcast of the event (rather than the event itself);
- sponsoring sub-categories within the event (for example, sponsoring a team rather than the event itself);
- buying advertising time around relays of the competitor's event (for example, during televised broadcasts); and
- staging major promotions that coincided with the event.

Despite the risk of 'ambush', sponsorship can be a hugely successful tactic. But like all tactics it should not be considered in isolation. Sponsoring organisations need to leverage their sponsorship with promotional expenditure in addition to their sponsorship investment. It is not unusual for a company to invest four times the sponsorship value in supporting promotion, marketing and public relations activity. So, while a sponsorship package may cost $10 000 for defined benefits, an astute organisation will invest a further $40 000 to leverage the sponsorship to ensure its key messages are communicated and the threat of ambush minimised. One popular tactic, which may be a part of a sponsorship package or a logical allied tactic in the public relations mix, is the special event.

Event management

The number and range of events that a practitioner can choose from is enormous. The range includes conferences, sports activities, launches, openings, community or political meetings, breakfasts or dinners, lectures—everything and anything imaginable. Strategy will help guide the choice of event that will most suit the purpose. Events are an opportunity to make news, but if badly planned or lacking in a good creative angle, the media will not be interested in them.

A carefully managed special event can achieve a variety of public relations goals and objectives. Common reasons for staging an event include the generation of media coverage, creating a platform for product demonstration, corporate/client entertainment and revenue generation.

Research conducted by Rob Tonge (1999) reveals that successful events have a number of common characteristics. A successful event has the full commitment of all members of the organising body. It features strong leadership, an efficient event committee, and effective subcommittees with clearly defined responsibilities. A successful event has clearly defined objectives and priorities as well as a strong event theme and image. Success depends also on allowing adequate planning time, and on successfully implementing, monitoring and evaluating detailed action plans. Events can be expensive, so an adequate budget is necessary, along with strong financial management. This can require good sponsorship support and credibility in the eyes of the sponsor.

Staffing is vital. Large events will require paid secretarial assistance and enthusiastic volunteer resources. Sufficient staff will be crucial to provide attention to detail, effective communication with stakeholder organisations and comprehensive post-event analysis.

Tonge's research also shows the characteristics of *unsuccessful* events. He found that events failed due to a combination of two or more of the following factors:

- failure to allow sufficient planning time;
- inadequate planning;
- problems within the organising committee—for example, power struggles, infighting, a lack of skills;
- inadequate market research;
- clashing of event dates;
- an ad hoc approach to marketing (lack of a marketing plan);
- lack of a sponsorship plan;
- inadequate budget and/or poor financial control;

- failure to meet spectator and/or competitor expectations; and
- failure to adequately make provision for inclement weather conditions (Tonge 1999).

Another vital factor in special event planning is the need for a comprehensive public relations strategy, designed specifically for the event, that follows the ten-point process for planning outlined in Chapter 6. Beware of restricting the primary focus of the event to the generation of publicity, as this narrow focus can result in lost opportunities for achieving other public relations objectives.

Media coverage

In media terms, special events can be visual, unusual, provide human interest, spectacle or famous faces. Through such elements, they can become news. 'News is anything that makes a reader say, "Gee whiz!".' This famous definition by Arthur MacEwen, editor of William Randolph Hearst's San Francisco *Examiner* (in Boorstin 1961: 8), illustrates simply the need for grabbing the reader's attention. Special events usually provide this opportunity for only a short period of time, so practitioners must work carefully to maximise these 'gee whiz' opportunities— before, during and after the event.

Ryan and Lemmond (in Wilcox et al. 1998: 313) point out that: 'Cynical consumers are zapping commercials and ignoring printed ads and are more receptive to the editorial message. The "third party endorsement" allows advertisers to sell a new product while enveloping the commercial message in a credible environment.' Special events can create such a credible environment.

Event publicity aims to extend the target audience beyond the event's spectators and participants. Media coverage is considered by many sponsors to be a crucial sponsorship component, and the event manager should consider tactics to generate publicity for the event and the sponsor. Richards (1998: 93) recommends that:

- a media release be issued about the event and sponsorship;
- media functions be staged within the event;
- an event handbook be distributed to the media; and
- event tickets be made available to the media.

Most major events set up a dedicated media centre as a central point for distribution of media information. It is important that this media centre is always staffed by at least one public relations professional to deal with telephone inquiries by media representatives who cannot attend the event. Journalists become infuriated when they have to rely on information provided by other journalists (sometimes from opposition publications) because the media centre has not been adequately staffed.

Due to the short-term nature of most events, it is not uncommon for media centres to take the form of tents or temporary offices. Regardless of the surroundings, every media centre should offer the following facilities: electricity (with extra power outlets for mobile phone chargers and laptop computers); a photocopier, a fax machine and at least one computer (with internet access); a printer, ample desks and chairs, catering, spare stationery, film, etc.; a first-aid kit; a lock-up area for cameras and personal equipment; a message board or personal pigeonholes; ample event information (background, competitor and sponsor information, results, past records); non-copyrighted photographs; a television and VCR; television monitors (if your event is being broadcast live); and access to transportation (such as media boats, motorcycles, helicopters).

Product demonstration

A special event can be an ideal forum for a company to launch or market a specific product with a view to attracting future sales as well as generating publicity. For example, a sports drink company might stage a fun run and give competitors free samples, as well as serving its product before, during and after the event. The publicity generated for the event would then include vision/pictures of competitors using the product.

Product demonstration can present opportunities for credible third party endorsement of a particular product. A sports hero could be contracted to wear a certain brand of clothing for an event or in media interviews about the event— giving this new brand of clothing instant credibility.

Corporate/client entertaining

Some events are staged simply as an opportunity to impress key clients and develop business opportunities. While corporate and client entertaining is rarely the sole objective in staging a dedicated event, it is a valuable sponsorship benefit. An event formulated with the key objective of entertaining could be a hotel hosting a wine tasting and dinner to entertain major clients and/or to demonstrate its unique food and beverage facilities (with a view to generating future business). Many organisations use major sporting events as an opportunity to get closer to their clients and key publics through the purchase of corporate hospitality.

Revenue generation

Special events can make money if they are carefully planned and budgeted for. Tourist and retail facilities often stage events to generate business in low-season periods. A ski resort might stage a summer music festival to encourage visits at a traditionally quiet time of the year.

It is not uncommon for the public relations department of an organisation to be viewed as a cost centre, which does not generate any direct revenue for the company. Special events have the potential to generate revenue as well as achieve objectives such as publicity, goodwill and future business opportunities.

Creating events

Tonge (1999) proposes four steps to follow to create a successful event: feasibility, planning, execution and evaluation.

Feasibility

Before you start planning an event, it is essential to undertake some fundamental research to determine the feasibility of the event. During this analysis, important factors can be analysed, including:

- how much the event is going to cost;
- whether it offers an opportunity to raise revenue;
- the effect of the event on the organisation's key publics;
- why the event is being staged;
- what the organisation can gain;
- how participants will be sourced; and
- when the best time to hold the event would be.

Planning

After the event has been assessed, the planning process begins. The easiest way to determine the time it will take to organise the event is to work backwards from the event date and formulate a list of duties and a time management plan for implementation. Some considerations include:

- generating sponsorship (including the preparation of a sponsorship plan, preparing sponsorship proposals, securing sponsors);
- servicing sponsors (such as provisions for corporate hospitality boxes, signage, media promotion, etc.);
- formulating the event budget;
- preparation and implementation of a promotional/marketing plan;
- preparation and implementation of a public relations strategy;
- developing the schedule of events;
- formulating event rules and procedures;
- appointment of key officials, judges and personnel;
- determining the amount of equipment needed to stage the event;
- organising event services such as electricity, audio visual, water and toilets;
- securing permits (e.g. council, police, etc.);
- organising security;
- arranging catering services;
- food and beverages for VIPs, sponsors, etc.;
- incorporation of a social schedule (for conference delegates and partners);
- organising key functions (e.g. welcome cocktail party, presentation dinner);
- liaising with accommodation providers;
- booking accommodation and travel for participants, sponsors, etc.;
- processing entries;
- coordinating registration of participants;
- securing merchandising; and
- organising insurance and implementing a risk management strategy.

It is unrealistic to expect that a public relations practitioner will have the expertise to carry out all of these duties, so it is common practice for an event committee to be formed, with the public relations practitioner assuming the role of chairperson. Committees can present their own challenges, however—the saying that a camel is a horse designed by a committee has some truth to it. To maintain the effectiveness of any committee, it is best to define clear roles for all members and to create, implement and monitor action plans for each task. A checklist is a helpful tool for planning any event.

Execution

The planning process should be completed as far in advance of the event as possible. Time needs to be allocated for any last-minute obstacles and to put the finishing touches on the operation. It is vital that all staff and volunteers know what they have to do and that their job expectations are clearly established before the event starts.

If the planning process has been successful, and lines of communication have been clear and open, the event should go smoothly. If something unforeseen happens, the key people on the event committee should be trusted to deal with the mishap as planned. On the event day, the committee chair needs to remain free to oversee the entire operation.

Preparation of a *critical path*—which details exactly what should be happening at any time—is fundamental to the effective management of an event (see box below).

World Cup Triathlon critical path

4.00 a.m.	Arrive at the event site. Ensure all media centre and registration equipment is operational.
4.30 a.m.	Key officials and registration staff arrive.
4.55 a.m.	Staff briefing. Event operations advise that all hire equipment is in working order.
5.00 a.m.	Medical staff and some entrants arrive. Caterers begin preparation of media and VIP breakfasts.
5.30 a.m.	Registration begins. 600 athletes.
5.30 a.m.	Some media and VIPs arrive. Media and VIP catering is available.
6.30 a.m.	Water police and Air Sea Rescue arrive.
6.45 a.m.	Registration finishes. All athletes to move to swim start.
6.45 a.m.	Various radio media crosses.
6.50 a.m.	Media boat leaves beach.
7.00 a.m.	Event start (swim).
7.00 a.m.	All marshals and waterstations on cycle course in place.
7.05 a.m.	Police in position along cycle course to assist with road closures.
7.05 a.m.	Motorcycles arrive to escort camera crews around course.
7.20 a.m.	First swimmer leaves water and starts cycle.
7.25 a.m.	Media transfer from boat to motorcycles.
7.30 a.m.	Media and VIP breakfast begins.
7.45 a.m.	Various radio crosses.
8.00 a.m.	All marshals and waterstations on run course in place.
8.30 a.m.	First cyclist back to transition zone.

8.31 a.m.	First runner leaves on course.
8.35 a.m.	Masseurs and post-race staff in place.
9.10 a.m.	Winner expected.
9.30 a.m.	Winner's media conference.
9.30 a.m.	Provide media with unofficial results.
9.45 a.m.	Various radio media crosses.
10.30 a.m.	Last competitor expected to finish.
11.00 a.m.	Provide media with official results and distribute event release and photography.
11.30 a.m.	Clean-up begins.
2.30 p.m.	Reconfirm details with venue for presentation banquet.
3.30 p.m.	View rushes of event video to be screened at presentation banquet.
4.00 p.m.	Transport trophies, prizes, etc. to event venue.
6.00 p.m.	Presentation banquet begins.

Source: Courtesy of Multi-sport Marketing

Evaluation

For a major sporting event such as the World Cup Triathlon, three primary methods of evaluation can be used: a debriefing meeting; event assessment; and business activity assessment.

Debriefing meeting

Tonge (1999: 50) suggests staging a debriefing meeting of the main committee and sub-committee as soon as possible after the event:

> The aim of this meeting is to review each aspect of the event planning management and marketing, examine any problems and identify ways future events can be improved. Importantly, the event outcomes should be evaluated against the goals.

Event assessment

The next step in Tonge's analysis is examining the event in terms of patronage and financial performance, by determining factors such as the number of spectators and/or participants and their origin, merchandising, ticket and program sales, and food and beverage sales.

Business activity assessment

This stage of the evaluation process looks beyond the event to gain an indication of the benefit to local businesses by investigating business activity during the event. This can be done through formal and informal research to obtain information on accommodation, airline, coach and rail bookings, and restaurant and retail sales over the event period. Businesses can be surveyed on whether they received an increase in patronage or revenue during the event and how this compared with previous years.

Further methods and approaches to evaluation can be found in Chapter 6.

Budgeting

Careful budgeting is the backbone of any successful special event. Unlike budgeting for other public relations activities, special events budgeting requires an eye for operational detail and consideration of items not usually included in the primarily administration-focused public relations budget.

The two main areas of special event budgeting are income and expenditure. The income budget calculates all revenue received from the event. Examples of revenue include grants/underwriting, sponsorship, ticket sales, merchandising and the sale of fixed assets at the end of a one-off event.

The expenditure budget covers all expenses associated with the event, which can include administration, insurance, the purchase of fixed assets, travel and accommodation, salaries and professional fees, event evaluation/bid costs, sanction fees, facility or venue fees, expenses associated with ceremonies (e.g. trophies), merchandising, printing and production, marketing, advertising, public relations and operational costs.

Risk management

Event management requires the adoption of strong crisis and issues management practices (as covered in Chapter 12), but also a dedication to risk management. O'Toole (2002) says changes in the general business environment, such as deregulation, globalisation and the pervasive growth of information technology, can result in a detailed plan for a special event being out of date before it actually occurs, so risk may be considered in the broader context of foreshadowing failure as well as something going wrong.

Event risk management plans are becoming standard and are a further management tool to position an event prominently in the eyes of stakeholders such as insurers, financiers, sponsors, clients and employees.

The rising costs of public liability insurance have brought risk management to the forefront of event planning. The O'Toole and Mikolaitis (2002) process of 'Identify→assess→treat→monitor→evaluate', and at the same time document, is a recommended model for event risk analysis (see Figure 13.1).

Figure 13.1 Risk analysis—a continuing process

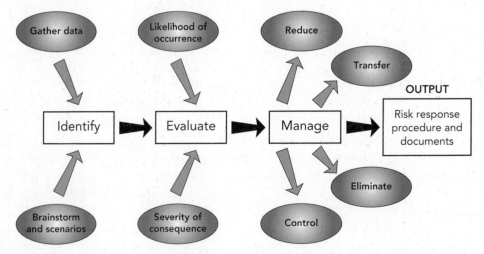

Source: Adapted from O'Toole and Mikolaitis, *Corporate Event Project Management*, 2002. Reprinted by permission of John Wiley & Sons, Inc.

Conclusion

Special events and sponsorship (or corporate partnerships) represent a high-profile aspect of public relations that focuses public attention on an event, organisation or product intensely over a short period of time. They are often highly visual, and for that reason offer strong media opportunities—especially for television and colour print publications. But sponsorship is a two-way street, with responsibility for positive benefits being taken by the event organiser as well as the sponsor. Sponsorship offers no guarantee of recall by the public. Similarly, events are so commonplace that they must truly be 'special' in order to gain interest and attention. Nevertheless, these fields of public relations can offer the practitioner unique opportunities for media management and exposure, while demanding the best the practitioner has to offer in the fields of research, planning, scheduling and creativity.

Case studies 13.1 and 13.2 were presented at the 2002 Meeting Industries Association of Australia (MIAA) conference (Connell 2002).

Case study 13.1: SOCOG sponsor dinner

Source: Presented by Keri Chittenden, David Grant Special Events

The brief

A sit-down dinner for 450 people in a unique harbourfront venue with attendees from every major Olympic sponsor and SOCOG, International Olympic Committee members, etc.

The hiccup

The venue chosen was a marquee on Goat Island in Sydney Harbour. The day before the event, Sydney was hit with the worst rain since 1911. The venue was an absolute washout and totally unusable.

The solution

An unused shed on a Sydney wharf was sourced and in under 24 hours was cleaned and then fitted out for the function. This included installation of lighting and audio, décor, kitchens, toilets, generators, tables and chairs—the lot. Most of the equipment on the island could not be salvaged in time for the event, so it had to be produced virtually from scratch.

Post-mortem

Have faith in your suppliers and be prepared to 'pull a rabbit out of a hat'.

The payoff

After showing they could cope with such a 'disaster', David Grant Special Events (DGSE) showed SOCOG, the IOC and the sponsors that they were truly professional and capable of almost anything. After that event DGSE ran a very successful corporate hospitality program during the Sydney Olympics and followed that with more work in Salt Lake City.

Case study 13.2: Saltimbanco opening night party for Cirque de Soleil and the Sydney Festival

Source: Presented by Brigid Paton, tp Events

The brief

An after-show party for 2000 guests, performers, and festival staff in January 1998.

The challenge

The venue is not air-conditioned; the event is in the middle of summer.

The solution

Install portable air-conditioning and, as there is insufficient power, install generators as well.

Hiccup # 1

Generator breaks down before the event, meaning that the air-conditioning cannot be used.

The fix

Source, through the generator hire company, a technician to fix the recalcitrant machine. The company also puts another generator on standby ready to get it to the location.

Hiccup # 2

The generator is fixed but now the guests are on their way and the hall is still warm.

The fix

Rearrange the running order and focus of the event. Guests are first greeted with a stiff drink and then ushered through the hall to an outdoor area. By the time the guests are ready to hit the dance floor, the hall has been cooled sufficiently.

Post-mortem

Budget for a technician through the event, or at least have after-hours contact numbers. Assess refuelling needs if overtime is likely. Budget for backup power source if possible.

Case study 13.3: Taronga Zoo 'Partners in Conservation' sponsorship program

Background and overview

The sponsorship program at Sydney's Taronga Zoo is a major source of revenue for the zoo. The program runs at three levels:

1   corporate sponsorship;
2   ZooParents (or individual sponsors);
3   philanthropy.

Animal sponsorships began in 1977, following a telephone call from a visitor asking how they could help the zoo. Soon the idea of animal sponsorship captured the imagination of people of all ages and in 2002 the ZooParent program raised more than $400 000 from individuals, families, schools, community groups and small companies. The corporate sponsorship program also began in the early 1970s. There are currently 68 corporate sponsors who are members of the 'Partners in Conservation' program, run through the Taronga Foundation.

Taronga's sponsors contribute a large part to the daily running of the zoo. With 2200 animals in the animal family, the weekly grocery bill is around $10 000. Among the weekly deliveries are 260 kilograms of apples, 650 kilograms of carrots, 40 kilograms of grapes, 90 kilograms of watermelon, 4.4 kilograms of mung beans, 20 kilograms of coconuts, 10 kilograms of curly parsley, 250 kilograms of leeks and 100 kilograms of sweet potatoes. And that's just for the herbivores!

Sponsors head the growing list of individuals and organisations contributing to the quality of life of animals as ZooParents or corporate sponsors. Taronga's stakeholders include:

- sponsors;
- animal sponsors;
- ZooFriends;
- Taronga Foundation patrons;
- visitors;
- councils;
- government;
- National Parks and Wildlife;
- media;
- volunteers;
- board members; and
- animal collection.

ZooParent program

The ZooParent program lets individuals or small groups sponsor just about any kind of animal. The list of animals available for sponsorship is wide and varied, from Asiatic elephants and pygmy hippopotamus to cobras and finches.

ZooParent sponsorships operate at four levels, starting with the $70 Amber Membership, through to Diamond Membership of up to $4999. Benefits to the ZooParent include:

- entry to Taronga Zoo (or Western Plains Zoo);
- a naming certificate;
- stickers;
- free parking;
- shop discounts;
- a subscription to the glossy magazine *Zootopia*; and
- at a certain level, a bronze plaque in the zoo identifying the ZooParent.

How does the zoo attract ZooParents for its less-than-cuddly animals? The Summer 2002 edition of *Zootopia* includes a profile of one such animal—the Gila Monster. Headlined 'Sponsor a Monster', it points out that the Gila Monster is the zoo's least sponsored animal, but that it is just as adoptable (if not as adorable) as its park friends.

Mother and baby rhino are part of the sponsorship program. (Photo courtesy of The Taronga Foundation)

Corporate sponsors

Corporate sponsorship begins at $5000 per annum in cash and/or contra, with major sponsors coming in at between $50 000 and $200 000 plus per annum. The sponsorship arrangement varies according to the financial level of sponsorship over a period from one to ten years.

Corporate sponsors operate at six levels, from Supporter Sponsor over one year to Principal Partner over five years. The value-chain of benefits to the partner increases with the level of sponsorship. Benefits to the corporate sponsor can include:

- a sponsorship launch;
- recognition in the annual report;

- a feature story in *Zootopia*;
- a hotlink to the zoo website;
- naming rights;
- signage at the zoo and on zoo collateral;
- acknowledgment at talks;
- single or Gold Pass tickets to the zoo; and
- discounts at zoo facilities.

In recent years, sponsoring organisations have tied their sponsorships to staff rewards and incentive programs. In what might be seen as the equivalent of the corporate box at a major league game, available to corporate executives and their partners, Taronga offers a family-friendly day out to executives from corporate sponsor organisations. Companies that compete for top-level staff can therefore include Taronga memberships as part of their incentive or salary package. Such incentives include family trips to the zoo, entry to functions such as Christmas Carols at the Zoo, Christmas party discounts and access to lecture theatres.

In addition, the trend toward corporate social responsibility offers a strategic partnership between the sponsor organisation and the zoo—a front-runner in the field of conservation and environmental care. Thus organisations can flag their involvement with the zoo by including their sponsorship on their own letterhead or in publicity collateral.

'Backyard to Bush'

In selecting their best-fit sponsorships, organisations may seek a strategic tie-in with the part of the zoo they sponsor. This is illustrated in the 'Backyard to Bush' exhibit, opened in mid-2003, which is sponsored by Sydney Water. 'Backyard to Bush' features a range of interactive environments from the house to the bush, with a primary focus on sustainability and conservation. This follows Sydney Water's previous award-winning Seal Bay sponsorship at Taronga.

Designed to encourage interaction between visitors, animals and staff, 'Backyard to Bush' is based on the 'Keen family', highlighting conservation, sustainability and living in harmony with the world around us. This interactive exhibit is presented in four stages:

1 *Urban house*. Reveals the animals within a normal suburban house (cockroaches, ants, worms, spiders, termites, beetles, moths, silverfish, skinks, possum, mice, bees) and includes teaching and presentation spaces.

2   *Backyard*. Demonstrates our connection to nature (plants, vegetables and animal composts, rainwater irrigation, rabbits, guinea pigs, budgerigars, lizards, rats, worm farm, maze, ponds, frogs, citrus grove).

3   *Rural living*. Demonstrates the importance of domestic animals (water system, plants, organic vegetable garden, fruit trees, beehive, chickens, ducks, shearing shed demonstrating shearing, honey bottling, cheese making, goats, pigs, rabbits, guinea pigs, pythons, owls).

4   *Bush*. Creates 'unfamiliar' territory and a place to relax (wombats, dingo exhibits, free-ranging animals including emus, wallabies, koalas, echidnas, kangaroos, yabbies) in a natural environment of streams, rocks and native flowers.

The journey of discovery through the four stages aims to immerse visitors in the experience, rather than have them as passive observers. This is consistent with the changing ethos of zoos, from the simple zoological park and living museum model of the nineteenth century, to their current and future directions as holistic, environmental resource centres with immersion exhibits that look at ecosystems and survival of the species. Taronga's award-winning sponsorship program ties in closely with this trend.

Source: Material supplied by Taronga Zoo.

Case study 13.4: Qantas and the Sydney 2000 Olympic Games

The official airline sponsor of the Sydney 2000 Olympic Games was Ansett Australia, although a poll conducted by Woolcott Research in July 1999 found that 58 per cent of those surveyed were sure that Qantas had signed up as sponsor of the Sydney 2000 Games compared with 38 per cent for Ansett (Lehmann 1999: 29).

Prior to the Olympics, ABC Radio reported that Ansett paid between $40 million and $50 million to be an Olympic sponsor, and expected a five-fold return on its sponsorship investment (Barrett 2000). Richards (1998) notes that Qantas was one of a number of organisations accused of ambushing three years before the 2000 Olympics by using high-profile athletes in advertising campaigns.

Just eleven days before the start of the 2000 Olympic Games, Ansett launched legal action in the Federal Court to stop Qantas from associating itself with the Games. Although the hearing commenced, it settled after several hearing days without a decision from the court.

In the leadup to, and during, the 2000 Olympics, Qantas used a $7 million television advertising campaign featuring its 'I Still Call Australia Home' theme song and an array of Australian athletes including Cathy Freeman and Kieren Perkins. On 29 and 30 August 2000, the airline published two advertisements in the *Sydney Morning Herald* and *The Age*. One of the ads was published in a souvenir team guide and featured a picture of Cathy Freeman with a reference to the Olympic Games and the Qantas logo printed across the bottom. Qantas also purchased a $7 million Olympic advertising package from the Seven Network to run during the broadcaster's telecast (Jackson and Hornery 2000).

Qantas defended its marketing activity, with Qantas's deputy chief executive officer Geoff Dixon quoted in the *Sydney Morning Herald* on 5 September: 'We had this marketing strategy before Australia was even given the Olympics. Qantas had a very consistent strategy to associate ourselves with Australians through sport and that has included using Olympic sport.'

From an operational perspective, Ansett prevented the use of the Peter Allen song 'I Still Call Australia Home' from being used in the Opening Ceremony because of its association with Qantas advertising (Townsend 2000).

Richards identifies a range of previous activities by corporations who were not official Olympic sponsors:

> *1992 Barcelona Games*: Toyota was Australian team sponsor, but Holden offered a golden car to any Australian athlete who won a gold medal, thus receiving greater exposure.
>
> *1996 Atlanta Olympic Games:* Reebok was a sponsor but Nike was accused of ambushing by tactics such as purchasing considerable signage around Atlanta and building an entertainment complex overlooking the Olympic park.

Some of the strategies that were in place at the Sydney Olympics to minimise ambush marketing were:

- The Olympic Insignia Protection Act protected the unauthorised use of the Olympic symbol and registered Olympic designs.
- The Sydney 2000 Games (Indicia and Images) Protection Act prohibited the unauthorised use of a large number of Olympic words and phrases for commercial purposes.
- SOCOG developed strategies to prevent ambush by crowd marketing and from the air.
- SOCOG implemented a sponsor awareness campaign to diminish the impact of marketing by non-sponsors.

- The Olympic Charter and Athlete's Agreement contain a number of restrictions on the manner in which an athlete can be used in advertising and promotions.
- An agreement between the IOC and the World Federation of the Sporting Goods Industry seeks to prevent ambush by sporting goods companies.
- For the 2004 Olympic Games, the host city is required to control all outdoor advertising sites. (Richards 1998)

Discussion and exercises

1   Choose a major sporting, cultural or social event being held in your state or city during the semester. It may be a one-day event such as the Melbourne Cup or held over several days, such as the Indy car race on the Gold Coast. By monitoring local newspapers, radio, television, billboards and other media, identify a list of sponsors for the event. After the event, contact the organisers and request a list of sponsors, comparing the 'actual' list to your class list. How do they compare? What level of exposure/promotion did each sponsor achieve?
2   Define and give examples of three different types of sponsorship. Analyse how these benefit both the sponsor and the organisation being sponsored.
3   Develop a sponsorship proposal for an upcoming event at your tertiary institution, identifying appropriate target sponsor organisations for different parts of the event. For example, a writing festival might require in-kind support from an office supplier, sponsorship of writing awards and the award ceremony/dinner.
4   Define ambush marketing. Can you identify an example of this tactic in your experience? Using Richards' list in Case Study 13.4 as a starting point, make a list of ways to prevent an ambush.

Further reading

Boorstin, Daniel (1961) *The Image: A Guide to Pseudo-Events in America*, Atheneum, New York.

Geldard, E. & Sinclair, L. (1996) *The Sponsorship Manual: Sponsorship Made Easy*, Sponsoring Unit, Melbourne.

Goldblatt, Jeff (1997) *Special Events: The Art and Science of Celebration*, Van Nostrand Reinhold, New York.

Richards, Craig (1998) *Structuring Effective Sponsorships*, LBC Information Services, Sydney.

References

Austin, S. (2002) 'What makes a good sponsorship proposal', *Australian Sponsorship Marketing Association Sponsorship Report*, December.

Barrett, R. (2000) 'Ansett sues Qantas over Olympic Sponsorship', *The World Today*, ABC Radio, 4 September.

Boorstin, Daniel (1961) *The Image: A Guide to Pseudo-Events in America*, Atheneum, New York.

Burbury, R. (2000) 'Ambush! All's fair in adland wars', *Australian Financial Review*, 28 September.

Connell, T. (2002) 'Keeping out of hot water', <http://pandora.nla.gov.au/pan/14340/20020710/www.specialevents.com.au/magazine/pagesjune02/featjune02/hot.html>.

Geldard, E. & Sinclair, L. (1996) *The Sponsorship Manual: Sponsorship Made Easy*, Sponsorship Unit, Melbourne.

Gotting, P. (2003) 'Cup organisers gear up for ambush tactics', *Sydney Morning Herald*, 13 March.

Jackson, A. & Hornery, A. (2000) 'Ansett takes legal action to stop Qantas sports ads', *Sydney Morning Herald*, 5 September.

Kendall, C. & Curthoys, J. (2001) 'Ambush marketing and the Sydney 2000 Games', *E Law—Murdoch University Electronic Journal of Law*, vol. 8, no. 2, <www.murdoch.edu.au/elaw/issues/v8n2/kendall82.html>.

Lawson, A. (2002) 'Tennis tops sponsorship stakes', *The Age*, 5 June.

Lehmann, A. (1999) 'Olympic hijack', *Weekend Australian*, 4–5 September.

Ligerakis, M. (2003) 'Ambush a no no', *B&T Weekly*, 18 March.

O'Riordan, B. (2002) 'Organisers get tough with ambushers', *Australian Financial Review*, 12 December.

O'Toole, W. (2002) *Special Event Risk from a Project Management Perspective*, <www.personal.usyd.edu.au/~wotoole/conferen/isesrisk.htm>.

O'Toole, W. & Mikolaitis, P. (2002) *Corporate Event Project Management*, Jacaranda Wiley, New York.

Richards, C. (1998) *Structuring Effective Sponsorships*, LBC Information Services, Sydney.

Sponsorship Solutions (2003), 'Thorpe and the Australian Open stay on top', media release, <www.onsport.com.au/top40.htm>, July.

Telstra (2003) 'Sponsorships and awards', <www.telstra.com.au/sponsorship/requests.htm?tR=3at>.

Tonge, R. (in partnership with Tourism Queensland, Queensland Events Corporation and Arts Queensland) (1999) *How to Organise Special Events and Festivals in Queensland*, Gull Publishing, Coolum.

Townsend, P. (2000) 'Olympics a boon for lawyers', *Sportslink*, <www.petertownsend.com.au/_11_legal_issues_at_the_Olympics.pdf>.

Turner, B. (2003) 'Corporate Partnership Awards', *Australian Financial Review Magazine*, <www.afr.com/sponsorawards>.

Wilcox, D., Ault, P. & Agee, K. (1998) *Public Relations: Strategies and Tactics*, 5th edn, Longman, New York.

PART 5
PUBLIC RELATIONS PRACTICE

14 PUBLIC RELATIONS IN BUSINESS

Rebecca Harris

In this chapter

Introduction
Public relations and organisational profits
Investors as special publics
Consumers and customers as special publics
In-house practice versus outsourcing expertise
Public relations and knowledge management
Corporate public relations
Public relations and corporate social responsibility
Conclusion
Case study 14.1: The 'Omo New Mum' contest
Case study 14.2: Mother and Baby doing well—private health and public
relations

Introduction

This chapter considers the special role of public relations and public relations practitioners in business. Of course, other chapters in this book deal with public relations practices that are used in business—such as media relations, crisis and issues management, internal and community relations. But this chapter focuses on unique business needs that require public relations strategies and tactics. It also deals with particular characteristics of businesses that public relations practitioners have to be aware of when they practise in the business sector.

Public relations and organisational profits

So what is a business? A business is an organisation that operates to generate profits, usually for its owners. Those owners may be a private individual or individuals, a group of individuals who form a partnership, or a wider group of people with a financial interest in the business and its profits because they are shareholders or members. What a business does to generate those profits can vary. It may manufacture goods for sale or trade, import or sell goods and products, or provide services to people or other businesses.

Public relations has several important roles in a business. It can make people aware of what the business is able to provide (goods and services), help the business communicate with the people who have an interest in it (e.g. owners, customers, employees and the community), and help the business develop an image and reputation within its environment. Public relations practitioners are in constant contact with publics that affect the activities of an organisation. Because of this, public relations practitioners can be an important source of information on how people regard the business and its activities. This is part of the *boundary-spanning role* of public relations. A boundary spanner is an individual who creates links between different publics and the organisation. They metaphorically span a boundary between an organisation and other groups of people through facilitating communication.

Some special publics are vital to business operations because they directly affect profits through financial transactions. These are investors (or shareholders) and customers. Of equal importance, but covered elsewhere in this book, are publics who influence profits indirectly through opinion and action—employees, the community and the media.

Investors as special publics

For some businesses (notably privately owned ones and small businesses), it can be said that the most important public to consider for the continued life of the business comprises the people who engage in trade with the organisation through the purchase of products or services. However, when a company becomes 'public' through listing shares for sale on the country or region's stock exchange, another public—investors—will demand regular communication.

Businesses are responsible to owners, and owners need information about the business operations of the organisation on a regular basis. For companies listed on the stock exchange, their wealth and operating viability are determined by judgments about their performance. Reports to the financial community help to form those judgments, and these judgments and opinions reflect the prices of the shares that are owned and traded through the stock market.

When people (individuals or corporate investors) own shares in a company, a proportion of the organisational profit is periodically divided up among all shareholders, giving them a dividend. The more net profit a company makes, the higher the dividend is likely to be. If a company is performing well or is judged to have the potential to perform well and make healthy profits, it is likely that the shares will become popular to purchase. Investors will want to buy them, and the share price will rise through competitive trading. As share prices rise, more investors are attracted to the shares, sometimes purely for the purpose of buying the shares at one price and selling them for a higher price later on. Share trading, when it leads to higher share prices, creates greater revenue for the company. The converse is also true: if a company performs poorly, the share price is likely to drop.

Although the stock market is far more complicated than this, it is easy to see that opinion and commentary play an important role in influencing how people respond to trading shares in various companies. Many sources of information can be used by investors to make judgments on buying and selling shares. Company information, the opinions of financial specialists, the knowledge of the share brokers and media commentary together paint a picture of how the business is performing. And the work of the public relations practitioner is crucial to all of them.

It is critical to many companies' long-term goals to ensure that financial publics are informed about business activities. Investors, potential investors, financial analysts and financial media need specialised information about the organisation in order to judge the performance of their investment and the company's potential for future investment. These financial publics can be called *active* or *information-seeking* (Grunig and Hunt 1984). They will look for specific information on which to base their opinions and decisions.

Public relations practitioners should be aware of the special information needs of specialist publics and media, and construct material for these publics accordingly. Steve Mackey's description of agenda setting theory in Chapter 2 is important to understand here, especially in relations with the financial media. Public relations practitioners need to know how to put their clients' or companies' interest on the media agenda. Financial information needs to be comprehensive and able to deal with the complex issues of fiscal performance in a competitive national and international market. Most of the time, especially when dealing with analysts and the media, the public relations practitioner is writing detailed information for a target public that has a special understanding of finance and uses particular jargon. As with any other highly specialised area of public relations practice, the practitioner needs to know the meaning of a variety of special terms and talk to experts in their own language. In order to share understandings with experts, practitioners can develop their background knowledge in finance and economics to more effectively specialise in financial public relations. (At the end of this chapter is an exercise using some of the terms the practitioner might find in financial and business public relations.)

Annual reports

One of the most direct ways to communicate with investor publics is through the company's annual report. Legally, every company listed on the stock exchange must publish an account of its performance during the year. This must include a detailed audited balance sheet of all the income and expenditure of the company, the names of the principal officers of the company, and details of where and when an annual meeting of investors and other interested parties is to be held. The Australian Securities and Investment Commission (ASIC: <www.asic.gov.au>) is the Australian authority that administers the rules pertaining to public companies and, among other things, the annual reports they produce. Elsewhere in the Asia Pacific region, the following authorities regulate the corporations:

- China: the China Securities Regulatory Commission, <www.csrc.gov.cn>;
- Hong Kong: the Securities and Futures Commission of Hong Kong, <www.hksfc.org.hk>;
- Indonesia: the Indonesian Capital Market Supervisory Agency (Bapepam), <www.bapepam.go.id>;
- Japan: the Financial Services Agency of Japan, <www.fsa.go.jp>;
- Korea: the Financial Supervisory Commission, <www.fsc.go.kr>;
- Malaysia: the Securities Commission, Malaysia, <www.sc.com.my>;
- New Zealand: the Securities Commission New Zealand, <www.sec-com.govt.nz>;
- the Philippines: the Securities and Exchange Commission, <www.sec.gov.ph>;
- Singapore: the Monetary Authority of Singapore, <www.mas.gov.sg>;
- Thailand: the Securities and Exchange Commission, <www.sec.or.th>.

Public relations practitioners should always keep up to date with any changes to legislation that will affect the production of the annual report, or any of the company's other financial documents or information. For instance, there are regulations governing the type (font) size of financial statements that must be adhered to, and certain headings and information must be included. It is wise to check these regulations on an annual basis, or at least before the production of any major financial publication.

It is the responsibility of the public relations staff of the company to oversee the production of the annual report. In addition to the requirement for it to include a financial summary of business operations and other mandatory statements, almost all annual reports incorporate a narrative description of yearly events. This trend began in the 1950s and has continued to the present, with the annual report assuming often elaborate and expensive forms—sometimes involving over 100 pages of text, full-colour glossy printing, sophisticated photography and lengthy descriptions of company activities. More recently, the trend has also been to mount the annual report on the company website.

Whether an online or printed version, the annual report is a challenging document to write and publish. It is generally considered to be one of the most important documents produced by the company. It typically involves coordinating written material from many sectors of the organisation; liaising with graphic designers and printers; establishing message and theme strategies in conjunction with senior management; and managing a tight and complicated time schedule and deadlines.

Because it is such an important communication vehicle, one of the difficulties of writing and producing an annual report involves taking other people's ideas and different writing styles and unifying them into a single coherent document to be read by a very wide audience. Juggling the demands of a wide variety of contributors to the annual report can also be a management challenge for public relations practitioners. It is a good idea to gain agreement and consensus on the directions of the annual report right from the start. This can avoid too many deadline-halting changes down the track.

Public relations often uses targeting strategies to hone a message to differentiated publics. However, the audience for an annual report is so diverse that it must appeal to a very 'general' public. In recent times, many large companies have started to produce the annual report in a number of versions, providing a different annual report for each audience. Australia Post produces a special employee annual report, which is simpler, shorter and cheaper to produce than the main annual report (this is discussed further in Chapter 8). Other companies produce summary annual reports, which give brief yet comprehensive financial information without too much description of yearly events. This can be helpful for publics whose only interest is in the bottom line. Others release two publications—one containing the narrative description of events, and the other the financial statements.

Large annual reports can often take a full year to prepare, so managing the deadlines and flow of information that constitute the annual report can be a difficult job. The tenets of print production management apply to this as they do to any other print job: build deadlines from the finished printed delivery date backwards, factoring in contingencies to allow for unexpected problems and judging deadlines for contributors accordingly.

It is a legal requirement that companies produce a printed version of the balance sheet. Today, however, while most still produce a printed version of the narrative component of the annual report, many organisations are experimenting with other formats for this. With varying success, online annual reports translate this communication vehicle to newer media. For many large corporations, online annual reports are now the norm. Obvious savings result from reducing the print run of an expensive high-end document. However, some organisations do little more than put the text and images of the printed report into a web format, which is not necessarily good use of web-based media. The more successful versions of online annual reports embrace interactive components that make full use of the online environment. Newer programming languages like eXtensible Business Reporting Language (XBRL) will help enhance the structure and delivery of annual reports. It appears that the trend to online annual reports will continue and increase for larger companies. Smaller companies may not have the resources required for elaborate online reports, nor will online formats always be the best choice for all audiences and publics. Because of this, while online annual reports will become more common, the print-based version is unlikely to disappear too soon. Public relations practitioners need to be able to work across both formats and liaise with relevant professionals in both online and print-based design and production to successfully meet the challenges of traditional and newer media. Look at the end of this chapter for an exercise that compares different online annual reports internationally.

Annual general meetings

Another obligation of a public company is to hold an annual meeting of shareholders. This meeting gives investors a chance to ask questions of management and to vote on changes to company rules, and gives them a voice within the company. Annual general meetings (AGMs) and other special or extraordinary meetings of shareholders are usually organised and coordinated by public relations staff. They plan the venue, estimate numbers, and liaise with interested media and shareholders.

While many annual general meetings are considered a formality, public relations practitioners should not treat them lightly. There are many examples of AGMs causing imminent crises for companies when directors are confronted by angry or disgruntled investors. Sometimes potentially difficult AGMs can be predicted by the occurrence of other organisational events. Companies need to be prepared for such events in order to deal strategically with negative media opinions, respond openly and frankly to shareholder questions, and provide explanations for management's actions. This involves extensive briefing of all executive staff involved, usually with the advice of legal counsel. Where possible, thorough media briefings should form a part of the communication strategy.

With the advent of the online annual report, the practice of video streaming of annual meetings or special meetings is also looming on the horizon as an increasingly popular use of this technology. Webcasting and video streaming will potentially change the nature of participation of shareholders in company decisions and votes.

Financial analysts and the media

In addition to communicating with potential shareholders, it is crucial to keep the financial media well informed about share issues and organisational actions that might affect share prices. Financial analysts are independent specialists who can assess the 'paper' or share value of a company, which can subsequently be reflected in its share prices. These assessments are very important when a company first lists its shares on the stock market and to support continued trading. A bad assessment from influential analysts can cause immediate and sometimes dramatic drops in share prices. Maintaining a good relationship with both financial analysts and the financial media is an excellent way to keep a responsive and high-volume flow of information out in the marketplace for existing and potential shareholders to read and assess while making their share-buying decisions. The basic principles of media relations are just as applicable to financial specialists as they are to other specialist media sectors.

Consumers and customers as special publics

Businesses generate profits through trade. A necessary component in the trade equation involves the consumer or customer who wants to buy the products or services produced or delivered by the company. While organisations have many publics to consider in the day-to-day running of their business—the community, employees, investors and so on—customers are necessary to enter into some sort of purchasing relationship with the business or it will fail. Customers as publics have different needs to other groups and business must cater for them. They have quality demands about products and services; they can exercise choice in their purchasing decisions; and they can complain and litigate. They can decide to return to the business for further purchases or try some other similar product or service. Whether the transaction is a one-off purchase or an ongoing relationship, one of the responsibilities of public relations practitioners in business is to ensure that the lines of communication are open between the organisation and its customers, and that the needs of those customers are known and can be met.

Marketing public relations

The ability to understand and relate to customer publics is the part of public relations practice that is inextricably linked to marketing. Marketing has at its core the need to manage customer relationships for the purpose of generating profits. Any marketing textbook contains reference to the 'four Ps' of marketing: product, price, place and promotion. Promotion is where public relations has links to marketing. In addition to advertising, point-of-sale material and other forms of promotion, the specialist talents of public relations practitioners in media and public liaison are important to the marketing mix.

All the strategies and tactics referred to in other chapters of this book can be applied to product or service promotion in the marketing mix. The range of public relations strategies and tactics used to enter into dialogues with publics can be integrated in the information and feedback that surrounds the purchase of products and services. Publicity, special events, launches, sponsorships, endorsements, printwork (brochures, flyers, direct mail, etc.) and other tools are all utilised extensively in marketing, often by public relations practitioners working with, or attached to, marketing departments. Chapter 8 discusses these in more detail.

The danger (and often the dominant misconception) is that this is all public relations practitioners do within a business environment, and that the public relations function should therefore be subsumed by marketing. While public relations is important within the marketing function, it has many roles in business that are not marketing-related. Another issue is that marketing departments tend to take management control of the marketing campaign, including all the communications components. They may call on the public relations staff only when specific duties need to be performed (a media release, organising an event and so on).

This situation highlights the dichotomy between the 'manager' and 'technician' roles of the public relations practitioner, discussed in Chapter 1. By treating public relations as purely technical rather than as managerial and strategic, marketing can miss out on facilitating the valuable relationship between the organisation and external publics that is the core of professional public relations communication. Using only the technical skills of public relations may result in a much longer time frame for briefing about and understanding the issues. Inevitably, this leads to an inferior approach to overall communication. A preferred approach is to include public relations counsel in the original planning and research for the marketing campaign. This problem can begin to be tackled by the approach of integrated marketing communications.

Integrated marketing communications

To explore the public relations function in business and marketing further, it is useful to consider the perspective of integrated marketing communications (IMC). Schultz et al. (1993) describe IMC as:

> a new way of looking at the whole, where once we only saw parts such as advertising, public relations, sales promotion, purchasing, employee communication and so forth. It's realigning communications to look at it the way the customer sees it—as a flow of information from indistinguishable sources. (1993: xvii)

IMC has grown out of a dominant perspective about the consumer environment in the late twentieth century. In today's marketing environment, objective product differentiation is marginal. Product and pricing change for the purposes of competition is rapid. The only thing that separates one brand from another in the mind of the consumer is brand image. Brand image comprises various value judgments made on the basis of information about the brand. For example, look at the wars between Coke and Pepsi; Nike, Reebok and Adidas; Hyundai and Daewoo in the budget-priced car market; Dine and Go Cat, Pal and Chum—and so on with most other consumable products. In this way, marketing *is* communication. The only factor left in this 'parity' marketplace to win the hearts and minds (and wallets) of the customer is whether they perceive or believe one brand image to be better than or preferable to another.

Whereas the emphasis of many marketing campaigns was traditionally on mass media advertising, IMC recognises the multiple bodies of information available to customers about brands. Customers receive and process brand information from various sources, including point of purchase, advertising, company image, the media, friends and TV programs. The principle of IMC is to make all those sources work in a unified way to strengthen brand perception and therefore influence purchasing decisions. The ability of public relations to expand and enhance marketing promotion in areas other than mass advertising is developing with the increasing maturity of the public relations profession itself. One of the essential components of IMC is to integrate all participants' understanding of the overall goals and objectives of marketing efforts as closely as possible in the inception of the campaign. In this way, the integrated approach can streamline communication channels and messages so they are unified in campaign implementation.

As with financial and other specialised forms of public relations practice, a career in marketing public relations requires the development of specialised knowledge in the area of product and service marketing. Knowledge of marketing approaches, marketing jargon and the fundamentals of consumer behaviours can help develop better ways of including public relations expertise in integrated marketing communications.

Product placement and branded entertainment

One of the features of the late twentieth century is the individual's ability to tune out to mass advertising material. Increasingly, this has led to the rise of a phenomenon called *product placement*. Rather than raising brand awareness through paid advertising space, companies seek to include their branded products in more 'naturalistic' settings—or at least, settings that are not clearly identifiable as advertising as we have known it. In the process, they blur the divide between advertising and popular culture. Placing products and commercial messages in movies has been happening since the 1950s, but the practice is clearly increasing and becoming more sophisticated. By placing products into movies and television shows, companies can avoid the ad break tune-out of television and insert product messages into feature films where none previously existed, thus colonising formerly unused advertising viewing time. In return, studios and production companies have realised an untapped source of revenue. Macklem (2002) tells us that Stephen Spielberg's film *Minority Report* created a branded world and in the process earned one-quarter of the film's US$160 million budget from over fifteen different brands.

The growing field of product placement is prominent internationally and has also attracted specialist communication companies to handle the process. In November 2002, Universal Studios created a division to work with 'branded entertainment' around the movies it produces (Gotting 2003). Taking the paradigm one step further, advertisers and marketers are also creating the popular culture vehicles for their products, tailoring the programs to what they know their consumers want, believing them be more appropriate platforms for their brands. Gotting (2003) reports that Johnson and Johnson, Unilever, Ford, Kellogg and Proctor and Gamble have funded the development of shows like *The Gilmore Girls*, which has been shown internationally, including in the Asia Pacific region.

Strategic alliances and partnerships

Another development in business is the increasing appearance of *strategic partnerships* between organisations. Drawing on the premise of a parity marketplace that has led to the rise of IMC, another strategic advantage for the organisation is to form relationships with other organisations that can give it a competitive edge. For example, the manufacturer of a drug-delivery device in the health care industry might form a strategic partnership with a pharmaceutical company. Neither has the same capability as the other. However, in a strategic partnership, the manufacturer can sell the device to the health care system with the assurance it will deliver a range of drugs easily. The pharmaceutical company can develop drugs to sell to hospitals knowing there is a device that can deliver them (Sharma 1999).

It is important to include public relations communication at every stage in the formation of strategic alliances. Sometimes the relationships are complicated, and benefits need to be communicated to customers in innovative ways. Public relations practitioners need to be in on the ground level for all such ventures, to maximise promotional and publicity opportunities and to brief media. Launches, special events and regular newsletter communication with participants are all prominent features of strategic alliances and partnerships that can enhance their effectiveness.

Global strategic partnerships can inject growth into industries. As a gateway to Asia Pacific markets, foreign insurers are embracing Australian and New Zealand insurers and investing in them because of their potential to build East–West strategic partners through existing trade and investment relations (Man 1998). In the software market, a consultant in San Francisco has a whole business devoted to helping small software developers form strategic partnerships with Microsoft (Kirkpatrick 1998), to enhance their ability to sell into the expanding computer markets.

E-business, the increasing trend towards using the internet for business, has changed the landscape for everyone participating in corporate environments in both the public and private sector. As the internet permeates all aspects of our daily life, public relations also is adapting to the demands of newer media, dictating the changes to business practices between organisations and their publics and between organisations.

Relationship marketing and loyalty programs

In an effort to build a solid base of customers who adhere to brand purchases over longer periods of time, companies have turned to different forms of marketing and public relations to realise their goals. Rather than striving for a single-choice purchase of a product or service, companies want to build relationships between their brands and consumers. There are many ways of constructing these relationships (see the Omo case study at the end of this chapter for an example), but one way that has become prominent internationally is through *loyalty programs*. Said to be one of the most important promotional currencies in the world, loyalty programs reward consistent long-term brand choice among customers by awarding gifts, discounts or other incentives.

While loyalty programs are now widespread, one cautionary note comes from the Australian experience of Coles Myer. Having established a highly successful loyalty program where the purchase of a minimum package of company shares entitled the shareholder to discounts at the various Coles Myer retail outlets (including supermarkets, liquor stores, clothing stores and department stores), the company decided to rack down and phase out the program. The Australian community's reaction was negative and subsequently loyalty programs have been greeted with a degree of suspicion. The collapse of Australia's 'second carrier' airline, Ansett, also left customers with unused and unusable frequent flyer points built up through its loyalty program. The lesson to be learned for public relations is that, while loyalty programs can drive revenue generation, the relationship built with the constituent publics of the loyalty mechanism is one that must be maintained and honoured. If not, serious damage can be done to long-term market strategy.

In-house practice versus outsourcing expertise

No matter how large or small the organisation, businesses can divide public relations work between employees of the company and external contractors or consultants. There are reasons for using both. Sometimes, as in small organisations, it can be beyond the scope of employees to perform certain specialised public relations tasks—for example, complex desktop publishing or design work, or crisis management. It is often wiser (both practically and financially) to contract experts in the area to help. Another reason to use external contractors is where psychological 'distance' from the organisation is required—for example, when conducting communication audits, community consultation or some forms of communication research. Specialists who have no vested interest in the organisation can bring more objectivity to bear in these circumstances.

On the downside, bringing in an external consultant comes with its own problems. The consultants may not know a lot about the organisation and its idio-syncrasies, and it may take time to brief them on all the pertinent issues. Even then, they may have at best a superficial understanding of the business and the specific issues relating to the problem at hand. Consultants also tend to be expensive, and negotiating the amount of time spent on each project may be difficult. Expectations should be delineated clearly. The relationship between client and consultant is a delicate one. There is a need to understand the importance of disclosure, trust, confidence and frankness. It can be to a company's advantage to develop an ongoing relationship with public relations consultants if possible, so they are more sensitive to and aware of the organisation's needs and history. As with all decisions affecting the communication capability of the company, the decision to choose public relations consultants should be made with the help of public relations staff. If companies spend time developing relationships with public relations counsel, the outcome can be satisfying, fruitful and good for the organisation.

Public relations and knowledge management

Knowledge management is a term that includes the coordination of knowledge and information resources for the advantage of the company in business and other strategic activities. It includes capturing, transferring and accessing the right knowledge and information when needed to make better decisions, take actions and deliver results. The ongoing role of the public relations practitioner involves knowing the wants, needs and opinions of the various publics that surround and interact with the organisation. Feeding this knowledge into the dominant coalitions and management structures of the organisation can enhance business effectiveness.

Knowledge management is not only about sourcing, sharing and processing information, but is a core business principle that should be at the heart of the business structure of the organisation. A disposition towards the strategic use of knowledge to enhance business activities should underpin the organisational culture to effectively manage information in the organisational environment. While 'knowledge' can come from many places and may be stored and used by many individuals, public relations practitioners should address systematised strategic knowledge to enhance communicative activities.

Corporate public relations

While financial publics and customers enjoy special consideration within businesses, there is another function that is important in business organisations. *Corporate public relations* deals mainly with the overall image and standing of the company or organisation as an entity in its environment. Marketing public relations is often concerned with the brands the company produces, and financial public relations with who puts money into (or takes it out of) the company. Corporate public relations can affect both these publics and many others by maintaining the profile of the organisation through interaction with various groups.

Sometimes this function is called *public affairs* and involves a myriad of activities. Government lobbying, sponsorship of major events using the company name, organising senior executives to serve on public boards and committees, managing the corporate image and the corporate identity, advertising and promoting the company's image and what it stands for, forming associations or partnerships with other companies, and managing the overall information and dialogue relating to major company announcements or changes are all functions that are subsumed under the rubric of corporate public relations.

Depending on the size of the company, the corporate function can govern many of the other public relations activities covered in this book. Managing long-term issues, ensuring that a crisis management plan is in place and updated, determining policy on public issues, and proactively initiating community consultation all go towards ensuring that the business is suitably integrated with its environment.

Industrial lobbying

Moloney (1997: 169) provides the following definition of lobbying: 'persuasive activity to change public policy in favour of an organisation by groups of people who are not directly involved in the political process'. He expands that definition to say that lobbying is 'monitoring public policy-making for a group interest; building a case in favour of that interest; and putting it privately with varying degrees of pressure to public decision-makers for their acceptance and support through favourable political intervention' (1997: 173–4). Moloney's inclusion of groups and organisations in his definition relates to the discussion of public relations in business. Whether through internal staff or external specialist lobbyists, there are many occasions when businesses need to lobby government to influence public policy formation for the benefit of organisational profits, continued growth and survival. While the general principles of lobbying and working with government are covered in the next chapter, it is worth noting a few recent examples pertinent to the business sector.

In Sydney, Fox Studios lobbied the New South Wales state government and the Sydney Organising Committee for the Olympic Games (SOCOG) to change the route of an Olympic cycling event from outside its front door. Fox claimed the closure of the road would affect its business and estimated a dollar value of the money it would lose. Fox threatened to sue the government for this loss of business if the route was not altered. Its efforts were successful, and the route and location were changed. The Australian Banking Industry has spent several years lobbying the federal government to relax merger and acquisition laws to allow the 'big four' banks (National Australia Bank, Westpac, the Commonwealth Bank and ANZ) to effect mergers, which would facilitate increased profits and service customers more effectively. Its lobbying efforts have been unsuccessful, and legislation still prevents such mergers in the interests of preserving adequate competition in the banking market.

Lobbying for public policy change is complicated and sometimes a very long-term activity. In most cases—particularly for one-off issues—companies would be well advised to seek the counsel of independent experts.

Public relations and corporate social responsibility

When we think of 'business', we think of selling, profits, marketing and activities driven by the health of the so-called 'bottom line'. While this is an undeniably important aspect of business success, businesses still have to live and exist within communities of people who have priorities and imperatives that may not be linked to the pursuit of organisational profits. It is no longer acceptable for organisations to pursue their missions to the exclusion of other people around them. Businesses need to behave as citizens in their communities, just as we all do. Rather than an optional extra, *corporate social responsibility* (CSR), or corporate citizenship, is becoming a vital aspect of business public relations. Business citizens should give consideration to how they can interact with and exist in their host communities. While this obviously includes preventing environmental pollution, not compromising public facilities and not harming or damaging the surroundings, it can also involve small-scale activities that establish a business as a good corporate citizen.

Proactive public relations activities can enhance social responsibility. Corporate social responsibility encompasses fairness, transparency and openness to all stakeholders and should be a core part of the businesses goals and activities rather than being seen as a one-off marketing or public relations exercise using a charitable or worthy cause as a strategy. By building CSR into the business as a long-term value, publics are more inclined to accept the trustworthy intentions of a company, even in times of crisis. By operating in a trusting relationship with a variety of publics, corporate reputation can carry an organisation through a crisis with greater goodwill than an organisation that neglects its responsibilities as a citizen. Another important consequence of an embedded commitment to CSR is how the performance of the company is judged as an investment prospect.

In Australia, the *Financial Services Reform Act 2001* includes a requirement for investment products to disclose factors like labour standards, environmental considerations, and social and ethical practices that are tied to the investment. It also allows for the Australian Securities and Investment Commission to begin to discuss guidelines for disclosure in these areas. Such formal mechanisms allow investors to transparently and competitively assess a company's performance of a variety of elements that pertain to CSR. Corporate social responsibility is discussed further in Chapter 5.

Corporate philanthropy

L'Etang (1996) tells us that philanthropy implies benevolent actions that are not legally required or otherwise necessary. She places corporate philanthropy in the realm of those voluntary acts performed by a company that are neither expected/ demanded by the recipient out of a sense of duty to the community nor a specific obligation of the organisation. In this sense, it is differentiated from what might be called 'social responsibility', which implies 'a relationship . . . [of] reciprocal rights and duties' (1996: 85).

The fine line between social responsibility and philanthropy is often blurred in modern business. For the public relations professional, it is worth noting the difference, because the implications of philanthropic actions can affect an organisation's role in the community. L'Etang (1996) also draws from philosophical and social theories about how we interact with each other, pointing out that philanthropy and benevolence imply a certain type of power relationship. Gifts and welfare often build dependent communities who have no say in what benefits are given and when, and withdrawal of those benefits (for whatever reason) can bring about altered social conditions—often hardship and suffering. In entering into philanthropic relationships with communities or publics, the public relations professional needs to be aware of the moral implications of the organisation's actions.

On the positive side, philanthropic acts can be of great benefit to many sectors.

The National Gallery of Victoria, for instance, relies on philanthropic gifts to, among other things, enhance its collection. In 2001, Rio Tinto donated a corporate collection of paintings by Fred Williams that had hung in its Melbourne offices since 1982. The Pilbara series of 31 paintings is valued at more than AU$6 million and is said to rival Sidney Nolan's Ned Kelly series. This philanthropic act has made one of the greatest landscape series accessible to the Australian and international community. Philanthropy and corporate sponsorships (or partnerships) are discussed further in Chapter 13.

Conclusion

This chapter highlights the relationship between public relations and marketing, showing how important strategic alliances are within the business sector and how businesses must remain socially responsible to maintain public confidence. Many of these functions of business are the responsibility of the public relations practitioner, who works with publics, both internal and external, in the most effective way. From dealing with stockholders and staff internally, to developing strong partnerships with other organisations externally, the practitioner will need to be multi-skilled in the fields of management, promotions, media and finance. Furthermore, the business sector represents one of the key job markets for the public relations graduate, and a sound knowledge and understanding of business is therefore a valuable asset.

Case study 14.1: The 'Omo New Mum' contest

This case demonstrates an approach towards brand identity among consumers that goes beyond an awareness of the functional qualities of the product itself. The manufacturer of Omo washing powder, Unilever, was not content with the product enjoying the number one position in the laundry powder market in China. They wanted the brand to be associated with deeper emotional and social qualities to further differentiate it from competitive products, strengthen the consumer's relationship with the brand itself and enhance brand loyalty.

Following a successful introductory campaign based on the perceived qualities of the consumer who used the product, the 'Omo New Mum' contest was launched. Fitting with Unilever's global imperatives for the Omo brand, a uniquely Chinese interpretation was mounted based on the slogan 'No stain, no learning'. While the translation of this slogan into English may seem initially clumsy, the spirit of the phrase has significance for Chinese approaches to parenting. In a country with a one-child family policy, there is a heightened attitude to children's safety and development. This can be manifested through an over-protective attitude, increased pressure to do well academically and shielding young people from danger. So the campaign's message conveys the idea that getting dirty is part of a child's growth process and that the 'modern parent' in China shouldn't worry about this, but rather encourage experimentation and learning through experience. The product is seen as reinforcing these values and existing as the backup to help the modern parent with limited time and resources 'clean' the results of children's natural learning processes.

One of the imperatives of the campaign was not only to embody the brand values but to create media interest. So, in keeping with Daniel Boorstin's concept of the pseudo event, the 'Omo New Mum' contest was conceived. The target audience comprised the consumers of the product: females aged 25–30 with a child aged two to fifteen years and a monthly income of RMB 2000 (A$500). As China is such a large and diverse market, the campaign was directed to seven key cities/provinces: Shanghai, Beijing, Jiangsu, Zhejiang, Sichuan, Hubei and Hebei.

The specific public relations objectives were to:

- maximise media exposure in the target market;
- target TV ratings of the final contest for television in Shanghai, which should be no less than 7 per cent (ACNielsen is the appointed source for TV ratings audit);
- promote the 'No stain, no learning' concept among target consumers; and
- introduce a brand new family education concept to Chinese mothers in the target markets.

The public relations consultancy took control of the entire process for Unilever, including all organisational aspects as well as evaluation. Importantly, it secured the patronage of the All-China Women's Federation, the most influential voice of women in China and also a key state organisation, which is very highly regarded. It also secured the sponsorship of Shanghai Oriental TV, thus ensuring the eventual media coverage that was required for the campaign

Women from the target provinces entered the contest, which revolved around the ideal qualities of the modern Chinese mum (motivating, open-minded, tolerant and versatile), reflected in the brand characteristics of Omo. Elaborate preliminary and semi-final contests in the seven target provinces/ cities occurred over a period of two months. The whole project ended with a large, televised final contest shot in Shanghai and broadcast in the seven provinces/cities. The media were invited to witness each phase of the project, making the contest a hot media topic throughout its execution. It encouraged modern mums to give their children more freedom in growing up, so helping them develop to become 'more courageous, creative, adaptable and responsible adults'.

Due to its positive social influence and effective publicity, the 'Omo New Mum' contest generated active involvement from consumers. There were over 10 000 applicants via mail, telephone calls and the internet. The event also won full government support and authorities in education also gave their advice regarding the organisation of the project. In China, this is an extremely important element. State support of a project such as this is crucial in influencing target audiences and legitimising the campaign.

Logistically, the campaign was extremely demanding, and the consultants had to balance the high participation rate, liaison with government authorities, briefings, extensive travel throughout the target provinces, the eventual rehearsal for the contestants and their families, high-level event and media management, market research, an essay competition, sponsorship and contra deals and, finally, managing the four-hour live broadcast of the contest final on Mothers' Day 2001, which aired for 90 minutes on Sunday night prime-time TV.

The campaign far exceeded the objectives set for media coverage, resulting in double the projected word count in print media. Radio and TV exposure reached sixteen TV stations and two radio stations, with a total broadcast time of over a thousand minutes. The TV ratings for the final contest were 8.4 per cent in Shanghai, exceeding the objective of 7 per cent. Other statistics included internet hits: 36 internet portals with 10 619 144 normal impression and 44 573 normal clicks in total online; contest hotline: 1215 calls. Top-of-mind brand awareness in Shanghai increased from 45 to 48 per cent, and in Chengdu (the capital city of Sichuan Province) it increased from 38 to 46 per cent. From both the objective evaluation and client satisfaction, the campaign was deemed extremely successful, and it has been followed up with another initiative focusing on children's educational and career growth.

Source: Juliana Zhu, General Manager, Shanghai Felix Public Relations Consulting Co Ltd, Shanghai, China. This campaign won the 2001 IABC Silver Quill Award for the category Marketing Communication—Industrial, Manufacturing, Commercial, Retail Sales.

Case study 14.2: Mother and Baby doing well—private health and public relations

Sydney Ultrasound for Women (SUFW) is owned by six partners who are specialist medical practitioners in obstetrics and gynaecology. They have seven offices across the Sydney region. However, the market for health services is highly competitive, characterised by hard sales tactics, and they felt over-shadowed by the large corporate health companies with their high and aggressive exposure to the target publics (general practitioners and other obstetricians and gynaecologists who refer women for ultrasound services). They felt they had something special to offer potential referring doctors and their patients in terms of expertise and a comprehensive and caring service.

Through research, communications consultancy 2iC found that, amongst their key audiences, SUFW lacked a strong brand image and logo; that aware-ness of them and their services was low among non-users; and that doctor and patient recall of its name was low (preventing word-of-mouth communication). However, users of the service had high awareness and appreciation of the company, and doctors valued the interpersonal support shown by the company during the referral and ultrasound process. Research also showed that the most appropriate ways to communicate with referring specialists were personal letters, communication through GP associations, newsletters, educational presentations, personal meetings and articles in vertical medical magazines. Consumer brochures on services were also welcomed.

The goals and objectives of this case are worth noting in detail. The goal of the communication strategy was to ensure that SUFW would be perceived by general practitioners, obstetricians, gynaecologists and end-users within the Sydney metropolitan area as offering the most thorough, reliable and informative obstetric and gynaecological ultrasound service available, and remain or become their service provider of choice.

Specific process objectives of the strategy were to:

- manage the rebranding of 'the Sydney Obstetric and Gynaecological and Ultrasound Service' (the company's old name) to SUFW;
- initiate at least three media programs per year with all relevant support material;
- manage the production of a bi-monthly newsletter for medical audiences;
- arrange for SUFW to speak at four general practitioner education events per year;
- manage the reproduction of new and updated SUFW promotional literature;
- position SUFW in the media as expert commentators on ultrasound issues; and
- manage at least two mailouts per year to Sydney's 5500 general practitioners.

Specific outcome objectives of the strategy were:

- to increase SUFW income by 15 per cent from 1999/2000 to 2001/02;

- to increase referrals to SUFW by 15 per cent from 1999/2000 to 2001/02;
- to identify and institute new ways for SUFW to increase revenue and provide extra value to its patients;
- for SUFW to be quoted in the media at least six times in 2001/02; and
- To have an ongoing presence on a media website by June 2002.

It is clear from the construction of these objectives how specific and measurable they are.

SUFW was put forward not as 'the best'—which was considered too hard a 'sell' for the target audience; rather it was profiled as 'a willing provider of information and assistance on obstetric and gynaecological ultrasound issues'. In addition to the target audience of referring doctors, a targeted consumer media program became part of the strategy, to influence the awareness of women who would ultimately be referred to the service. A key part of this strategy was to build the credibility of SUFW within the health media, ensuring that they sought comment from SUFW partners as experts in their field.

As a result of the research, SUFW accepted 2iC's recommendations to rebrand the company, including a new logo and office fitouts; produce a range of brochures; and write a bi-monthly medical newsletter. It also agreed to be more assertive in securing general practitioner educational speaking engagements and to become more strategic, targeted and proactive with the media.

Since the implementation of the rebranding and communication strategies early in 2001, income generated by SUFW has increased by over 23 per cent. Comprehensive evaluation of all the objectives showed the full program to be extremely successful in all areas of communication, including media and educational programs. 2iC also negotiated with a publisher for SUFW to contribute its expertise to a book which will generate royalties for SUFW.

Source: 2iC Integrated Communications, in conjunction with Leapfrog Research. This campaign won a PRIA Golden Target Award for best in the Comprehensive Communication Category.

Discussion and exercises

1   Go to the website <www.mercommawards.com> and click on its annual reports link. This is an awards site for annual reports. Navigate to the online category and click on the winners' websites to find the annual reports that have been awarded in this category. See which ones have been commended for their

design and use of electronic media. Look at the judging criteria for the reports and see if you agree with the judges' decisions.

2   *Product placement:* Take two television programs you regularly watch (drama, comedy, etc.) and two movies you have seen recently or are planning to see. Write down all the brands that appear in these shows or movies and the way in which they appear. Make a decision on whether they have been placed there through deliberate brand strategies.

3   After reading Case study 14.1 about the 'Omo New Mum' contest in China, write down any differences you see as necessary to conduct this campaign in another country or culture like Australia or New Zealand. What elements are important for conducting this campaign in the Chinese market?

4   Look through the business and finance section of *The Australian*, the *Australian Financial Review* or your state's or region's major metropolitan daily newspaper (or look at the following newspaper internet sites for an online paper: e.g. <www.fairfax.com.au>; <www.news.com.au>). Look for some or all of the following specialist terms and write a short definition: write off; writedown; the day's high; discretionary fund; NASDAQ; Nikkei Dow; GDP; All Ords; blue chip. Note down any other financial terms that you would regard as specialist concepts in business and finance. What are they and what do they mean? Why is it useful to employ jargon in public relations writing when communicating with specialist audiences and publics?

Further reading

Haywood, R. (1998) *Public Relations for Marketing Professionals*, Macmillan, London.

Mayhew, L. (1997) *The New Public: Professional Communication and the Means of Social Influence*, Cambridge University Press, Cambridge.

Schultz, D., Tannenbaum, S. & Lauterborn, R. (1993) *Integrated Marketing Communications: Pulling it Together and Making It Work*, NTC Business Books, Chicago.

Spicer, C. (1997) *Organisational Public Relations: A Political Perspective*, Lawrence Erlbaum, New Jersey.

References

Gotting, P. (2003) 'Ads come branded as entertainment', *The Sydney Morning Herald*, 13 January.

Grunig, J. & Hunt, T. (1984) *Managing Public Relations*, Holt, Rhinehart & Winston, New York.

Haywood, R. (1998) *Public Relations for Marketing Professionals*, Macmillan, London.

Kirkpatrick, D. (1998) 'These days, everybody needs a Microsoft strategy', *Fortune*, vol. 137, no. 1, January, pp. 134–35.

L'Etang, J. (1996) 'Corporate responsibility and public relations ethics', in J. L'Etang & M. Pieczka (eds), *Critical Perspectives in Public Relations*, ITP, London.

Macklem, P. (2002) 'They make a different brand of movie in Hollywood', *The Sydney Morning Herald*, 14 February.

Man, S. (1998) 'Gateway to Asia', *Best's Review (Life/Health)*, vol. 99, no. 2, June, pp. 50–53.

Mayhew, L. (1997) *The New Public: Professional Communication and the Means of Social Influence*, Cambridge University Press, Cambridge.

Moloney, K. (1997) 'Government and lobbying activities', in P. Kitchen (ed.), *Public Relations: Principles and Practice*, ITP, London.

Schultz, D., Tannenbaum, S. & Lauterborn, R. (1993) *Integrated Marketing Communications: Pulling it Together and Making It Work*, NTC Business Books, Chicago.

Sharma, A. (1999) 'Central dilemmas of managing innovation in large firms', *California Management Review*, vol. 41, no. 3, Spring, pp. 146–64.

Spicer, C. (1997) *Organisational Public Relations: A Political Perspective*, Lawrence Erlbaum, New Jersey.

15 PUBLIC RELATIONS IN GOVERNMENT

Stephen Stockwell

In this chapter

Introduction

Abraham Lincoln described democracy as 'government of the people, by the people, for the people'. It is thus hardly surprising that the people-oriented techniques of public relations play such an important—if little understood—role in the work, control and formation of democratic governments.

The growing public interest in the mechanics of public relations in government is reflected by the commercial success of documentaries such as David

Pennebaker's *The War Room*, an account of the 1992 Clinton campaign for the US presidency, together with movies such as *Primary Colors*, *The Distinguished Gentleman*, *Speechless* and *Wag the Dog*, and even situation comedies such as *Spin City* and *Yes, Minister*. People are interested not only in what governments tell them, but also in how governments decide what they will communicate. By laying out some of the elements of public relations in government, it is possible to move from experiencing politics as a rush of media items to an appreciation of the mechanics of these events that provides us with a deeper understanding of the workings of contemporary democracy.

This chapter considers the three main ways in which public relations intersects with democratic government. These are:

- the use of media management by government to pursue its political and policy objectives;
- the use of public affairs/lobbying by interest groups to affect government decisions; and
- the use of campaign techniques in the elections required to form governments.

Further, it provides an analysis of some of the language used in the context of public relations in government—both in current times and as it has been viewed in the past. Finally, it develops some key areas of public relations in this field, including strategy, research, direct mail and voter contact.

Rhetoric, persuasion and propaganda

Public relations in general, and the government use of public relations techniques in particular, is a contemporary development of political rhetoric, which was defined by the ancient Greek philosopher Aristotle as 'the power to observe the persuasiveness of which any particular matter admits' (1991: 1355b). Aristotle was writing in the context of Athenian democracy, where native-born, adult males collectively made political decisions in a sovereign Assembly which convened 40 times a year. In analysing the persuasive arguments made in this forum, Aristotle identified three categories of rhetorical proofs: those from reason, character and emotion. Aristotle understood that persuasive arguments made not only logical sense, but also a psychological connection with the target audience—an insight that remains relevant today.

Despite Aristotle's enduring relevance, 'rhetoric' has become a term of abuse, used to suggest that one's opponents are using glib phrases in the cynical pursuit of their own self-interest. Theorists have given some content to this negative reading of rhetoric: Edward Herman and Noam Chomsky (1988) suggest that public relations, and the mass media generally, are tools used by governments and corporations in the manufacture of consent. Jurgen Habermas (1989) argues that public relations techniques have closed the public sphere to the free-ranging debate that is a vital part of an effective democracy. Postmodernists such as Pierre Bourdieu (1978) have criticised notions such as 'public opinion' and 'will of the people' as empty ideals, which mask the diversity within contemporary societies and the exercise of power over citizens that constitutes the actual practice of government. There is something in these critiques, but they do not explain the possibilities offered by contemporary democracy, which provides for the representation of diverse viewpoints by the opposition, minor parties, independents, interest groups and concerned citizens. The rule of government is tempered by the plethora of voices heard in the decision-making process.

A useful distinction to make at this point is between the persuasion of *rhetoric*, which seeks to find compelling arguments to convince people, and the coercion of *propaganda*, which insists people believe certain things or act in certain ways by using communication techniques to end discussion. The term 'propaganda' was coined by the Catholic Church in 1622 when it established the *Sacra Congregatio de Propaganda Fide* to respond systematically to arguments expounded by the Protestant Reformation by propagating church doctrine (Ward 1995: 21).

The term was used in a neutral fashion to denote any political communication until World War II, when it acquired a more negative connotation informed by the practices of Nazi Germany and its Minister for Public Enlightenment and Propaganda, Joseph Goebbels. With an instruction to mould mass public opinion in the interests of the Nazi regime, Goebbels took charge of all mass media in Germany, introduced blanket censorship and provided every home with a radio. He pursued a comprehensive program to ensure that all information flow was in the interests of the regime. He insisted on direct access to the highest level of intelligence so he could tailor propaganda to produce required responses in Germany and among the Allies. On the home front, he attempted to steer a path between frustration and unsustainable hope, to create 'an optimum anxiety level' (Doob 1954: 519). He appreciated that 'propaganda cannot immediately effect strong counter-tendencies' (Doob 1954: 521), but realised that, by repeatedly labelling people and events with easily learnt phrases and slogans, he could touch the audience's existing emotions to evoke the desired response.

This is not to say that Goebbels saw his work as the perpetual production and distribution of political slogans. He knew that 'to be perceived, propaganda must evoke the interest of the audience' (Doob 1954: 513). The movies made under his control worked within existing genres, particularly the musical, to spread the Nazi message with some subtlety. He is reported in the documentary *We Have Ways of Making You Think* (ABC-TV, 4 February 1993) to have told one producer: 'Don't come to me with political films.' Goebbels conceived propaganda as the production of a total world-view that, once inculcated in the populace, would produce instinctual responses that matched the requirements of the regime.

George Orwell explained the power of mass media propaganda by analysing the content of political language and revealing how it could be over-inflated with extended metaphor, pretentious diction and meaningless words 'to make lies sound truthful and murder respectable, and to give an appearance of solidity to pure wind' (1970: 170). In his novel *1984*, Orwell further developed his critique of propaganda through the mass media with his concept of 'newspeak': a language with a shrinking vocabulary designed for use by the media to make heretical thoughts, particularly against the state, literally unthinkable.

To combat the totalitarian certainty of propaganda and the 'dumbing-down' of the media that Orwell foretold, active citizens can make use of rhetorical persuasion to offer alternative arguments and extend the debate. The point of the speech in the ancient Athenian Assembly, and of public relations in government today, is to persuade the citizen-audience to points of view that allow majorities to be formed and ideas to be turned into action. Rhetoric aims to approach this persuasion scientifically—or at least systematically—and is thus a necessary condition for the effective operation of a healthy democracy.

It can be seen that rhetoric and public relations have a positive role to play in facilitating the debate required before democracy can come to decisions about collective action.

Media management

Modern governments seek to manage their interactions with the mass media strategically in order to build a consensus of support for the government's policies that will ensure its re-election. Thus, as Sidney Blumenthal (1980) argues, the process of government has become a permanent campaign for electoral support. Government media management techniques involve building support for the government by advancing arguments, engaging in debate and taking every opportunity to manipulate media output (Carey 1995; Tiffen 1989). In Australia, where the federal government has a regulatory role over the media, it sometimes appears that government media policy is designed to satisfy media proprietors who respond by ensuring that their media outlets are not particularly critical of the government's other policies.

Governments' media management takes two forms: dissemination of political information, and dissemination of public information. Political information is spread via press secretaries (or 'minders')—members of ministerial staffs who seek to promote their ministers' actions. Press secretaries are often ex-journalists, who use their journalistic skills and knowledge of media work practices to develop and place news stories for party political advantage and electoral success. As one 'minder' remarked of his move from journalist to media manager: 'the transition from poacher to gamekeeper was simple: you use the same weapons, you just point them the other way' (Atkins, in EARC 1992: 17). A lot of their energy goes into convincing opinion leaders of the validity of their minister's position, but they are also responsible for ensuring that their ministers' lines are phrased to maximise political impact and that these lines are communicated to all interested media.

The techniques of media management are covered in Chapter 10, but a few points need to be made in the context of the press secretaries' responsibilities. To earn editorial coverage, press secretaries mould their material to the needs of busy political journalists, who have to meet tight deadlines while being pushed by editors to produce more with fewer resources. Because journalists find themselves reacting to news with little time or support to fully understand it, the press secretary seeks to assist journalists to comprehend, write and file stories, hoping that this will portray the government in a positive light. Press secretaries can make a major contribution to the quality of coverage the government they represent receives, by providing:

- press releases that explain issues simply;
- well-researched background material;
- strong photo opportunities;
- spokespeople for community groups with different (though generally supportive) viewpoints; and
- opportunities to file stories by deadline.

The press secretary must establish a media contact system based on a media list of all relevant journalists, their phone numbers, deadlines, direct work numbers and even home numbers. This list needs to be constantly updated and programmed into a computer that can quickly send press releases by fax or email (depending on newsroom requirements). But pumping out press releases is pointless without personal contact; developing close relationships with key journalists and media executives will allow the press secretary to contribute to the setting of the media agenda and thus ensure positive coverage of the minister's media events.

Public information is achieved via departmental publicity officers—public servants employed by government departments to assist in the dissemination of information on government policy and operations. Departments use publicity techniques to:

- inform the public about their rights and obligations;
- acquaint the public with available benefits and services;
- educate the public about departmental initiatives;
- clarify and explain the impact of legislation;
- foster debate; and
- aid recruitment.

Publicity officers utilise a broad range of techniques to identify and communicate with a diversity of audiences. While their work involves some day-to-day press liaison, publicity officers also seek to communicate directly with the public by commissioning advertising, coordinating community events, ensuring a web presence, and designing and distributing brochures and other information materials.

One important tool used by departmental publicity officers in pursuit of their departmental work is the information campaign. Governments employ the techniques of election campaigning (discussed in detail later in the chapter) to make people aware of information that assists in attaining policy objectives and, in particular, to persuade people to adopt healthy behaviours. There is clearly a significant cost benefit for governments from preventing health problems before those problems start taking up space in expensive hospital beds.

In the past 30 years, governments have run or sponsored information campaigns which have warned of the dangers of smoking ('Every cigarette is doing you damage'), drinking alcohol, and abusing other drugs; and which have taught people how to recognise early symptoms and avoid skin cancer ('Slip, slop, slap'), breast cancer and venereal disease. Road safety campaigns, combined with prominent enforcement activities, have targeted drink-driving, speeding, seatbelt compliance and driver fatigue (as discussed in the 'If you drink' case study at the end of this chapter). Positive campaigns have encouraged people to stay active ('Life. Be in it') and eat a healthy diet.

Perhaps Australia's greatest success has been the AIDS awareness campaign. It has used a variety of techniques, from mass TV advertising (to generate public discussion and sympathy towards victims) to very specific harm-minimisation tactics (at the locales and in the subcultural media relevant to those who may engage in infectious activities). The breadth and intensity of the AIDS campaign have led to a significant drop in new infections, and the campaign is regarded as world best practice.

Other government departments have used public information campaigns to send simple messages through a complex array of communication channels, to confront sexism in the workplace, combat bullying in schools, promote tourism and public transport, and advocate compliance with plant and livestock quarantine. It has reached the stage where every minister needs to have a public awareness campaign underway so they can be seen to be active in their portfolio. There is the danger of departmental publicity activities becoming focused on departmental image-building and political persuasion rather than providing factual and balanced information. These issues become particularly pertinent as elections approach, and often require the use of bureaucratic skills to ensure that departmental budgets are not used for political purposes.

Public affairs/lobbying

As society becomes more complex, so does the work of government. Federal, state and local governments are constantly making decisions that affect people's lives, so individuals and interest groups (from local environmental organisations to large corporations) seek to influence the outcome of government decisions by lobbying politicians and public servants. The term *lobbying* comes from that area just outside the parliamentary chambers where citizens traditionally meet politicians. The systematic development of sustained lobbying campaigns utilising not only personal and institutional contact, but also media management and coalition-building among supporters, is described as *public affairs*, and has now become a standard part of the democratic control of governments.

The traditional lobbyist was typically a retired 'minder', journalist or public servant, who could tap the 'old boys' network' to have a word in the client's interest to the right person in the right place at the right time. The changing nature of government and the intensity of media scrutiny means that lobbyists now have to organise complex campaigns to advance their client's position. Today, lobbyists are more likely to be communications graduates, who can utilise new information technologies to research and deliver decisive arguments in the appropriate forums at the right moment. This work requires a high degree of flexibility. A typical day might see the lobbyist pitching stories to breakfast radio, appearing with a client before a government inquiry, commissioning research, lunching with prospective clients or contacts, drawing diverse materials into a submission to government, writing and coordinating a direct mail push, and making introductions between clients and contacts over dinner.

While international companies like Burson Marsteller dominate the lobbying industry, there is still plenty of opportunity for small operations or individual practitioners to develop expertise and contacts in particular areas that give them a competitive advantage over the large organisations. Industries that depend on government financial support and regulation have become particularly adept at lobbying. The pharmaceutical industry is a good example: it both requires government approval to introduce new drugs and receives government financial support through subsidies that make its products generally affordable. Thus the pharmaceutical industry, and particular pharmaceutical corporations, can be observed lobbying vigorously to expedite the often lengthy approval processes for drugs with a ready market (for example, Viagra), or to seek the inclusion of particular drugs on the list of government-subsidised pharmaceuticals.

The tobacco industry has run a long campaign against government plans to restrict the sale and advertising of cigarettes. This has effectively been countered by those concerned with the health effects of cigarette smoking, such as the Australian Medical Association (AMA). Of particular interest here was the counter-lobbying organised by BUGAUP (Billboard Utilising Graffitists Against Unhealthy Promotions), which pursued a campaign of defacing cigarette advertising to turn it into anti-cigarette advertising while simultaneously confronting governments with scientific evidence about the dangers of the habit. While the efforts of the tobacco industry have been dictated entirely by commercial concerns, it has had some limited success in diluting planned government restriction by refusing to discuss the scientific evidence and raising other issues in politically adept ways. It has used arguments in favour of free choice, raised questions about the economic future of tobacco-growing regions (which is of particular political relevance where those regions are in marginal electorates), and used the sponsorship of international sport to circumvent national regulations. The success of tobacco industry lobbyists is evident in the rising consumption of cigarettes by young people.

Lobbying requires a constantly updated contact system that lists politicians, journalists and public servants relevant to client interests. Lobbyists must be able to monitor current events continually, with particular attention to shifts in political factions and bureaucratic alignments that may affect on their clients' interests. They must also remain informed about the minutiae of government decision-making processes and the progress of policy initiatives, legislation and regulation through parties, governments, cabinet and parliament. Access to a comprehensive database of relevant historical material is useful, as is the technology to turn all this raw data into timely intelligence for the client.

Areas of specialisation for lobbyists include trade, defence and the environment. Their work entails not only presenting clients' views and promoting them in the media, but also serving as a source of information for governments and keeping clients informed of often-subtle developments that affect their interests. Lobbyists have become the conduits between government and a diverse range of interests in society.

While an awareness of policy initiatives and the capability to intervene in the policy-making process will remain key work for lobbyists, more and more public affairs campaigns are about developing and utilising public opinion. Through media management, advertising, direct mail and strategic use of the internet, those involved in public affairs campaigns seek to develop popular support for a position. They then seek to turn public opinion into a political force by using grass roots networking to encourage supporters to communicate key messages direct to politicians and public servants so that government appreciates the strength of public sentiment (see Bonner et al 1999: 22–26). Anyone who has ever been asked to sign a petition or write a letter to their local MP has been asked to participate in a grass roots campaign. Community groups, and their use of public relations techniques, are discussed further in Chapter 16.

Election campaigns

The cross-development of political and commercial persuasion techniques this century has produced a distinct election campaign industry (Blumenthal 1980; Mills 1986; Napolitan et al. 1994). As already shown, media managers and public affairs lobbyists are now expected to be able to plan and organise complex campaign activities, so much of the material below is crucially relevant to their work.

Political campaigns are now often orchestrated by *campaign directors*—professional 'guns for hire' who employ techniques derived from mass marketing, organisation theory, strategic game play and psychology. They are assisted by recent developments in telecommunications and computers which allow pollsters to quickly assess specific audiences' quantitative and qualitative responses to the

The inexpensive counter-lobbying techniques used by BUGAUP turned tobacco advertising against itself.

BUGAUP's campaign extended to a more general critique of the media's role in society. (Photos courtesy of BUGAUP)

ideas, issues, personalities and events operating in any political situation. Campaign directors utilise the skills of media consultants to position and reposition their candidate quickly and effectively by putting a favourable interpretation on developments and 'massaging' precisely those segments of the audience needed to win an election. Advertising and direct mail, as well as more traditional forms of communication such as speeches and door-knocking, are also used to deliver messages designed to elicit appropriate intellectual and emotional responses at the ballot box.

No matter how big or small the campaign, fundraising is a vital part of it. The fundraising plan should be written into the overall campaign plan at the outset and key personnel given responsibility for ensuring that the plan is executed. Besides direct approaches to companies, organisations and individuals, the campaign should stage fundraising events where the price of admission becomes a de facto contribution. While direct mail is used extensively for political fundraising in the United States, this is not yet the case in Australia, where it is more often used for persuasive purposes. However, this could change. The Australian and various state Electoral Commissions provide electoral funding to political parties in proportion to the number of votes each receives. Thus emerging political groups who don't have the track record of the established parties or their existing affiliations for fundraising (the Australian Labor Party, for example, has formal arrangements with the union movement to gather funds) may turn increasingly to direct mail to raise campaign funds.

Political strategy

The crucial element in campaign work—the thing that makes it a campaign—is a commitment to consistency and strategic effectiveness: all campaign activity should cohere to the central message and be directed towards achieving the desired result.

The two main forms of electoral campaigning are dictated by the starting position of the candidate: there is the *insurgent campaign* where the candidate seeks to win a position for the first time, and the *incumbent campaign* where the candidate already holds the position.

The concept of insurgency comes from the conduct of rebellions and revolutionary wars. When confronted with the superior forces of Hannibal, the Roman general Fabius Maximus adapted the tactics of rebellious tribes against whom he had fought: by avoiding open battle, he used the terrain to bog down and dissipate the stronger enemy. In modern times, insurgency is typically waged as guerilla war conducted by irregular forces with weapons stolen from their opponents, fighting on territory favouring their struggle, using constant mobility to find a tactical means of achieving relative superiority. Sam Rubesohn was Liberal Prime Minister Robert Menzies' advertising agent in 1949, and he understood the functions of insurgency: 'vigorous attack directed against chinks in the other man's political armour is of vital importance in assuring the effectiveness of election advertising . . . non-militant advertising . . . is ineffective' (quoted in Mills 1986: 89). By refusing to play the incumbents' game, by attacking their weaknesses and distracting them from their agenda, the insurgent campaign creates its own game, which it just might win.

Just as the successful insurgent campaign has much to learn from guerilla warfare, the successful incumbent campaign has much in common with defensive siege warfare. Ancient walled cities resisted invaders by strengthening defences to close gaps and reinforce weak spots, by preparing supplies of incendiary mixtures and even swarms of bees to be dumped on attackers, and by ensuring a steady supply of such resources as food and water. In the 1700s, the art of fortification was refined into a geometric exercise, with city walls built at acute angles so that all parts of them could be covered by outflanking fire from another point on the walls. Similarly, the incumbent campaign today must blunt the opposition's attack by parrying it with all available resources while simultaneously looking for every opportunity to outflank it or turn it back on itself. The incumbent campaign has little choice over terrain. Its very incumbency has locked it into a set position. The challenge is to use this position most effectively. Incumbents must exert such complete control over the terrain that the certainties they offer seem safe and secure compared with the radical plans of their opponents.

In putting together a campaign strategy, the campaign director is seeking to construct a complex metanarrative that sends a multiplicity of variations on the key campaign message to a variety of targeted audiences in various configurations by assorted media over the length of the campaign. The complexity of the strategy is further enhanced by the continuing need to address the three core elements of a persuasive argument identified by Aristotle: reason, character and emotion. What Aristotle called 'arguments from reason' now centre around developing and refining the message of the campaign. As Ron Faucheux puts it in *Campaign and Elections*: 'The Message is the central strategic rationale as to why a candidate or issue position is the right one at the right time and is preferable to other alternatives.' (1993: 26)

The message may be summarised in slogans such as Gough Whitlam's 'It's time', Bill Clinton's 'There's a place called Hope' and John Howard's 'Warm and comfortable government'. In these examples, the message is simple, concise and direct, yet with enough narrative texture to allow the citizen-audience to produce its own complex readings. The message is then developed into the lines of argument about particular issues important to the voters, which are delivered to the media at the ideal rate of one a day. Then, in the final days of the campaign, key lines that have tested well in the research are developed into tight, cohesive argument that substantiates the message, and that argument is repeated by the candidate as a mantra in all available forums.

An important element in the construction of the metanarrative of the campaign is ensuring that its logical arguments gel with what Aristotle called the character of the candidate—or, to put it in contemporary terms, that the candidate's image reinforces the message and is reinforced by it. In a mass society, most citizens do not have the opportunity to know the candidate intimately, so they construct their own 'intimate' relationship with the candidate based on their observations of the candidate's persona through the media, fitting that relationship into their personal system of relationships as best they can.

The campaign creates the candidate's persona by highlighting the characteristics to which swinging voters, as well as stalwart supporters, will be attracted. Daniel Boorstin (1961) identifies the key characteristics of the image: constructed to achieve certain goals, it credibly appeals to the values and common sense of the electorate. It is vivid and concrete, but still ambiguous enough for voters to supply their own interpretations and draw their own conclusions about the worth of the candidate.

Regardless of what the candidate says, it is the candidate's presentation (clothes, hairstyle, speech, posture and attitude) that will be read by the citizen-audience as they decide what kind of person he/she is. Honing a candidate's image involves everything from deciding on the appropriate glasses frames to elocution lessons. There is no exact formula in this area—it depends on the electorate. In some electorates, candidates should never be seen without a suit; in others they might succeed *because* they do their door-knocking in thongs and tee-shirt.

While the election campaign cannot absent itself from the policy debate, one key function of the campaign is to elicit an appropriate emotional response at the moment of voting. Technological change has provided powerful means to touch human emotions: personally addressed direct mail, radio, computer-assisted tele-marketing and, most significantly, television. Where once TV producers used loud, raucous repetition to attempt to lodge the message in the subconscious of the audience, they now look for an instinctual response by selecting music, lyrics, words and images that gently 'stir' the subconscious and resonate with the audience. That is why many advertisements mirror dreams and how, while individuals cannot verbalise the impact of an ad, that impact can be observed in their behaviour.

The emotional potency of candidates talking quietly and candidly about their private life on television became evident in 1952, when the future US President Richard Nixon deflected concern about improper campaign donations in his famous 'Checkers' speech. He went on national television with his dog, Checkers (which had supposedly been given to his children as a gift), and appealed for public sympathy because he was operating under a set of rules that would force him to give back the dog and deprive his children (Diamond and Bates 1984: 66–75). Television is an excellent medium with which to elicit an emotional response that reinforces a hard political message or distracts from some policy shortcoming. In traditional speechmaking before a large crowd, the production of charisma involved the expression of an overbearing, almost arrogant demeanour. But on television the most effective delivery involves talk directed to the emotions, using a soft voice and colloquial language that suggests the candidate is communicating intimately with viewers in the privacy of their living rooms.

Campaign research

The speaker in the ancient Greek Assembly knew the opinions and attitudes of many of his audience, and could just look around to judge its characteristics in terms of relative age, class and wealth. This allowed the speaker to adapt the speech to the crowd. But, because the modern audience is on the other side of a TV transmission, the contemporary candidate in a mass society needs to employ complex research strategies to achieve the same result.

In the pre-campaign phase, the candidate and key advisers research the demographics and past voting habits of the electorate. Australian Bureau of Statistics (ABS) and Australian Electoral Commission (AEC) publications provide this information, and it should be consolidated into a document that provides a comprehensive overview of the electorate. The campaign then needs to retain opinion pollsters who have quantitative and qualitative models and access to the computer programs and banks of phone lines required to assess the electorate's response to the ideas, issues, personalities and events operating in a campaign. To be effective, pollsters should operate within the principles of targeting and tracking (Mills 1986: 8–13). Thus they assist the campaign to develop messages targeted at the swinging voters in the marginal electorates required to win the election, then track (or evaluate) the targeted voters' response to those messages in further research.

Quantitative polls provide a statistical measure of the level of a candidate's support, the strengths and weaknesses of their arguments, and which issues are important to various segments of the public. Polls can only ever measure the support for a candidate at the moment they were taken, and so should not be seen as a prediction of the outcome of the election, but rather as a tool for setting the future direction of the campaign. What the polls tell the campaign is secondary to what the campaign does with them. For campaign teams, the most important thing is to gauge the mood and preoccupations of the undecided and minor party voters in marginal seats, and thereby the field of opportunity to persuade those key voters to support the campaign with either their primary or preference vote.

It is important to remember that polls can be wrong. An option is to retain a second polling company to check on the accuracy of the first, but this is expensive and time-consuming. Sources of error include non-random or incomplete samples, and prejudices in writing and interpreting questions and answers. These problems can be avoided if the campaign director insists on an objective stance when briefing the pollster. Campaign directors should also insist on access to the raw data so they can analyse those data themselves with a critical eye. In the 1991 Brisbane City Council lord mayoral race, the incumbent Liberal Sallyanne Atkinson was seemingly impregnable in early Labor Party research. It was only close analysis of the raw data that allowed the campaign team of challenger Jim Soorley to notice a small number of minor negative responses about Atkinson. Those responses hinted that her other ambitions, international interests and presidential style (with a pay packet to match) might be construed as lack of interest in the day-to-day affairs of the council. Soorley achieved a surprise upset victory over 'Salaryanne'.

While quantitative polling reveals the big picture, it is not so effective in monitoring the minutiae of motivation. To probe the values, emotions and feelings that will determine the voter's choice, another more qualitative form of research is useful. Qualitative research is based on the interaction of small focus groups of undecided voters from marginal electorates. Facilitators of focus groups use discussion, observation and analysis to understand the psychological motives that underpin political attitudes and behaviour.

The success of small-group research is dependent not on statistical validity, but on the abilities of the facilitator to foster debate with casual but incisive questioning that probes people's motivations and develops solutions for the campaign's problems. Whenever possible, campaign staff should also observe discussion, reading body language and tone of voice first-hand, to find the lines and positions that ring true and produce strong reactions. Another important use of qualitative research is in testing the effectiveness of advertising by showing it to small groups and observing their responses before it is broadcast.

Good voter research is reading the mind of the electorate as it is being persuaded. It not only records the current state of voter opinion, but is a simulation of the campaign, testing the effectiveness of various strategic feints. The campaign must use the polls to reposition itself, not by changing its policies but by choosing which ones to emphasise and then reinventing, reinterpreting and repackaging them in ways that maximise their appeal.

A final form of research is that required for negative campaigning on an opponent's shortcomings. It is a dangerous area that can all too easily backfire on a campaign. It should be based on rigorous 'opposition research' of the opponent's public record to identify hard information of contradictions between their statements and actions or other reasons why they should not be elected (Persinos 1995: 20–23). It is most effective when it attacks the opponent's policy positions, but it can even be useful in repositioning the opponent's character. Opposition research on the campaign's own candidate should be done so the staff are prepared to respond to adverse material that will probably turn up at some time during the campaign. Research is discussed further in Chapter 6.

Mass media

In a mass society, the most obvious way for the campaign to connect with the audience-electorate is through the mass media. But, rather than dispersing a random selection of messages and images into the mediasphere, a good political campaign seeks to develop a strategy that positions the candidate to most effectively appeal to targeted voters. It then communicates with that group through every available means: free editorial coverage and paid advertising in the mass media, and more personal contact through direct mail and door-knocking on the ground.

The term *position* is borrowed from concept evaluation techniques used in product marketing, where researchers analyse consumers' perceptions of existing and potential products and rank consumers' preferences to determine the market position of a new product. The political campaign similarly seeks the most effective and efficient ways to maximise voter support and persuade the swinging and undecided voters required to win targeted electorates by identifying the themes that concern those voters and then using the media to position the campaign, its message and the candidate's image. While no campaign can position itself as something it is not, it can certainly position itself as anything it might become.

The day-to-day media work of the campaign involves the constant repetition, refinement and redevelopment of the candidate's positions in light of the latest statements from the opposition, external developments and, most importantly, research. This complex work is sometimes summarised as the application of 'spin', and is particularly relevant when the campaign has to manage a crisis or go into damage-control mode. Every campaign teeters constantly on the edge of disaster, and to turn each day into an opportunity to improve public support for its position, the campaign needs to promote its positive agenda enthusiastically while remaining flexible in its media strategy, ready to admit its shortcomings where necessary and able to turn those shortcomings (or at least the admissions) into positive things about the candidate.

A few further points may be made about earning editorial coverage in a campaign context. The campaign should issue daily a press release setting out the message, image and media event for the day in clear terms, not just for the media, but for the campaign itself:

- Direct quotes from the candidate in the release should form the basis of a 10–20 second grab for radio and television.
- Ensure that the press release has the correct date and effective contact phone numbers.
- Follow up by lobbying key journalists, particularly the political reporter at the AAP wire service, for coverage of the story.
- Build relationships with key journalists by social contact and casual backgrounding off the record, explaining the 'real story' of the campaign.
- Ensure that journalists have phone numbers to reach the campaign for comment at all times.
- Develop similar contacts with opinion leaders active in the media—proprietors, management, editors, chiefs of staff and radio announcers, as well as other commentators, church leaders and key community figures.
- Ensure that the campaign will be the subject of discussion among those with power and influence in the media, so creating the potential to edge campaign issues on to the news agenda.

To produce a story, journalists need an image and an interesting quote. One way to make both available is to hold a media event. In its simplest form, the media event may be just the candidate making a comment at a doorstop. By holding the press conference in an appropriately decorated room or at a symbolic external location, the campaign can exert more control over the backdrop and so reinforce the verbal message of the candidate.

Well-researched advance work is required at external locations to ensure that the candidate is not embarrassed. For example, former Labor Prime Minister Paul Keating found his positive pitch turned into a negative during the 'cake shop incident' of the 1993 Australian federal election. He visited a bakery with a full media contingent to criticise his opponents' confusion over how their planned goods and services tax would affect the price of a shop-bought cake. Keating's advance team had not ascertained that the proprietor was a Liberal supporter with well-informed criticisms of the Labor's own tax regime, and Keating was seen to be wrong-footed on national TV news that night.

Major events such as campaign launches, significant addresses, rallies, debates and candidacy announcements need to be even more meticulously planned than simple media events. Media coverage is the key outcome, so the events should be planned to fit into media schedules, the candidate's message should be clear and easily understood, and the media should be given all possible help. Careful preparation of the candidate is required for all major events so they don't 'slip up', which can *become* the news and so obscure the message.

It is easy for a campaign to become obsessed with its appearances on the evening TV news and in the daily papers, but these are only two sources of news. Alternatives such as local community newspapers, the internet, chat shows, and breakfast and talkback radio are all valid—and sometimes more effective—ways of getting the campaign message across. As the electronic media diversify into new forms, the power of the evening news and the morning broadsheet will decline and new points of entry will become available to campaigns that stay aware of what their target audience is doing.

Advertising has become the most significant site at which political rhetoric occurs, because it is there for all to see in the dominant media forms and, more importantly, because it is effective. Whether communicated by television, radio or newspapers, political advertising seeks to bond ideas, images, policies and arguments together in a moment of 'emotional exchange' (Miller, in Diamond and Bates 1984: 10). Advertising aims to crystallise moments of meaning which answer the concerns of undecided and third-party voters and leave them more inclined to vote for the campaign's candidate (or less inclined to vote for the opponent). Witherspoon (1989: 61–74) identifies the various uses of campaign advertising thus:

- *identification*—simple name/face recognition to establish the candidate's presence in a campaign;
- *biography*—documentation that establishes the candidate's achievements, character and family situation;
- *issue* definition—informative material positioning the campaign on issues;

- *attack*—negative attacks on opponents and their policies, which work best when they reinforce the campaign's positive positions;
- *comparison*—contrasting policy positions and character, where the voter is invited to choose;
- *vision* spots—where the candidate summarises character, themes and issues in a statement of their aims and objectives; and
- *11th-hour blitz*—in the final phase, the campaign being ready to respond quickly and effectively to developments, shifts and the final tracking research.

Direct voter contact

In the frenzy of modern campaigning, personal contact is often overlooked as an effective means of establishing a relationship with the voters. In the past fifteen years, personally addressed direct mail has become a serious challenger to TV advertising as the most significant campaign tool in Australia. It is more expensive per contact than television advertising, but it can be targeted to make a connection with just those swinging voters in the key marginal seats who ultimately decide the outcome of an election. Of course, direct mail works most effectively where it reinforces and is reinforced by the advertising campaign.

Direct mail should be distinguished from unaddressed campaign materials, which are useful to trawl for postal and absentee voters but are generally ineffective. Direct mail, by contrast, arrives at the targeted voter's home in a personally addressed envelope, usually from the candidate, talking directly to the voter within the codes of correspondence but with a letterhead and overall design to communicate key messages even to those who do not read the text. The aim is to build a relationship that will be decisive in the polling booth. Australian political campaigns have refined the use of direct mail as a persuasive medium. In close contests such as the 1990 and 1993 Australian federal elections, the effectiveness of direct mail was decisive.

The overriding principle of direct mail is personal intimacy: the campaign should not only personalise letters so they are addressed to the intended recipients, but the text of the letter should contain references to the recipients ('Dear John and Mary . . . as I'm sure you will agree, John and Mary') and their street and suburb. Signatures and postscripts should be in the candidate's handwriting, and be printed in fountain-pen blue. The letter is only one element in the communication, and the complete package should be carefully developed: the mailing envelope should not turn off the recipient. A return address is required by Australia Post regulation, and it is best to leave external messages at that so the recipient cannot 'pick' the communication as being from a political candidate. A window envelope with the address printed on the letter is the cheapest approach and gets around the problem of double-checking that each letter is in the right envelope.

Just as important as what you mail is to whom you mail it. Where the campaign can afford to canvass the entire electorate, it can delete opposition supporters and produce separate lists for the campaign's confirmed supporters, third-party supporters and undecided swingers, and mail appropriate material to each group. Responses to surveys, incoming constituent phone calls and candidate contacts provide 'in-house' lists which can be used to mail letters on specific issues. Too often, individual voter contact is treated as a nuisance by campaign workers. But a systematic approach to this contact, combined with an application of computer technology, can produce lists that can have a big impact.

Writing direct mail may look easy, but it requires discipline to stick to the research, care that the language clearly conveys what needs to be said, and a determination to get the message across.

Ten commandments for effective direct mail

1. Keep it simple. 'Expenditure' is hard, 'spending' is easy.
2. Keep it short. One page or seven paragraphs is plenty.
3. Keep it positive and voters will feel better about the candidate.
4. Be emotive. The writer should 'pull at the heart strings'.
5. Be direct. Use active verbs and short, 'bouncy' sentences.
6. Be local to show the candidate is aware of pertinent issues.
7. Be personal. Build a one-on-one relationship.
8. Stick to the message. Keep it consistent with all other media.
9. Make the first paragraph count. It may be the only one that is read.
10. Check everything. Your opponents read this letter.

The telephone is an even more personal form of communication. Commercial and charity organisations in Australia already use the phone to sell products and raise money. Doing these things systematically is called *telemarketing*. The political possibilities for telemarketing include targeting campaign contributors, recruiting and supervising volunteers, taking polls, canvassing the electorate and persuading voters to support the candidate (Boim 1989: 100–105). Integrated computer–telephone systems improve the efficiency of the telemarketing process by having the next call ringing as the last is finished and by screening out fax machines and disconnected or busy phones. They can prompt the caller with scripts, record results and produce instant tabulations. They can also print out direct mail follow-up that reflects the candidate's positions on the voter's interests and preoccupations.

Telemarketing technology can also be used for 'push-polling'. This is when pollsters conduct pseudo-polling directed at identified swinging voters and designed not to gather information but to highlight the opponent's negatives in the period immediately before an election. Most established pollsters reject this practice as unethical.

While the campaign is working the electorate on a macro scale, the candidates' most effective contribution is to work at the micro level by involving themselves as the spokespersons on local issues, speaking to community organisations and local opinion leaders and door-knocking the electorate. Every opportunity should be taken to meet the voters and personally communicate the campaign's message.

Interaction with community groups on local issues 'fleshes out' the image by giving the candidate the opportunity to actualise the one-on-one relationship that mass media and direct mail activities strive for but can never really deliver. Just as the campaign establishes good relationships with the owners and editors of local news-papers, the candidate should contact local opinion leaders: religious and community leaders, headmasters, police commanders, publicans, and any other local identities with a high profile. They will not all warm to the candidate, but at least the candi-date has set up a personal contact so if the opinion leaders have a problem there is a chance they will come direct to the candidate rather than spreading the problem to everyone they meet.

Door-knocking is still the best way for candidates to meet the voters, particu-larly if it is done systematically (Duquin 1989: 41–45). Using ABS information supported by campaign canvassing, supporters, opponents and swinging voters can be identified. Supporters can be invited to meet the candidate in a local park, opponents can be left with a pamphlet extolling the virtues of the candidate and highlighting the opponent's negatives, and swingers can receive personal attention from the candidate.

Not all votes are cast on election day. Many people are too infirm to get to the polls or will be absent from the electorate on polling day. They can use postal or absentee section votes, and it is crucial that the campaign utilises local knowledge to get the best result here. The more people who are assisted by the campaign to exercise their vote, the better the candidate will do in this segment of the electorate. The campaign must be ready to mobilise to assist in the application for postal or absentee votes as soon as it is legally possible, so as to beat opponents to them.

Conclusion

The potential for political rhetoric to manipulate the electorate is an abiding concern for all democratic institutions, and the success of public relations techniques in managing political debate highlights one of the main limitations of the two-party system of representative democracy which is often seen to exclude alternative viewpoints in the rush to win or use power. But, in rethinking and remaking democracy for the twenty-first century, the techniques and technologies offered by campaign processes suggest some means by which contemporary representative institutions may be transformed into more effective democratic tools.

Central to this transformation is the responsibility of citizens generally to find ways to exercise their voice by communicating their ideas and opinions to other citizens. To produce a participatory and deliberative democracy in a mass society, usually passive audiences must transform themselves into citizens of the global media, with the requisite public relations skills to utilise the opportunities provided by the gaps in the mass media and by the rapidly developing new media to create new forms of discussion, debate and political organisation.

Case study 15.1: Australian federal election, 2001

Prime Minister John Howard first led the Liberal-National Party coalition to government in 1996 as blue-collar voters reacted against Paul Keating's perceived arrogance and thirteen years of Labor government. Howard was re-elected in 1998, but many of his blue-collar supporters had turned to Pauline Hanson's One Nation Party to register their dissatisfaction with Howard over his guns buy-back scheme and the goods and services tax (GST). The GST was introduced in July 2000 and many of Howard's small business supporters were upset by the extra work it entailed for them. Winning a third term is traditionally hard for an incumbent government. Howard had a big job ahead of him to win the 2001 Australian federal election, and the way he rose to the occasion has much to teach us about how political campaigns work.

Howard's year had not started well: his party was behind in all opinion polls and Labor's Kim Beazley was beginning to outrank him as preferred Prime Minister. Then the Liberals lost the Western Australia state election and the conservatives were white-washed in Queensland as Howard's Liberals won only three seats in the 89-member Parliament. And then, in a by-election on 17 March, the Liberals lost their heartland federal seat of Ryan. But Howard's middle name is Winston and he provided a Churchillian fightback. His first step was to look at the research, which revealed that education, health, unemployment, environment and family issues were the most important concerns of voters and that Labor was seen to be the best party to handle each of these issues (Newspoll 25/1/01). The only issues on which the government maintained a lead were tax, economics, defence and immigration. Howard sought ways to use his lead on these issues to win back small-business and blue-collar voters. He commissioned a report from the federal Liberal Party President, Shane Stone, which said that Howard was seen by the voters as 'mean and tricky, out of touch and not listening'. The report was leaked so that the Prime Minister could respond that he was addressing these issues and would mend his ways.

Then Howard began the process of 'wedge politics', appealing to target groups crucial to holding government while disregarding the rest. As the GST had raised more tax than was expected, Howard could afford to be generous. Appealing directly to the male, working-class 'battlers' who supported One Nation, the Prime Minister ordered cuts to taxes on beer and petrol. To lure back small business, he dropped his hard-line approach against any changes to the GST and made the tax collection process simpler and less time-consuming for small business.

But most significant were his moves on immigration and defence. In late August, the government began taking a hard line against refugees, informing the Norwegian ship *Tampa* of refugees in distress and so obliging them to take them on board and then refusing the *Tampa* permission to land them on Australian territory. Most significantly, the government immediately implemented a strict media management regime and prevented journalists from talking to the refugees and photographers from getting shots that may have humanised the refugees. For weeks, newspapers and TV only had the one long shot of distant figures on the deck of the *Tampa*, taken shortly before flight restrictions were placed around the boat. And, while the *Tampa* stand-off continued, the events of September 11 occurred and Australian troops were committed to America's 'War against Terror' in Afghanistan.

Then the federal election was called in early October, and within days the Prime Minister was lambasting refugees for 'throwing their children overboard'. When called on to substantiate this claim, a photo was produced of a number of figures in the sea with their faces digitally removed. Only after the election was it conclusively confirmed that this photo was taken during an unrelated Navy rescue and that no children had in fact been thrown overboard.

Howard skilfully managed the refugee issue for maximum electoral effect, promoting a moral panic about the uncontrolled influx of immigrants, subtly shifting the designation of these people from refugees and asylum seekers to illegal immigrants and queue jumpers. Labor, by way of contrast, was caught flat-footed. It did not offer a strong insurgent campaign. It had hoped that disquiet about the GST and Howard's mean and tricky ways would create such opposition in the community that it would be elected by default. But Howard did not give it that opportunity. He manufactured his own fortune, convinced targeted voters that he had their interests at heart and won an increased majority.

Case study 15.2: If you drink, then drive, you're a bloody idiot

Considerable progress has been made in improving road safety in Australia in recent years. Road fatalities have more than halved since 1971, while road traffic has almost trebled in the same period. The careful analysis of safety problems, the application of practical counter-measures in an integrated fashion and the evaluation of counter-measures and programs have resulted in an effective and sound road safety strategy. It is useful to consider the influence of public relations techniques and media awareness campaigns in producing these outcomes, together with the potential for too much publicity to produce contrary results.

In 1989, the growing road toll was causing widespread concern. The key players in setting the road safety agenda in Victoria—VicRoads, Victorian Police and the Traffic Accident Commission (TAC)—adopted an integrated approach to tackling road trauma. The TAC launched a number of publicity campaigns with drink-driving themes to support police enforcement, especially the program of increased random breath testing (RBT) using highly visible 'booze buses'. The TAC decided to adopt a more aggressive approach to its marketing role in attacking the key causes of the road toll: drink driving, excessive speed, poor concentration, fatigue and not wearing seatbelts (Cameron and Newstead 1996).

In November 1989, the TAC engaged a Melbourne company, Grey Advertising, to develop a campaign that would challenge drivers to rethink their personal attitudes to road safety and change their driving behaviour. The first task was to develop 'product' or 'brand' names that would give road-safety campaigns a strong presence and encourage motorists to 'buy' the TAC message. Such names would have to be memorable, striking and short. Each name had to sum up a particular theme or issue, as no single advertisement could deal effectively with all these issues at once.

The advertising campaign used the following slogans to act as the 'brand names' of the campaign (see Table 15.1).

Table 15.1 Advertising slogans

Issues	Slogans/brand names
Drink driving	If you drink, then drive, you're a bloody idiot
Speed	Don't fool yourself, speed kills
Fatigue	Take a break, fatigue kills
Concentration	It's in your hand, concentrate or kill
Seatbelts	Belt up, or suffer the pain
Rural areas	Country people die on country roads

The first TAC campaign went to air during the 1989 Christmas period and placed drink driving firmly on the public agenda by graphically illustrating a potent deterrent—the fear drink drivers have of finding themselves responsible for the death or serious injury of another human being. The ad, called 'Girlfriend', was set in a hospital casualty ward, where the parents of a maimed girl confronted the boyfriend whose drink driving was to blame. The naturalistic style and emotional intensity achieved in the ad gave force to the slogan 'If you drink, then drive, you're a bloody idiot', which rapidly became part of the national idiom.

The message was reinforced by a string of ads repeating the slogan. The TAC also supported the Victorian speed camera program, with mass media publicity promoting the slogan 'Speed kills', also in a series of TV ads. Details of these campaigns can be seen on the TAC website (at <www.tac.vic.gov.au/DOCS/b4.htm>).

The combined effort by road-safety stakeholders has produced dramatic results in Victoria. Road deaths have more than halved since 1989, dropping from around seventeen to eight per 10 000 population. An evaluation of the speed camera program found statistically significant relationships between levels of TAC publicity and reductions in casualty crashes in Melbourne when other key factors were taken into account (speed camera operating hours, numbers of speeding tickets issued and unemployment rates). The methods used in that study were also employed to examine the effects of TAC publicity on casualty crashes, with drink-driving themes supporting the RBT program (monthly variations in RBT activity, alcohol sales and unemployment rates were taken into account). The strongest effects were found when the publicity was measured by a function that represents cumulative awareness due to current and previous advertising levels.

The economic value of the publicity was measured using average costs of the crashes saved and the costs of development and placement of the TV advertisements. The reduction in accidents from 1989 to 1996 is estimated to have saved the Victorian community more than $2.9 billion.

However, in November 1993, the Victorian police in conjunction with TAC launched a major program in country Victoria in an effort to increase the number of random breath tests to at least 700 000 tests in a twelve-month period. They supported the enforcement operations with mass media publicity (Cameron and Diamantopoulou 1998). The intensity of the supporting publicity was also measured, both by amount over time and in terms of awareness levels. The outcomes were significant. There was a 9 per cent reduction in serious casualty crashes below expected levels in country Victoria during the program.

Crashes in smaller areas of country Victoria influenced by the RBT activity were analysed so that the effects of styles of RBT operations, and the interactions of these effects with the levels of publicity awareness, could be seen. A statistically significant reduction in serious casualty crashes was found when RBT was conducted by police cars operating alone and without significant publicity. Medium levels of publicity appeared to increase the effects of the 'car-only' enforcement operations. However, when both police cars and 'booze buses' were deployed and high-level publicity accompanied the enforcement, a statistically significant increase in serious casualty crashes occurred.

These somewhat surprising findings led to further evaluation, which found that some drink drivers faced with intense enforcement and intense publicity changed their travel behaviour and used relatively unsafe minor roads where RBT enforcement was not common, with negative consequences for road safety. The result is that Victorian police now schedule RBT operations on minor as well as major roads during periods of intense publicity.

Source: Traffic Accident Commission.

Discussion and exercises

1   Run a small focus group to assess the effectiveness of a political or government TV advertisement. Gauge the general characteristics and attitudes of the group before showing the ad. What are the ad's strengths and weaknesses? What is the message it is designed to communicate? Does this differ from the message that is communicated? Test alternative images, slogans and 'lines'. Write a report on the effectiveness of the ad, with suggested changes.

2   You are the campaign director for a local government candidate. Prepare the candidate for their first media conference. Taking into account the demographics and voting habits in the constituency, and key issues affecting the area, develop your message and key lines. Develop the candidate's image. School the candidate, brief the class on their role as the local media and present the candidate to them. Be ready to step in when things get too hot.

3   What are the arguments for and against the efficacy of quantitative opinion polling in the political arena?

4   You have inherited a client which is an interest group espousing positions that you personally oppose (e.g. they want gun control and you think all responsible citizens should have access to their weapon of choice, or vice versa). How do you handle this? Discuss with reference to various formal ethical codes and a selection of philosophers, religious thinkers and practitioners.

Further reading

Barrett, H. (1987) *The Sophists*, Chandler & Sharp, Novato.

Bremmer, J. & Roodenburg, H. (eds) (1993) *A Cultural History of Gesture*, Polity Press, Cambridge.

McGinniss, J. (1970) *Selling the President*, Andre Deutsch, London.

Machiavelli, N. (1961) *The Prince*, Penguin, Harmondsworth.

Matthews, C. (1989) *Hardball*, Perennial Harper & Row, New York.

Morris, D. (1996) *Behind the Oval Office: Winning the Presidency in the Nineties*, Random House, New York.

Richardson, G. (1994) *Whatever it Takes*, Bantam, Sydney.

Sabato, L. (ed.) (1989) *Campaigns and Elections: A Reader*, Scott Foresman, Glenview.

Thompson, H.S. (1973) *Fear and Loathing on the Campaign Trail*, Popular Library, New York.

References

Aristotle (1991) *The Art of Rhetoric*, Penguin, London.

Blumenthal, S. (1980) *The Permanent Campaign*, Beacon Press, Boston.

Boim, D. (1989) 'The telemarketing centre', in L. Sabato (ed.), *Campaigns and Elections: A Reader*, Scott Foresman, Glenview.

Bonner, J., Grete, E. & Minard, R. (1999) 'Trends in grassroots lobbying', *Campaigns and Elections*, February, pp. 22–25.

Boorstin, D. (1961) *The Image*, Atheneum, New York.

Bourdieu, P. (1978) 'Public opinion does not exist', in A. Mattelart & S. Siegelaub (eds), *Communication and Class Struggle*, IG/IMMRC, New York.

Cameron, M. & Newstead, S. (1996) 'Mass media publicity supporting police enforcement and its economic value', *Public Health Association of Australia Annual Conference*, 30 September, <www.general.monash.edu.au/muarc/media/ media.htm>.

Cameron, M. & Diamantopoulou, K. (1998) Evaluation of the *Country Random Breath Testing and Publicity Program in Victoria, 1993–1994*, Report #126, Monash University Accident Research Centre, Melbourne.

Carey, A. (1995) *Taking the Risk out of Democracy*, University of NSW Press, Sydney.

Diamond, E. & Bates, S. (1984) *The Spot: The Rise of Political Advertising on TV*, MIT Press, Cambridge.

Doob, L.W. (1954) 'Goebbels' principles of propaganda', in D. Katz et al. (eds), *Public Opinion and Propaganda*, Holt, Rinehart & Winston, New York.

Duquin, L.H. (1989) 'Door-to-door campaigning', in L. Sabato (ed.), *Campaigns and Elections: A Reader*, Scott Foresman, Glenview.

Electoral and Administrative Review Commission (EARC) (1992) *Proceedings: Public Seminar on Review of Government Media and Information Services*, EARC, Brisbane, 16 June.

Faucheux, R. (1993) 'Great slogans', *Campaign and Elections*, June/July.

Habermas, J. (1989) *The Structural Transformation of the Public Sphere*, Polity Press, Cambridge.

Herman, E.S. & Chomsky, N. (1988) *Manufacturing Consent*, Pantheon, New York.

Mills, S. (1986) *The New Machine Men*, Penguin, Ringwood.

Napolitan, J., Reese, M., O'Leary, B. & Edmonds, T. (1994) 'The political campaign industry', *Campaigns and Elections*, December/January.

Newspoll (1995) *Australian*, 15 July, p. 10.

Orwell, G. (1970) 'Politics and the English language', *Collected Essays, Journalism and Letters*, vol. 4, Penguin, Harmondsworth.

Persinos, J. (1995) 'Gotcha!', *Campaigns and Elections*, August.

Ramsey, A. (1995) 'Countdown to an election', *Sydney Morning Herald*, 31 May.

Tiffen, R. (1989) *News and Power*, Allen & Unwin, Sydney.

Ward, I. (1995) *Politics of the Media*, Macmillan, Melbourne.

Witherspoon, J. (1989) 'Campaign commercials and the media blitz', in L. Sabato (ed.), *Campaigns and Elections: A Reader*, Scott Foresman, Glenview.

16 PUBLIC RELATIONS IN THE THIRD SECTOR

Kristin Demetrious

In this chapter

Introduction

Wired global communities are massing, moving, and shifting the social and political contours of the twenty-first century, producing new ways of seeing power and change. From the regions of Cambodia to the suburbs of Australia, the Third Sector—comprising non-government organisations (NGOs) and community action groups (CAGs) —is growing and will increasingly play an important role in shaping those changes.

Separate from the state and business sectors and operating largely with voluntary labour and a nonprofit agenda for the 'common good', the Third Sector has experienced recent, rapid growth, at the same time diversifying in scale and size. While many commonalities and intersections exist between the two classifications of NGOs and CAGs, there are also specific issues and hurdles related to their organisational structural differences that influence the achievement of their communication objectives. NGOs include both radical and conservative organisations, from not for profits (NFPs) like clubs, societies and professional associations to political and ideologically driven organisations in areas such as health and human rights. They are generally characterised by their larger size, proactivity, more broadly based agendas, levels of established 'legitimacy', greater rigidity, access to infrastructure and resources, established chains of command and long-term survival. CAGs, on the other hand, range from small grass roots activist groups to widespread community collectives. They are generally characterised by short-term reactivity, a direct relationship to a specific issue, nascent 'legitimacy', decentralised 'organic', non-hierarchical organisational structures, informality and adaptability, and their disappearance from the public sphere when the issue is 'over'.

What brings the Third Sector together is its components' separateness from state and the business sectors. Third Sector organisations increasingly utilise strategies developed by these two sectors, but what sets them aside is the use of tactics such as activism. It is important to understand the relationship between the Third Sector and the other more traditional sectors, particularly the degree to which the Third Sector has been able to utilise strategies and tactics more commonly associated with more traditional organisations. In turn, more traditional organisations have had to recognise, accept and create relationships with the Third Sector.

Meltdown: new soft world order

Ulrich Beck's book *Risk Society Towards a New Modernity* (1992) discusses the notion of risk society and a new era, one of 'reflexive modernisation'. His theories forecast the growth of the Third Sector and its capacity to generate influence in society. They provide a key to understanding the types of issues that grass roots activists seek to promote and the reasons why they are gaining relative power in this area. Beck describes how old hierarchies of social order based on rigid, centralised mechanistic, economic power structures have changed to a new order of decentralised knowledge, social and political power. According to Beck, the 'dictatorship of scarcity' (1992: 20)—that is, the premise that 'need' or 'lack' of any commodity required for our survival dictates production—has given way to a new reality. The world is in a nascent state where 'hazards' like the greenhouse effect, acid rain and toxic contamination are the growing, powerful and threatening by-products of the sophisticated techno-economic production processes which have developed to an extent previously unknown. Beck characterises risk in this sense as impacting widely on humanity. But, rather than having its genesis in 'underproduction' and the practice of 'making nature useful' that characterised the 'scarcity society', this new risk will have its basis in the 'overproduction' and 'modernisation' practices of our society.

What are the consequences of this for people? What happens, for example, if the unintended and unwanted by-products of genetically modified foods spill out into global ecosystems, unable to be contained? For Beck, the powerful institutions of industrial society, such as governments and corporations, produce these global risks and hazards (1992: 21). However, the impact of the risks they create will not solely be absorbed by disempowered publics, as was the case in the scarcity society. According to Beck, risk will cross over traditional class boundaries that in the past have protected power elites from consequences of their actions. Global and local NGOs and CAGs will rise. They will represent articulate, vigilant and cynical publics who can organise sustained and effective action on diverse issues. These groups will have access to new communication technologies and information. Their knowledge, understanding and management of the communication process are essential to the success to that role. The Third Sector's relationship to public relations is balanced at a critical point.

The Third Sector and citizenship

Collective community action by NGOs and CAGs can be a sign of a confident and articulate civil society that seeks to communicate outside governments, or private institutions like businesses. In the past, community action has contributed to a fairer and more democratic society, leading to new laws and views of society—for example, feminist and anti-racist issues.

However, there are many other instances where activist groups' self-interests and relationship with society are fraught with tension. 'Community activism' can also be seen as civic dysfunctionality and be associated with extremist groups like the Klu Klux Klan. 'Activism' is not in itself inherently good or bad; it is a tool to achieve a goal. One useful way to see activism and make a judgment on its value is through its relationship to citizenship. But what is citizenship and why is it important to understand its relationship to community activism? The answer is that the activities of NGOs and CAGs impact on their local, regional and global communities. Therefore, like any other sector in our society—including business and government—these activities are subject to scrutiny and need to be viewed through an ethical framework. The notion of citizenship is a central tenet of a liberal democracy. Citizenship can be defined as a belief that everyone within the democracy has an equal right to become a fully participating member of the community. This means that, while a community group may make legitimate challenges, the group itself must respect the citizenship rights of others. Marshall (1950: 28) discusses this idea of citizenship, but says that there is no one rule that says what these rights and responsibilities will be; rather, by embracing the idea of citizenship, we will have a clearer idea of where to aim.

Citizenship can be seen as a status bestowed on those who are 'full members' of a community. All who possess the status are 'equal' with respect to the rights and duties with which the status is endowed. There is no universal principle that determines what those rights and duties shall be, but societies in which citizenship is a developing institution create an image of an ideal citizenship against which achievement can be measured and towards which aspiration can be directed (Marshall 1950: 28).

The idea of equal rights in democratic societies extends beyond just voting and the right to a free education. We might, for example, all have the right to a universal vote—but does that make us equal citizens? Aren't some people in society more inherently privileged because of good fortune, position and power? Many activists enter the debate at this point and argue that, although things appear to be equal, in fact this is not the case. Taylor (1994) discusses the notion of first- and second-class citizens. He maintains that we should adopt the view that, rather than saying we are all equal when clearly we aren't, we need to look at what he calls a 'universal human potential': 'The politics of equal dignity is based on the idea that humans are equally worthy of respect.' (1994: 41) Both NGOs' and CAGs' activities can be viewed through their contribution to full citizenship rights. Adopting the notion of citizenship helps define and delineate the type of activism that contributes to a more democratic society.

The public sphere, power and activism

Foundations of ethics in communication have been developed by Jurgen Habermas and can now be viewed in relationship to citizenship and the Third Sector. Habermas's idea of the 'public sphere' is as a free and open space to discuss the common good. Habermas argues that the whole notion of the public sphere is under threat as modern world discussion is 'anchored' by self-interest: 'Competition between organized private interests invaded the public sphere . . . The consensus developed in rational-critical public debate has yielded to compromise fought out or simply imposed nonpublicly.' (Habermas 1989: 179) The specialised discourses degrading the public sphere have resulted in what Habermas terms 'cultural impoverishment' (Dodds 1999: 116). For example, newspapers increasingly represent organisations' self-interests as 'news'. This is facilitated through the use of the same techniques as used by more traditional organisations. The result is cultural impoverishment where citizens' understanding of the world is increasingly framed within commercial discourses. With a strong relationship to citizenship, it is possible that NGOs and CAGs can revitalise the public sphere and balance the barrage of specialised self-interest of governments and corporations. However, again the Third Sector's own activities must be viewed and scrutinised as well as others. (A fuller analysis of the public sphere is found in Chapter 3.)

Activism in its many forms is more visible than ever before. In the past, 'activism' was a marginal activity practised by isolated publics on the fringes of the 'legitimate' institutions, as government or corporate institutions proclaimed their right to exercise power either by public mandate, or by the provision of products and services of 'benefit' to society. But the Third Sector now uses corporate and government methods to send its messages and achieve its objectives. Is this creating a fairer and more equal society by contributing to the 'common good', or just adding to the clutter of self-interest competing for our attention in our daily lives? 'Activism' is historically a problematic area for the public relations industry, and 'public relations' is problematic for activists. Interestingly, when activists discuss 'public relations', it is often only to portray themselves as *victims* of the public relations industry. When public relations discusses 'activism' it is often only as a *challenge* to organisations. Today the use of sophisticated public communication techniques is not the exclusive tool of large corporations and governments. All organisations, including CAGs, can and do exercise influence through effective communication campaigns and the use of public relations strategies.

Ewen (1996) discusses the idea of the public relations industry as a mechanism for control in society. He argues that the intersection between democracy and the rise of the media has resulted in public relations as a new controlling force in society. This helps explain why activists associate 'public relations' with the corporate world and the 'domination' of workers. The legacy of this influence is palpable. Activists who mount campaigns often view corporations as capitalist structures with simplistic exploitative relationships to communities. Hostility erupts and each party reacts with predictable communication tactics and strategies. The contested idea of power and agency is at the heart of this tension. Much collective community action is reactive, time- and resource-poor and cobbled together under intense pressure. Added to this power asymmetry are corporate anti-activism tactics. These in turn have led to further distrust of public relations and a perception of underhand responses to threats by corporate power elites. Public relations practitioners in traditional organisations need to be aware of these attitudes and the history that has created them.

Grass stains and dirty tricks: corporate anti-activism

Strategies such as 'astroturfing' and 'greenwashing' practised by unethical organisations and aimed against activists explain some of this antipathy.

Astroturfing

Astroturfing is 'fee for service' artificial grass roots public support offered by public relations companies. It manifests itself as 'genuine' public support of corporate programs channelled through the mass media. For example, a talkback radio segment might be bombarded with calls from 'genuine' concerned citizens claiming to support a contested fast food development; in reality, these people are 'stooges' working for the organisation. In *Global Spin: The Corporate Assault on Environmentalism*, Beder argues that 'manufacturing grassroots' is accelerating with the advent of new technologies. In a classic case, she tells how one of the world's largest cigarette manufacturers, Philip Morris, and international public relations giant Burson Marsteller used their grass roots lobbying unit to create the National Smokers' Alliance in 1993. These two organisations used the group as a vehicle to increase membership, eventually claiming three million members, sending pro-smoking messages using sophisticated communication techniques like advertising and direct telemarketing (Beder 1997: 34).

Scientific grass roots or 'astroturfing' campaigns that mislead and manipulate perceptions of genuine public support contribute to a growing perception of global organisations' power and access to sophisticated communication techniques, and their entrenched and dominating influence in the public sphere. The negative effects can disempower and erode citizens' preparedness to engage in community debate, therefore weakening the integrity of the public sphere.

Greenwashing

Greenwashing is the use of public relations to manipulate public views that corporations are acting in environmentally responsible ways. For example, a mining company may produce attractive brochures espousing their ecological 'values', or sponsor an indigenous revegetation program as a *tactic* to disguise their true objectives and deflect criticism from key groups. Beder refers to the 'green' Sydney 2000 Olympic Games on the site of Homebush Bay, a former toxic dump. Beder accuses the public relations around the Olympics of 'greenwashing' the event by communication tactics such as 'Olympic Neighbours Day' (1999b):

> Titled 'the Big Clean–up', the event took area residents on a tour of the nicely-landscaped Olympic site, while avoiding mention of the toxic wastes buried underneath the new lawns and shrubbery that will be slowly contaminating these neighbours' groundwater for years to come. (Beder 1999b: 3)

It is important to note that such activities are unethical and are rejected by the PRIA and other professional organisations around the world.

Stauber and Rampton's *Toxic Sludge is Good for You!* (1995) presents a view of public relations as unethical and manipulative in relation to activism. They argue that public relations practitioners bow routinely to the self-interest of their employers. This leads to unscrupulous behaviour and deliberate harm to the reputation of the opposition (1995: 3–4). These practices have entrenched an intrinsic tension between activists and the 'public relations' industry. They have also raised an urgency to examine the role of public relations and the future of democracy. However, if the notion of citizenship is introduced, there is new ground for these spheres of activity to meet. Resources for activists can now be pooled in global communities using new tools of electronic technology. By adopting the outlook of citizenship, novel alliances can be forged that cross traditional boundaries to achieve objectives. Recast, these domains can view themselves as collaborators in reshaping the political area, rather than as simple adversaries.

Corporate citizenship

Corporations and the activities of corporations have the power to change the lives of those around them. For this reason, the notion of citizenship and its implications of rights, responsibilities and full participation in society can also be applied.

Corporate citizenship goes beyond conventional ideas of sponsorship, charity and philanthropy, which some see as little more than cynical marketing and branding strategies to promote products and services. The notion takes a more complex view of building relationships and partnerships, developing trust and defining value in communities. Corporate citizenship takes a long-term view of business viability. It suggests that the organisation is dependent on the host community (see box). Therefore, to survive, prosper and maintain consent, it must conform to the expectation of the community beyond just 'making a profit'. The organisation also has a social and environmental responsibility. This trio of economic, social and environmental responsibility is known as 'the triple bottom line' (also known as profit, people and planet).

Corporate citizenship benefits

- Stronger and integrated partnerships that result in creativity, inclusiveness and confidence, reputation, credibility and legitimacy to operate.
- Harmonious internal employee relationships creating an employment base that attracts the best candidates, stability that delivers long-term value to shareholders, further strategic development opportunities within the host community as its 'preferred' organisation.

The Millennium Poll (1999) on Corporate Social Responsibility (CSR) surveyed 25 000 people in 23 different countries. The poll found that respondents believed that companies in the twenty-first century should:

- demonstrate their commitment to society's values and their contribution to society's social, environmental and economic goals;
- fully insulate society from any perceived negative impact of company operation; and
- share the rewards of company benefits with key stakeholders as well as shareholders.

The broad support signalled in this poll is significant. It indicates a strong perception that corporate responsibility will build confidence that in turn makes business profitable. One example of a corporation that has adopted this approach is international mining company Rio Tinto, formerly CRA. This company has undergone a massive cultural change from the days when they 'were out on the hustings, vigorously opposing the indigenous people's interests' (Birch 2001: 27). In 1995, Leon Davis, CRA's Managing Director, signalled the change of attitude in this historic speech:

> Let me say this bluntly. CRA is satisfied with the central tenet of the Native
> Title Act. In CRA we believe that there are major opportunities for growth in
> outback Australia which will only be realised with the full cooperation of all
> interested parties. (Birch 2001: 27)

Today, Rio Tinto's operations require the company to produce five-year community plans with detailed assessments of the social, economic and cultural characteristics of each local community, as well as the means by which they consult with local people. Rio Tinto provides funding for health and education employment and business development programs while integrating local needs. In the Ngukurr region in Arnhem Land, respiratory health issues for the local community were being caused by dust. Rio Tinto's first response to the problem was to 'send in some dozers', but that wasn't what the community wanted. Consultation revealed that the local community wanted to re-establish 'medicine trees' in their lands with a mix and pace that was significant for them—much slower, 'but with their ownership and their custodianship' (Birch: 2001: 27). In this example, Rio Tinto recognised that, although it had the technology to facilitate a 'quick fix', it was not an appropriate solution to address wider, more complex and sensitive local community issues.

Challenges for organisations that don't embrace corporate citizenship are significant. They could include consumer boycott of products and services, highly visible media and information campaigns to spotlight an offending company, loss of reputation and credibility, diminished value as an employee base, loss of share value and ongoing global reputation ramifications. Embracing corporate citizenship enhances an organisation's reputation by demonstrating that it is an active participant in a society that provides safety, security and economic well-being for all. Community relations then becomes a mutual investment for both the corporation and the host community. (CSR and community relations are discussed further in Chapters 11 and 14.)

The rise of consumerism

> Until the sixties, science could count on an uncontroversial public that believed in science, but today its efforts and progress are followed with mistrust. People suspect the unsaid, add in the side effects and expect the worst. (Beck 1992: 169)

Ralph Nader

In 1965 US lawyer Ralph Nader published *Unsafe at Any Speed: The Designed-in Dangers of the American Automobile*. This book targeted US automotive giant General Motors and its product, the Corvair. Nader described consumers as victims of a policy vacuum that enabled systemic and routine industrial irresponsibility:

> The American automobile is produced exclusively to the standards which the manufacturer decides to establish. It comes into the marketplace unchecked. When a car becomes involved in an accident, the entire investigatory, enforcement and claims apparatus that makes up the post-accident response looks almost invariably to driver failure as the cause. (Nader 1973: 35)

After four years in the public spotlight, the Corvair was taken off the market after a 93 per cent sales decline (McCarry 1972: 28). Nader went on to successfully lobby Washington for structural reform in the automotive industry. In 1966 the National Traffic and Motor Vehicle Safety Act was passed as law. This important legislative milestone changed the position of buyers and set the agenda for active consumers for the next three decades.

In today's brand name-dominated culture, whistle-blowing consumer activists ask questions, know their rights and take action. They form powerful consumer advocacy and watchdog groups who advise publics about what to buy and when to sign on the dotted line. But the prospect of 'globalisation' and vast borderless trading markets has given the consumerism debate a sharp new edge. Consumer activists now collectively act on complex global issues like corporate monopolies, exploitative labour policies and practices and the cultural side-effects of rampant consumerism. While the idea of a 'smart consumer' is now accepted, the move towards consumerism has been gradual and diffused. However, some key events happened in the 1960s that influenced the rise of consumerism protection. One of these was the change to the way we viewed the notion of *caveat emptor*. *Caveat emptor* means 'let the buyer beware'—that is, the buyer bears the onus of responsibility to check goods for quality, price and safety. Until the 1960s, there were limited advocacy opportunities for consumers. The shopper who bought a 'lemon' had few redresses to put things right. Generally this culture was a basic precept for running a business. Increasingly, legislation protects consumers and reflects the new way society now regards the act of buying and selling. *Caveat emptor* can no longer be used as a basis for running a successful long-term business. Indeed, the 'seller' now has the onus of responsibility to check the quality and safety of their goods and ensure they have not deceived or misled consumers.

Australian consumer protection

Getting 'ripped off' by a trader or 'baited' by false advertising is not acceptable in Australia. Citizens' right to a fair and competitive marketplace is now regulated by state and federal legislation, and organisations and associations can lobby on behalf of individuals.

The Australian Competition and Consumer Commission (ACCC) is a statutory authority that independently administers the Trade Practices Act for all Australians. Individual states and territories have their own laws that govern fair trading and consumer protection, and these complement the national agency. The role of the ACCC is to promote competition and fair trading and provide for consumer protection. The key roles of the ACCC are to monitor:

- anti-competitive and unfair market practices;
- mergers or acquisitions of companies;
- product safety/liability; and
- third-party access to facilities of national significance.

(Details can be seen at the ACCC's website: <www.accc.gov.au>.)

In 2002, the Federal Court fined personal and household cleansing product suppliers Colgate-Palmolive Pty Ltd $500 000 for trying to stop a discount retailer in Tasmania from advertising its products at bargain prices. Colgate had refused to supply more stock unless the discount retailer agreed to sell it at 'normal' price.

The discount retailer rejected the bid and Colgate cut off any further supply. Additionally, the court ordered Colgate to pay the ACCC's costs and placed a five-year injunction 'restraining the company from engaging in similar conduct in Australia' (ACCC: 2002: 23). Cases like these can leave a distinct impression of unbalanced and unfair power relations in favour of corporations. With so much choice available on supermarket shelves, smart consumers can recognise their power and easily make a statement by preferring another brand.

Activist stakeholders

Other organisations have also developed which provide information and advocacy to consumers and stakeholders. The Australian Shareholders' Association (ASA) is an example of a specialised consumer protection advocacy group. Established 40 years ago, the ASA now has 7000 members. It sees its role as protecting and advancing the interests of shareholders. This means monitoring companies and calling for explanations for poor performance. Among action it has taken in the past has been urging NRMA members to direct their votes away from the incumbent president of the road service organisation with concerns about the board's size, lack of disclosure of information and other issues. In 2003, a strong message from share-holders saw all NRMA directors voted off the board. (Details can be seen on the ASA's website: <www.asa.asn.au>.)

The Australian Consumers' Association (ACA) is well known for communicating with its publics through its popular magazine *Choice*. With its mission 'We test, inform, and empower consumers', the organisation has been active in many consumer issues since it was founded in 1959. It is well known for its regular safety testing of items like fridges, irons and drills, and also plays an active role in complex and contemporary debates such as the right to sufficient genetically modified (GM) food labelling and information technology issues, including the impact of the new digital signal on ana-logue televisions. (Details can be seen on the ACA's website: <www.choice.com.au>.)

Impact of new technologies

New information technologies like the internet have changed the way the Third Sector operates and functions. Traditional media like print, television and radio are highly centralised, with editors acting as 'gatekeepers' selecting and signifying the messages that reach the public sphere. The internet, however, is characterised by two-way communication, interactivity, transmission efficiency and decentralisation of power. On the internet, individuals and groups can set up their own websites and send their message directly to a global audience, bypassing the media gatekeepers. Access to vast amounts of information and data creates an opportunity to table alternative views in online forums that promote interaction, discussion and networking. It is an ideal tool for collective community activists to mobilise and develop virtual communities through email groups and powerful websites. Dealing with pressure from the internet has forced multinationals to change policy. Whether the National Anarchist Conference or a Labor Day meeting, the internet can bring together activists to empower and connect individuals all over the world. Protest sites such as the Activists Handbook at <www.prtoext.net/activists_handbook> provide live links to global events, calendars and actions, as well as useful materials such as legal information for activists. From Fremantle to Brisbane, activists can locate details about meetings and events, both in person and on the net. This streamlines communication and facilitates rapid responses to mobilisation. One example was protests which were rapidly staged across Australia to stop the commitment of troops to the war in Iraq.

Electronic civil disobedience: hactivism

Are hactivists protesting cyber warriors creating meaningful social change, or delinquent cyber vandals infiltrating legitimate computer security systems and corrupting data?

In his article *The New Age of Hactivism*, Robert Lemos (2000) argues that one of the first effective examples of hactivism arose in Mexico in 1994 with the Zapatista democratic uprising for Indian rights. Since then the practice has proliferated, with companies and governments the targets of strategic campaigns where sites are defaced and business is derailed. According to internet analyst Gert Lovink: 'It can be to disrupt data traffic, to bring down servers, to hijack sites and emphasise other alternative content.' (Smith 2002: 2)

The power of internet activism in Australia was highlighted recently by a call from New South Wales Police Minister Michael Costa to ban a number of protest websites planning the disruption of the World Trade Organisation meetings in Sydney in 2002. The response followed an organised hactivist attack during the 1999 WTO Seattle conference. The 'virtual sit in' saw 50 000 global hactivists jam the WTO website, effectively shutting it down and disrupting business for hours. At the Seattle conference, the internet was also credited with the massive organisational task of mobilising the thousands of protestors and focusing their energies on the widespread and furious public demonstrations that successfully hijacked the media agenda. But, while the internet can and does offer a direct way of reaching target publics for activists, does it fundamentally change anything? The rapid growth of the World Wide Web means most organisations will now have the capability for a website. However, the quantity of information on the web can dilute the effectiveness of the medium. Evaluating a site by quantifying the number of 'hits' in isolation is limited. Poorly managed sites can be out of touch with target publics, but give the illusion that they are meeting their needs. An internet site has the potential to amplify activists' messages to global audiences or be just another piece of junk floating about in cyberspace.

Online activism

Well-known online activism campaigns have included Oxfam's Community Aid Abroad anti-Nike site and McSpotlight. Culture jamming the famous slogan 'Just Do It', the 'Just Stop It' campaign targets corporate clothing and footwear giant Nike to account for rights and working conditions in sweatshops (see it and other campaigns at <www.caa.org.au/campaigns/index.html>). McSpotlight was established in 1996 to counter McDonald's $2 billion image budget. With shades of PT Barnum, it describes itself as 'the biggest loudest, most red, most read Anti-McDonald's extravaganza the world has ever seen', with 21 000 files and one million hits per month (see it at <www.mcspotlight.org/>).

Development of NGOs

Non-governmental organisations (NGOs) have in increasing numbers injected unexpected voices into international discourse about numerous problems of global scope (Weiss and Gordenker 1996: 17).

Organisations like Greenpeace, Amnesty International, Medecins Sans Frontieres (MSF) and Oxfam have proliferated since the post-1945 social and political awakenings. Boutros Boutros-Ghali discusses how NGOs are now growing in their diversity and influence.

In France, 54 000 new associations have been established since 1987. In Italy, 40 per cent of all associations have been set up within the last 15 years. This phenomenon is also occurring in developing countries. Within a short space of time 10 000 NGOs have been established in Bangladesh, 21 000 in the Philippines and 27 000 in Chile. (Weiss and Gordenker 1996: 7)

NGOs can be characterised by their participation with the local community, their ability to learn from the past, transparency and accountability to the community, and local grass roots legitimacy. But beyond this, West (2001) adds their flexibility; unconventional approaches and borderless charters give them a responsiveness that places them well ahead of intergovernmental organisations (IGOs). Vast and influential, the United Nations (UN) is a global organisation established in 1945 by 51 countries committed to peacekeeping, security and humanitarian aid. However, Article 71 within its Charter enables the UN Economic and Social Council (ECOSOC) to develop special consultative relationships between other NGOs and the UN. This unique consultative status benefits more than 2000 NGOs who participate and have policy input in areas like human rights, health policy and food production. NGOs with this status have participated on apartheid and disarmament policy (Donini 1996), and played an important role in agenda-setting at the ground-breaking Rio Conference on Environment. This 'bottom-up' relationship, with grass roots issues and advocates, gives this massive organisation a critical integrity to maintain its own status as an NGO.

Often with their genesis in crisis, large NGOs can start life as a small CAG but evolve into a long-term issue-based organisation. Greenpeace was established in 1971 with a handful of activists on a one-issue mission. Today this organisation has nearly three million supporters, and defines and communicates global ecological and environmental risks with recent campaigns for genetic engineering, climate, nuclear disarmament and marine action. Greenpeace's public relations tools, like its annual reports and website, and the use of liberal 'photojournalism' visuals with captions in a handwritten script style, underscore its relationship to global communities, ecological protection and grass roots empowerment. (Details can be seen at the Greenpeace website: <www.greenpeace.org/history/>.)

Resourcing and financing

Resourcing of NGOs is complex and diverse. Some organisations like Greenpeace cite 93 per cent of their funds as coming from individual donations, while according to Weiss and Gordenker, others—like the International Committee of Red Cross and CARE—'rely on contributions from governments of rich countries for most of their operating funds' (1996: 31). Weiss and Gordenker also discuss the complicating political dimension existing between foreign-based NGOs and host governments who can limit or grant discretionary permission to use state infrastructure like roads and communications. While many NGOs are financed by a mix of government funding and public contributions, significant financial sources are vital for survival and to conduct programs.

The raising of funds to conduct programs is a major activity of the Third Sector and an important area of public relations. All NGOs face critical public relations challenges such as lack of corporate support, stiff competition, donor and volunteer fatigue, competition for media coverage and unexpected crises. However, the list of over-optimistic and costly fundraiser flops is growing. Fundraising incurs considerable costs and should therefore be planned and systematic in order to achieve a high organisational return to justify the use of resources.

The first step to a successful fundraising program is to identify prospective donors. Breaking down the donor target publics' demographics and psychographics is important to an applied, strategic approach. According to Dalton (2000: 20), the act of fundraising is more than a simple exchange or monetary transaction: it 'offers you something intangible, an opportunity to participate in something greater than yourself' (2000: 20). The increasing levels of fundraising activity in the crowded charity marketplace can result in over-solicitation of donors. Additional demands to support the effects of a humanitarian crisis such as a famine, or a natural disaster like an earthquake or tidal wave, can result in 'donor fatigue' or unwilling contributors. Managing the solicitation process to build a solid supporter base means considering how many times and in what ways a donor is asked for money—and respecting their wishes if they don't want to be approached. To maximise efficiency, Dalton (2000: 70) argues that it is critical that fundraisers set goals that define how much they want to raise, what and how much they are asking for, who they will ask, and finally, who will do the asking!

Fundraising

There are numerous ways fundraising activities can be conducted:

- *Face-to-face:* direct donation is one of the most powerful, low-cost and successful tactics to obtain a high return (Dalton 2000: 4).
- *Direct mail:* personalised letters asking for donation and support are sought. Opinion leaders are used to increase target audience appeal.
- *Regular donation programs:* these provide a good opportunity but require direct debit facilities for regular and ongoing donations. Used by large NGOs like Amnesty International.

- *Door to door*: raffles, goods drives, competitions, etc. External variables need to be considered when planning the scale and costs of these undertakings.
- *Major awareness events*: these are becoming more popular but also more competitive. A successful example is World Vision's annual 40 Hour Famine. Principally targeted at young Australians, this campaign creates physical and psychological awareness of going 'without', as well as raising funds.
- *Charity telemarketing*: the 'call centres' explosion has facilitated an increase in charity telemarketing. Evaluate high saturation levels, 'real' costs and donor privacy when considering this tactic.
- *Events*, such as balls, auctions, fetes: although some of these can be highly successful, there are no guarantees and many require long-term planning.
- *Sponsorship*: an increasingly complex area of resources and fundraising. Arts, education and health NGOs are forging complex and long-term partnerships with other businesses that run parallel to the redefined corporate citizenship role.
- *Private trusts and foundations*: independent philanthropic trusts that distribute investments operate throughout the world. An example is the massive global Rockefeller Foundation.

Volunteers

Volunteers are a critical part of Third Sector organisations. The tenets of corporate citizenship also mean that business and governments will encourage active partnerships, and participation in Third Sector activities. Feelings of unity and working for the 'common good' have significant rewards for individuals, and these feelings can be encouraged and nurtured by the organisation that relies on its volunteer base. Public relations managers who work closely with volunteers therefore need to be clear about the benefits to volunteers in order to develop and maintain a stable and long-term volunteer contingent.

What's in it for volunteers?

- skill building, training and education;
- establishing networks with people with similar values and concerns;

- transferable work experience and responsibilities;
- a variety of tasks to perform; and
- hours and times that suit individuals.

Volunteers need to feel respected and valued by the organisations they serve. These days, large NGOs will invite potential volunteers to participate in a formal application process in an effort to match people to skills and tasks. Once established, volunteers will need someone within the organisation who will talk, listen and act on issues that arise. Formal acknowledgment for service is also essential. Whether in the form of service badges, gifts, awards, a party to celebrate a milestone, or privileges such as free carparking, tangible recognition and rewards for hard work and dedication over long periods of time create clear and positive relationships between volunteers and the broader organisation.

Building a successful team will also include communicating a vision about the shared issue and group ideology, establishing the commitment level at which volunteers want to engage, setting clear goals and objectives, and developing regular communication.

Development of community action groups (CAGs)

> Challenger groups are often poorly funded and poorly organized; lack of organization, social power and resources in turn dictates reliance on less than optimal campaign strategies. (Salmon 1989: 25)

CAGs can develop out of a common cause, as individuals come together to achieve a shared goal. As Salmon (1989) notes, many 'challenger groups' can be poorly funded or organised; however, the rise of the risk society means some now mobilise in ways that were unusual in the past, using sophisticated communication techniques. CAGs utilising knowledge will find committed supporters who will work effectively on a shoestring budget and for no financial gain. CAGs have been instrumental in altering a wide range of national debates. Particularly well known are those involving the environment, which have on occasion forced governments to re-think decisions on major developments.

One of Australia's most historic and longest running community action campaigns was the 'No Dam' campaign against the proposed damming of the Franklin–Gordon rivers in Tasmania in the early 1980s. This campaign ran over several years through changes of state and federal government. It involved a massive community protest, with thousands of people taking to the streets, voters writing 'no dams' on election ballot papers, more than 1000 people arrested, rallies of support for the protest all over Australia and huge media interest and coverage. Blockaders carried out daily actions, including occupations and attempts to impede machinery. Indigenous Australians worked with blockaders and held their own protest at the destruction of their land. In February 1982, a rally in Hobart in opposition to the Franklin dam drew 20 000 people into the streets (Stephen 1992). In March 1982, the Hawke government ruled against the dam by banning work in the World Heritage Area. Soon after, the High Court ruled in favour of the Commonwealth against a challenge by the Tasmanian government (Stephen 1992). Senator Bob Brown, who was well known for his involvement in the famous Franklin–Gordon protests, made the following comment about the community blockade of the proposed dam:

> You must never, never, never, give up on something you feel strongly about, and where a great wrong is being done . . . bulldozers aren't always the strongest form of power. The hearts of people are a mighty strong force, and it's infectious. (*The Age*, 2002: online)

CAGs are often made up of a collection of disparate people brought together as a reactive response to a crisis or issue. The crisis or issue might be unrelated to anything familiar—for example, the relocation of overhead cables. These can involve understanding technical reports or the impacts on health and environment. Complex and unfamiliar issues may see the group struggle to do anything more than table the matter, getting a minor media 'splash'. Add to this lack of money and time and/or pressure from personal relationships and career, and it is not surprising that many activists walk away from participating, frustrated and disheartened by the arduous process of achieving their goals.

The very nature of CAGs and their *ad hoc* setting can mean it is tempting to dismiss formal organisational structures; however, attention to structuring the group and adhering to basic organisational precepts will help to achieve efficiency and effectiveness of output. Maintaining a positive focus and sense of momentum within community groups can be difficult. Once the group has formed, a strong strategic approach is critical for long-term success. Clear goals and objectives need to be set and pursued cohesively as a team. It is vital that the shared perspectives brought into the group are pooled to find a binding issue that crystallises the group goals. From there, the group should audit or establish resources like skills, time, equipment and access to facilities. Ultimately, CAGs need to present both themselves and their targets as belonging to the same community, sharing the same concerns.

Not in my back yards (NIMBYs)

Effectively communicating a local significance can promote CAGs' causes, rather than them being perceived as pushing a one-sided agenda as NIMBYs. However, other situational factors like political philosophy can affect how a 'cause' is interpreted more widely. Media may represent CAGs' concerns as localised and ignorant of broader public agendas. It is therefore essential for CAGs to research and fully investigate the background and history of a cause or issue before presenting it to the media. While situational factors make each CAG's task different, some basic tenets can help understand how best to manage circumstances.

Guidelines for community action groups

- Adopt a long-term view about the realistic achievement of objectives. This allows the group and individuals to 'pace' themselves, balancing the other pressures.
- Establish and facilitate member contributions in relation to skills and circumstances. Some will elect to leaflet drop, while others will write media releases or organise petitions.
- Use a chairperson, take meeting minutes and be clear about the responsibilities of office bearers like treasurers or secretaries. These structures create effective output and encourage full member participation.
- Build trust within the group by demonstrating core values of equity, tolerance and goodwill through member relationships. Share public recognition by using various media spokespeople.
- Value diversity. The single issue that binds group members doesn't mean members will think alike on all matters.
- Get to know the issue inside out. Access background information and master technical aspects. It may be important to become familiar with a range of private and state institutions and processes. Link and create lateral partnerships with other key groups and stakeholders to facilitate 'legitimacy' and generate creative alliances.

- Understand the issue within the broader local, state and federal political context. It is important to see things as they affect others. Structure sub-campaigns of action. For example, a 'letter to the editor' campaign needs to be dispatched in strategic concentrations at particular times.
- Write and adapt the group's message for a variety of documents. Learn the writing conventions of a media release, report, submission, newsletter, web writing, etc. In time, these become valuable records and reference points.

Conclusion

This chapter has discussed public relations and the Third Sector and outlined its relationship with the evolution of 'scarcity society' into 'risk society', the central tenets of citizenship and notions of 'public sphere'. While new technological developments make it easy to imagine that somehow we are different from other generations, issues of equity, fairness, tolerance and diversity have not changed.

By mounting long-term strategic campaigns, developing insight into communication processes and understanding situational factors, we can achieve collective goals.

The rewards will be long-term sustainability, a solid reputation, the ability to attract new members, gain support in unusual alliances, create novel and new ways of communicating, and to take on and describe issues often ignored. The Third Sector will continue to grow and become a powerful force in the twenty-first century. It has an important role to play in challenging and interrogating 'knowledge' and in dealing with critical power positions. Its relationship to citizenship will determine whether this is fair and democratic.

Case study 16.1: SIDS and kids

Today, the 'charity marketplace' is busier and more pressured than ever, as new groups join ranks and develop sophisticated approaches to communicate with publics and raise funds to reach their organisational goals.

The overall goal of the Sudden Infant Death Research Foundation Inc (SIDRF) is to eradicate the incidence of Sudden Infant Death Syndrome (SIDS) in our community. Statistics reveal that increased awareness and research undertaken in this area have a direct bearing on the dramatic decrease in child deaths. Other objectives are to provide support and counselling for families who experience SIDS, raise awareness, develop knowledge and research data to investigate the causes of the conditions of SIDS in the community, and develop educational programs for key groups at risk. One of the most successful fundraising events is SIDS and Kids Red Nose Day. The red noses have come to symbolise the fight to reduce the incidence of 'cot death', or SIDS. The first Red Nose Day (RND) fundraiser was held in 1988 and sold one million red noses. That same year, $36 335 was spent on research and $130 972 on national programs. The bright, playful plastic noses are popular with adults and children and have 93 per cent recognition level in the community (Quantum Market Research 2001). The campaign success can be judged by notification of sudden infant death notifications declining from 157 in 1985 (SIDRF Annual Report 1998: 5) to 24 in 2001 (SIDRF SIDSVictoria 2001: 3).

SIDS Red Nose Day 2000

While Red Nose Day is one of the most recognised national fundraising events in Australia, social and political variables as well as the competitive fundraising environment also affect it. In 2000, the Australian national focus was on the Sydney Olympic Games and the introduction of the Goods and Services Tax (GST), and this impacted on Red Nose Day. The outcome was disappointing, in part due to heavy advertising for the Olympics, alterations to health insurance and the advent of the GST, which occurred the day after Red Nose Day. Advertising was difficult to obtain, companies were committed to working on the introduction of the GST and families were concerned about the financial impact on their budgets (SIDSVictoria SIDRF Inc Annual Report and Accounts 2001: 8).

As a result, a number of regular communication opportunities available to assist the group with its annual fundraising appeal were squeezed out by the cluttered public agenda. These were 'free spot' advertising opportunities restricted by the concentration of GST advertisements and limited communication consultancy choice.

This demonstrates that, while there is a generally high recognition of a campaign, it does not necessarily translate to 'donor dollars'. It shows that fundraising is a competitive business and that donor fatigue may be compounded by a perception that there have already been sufficient inroads made into research. These can add new dimensions to challenges for not-for-profit organisations.

Case study 16.2: The Werribee Residents Against Toxic Dump (WRATD) campaign

On 13 November 1998, a contentious and sustained CAG campaign claimed success. That day, corporate building and sugar giant CSR announced to the community that it would drop its controversial plans to install a 'waste management precinct' or 'toxic dump' in the outer western Melbourne suburb of Werribee. Instead, CSR would sell the quarry site earmarked for the 'toxic dump' to Wyndham City Council. According to WRATD Chairperson Joanne Ryan, Werribee residents planned the 'biggest community party the city had ever seen'. The campaign began in April 1995 when a preliminary meeting of eight residents was held to consider the organisation of a group to oppose CSR's toxic waste disposal facility proposal. On 18 April 1995, Werribee Residents Against Toxic Dump (WRATD) was formed at a public meeting.

Definition of issues

Local Wyndham residents and businesses greeted the proposed location of the toxic waste disposal facility with dismay. As outlined by van Moorst (1998), the issues fell into these areas:

1   *Location and technology of the waste disposal facility.* Werribee is one of Melbourne's fastest developing municipalities. It is a designated growth corridor and the quarry would be 3 kilometres from the nearest housing estate. Industry in the area includes the Western Treatment Plant, air bases at Laverton and Point Cook, as well as a major market garden horticultural industry. Clay and plastic liners proposed for the disposal facility were deemed by WRATD to be inadequate and contained a risk of toxins leaching through into the water table and contaminating the environment.

2   *Reputation of CSR.* The reputation of CSR added to the unease as the company was responsible for ground water contamination at its timber processing plant at Dartmoor and numerous breaches of Environmental Protection Authority (EPA) guidelines.

3   *Democracy and issues of transparency and disclosure on the part of the statutory authorities.* Perceptions of the failure of 'legitimate' decision-making institutions to protect the environment (e.g. the state government and the EPA) gave momentum to those who questioned the policy decision. The WRATD debate reignited the same fears about citizens' rights that the Save Albert Park campaign had voiced several years earlier.

Agenda setting and not being NIMBYs

'This is not simply a case of not in our backyard but not in anyone's backyard,' said Joanne Ryan, Group Chairwoman, WRATD (*Herald Sun* 1998: 14). The fact that WRATD could be perceived as a group of NIMBYs was a central problem for the campaign. The Kennett state government had used the word 'NIMBY' to imply an anti-Victorian outlook, narrow and subjective views and an irrational fear of change itself. Against this political backdrop, WRATD sought to broaden the debate about the appropriateness of the toxic waste disposal facility and involve a number of 'legitimate' institutions such as the local council, the justice system, unions, other businesses and corporations, and the federal government.

Messages that sell

Grass roots activists act with limited financial budgets and time frames to develop key messages to reach their objectives. But, ironically, the pressured environment can lead to an accelerated creative process resulting in highly effective and memorable slogans. In this campaign, WRATD designed a range of communications to be broadly applied through text-based and verbal communication channels. WRATD's short, punchy key messages used repetition, rhythm and redundancy. Common language use established the shorter and more memorable term 'toxic dump' rather than CSR's awkward classification of 'prescribed waste landfill'. WRATD's messages included the following: the 'toxic dump' was the 'Wrong technology, the Wrong location and the Wrong company'; 'Dump the Dump'; 'Clean and Green—Not Toxic'; and 'Community Rights Not Toxic Profits'. These messages were readable in a single eye scan, short enough to be remembered verbatim and could be elaborated through successive exposure.

A range of other messages repeated the same words in other configurations and included: 'No Toxic Dump'; 'Dump Jeff'; 'Dump CSR'; and 'Dump Kennett, Toxic Govt'. These messages were displayed on bumper stickers, badges, caps, t-shirts, posters, pickets and signs. The very name of the group, 'Werribee Residents Against Toxic Dump', insured that the key message of the group gained maximum exposure through its use in common discourse amplified by the media.

The WRATD case study demonstrates how a community can successfully mobilise for community action and how public relations can be used to redress power asymmetry to achieve objectives. The group is notable for its use of unusual tactics, alliances and its challenge to 'scientific' interpretations of risk. This group did not allow the fact that it was a reactive social movement to prevent it from using sophisticated communication techniques to advance its position underpinned by the notion of citizenship. CSR and the state government were entrenched in their strong perception of public pressure as an unwarranted attack on their own legitimacy to instigate the proposal. This oppositional stance limited their views and understanding of the debate.

Discussion and exercises

1   Monitor the daily newspaper in your area (local, not state or national) and see what community groups are featured in news stories. This exercise can be undertaken over a period of time to gain an understanding of ongoing stories. What are their activities? Do they have one spokesperson? How effectively are they getting their messages across? Do you believe they have public support for their causes?

2   Is the 'public sphere' dead in risk society? What impact will the growing use of public relations by the Third Sector have on its future?

3   Is a hactivist who participates in a 'virtual sit in' engaged in a legitimate public act to achieve a social goal? Justify your response.

4   Examine the Oxfam CAA, McSpotlight or another protest website. Detail the specific ways these sites contribute to citizenship.

5   Local councils often provide booklets of community groups. Obtain a copy of such a booklet and identify community groups that your class members might be able to assist. As well as providing a basis for assignment work, this community-based work can provide a great addition to your CV.

Further reading

Beck, U. (1997) *The Reinvention of Politics—Rethinking Modernity in the Global Social Order*, Polity Press, Cambridge.

Castells, M. (ed.) (1997) *The Information Age: Economy, Society and Culture: The Power of Identity*, Blackwell, Massachusetts.

Franklin, J. (ed.) (1998) *The Politics of Risk Society*, Polity Press, Cambridge.

Outhwaite, W. (1994) *Habermas: A Critical Introduction*, Polity Press, Cambridge.

References

The Age (2002) 'Saved by those who gave a damn', 24 December, <www.theage.com.au/articles/2002/12/23/1040511005798.html>.

Australian Competition and Consumer Commission (ACCC) (2002) 'Colgate-Palmolive Pty Ltd resale price maintenance', *ACC Journal*, no. 39, May–June.

Activist Handbook (2003) at <www.prtoext.net/activists_handbook>.

Beck, U. (1992) *Risk Society: Towards a New Modernity*, Sage, London.

Beder, S. (1997) *Global Spin: The Corporate Assault on Environmentalism*, Scribe, Melbourne.

—— (1999a) 'Greenwashing an Olympic-sized toxic dump', *PR Watch* archives, vol. 6, no. 2, <www.prwatch.org/prwissues/1999Q2/olympic1.html>, accessed 1/13/2003, pp. 1–8.

—— (1999b) 'Selling a leaky landfill as the "world's best practice"', *PR Watch* archives, vol. 6, no. 2, <www.prwatch.org/prwissues/1999Q2/olympic3.html>, accessed 1/13/2003, pp. 1–3.

Birch, D. (ed.) (2001) *Proceedings of the Second National Conference on Corporate Citizenship*, 16–17 November 2000, Deakin University, Geelong.

Dalton, P. (2000) *The Key to Fundraising Success*, Wright Books, Melbourne.

Demetrious, K. (2002) 'People power and public relations', *Asia Pacific Public Relations Journal*, vol. 3, no. 2, University of Canberra, Canberra, pp. 109–20.

Dodds, N. (1999) *Social Theory and Modernity*, Polity Press, Cambridge.

Donini, A. (1996) 'The Bureaucracy and the Free Spirit', in T.G. Weiss and L. Gordenker (eds), *NGOs, the UN and Global Governance*, Lynne Rienner, London.

Eade, D. & Ligteringen, E. (eds) (2001) *Debating Development*, Oxfam, London.

Ewen, S. (1996) *PR! A Social History of Spin*, Basic Books, New York.

Grunig, J.E. & Hunt, T. (1984) *Managing Public Relations*, Holt, Rinehart and Winston, New York.

Habermas, J. (1989) *The Structural Transformation of the Public Sphere: An Inquiry into a Category of Bourgeois Society*, Polity Press, Cambridge.

Herald Sun (1998) 'Residents plan dump protest', 25 May, p. 14.

Lemos, R. (2000) *The New Age of Hacktivism*, <http://zdnet.com.co./2100-11-525390.html?legacy=zne>, accessed 13/1/03, pp. 1–2.

McCarry, C. (1972) *Citizen Nader*, Saturday Review Press, New York.

Marshall, T.H. (1950) *Citizenship and Social Class and Other Essays*, Cambridge University Press, London.

Nader, R. (1973) *Unsafe at Any Speed: The Designed-in Dangers of the American Automobile*, Bantam Books, New York.

Salmon, C.T. (ed.) (1989) *Information Campaign: Balancing Social Values and Social Change*, Sage, Newbury Park.

Smith, S. (2002) 'Internet activism changes face of protest movement', *Lateline*, ABC TV, <www.abc.net.au/latelline/s544247.htm>, accessed 4/02/03, pp. 1–2.

Stauber, J.R. & Rampton, S. (1995) *Toxic Sludge is Good for You! Lies, Damn Lies and the Public Relations Industry*, Common Courage Press, Monroe, Maine.

Stephen, Sarah (1992) '10th anniversary of the Franklin blockade', *Green Left Weekly*, <www.greenleft.org.au/back/1992/80/80p9.htm>.

Sudden Infant Death Research Foundation Inc (1998) *Annual Report*, Melbourne.

—— (2001) *Annual Report and Accounts*, Melbourne.

SIDS website: <www.sidsaustralia.org.au>.

Taylor, C. (ed.) (1994) *Multiculturalism: Examining the Politics of Recognition*, Princeton University Press, Princeton, New Jersey.

van Moorst, H. (1998) *The Proposed Werribee Toxic Dump and the Failure of Government Planning Practice 1998: The Best and Worst Examples of City Planning and Development*, People's Committee for Melbourne.

Weiss, T.G. & Gordenker, L. (eds) (1996) *NGOs, the UN and Global Governance*, Lynne Rienner, London.

West, K. (2001) *Agents of Altruism: The Expansion of Humanitarian NGOs in Rwanda and Afghanistan*, Ashgate, Aldershot.

APPENDIX

PRIA Code of Ethics

The Public Relations Institute of Australia is a professional body serving the interests of its members. In doing so, the Institute is mindful of the responsibility which public relations professionals owe to the community as well as to their clients and employers. The Institute requires members to adhere to the highest standards of ethical practice and professional competence. All members are duty bound to act responsibly and to be accountable for their actions.

The following Code of Ethics binds all members of the Public Relations Institute of Australia.

1 Members shall deal fairly and honestly with their employers, clients and prospective clients, with their fellow workers including superiors and subordinates, with public officials, the communications media, the general public and with fellow members of PRIA.
2 Members shall avoid conduct or practices likely to bring discredit upon themselves, the Institute, their employers or clients.
3 Members shall not knowingly disseminate false or misleading information and shall take care to avoid doing so inadvertently.
4 Members shall safeguard the confidences of both present and former employers and clients, including confidential information about employers' or clients' business affairs, technical methods or processes, except upon the order of a court of competent jurisdiction.
5 No member shall represent conflicting interests nor, without the consent of the parties concerned, represent competing interests.

6   Members shall refrain from proposing or agreeing that their consultancy fees or other remuneration be contingent entirely on the achievement of specified results.

7   Members shall inform their employers or clients if circumstances arise in which their judgment or the disinterested character of their services may be questioned by reason of personal relationships or business or financial interests.

8   Members practising as consultants shall seek payment only for services specifically commissioned.

9   Members shall be prepared to identify the source of funding of any public communication they initiate or for which they act as a conduit.

10   Members shall, in advertising and marketing their skills and services and in soliciting professional assignments, avoid false, misleading or exaggerated claims and shall refrain from comment or action that may injure the professional reputation, practice or services of a fellow member.

11   Members shall inform the Board of the Institute and/or the relevant State/Territory Council(s) of the Institute of evidence purporting to show that a member has been guilty of, or could be charged with, conduct constituting a breach of this Code.

12   No member shall intentionally injure the professional reputation or practice of another member.

13   Members shall help to improve the general body of knowledge of the profession by exchanging information and experience with fellow members.

14   Members shall act in accord with the aims of the Institute, its regulations and policies.

15   Members shall not misrepresent their status through misuse of title, grading, or the designation FPRIA, MPRIA or APRIA.

Adopted by the Board of the Institute on November 5, 2001, this Code of Ethics supersedes all previous versions.

INDEX